Other titles in the Jossey-Bass Nonprofit & Public Management Series:

Managing for the Environment

Managing for the Environment

Understanding the Legal, Organizational, and Policy Challenges

Rosemary O'Leary, Robert F. Durant,
Daniel J. Fiorino, Paul S. Weiland

Jossey-Bass Publishers
San Francisco

Jossey-Bass books and products are available through most bookstores. To contact Jossey-Bass directly, call (888) 378-2537, fax to (800) 605-2665, or visit our website at www.josseybass.com.

Substantial discounts on bulk quantities of Jossey-Bass books are available to corporations, professional associations, and other organizations. For details and discount information, contact the special sales department at Jossey-Bass.

Manufactured in the United States of America using acid-free Lyons Falls D'Anthology paper, which is a special blend of non-tree fibers and totally chlorine-free wood pulp.

Library of Congress Cataloging-in-Publication Data

Managing for the environment: understanding the legal, organizational, and policy challenges/Rosemary O'Leary . . . [et al.].—1st ed.
    p.   cm.—(The Jossey-Bass nonprofit & public management series)
  ISBN 0-7879-1004-X (acid-free paper)
  1. Environmental management. 2. Environmental policy.
3. Environmental ethics. 4. Environmental management—United States. 5. Environmental law—United States. I. O'Leary, Rosemary, date. II. Series: Jossey-Bass nonprofit and public management series.
GE300.M36   1999
363.7'05—dc21   98-36772

FIRST EDITION

HC Printing 10 9 8 7 6 5 4 3 2 1

The Jossey-Bass
Nonprofit & Public Management Series

CONSULTING EDITOR
PUBLIC MANAGEMENT AND
ADMINISTRATION

James L. Perry
Indiana University

CONTENTS

PART FOUR
Lessons

PREFACE

Consider the following scenarios: A community wants to build a new elementary school building and discovers that the land designated for the new school is contaminated with oil. A city manager receives a phone call at 1:00 in the morning informing her that the company with which the city has contracted to haul garbage is illegally disposing of the waste. A zoning board denies the application of a hardware store to expand, on the basis of fears that increased traffic will result in violations of the Clean Air Act; the zoning board is promptly sued. A regional hospital is no longer allowed to dispose of medical waste in a county incinerator. A leaking county landfill becomes the state's worst Superfund site.

These are only a few of the multitude of environmental challenges facing today's public, nonprofit, and for-profit managers. To an unprecedented extent, environmental dilemmas of these kind pervade every area of society, every level of government, and every sector of the economy. Indeed, one is challenged to imagine any type of organization—public, nonprofit, or for-profit—that has not confronted an environmental problem over the last decade. Nor can one easily imagine the circumstances under which any of these types of organizations might escape rigorous environmental scrutiny in the future. They may garner attention as regulators or regulatory targets; as public agencies, private contractors, or nonprofit grantees; as single organizations or as members of the service delivery networks of organizations (public, for-profit, and nonprofit) that must work together for public needs to be met (Luke, 1998). Moreover, as for-profits and nonprofits are called upon as "partners" to do the public's business, they will find citizens holding them to a decidedly broader, more complex, and often contradictory range of democratic values (such as efficiency, equity, due process, equality, and accountability) than that to which they are typically accustomed when meeting the demands of markets or boards of directors.

How can managers who are nonspecialists in this area best deal with the environmental problems they face? How can they best manage their scientific and technical staff, as well as their contractors and grantees? How can they stay up-to-date on changes in environmental laws? When should they contract out their environmental programs and when should they not? How can they ensure that their contractors and grantees are environmentally responsible? How can they bring citizens into environmental decision making, and how can they resolve the environmental conflicts that emerge? How can they more effectively engage the media when environmental issues are involved? What do they need to know about the impact on their day-to-day activities of such concepts as total quality environmental management, market incentives, environmental justice, and sustainable development? Can they deal successfully with today's emerging emphasis on results-oriented and risk-prioritized environmental management without developing strategic information management capabilities in their agencies? How can they best assess the success or failure of their environmental initiatives? How can they stay abreast of new approaches to environmental management? These are some of the questions this book addresses.

Managing for the Environment is based on the premise that all managers must be aware of potential environmental problems and act proactively to address them if their organizations—and the interorganizational partnering networks in which they labor—are to thrive in the twenty-first century. This is true whether they are environmental specialists or nonspecialists, whether they are political appointees or career managers, and whether they are elected or appointed officials. All managers need to manage environmental conflict successfully. Doing so requires them to, among other things, adroitly and strategically manage employees, community relations, information resources, contractors, perceptions of risk, and media relations. At the same time, rapidly changing environmental laws require them to understand, develop, and refine new and effective strategies to cope with these vicissitudes. Meanwhile, the values cherished in a democracy require that they ensure environmental justice, an economically sustainable future, and accountability to the public for actions taken on their behalf. To do otherwise will put the public's trust in them at risk, jeopardize their organizations' missions, and alas, even imperil their careers.

Specifically, this book

- Explains how managers can incorporate environmental management concepts into their own, their subordinates', and their organizations' thinking

- Reviews the political, economic, and organizational obstacles that await managers when they try to incorporate environmental management concepts into their organizations

- Offers strategies and tactics for managers seeking to cope with sources of resistance
- Helps managers to understand the complex value trade-offs that are inherent in environmental management
- Alerts managers to the dangers involved in unbridled pursuit of environmental values
- Describes current issues and trends that managers must recognize, including interorganizational partnerships and implementation networks
- Explains what managers should know about environmental laws
- Critiques and offers suggestions to managers for implementing total quality environmental management
- Explains to managers why scientific and technical personnel are "different" and how they can best manage these types of professionals
- Provides guidelines to managers for deciding when to contract or subcontract out environmental programs, and how best to ensure that their contractors, subcontractors, and grantees are environmentally responsive
- Reviews how and when managers can best take advantage of nontraditional approaches to environmental regulation
- Provides tips to managers for dealing constructively with environmental conflicts
- Clarifies how managers can most effectively engage the media when environmental issues arise
- Discusses how managers can use risk communication with communities to build mutual understanding of environmental challenges, choices, and opportunities
- Provides managers with many examples of successful and unsuccessful environmental management practices
- Relates the entire discussion to the relevant research and literature

THE BOOK'S AUDIENCE

This book is written for three main groups. The first consists of career managers, elected officials, and political appointees who are responsible for, and want to learn more about, environmental management as it affects the operations of public, nonprofit, and for-profit agencies. This group includes both those who design and implement environmental policies and those who are regulated by them. The book will help them to understand what environmental management is, and how to apply the principles, practices, and priorities presented in the book to their organizations, partnering networks, and communities. Thus, policymakers and their staffs who will find the book useful at the local government level include mayors; city and county managers; city council, board, and commission members; public works directors and city engineers; sheriffs, police chiefs, and fire chiefs; and school board members, administrators, and teachers. Likewise, those who will profit at the state and federal government levels include chief executives, cabinet secretaries, agency heads and administrators, and state legislators and congressmembers. In the nonprofit and for-profit sectors, those who will benefit include presidents and vice presidents; chief executive and chief administrative officers; executive directors, deputy directors, and unit directors; and boards of directors.

The second major audience consists of academics and students of environmental management and policy, nonprofit management, and public management. Courses concerned in whole or in part with environmental management are growing in popularity at schools of government, business, public affairs, public policy, planning, public administration, public management, nonprofit management, environmental science, and environmental policy. This book offers to teachers and students who are not specialists in environmental management a useful blend of theory and practice. To those who are environmental specialists (such as wildlife biologists, engineers, chemists, and lawyers), the book affords an uncommonly integrated look at the political, economic, and organizational dynamics they confront daily in their work.

Finally, businesspeople, interest groups, and ordinary citizens concerned about environmental issues, values, and reforms will also find the book useful. They too can cull from it an understanding of how the present regulatory regime came into being, the challenges to effectiveness it poses for the regulatory, regulated, and contractor communities, and the promise versus the performance of a range of proposed strategies for coping with these challenges. Our aim is to foster a mutual understanding of why all parties involved in environmental management act as they do, and what can, and cannot, be done about it in an era of organizational downsizing, devolution of government authority to states and localities, and funding constraints. At the same time, our readers will gain an appreciation for what colleagues in other businesses, interest groups, and communities across the United States and abroad have learned about dealing cost-effectively, responsively, and equitably with environmental management issues.

ACKNOWLEDGMENTS

Any collaborative effort like this book project requires a positive working relationship. The authors have shared equally in designing, conceptualizing, integrating, and writing what you will read in this book—a truly collaborative effort in the finest sense of the term. Thus we are jointly responsible for the book's themes, contents, and arguments. We are especially indebted to Jennifer Durant and Marlys Shields for their untiring perfectionism in the technical preparation of our many drafts of the manuscript. Thanks as well go to Thomas Baca of the U.S. Forest Service for his suggestions on topical coverage in various chapters. Special thanks go to Thomas A. Darling, director of the Government and Technology Division of the William D. Schaefer Center for Public Policy at the University of Baltimore, for his coauthoring of Chapter Nine, on strategic environmental information systems. We are also indebted to Jim Carr of the U.S. Environmental Protection Agency (EPA), as well as to Lois Wise, the late Neil Nielson (former city manager), Dick Bauer (former EPA deputy regional administrator), A. James Barnes (former EPA chief of staff, general counsel, and deputy administrator), and many others at the School of Public and Environmental Affairs at Indiana University for their advice on Chapter Ten, concerning the management of scientific and technical personnel. We thank our anonymous reviewers for their thorough and insightful comments. Finally, we thank Jim Perry, series consulting editor, Alan Shrader and Jennifer Morley of Jossey-Bass Publishers, and Rachel Anderson of Satellite Publishing Services for their patience and guidance throughout this project.

January 1999   ROSEMARY O'LEARY
                                Syracuse, New York

                                ROBERT F. DURANT
                                College Station, Texas

                                DANIEL J. FIORINO
                                Washington, D.C.

                                PAUL S. WEILAND
                                Cambridge, Massachusetts

For my husband, Larry Schroeder, who patiently listened to me dream about writing this book ten years before it was written.—R.O.

For my grandson, Nicholas Blake Durant, and to the memory of Bruce K. Birch.—R.F.D.

To Tillie Fiorino, for a lifetime of encouragement and support.—D.J.F.

To the memory of Stanley Miles Weiland Jr.—P.S.W.

THE AUTHORS

ROSEMARY O'LEARY is professor of public administration at the Maxwell Graduate School of Citizenship and Public Affairs at Syracuse University. She also is a senior Fulbright scholar conducting research on environmental policy in Southeast Asia and an elected member of the National Academy of Public Administration. Previously she was professor of public and environmental affairs at Indiana University, and codirector of the Indiana Conflict Resolution Institute. O'Leary has served as the director of policy and planning for a state environmental agency in the Midwest, and has worked as an environmental attorney. She has also worked as a consultant to the U.S. Department of the Interior, the U.S. Environmental Protection Agency, the Indiana Department of Environmental Management, the International City/County Management Association, the National Science Foundation, and the National Academy of Sciences. She is the author of three books and more than sixty articles on environmental management, environmental policy, public management, dispute resolution, bureaucratic politics, and law and public policy. She has won five national research awards, including the Mosher Award, which she won twice, for best article by an academician published in *Public Administration Review*. She has won seven teaching awards as well, including the national Excellence in Teaching Award given by the National Association of Schools of Public Affairs and Administration, and she was the recipient of the Distinguished Service Award given by the American Society for Public Administration's Section on Environment and Natural Resources Administration. She has served as chair of the Public Administration Section of the American Political Science Association, and as chair of the Section on Environment and Natural Resources Administration of the American Society for Public Administration. She holds a Ph.D. degree in public administration from Syracuse University and a J.D. degree from the University of Kansas.

ROBERT F. DURANT is professor of public administration and public policy at the George Bush School of Government and Public Service and in the Department of Political Science at Texas A&M University. His research has focused on environmental policy, public management, bureaucratic politics, and the roles of professionals and privatization in service delivery. He has published in such leading disciplinary journals as the *American Journal of Political Science, Political Research Quarterly, Political Science Quarterly, Administration & Society, Public Administration Review, Journal of Public Administration Research and Theory, Journal of Public Policy, International Journal of Public Administration, American Review of Public Administration, Legislative Studies Quarterly,* and *Policy Studies Review.* He is the author of *When Government Regulates Itself: EPA, TVA, and Pollution Control in the 1970s* (1985) and *The Administrative Presidency Revisited: Public Lands, the BLM, and the Reagan Revolution* (1992). The latter was awarded the American Political Science Association's 1993 Gladys M. Kammerer Award for the best book published on U.S. national policy. Durant has also received the Jeffrey Pressman Memorial Award from the Policy Studies Organization for his research, and has been recognized for outstanding contributions to the literature on environmental and natural resource management by the Section on Environment and Natural Resources Administration of the American Society for Public Administration. He holds a Ph.D. degree in political science from the University of Tennessee-Knoxville.

DANIEL J. FIORINO is a political scientist with nearly twenty years of experience in environmental policy. His administrative experience includes assignments in regulatory reform, the rulemaking process, policy analysis, regulatory negotiation, and sector-based approaches to environmental protection. The author of *Making Environmental Policy* (1995), his articles on public policy and regulation have appeared in *Policy Studies Journal, Public Administration Review, Risk Analysis, Environmental Law,* and *Science, Technology, and Human Values,* among others. In 1989 and 1991, he won the Brownlow Award of the American Society for Public Administration, given annually for the best article by a practitioner published in *Public Administration Review.* Fiorino teaches public policy as an adjunct professor at George Mason University and American University. He is currently director of the emerging strategies division in the policy office of the U.S. Environmental Protection Agency. He holds a Ph.D. degree in political science from the Johns Hopkins University.

PAUL S. WEILAND, who is pursuing a J.D. degree at Harvard Law School, has a Ph.D. degree in public policy from Indiana University,

Bloomington, and a B.A. degree in international relations and political science from the University of Southern California. He is presently editor-in-chief of the *Harvard Environmental Law Review*. His research on environmental and natural resources law and policy has been published in numerous journals, including the *Environmental Law Reporter, Journal of Land Use & Environmental Law, Harvard Environmental Law Review, Public Administration Review, Publius,* and *American Review of Public Administration.*

INTRODUCTION

For every problem there is a
solution that is simple, direct and wrong.

—H. L. Mencken

The very concept of environmental management is thought by some scholars to be an oxymoron. They argue that if we take *environment* to mean the natural world and *management* to mean control, the concept is nonsensical. Their reasoning is straightforward: we are unable to control effectively that which we do not understand. And most assuredly humankind does not understand many aspects of the natural world.

To support their argument, critics point to countless examples of failed attempts at environmental management. Rarely do we know the extent and manner of disruption to the natural world that our actions will cause—particularly the synergistic effects of multiple actions. Consider, for example, the once highly touted "green revolution" of the 1960s. It yielded many benefits (primarily vast increases in food production), but its reliance on heavily subsidized fertilizers and pesticides, water supplies, and monocultured crops also had significant long-term environmental costs. Similarly, when scientists developed chlorofluorocarbons (CFCs) early in the twentieth century, the benefits of these seemingly benign and stable chemicals seemed to outweigh their costs significantly. Fifty years later, however, scientists began understanding the devastating effects of CFCs on the stratospheric ozone layer.

Despite how persuasive this argument can be in particular instances, we assert in this book that society has little choice but to refine, extend, and apply what knowledge it does have, or else pay the price for its inaction. By its very existence, humankind is part of, is affected by, and affects the natural world every day. Moreover, the scope and intensity of humanity's impact on the environment has increased many times over in recent decades, and shows no signs of abating in the twenty-first century. Indeed, so potentially large, negative, and rapid are the effects of these activities on public health, safety, and ecosystems that scientists now worry about the global impacts and adjustments these activities may auger for all species.

We argue that under these circumstances efforts to understand these effects, to mitigate them, and where possible, to avoid them altogether make eminent sense. And although everyone has a role to play in this endeavor, society has to look to its public, nonprofit, and for-profit managers to take the lead. Whether by chance or by choice, as regulators or as regulatees, reactively or proactively, these managers make choices daily that have profound effects on the environment. Thus their actions will help determine how wisely or wantonly, in environmental terms, our society pursues its social, economic, and lifestyle aspirations.

But if environmental management is not about controlling the natural world, what is it about? To us, *environmental management is an interactive process wherein we learn how social institutions can best reconcile humankind's needs and aspirations with the limits that the natural world imposes.* Thus, in this book we describe existing social institutions and their relationships to the environment, provide explanations of new and emerging social institutional arrangements that may improve (or in some cases detract from) environmental stewardship, and assess the potential utility of a number of tools that managers may use to assist them in realizing a sustainable future.

CHALLENGES, CHOICES, AND OPPORTUNITIES

What we do not suggest is that environmental management is new. It has been an integral aspect of public affairs in the United States for more than a century. Long before the term *environment* took on its modern meaning, government officials focused routinely on public health, safety, and environmental issues. Responsibility for dealing with such issues as sanitation, safe drinking water, and solid waste disposal rested largely on local government officials, with some state involvement and minimal federal involvement.

All this changed dramatically in the post–World War II era. During the 1950s and 1960s, the use of chemicals and petroleum-based products exploded. At the same time, scientific advances improved humankind's understanding of its own impact on the environment. In 1956, the report of the International Symposium on Man's Role in Changing the Face of the Earth was published, and in 1965 Harvard University Press reprinted a century-old book by George Perkins Marsh titled *Man and Nature*. Also in 1965, the White House Conference on Natural Beauty ("Beauty for America," 1965) and a conference on Future Environments of North America were convened. In 1968 and 1972, two major international conferences (the Biosphere Conference and the Stockholm Conference, respectively) occurred, signaling heightened awareness of environmental problems. In turn, a series of popular books—including Rachel Carson's *Silent Spring*, Aldo Leopold's *Sand County Almanac*, and Stewart Udall's *Quiet Crisis*—disseminated to the public the concerns that these scientific advances revealed.

In addition, a number of environmental disasters spurred public outcries and led to congressional action. In January 1969, an oil well blowout resulted in the discharge of 250 million gallons of crude oil into the Santa Barbara Channel. In June 1969, the Cuyhoga River burst into flames near Cleveland, Ohio. Throughout the late 1960s, scientists speculated that Lake Erie was dead. Intense commercial fishing combined with sewage inflows to greatly increase nitrates and phosphates, eutrophication, and damage to Lake Erie's aquatic life. Disasters also occurred internationally, the most notable being the *Torrey Canyon* oil spill of March 18, 1967.

Over time it also became apparent that localized environmental problems (such as sanitation, drinking water provision, and solid waste disposal) were not the only issues facing the United States. Transboundary and multimedia problems existed as well.[1] As a result, from 1969 to 1980 Congress established a statutory and regulatory framework for federal environmental protection. Major environmental statutes were passed, including the National Environmental Policy Act (1969), the Clean Air Act (1970), the Federal Water Pollution Control Act Amendments (1972), the Endangered Species Act (1973), the Safe Drinking Water Act (1974), the Resource Conservation and Recovery Act (1976), the Toxic Substances Control Act (1976), and the Comprehensive Environmental Response, Compensation and Liability Act (1980). Collectively these statutes provided a strong state and federal government role in environmental protection efforts, shifting environmental management from being an almost entirely local concern to being an intergovernmental concern. Accordingly, environmental managers began to fill the ranks of federal, regional, and state governments, as well as local governments.

Next came recognition that environmental problems also spanned national boundaries. During the 1980s and 1990s, global issues such as climate change, large-scale species extinction, and stratospheric ozone depletion emerged in the press and on political agendas worldwide. Environmental management accommodated this awareness by expanding to include such international efforts as the United Nations Environment Programme and the International Institute of Sustainable Development. Relatedly, the globalization of the world's economy has spawned the creation of voluntary environmental process standards by multinational organizations such as the International Organization for Standardization. Today, environmental management concerns exist at every level of governance, from the most local to the most global. Moreover, even managers who do not consider environmental management part of their job descriptions increasingly find themselves confronted by its challenges, choices, and opportunities.

PURPOSE AND CONTENTS OF THE BOOK

Despite this long, storied, and challenging history, there still is no single comprehensive and readily understandable source of environmental management information for managers who are not specialists in the field. Indeed, even environmental management specialists lack a single source they can consult that treats the topic with the interdisciplinary breadth (including legal, organizational, political, scientific, economic, policy, journalistic, and communication issues) and integration that successful environmental management requires. Those seeking comprehensive information on the subject have to turn to separate books dealing with, for example, environmental economics (such as Tietenberg, 1996), environmental law (such as Findley and Farber, 1996; Government Institutes, 1997; Rodgers, 1994), environmental policy (such as Fiorino, 1995; Portney, 1990; Vig and Kraft, 1997), and environmental science (such as Kupchella and Hyland, 1993; Henry and Heinke, 1996). Missing is a book with a coherent, integrated, and multidisciplinary set of environmental principles, practices, and priorities—a book that can help managers to address today's and tomorrow's environmental challenges in informed, deliberative, and strategically savvy ways.

We seek to fill this gap by providing present and future managers with precisely such a book. Our book embraces the notion that success in dealing with environmental issues requires three elements: understanding volatile and complex issues and trends, "coproducing" with communities methods for dealing with those issues and trends, and delivering those methods effectively in a dynamic, politically charged, and legally contentious environment populated by interorganizational networks of actors with often competing interests.

The first element refers to the need for managers to understand the nature of the environmental challenges, choices, and opportunities that confront them. Managers must see how a commitment to environmental values, learning, and innovations is in their own, their agency's, and the public's interest. To these ends, our book discusses what we see as compelling reasons for adopting a prudently effective environmental ethic in our organizations. Discussed throughout are the legal, economic, political, scientific, and policy reasons for doing so that we feel all managers must understand.

Coproducing environmental values means working strategically with stakeholders—both within and outside one's agency—to meet these challenges, choices, and opportunities in cost-effective, responsive, and equitable ways. This is often a very trying process, rife with mixed results and caveats, and hence flush with contingent recommendations. In ensuing chapters we convey a sense of the dilemmas inherent in this enterprise. Moreover, we review tactics and strategies that may be useful to managers dealing with these dilemmas. Stressed especially is acquiring a strong sense of the conditions under which various approaches are more or less likely to succeed in bringing about multimedia-focused, results-oriented, and risk-prioritized environmental management. To these ends, parts of Chapters Four through Eight deal with how managers can tailor total quality environmental management (TQEM), media, community relations, risk communication, and conflict resolution strategies to their environmental management needs.

Premised on the experiences of managers in the United States and abroad, the lessons culled and summarized in this book are sometimes encouraging, sometimes disappointing, and at other times outright chastening. But at all times they speak to the realpolitik that all savvy managers must understand. Otherwise, they will have little chance of meaningfully inculcating a strong environmental management ethic within their organizations, of creating a more informed set of stakeholders to help inform their actions, or of "greening" the interorganizational networks of agencies, contractors, and grantees within which they work.

Finally, delivering environmental values involves institutionalizing one's long-term strategic goals in an organization's day-to-day operations. This, again, is not a task for the meek, the impatient, or the politically unastute. Organizations accustomed to thinking solely in terms of their primary mission rather than in terms of combining it with environmental sustainability, pollution prevention, or environmental justice can find change traumatic. In addition, those accustomed to hoarding information within islands of functional autonomy will find the need to become "learning organizations" that share information—a sometimes distinctly alien and discomfiting proposition. At the same time, even those organizations that are bent on success, comfortable with change, and rife with environmental commitment will find the managerial innovations necessary for change quite challenging. Chapter Four and Chapters Nine through Twelve explore the nature of these new managerial approaches. Reviewed are various strategies for building the kinds of strategic environmental information systems (SEIS) that learning organizations require, as well as for increasing what we know about marshaling the scientific, technical, and contract management know-how to meet environmental challenges with new policy tools.

From all this, three primary, recurring, and important themes emerge: the dynamic nature of environmental management, the need for effective two-way communication, and the value of adaptive management.

The Dynamic Nature of Environmental Management

In Chapter One we identify cutting-edge policy issues that environmental managers are likely to face. Because of the dynamic nature of the field, at any given time issues that are unexplored in Chapter One may be in the spotlight. Alternatively, the salience of some of the issues identified may wane. Still, because of this dynamism, the tools identified in Chapters Four and Nine will be of continuous use to managers confronting environmental challenges, choices, and opportunities. TQEM and SEIS are process-oriented tools that assist the efforts of managers to organize and analyze new information and address emerging problems. Properly utilized, TQEM and SEIS allow managers to anticipate and cope with many (although certainly not all) of the environmental problems they encounter.

The Need for Effective Two-Way Communication

Chapters Four and Seven identify the need for quality communication as one facet of an effective environmental management strategy. In Chapters Five through Seven, we present methods for communicating effectively with the public. Chapter Five deals expressly with the media and with techniques that managers may use to maximize the likelihood of a professional, mutually advantageous, and deliberation-enhancing relationship between managers and journalists. Focusing on communities, Chapter Six argues that great advantages accrue to managers who develop a coproduction environmental ethic in their agencies. This is an ethic predicated on creating a prudently open, early, and meaningful stakeholder participation process. Finally, in Chapter Seven we address ways to fill the dysfunctional gap in risk perceptions that typically exists between experts and lay citizens.

The lessons from these chapters may result in managers' avoidance of many environmental conflicts. Some conflicts will inevitably arise, however, given scarce resources, value differences, and competing interests. Chapter Eight, therefore, provides a framework for environmental dispute resolution (EDR). Although EDR is not appropriate for all circumstances, it is a powerful alternative to the U.S. judicial process. The latter focuses on using the courts to resolve adversarially concrete disputes between parties. In contrast, EDR's strength lies in its ability to bring together multiple parties in a nonconfrontational, nonthreatening, and nonlitigious setting and to focus on common interests rather than rigid positions.

The Value of Adaptive Management

Adaptive management integrates learning into the management process (see Lee, 1993). As noted, we see environmental management as an interactive learning process between humankind's aspirations and the limits that the natural world places on them. As such, environmental management is perpetually adapting to these needs and limitations. Many of the tenets of TQEM described in Chapter Four apply to adaptive management. TQEM is process oriented and interactive, allowing (and in fact compelling) organizations to learn from their experiences and to integrate lessons learned into constantly evolving social institutions. Science also plays a critical role in adaptive management, based as it is on experimenting and then internalizing lessons learned. The management of scientific personnel described in Chapter Ten and the creation and maintenance of SEIS described in Chapter Nine are therefore important components of an overall adaptive management strategy.

Equally important as adaptations are our efforts to mold social institutional arrangements to the dynamic nature of environmental management. The results of that adaptation are moves over time toward creating networks of "partnered" public, for-profit, and nonprofit actors who work together to provide environmental protection. The use of contracts and grants (discussed in Chapter Eleven) and new approaches to regulation (analyzed in Chapter Twelve) are central to these developments. Both approaches seek to serve human interests better while protecting the environment. Yet each also offers to managers severe downsides that they can ill afford to ignore. As such, managers implementing or overseeing government contracts, grants, and new approaches to regulation should continually evaluate the ability of these tools to assist in attaining the public's interest in environmental quality.

CONCLUSION

Dynamism, communication, and adaptation—these will remain the catchwords of environmental management well into the twenty-first century. For this reason, we weave together in Chapter Thirteen the principles, practices, and priorities that tomorrow's managers can learn from the past to serve them well in the new century. Recognizing that simple solutions to both the immediate and long-term challenges posed by our interaction with the environment are likely to be wrong, we argue that managers must continually retool to address the issues as they emerge. In the interim, both today's and tomorrow's managers would do well to begin this career-long learning process immediately. The best place to start, we contend, is by understanding the evolution of several key issues framing contemporary environmental debates and the regulatory regime presently straining to deal with them. Thus we turn next, in Chapter One, to some of the most important issues, trends, and trade-offs that managers must come to appreciate.

PART ONE

UNDERSTANDING ENVIRONMENTAL ISSUES

1

ENVIRONMENTAL MANAGEMENT

Policy Issues, Trends, and Trade-Offs

There is a whole new generation of issues before us that will require a new approach to environmental management.

—Lee Thomas, former EPA administrator[1]

Staying abreast of emerging issues and trends is always a challenge to managers, whether they work in public, nonprofit, or for-profit organizations. It is an especially difficult task, however, when environmental management issues and trends are involved. Not only are environmental issues as multidisciplinary in scope and complexity as we described in the Introduction, but they also have three other traits that compound the problem. First, they are often plagued by extraordinary levels of uncertainty. As we shall see especially in Chapters Four, Six, Seven, and Eight, managers often must make decisions predicated on incomplete data bases, premised on uncertain cause-and-effect relationships, and amid shrill voices that sometimes distort information to suit their purposes. Second, resolving environmental problems often requires managers to act as intermediaries among scientists, technical professionals, politicians, stakeholders, and the general public. Finally, given the interdependency of many environmental issues, managers often find it difficult to know where to start in getting a handle on understanding the intricacies of these issues.

In this chapter we introduce readers to five cutting-edge issues in environmental policy that demonstrate these intricacies, interdependencies, and intrigues in vivid ways: accountability, ecosystem management, environmental justice, sustainable development, and unfunded mandates. As we explore these issues, their interdependencies will become readily apparent. For example, accountability is a critical component of ecosystem management, sustainable development incorporates notions of equity (and therefore environmental justice) among different segments of the present human population and between present and future populations, and unfunded (and underfunded) mandates provide a significant force behind efforts to develop more efficient nontraditional approaches to regulation. It is therefore important for present and future managers to recognize linkages among these issues and to consider their impact on efforts to manage the environment. Indeed, each issue will be a critical consideration in many of the environmental management principles, practices, and priorities we discuss later in this book.

We selected these particular cutting-edge issues in environmental policy for several reasons. First, each is a major and fundamental issue that all managers dealing with environmental management need to know about in order to function effectively. Second, for at least a decade, the salience of each of these issues has spiraled. Third, each of these issues promises to grow even more salient in the twenty-first century. Finally, together they afford an uncommon perspective on how their interdependencies present managers with difficult trade-offs among values that democratic societies cherish dearly.

ACCOUNTABILITY

As in all cases in which public managers exercise discretion, ensuring that agencies are held accountable for the decisions they make regarding environmental protection is critical in a democracy. As David Rosenbloom (1983) suggests, we hold public managers accountable for a panoply of often-competing values, including cost-effectiveness, responsiveness, and due process. Yet perhaps in no other policy arena are the uncertainties involved in exercising bureaucratic discretion more profound, and the trade-offs among competing democratic values so pronounced, as in environmental protection.

Two examples help illustrate the stakes involved in environmental management challenges, choices, and opportunities. First, consider the role of environmental managers in efforts to limit water pollution. As we discuss in more detail in Chapter Two, the Clean Water Act is the cornerstone of the nation's efforts to protect water quality. One of the goals included in the Clean Water Act (also known as the Federal Water Pollution Control Act) was achieving fishable and swimmable waters by mid-1983. Managers had to determine how to set regulations based on this vague goal. They had to determine what "fishable and swimmable" actually meant in practice.

Although defining these terms seems straightforward, it is anything but. Regulatory agencies, for example, had a whole host of decisions to make. For example, when measuring water quality, should they use physical and chemical data or biological data? Should they test continually or at intervals? If at intervals, should it be hourly, daily, weekly, monthly, or yearly? Should they report averages or extreme measurements? The answer to each of these questions has an important impact on how one assesses water quality, on what the costs are of enhancing it, and on who bears the benefits and burdens of doing so.

Relatedly, technical obstacles and the uncertainties they occasion also plague decisions about water quality. For instance, regulators often find it difficult or impossible to establish whether a body of water is swimmable and fishable in its entirety. Limited resources and other practicalities mean that they can collect data on only the *relative* quality of the water at various sites. They then either aggregate or extrapolate from these readings to categorize the entire water body. But how often, at what depth, at what location, and with what personnel should these measures be taken? Not only do the answers to these questions address cost-effectiveness concerns, but they address social justice concerns as well.

A second illustration of how straightforward operationalizations in theory pose a wide range of choices for agencies interpreting them involves setting goals for solid waste reduction. In the late 1980s and early 1990s, a number of state governments promulgated waste management acts mandating that their localities should better control and reduce wastes. As of 1993, forty-one states and the District of Columbia had legislated comprehensive recycling laws, and thirty-one states have adopted laws setting a specified target for waste reduction (Grogan, 1993). Most of these laws hold a specified local government unit accountable for developing a solid waste management plan and achieving specified reduction goals.

But what material should be categorized as waste? What baseline should be selected to assess progress? Should any special considerations be given to those local governments that had a solid waste reduction strategy in place before the law passed? In addition to these more obvi-ous issues (which legislatures often anticipate), other more difficult issues emerge. What strategy should be employed to meet the waste reduction goals set? How should governments allocate costs (and sav-ings) to reach these goals? To what extent and in what capacity should they allow affected parties (including private waste haulers, home-owners, and different generator groups such as schools, hospitals, and hotels) to help develop and implement a solid waste management plan?

The answers to many of these questions depend, in part, on the goal one is trying to achieve. If the goal is increased public education, re-liance on transfer stations and materials recovery facilities to meet tar-geted reductions would be ineffective. Alternatively, if the goal is to wed waste reduction and efficiency, a system of volume-based garbage pricing would be more logical than a flat-fee system. What is clear is that managers in both cases are faced with dilemmas for which an anxious and sometimes litigious citizenry, with competing values and interests, will hold them accountable. Clear as well is that accountabil-ity in environmental management depends on what gets measured and how it is measured.

Until recently, what got measured most when holding managers accountable for their environmental management decisions were pro-gram inputs (such as number of staff or amounts of funding budgeted) and outputs (such as number of notices of violations issued or number of court cases filed). As we chronicle in subsequent chapters, an epiphany of sorts has resulted from the obvious shortcomings of an exclusive focus on effort rather than on outcomes. For example, legislators now ask "How much cleaner is the water as a result of doing what?"

Indeed, managers dealing with environmental issues today are entering the brave new world of results-based, risk-prioritized, and geography-based environmental management. At the heart of these efforts within agencies are two movements: the environmental indicators movement and the total quality environmental management (TQEM) movement. And intergovernmentally, this "new accountability" is taking form in Environmental Performance Agreements (EnPAs) across the United States between the EPA and various states. In return for regulatory flexi-bility, states contract with EPA to meet agreed-upon performance goals.

None of this will be easy. For example, assigning responsibility for outcomes—good or bad—can be difficult given the transboundary migration of pollutants. Equally challenging to traditional modes of accountability of results is the dense, complex, and opaque nature of policy implementation networks today. Finally, although states are rushing to embrace the environmental indicators movement as a means for becoming more outcomes based, only a handful of states have the rudiments of a system that could be used in multimedia (that is, across media, including air, water, and land) environmental management ("Five States Map...," 1996). Perhaps the environmental management standards developed by the International Standardization Organization (discussed in Chapter Four) will help ameliorate these problems, but we simply do not know at this point.

In the interim, as James Bernard (1996), project manager of the State Environmental Goals and Indicators Project, puts it, "the cultural and bureaucratic shift to fully integrating environmental indicators into management systems is just beginning" (p. 27). Moreover, ongoing efforts still show a pragmatic tendency to develop quality indicators and program performance measures "within the context of programs that relate to individual environmental laws" ("Colorado, Utah Opt...," 1996, p. 12–13). Yet as Bernard argues, this must stop if EnPA is to succeed. Cross-media issues concerned with multiple programs must be identified, measured, and adroitly linked to management decisions. So far, however, statutory tethers have afforded ample justification for those within the states who oppose multimedia initiatives.

Likewise, a twofold problem quickly arose during the early years of the performance partnership program ("States Rebuff...," 1996). To begin with, the single-medium statutory approach taken by Congress, in terms of both regulation and intergovernmental grants, worked in direct opposition to this program. In the EnPA initiative, observers found that "infighting between state agency [program] staff over the pot of money created [was] becoming a hurdle" ("Colorado, Utah Opt...," 1996, p. 13). Indeed, even EPA and state officials "predicted [accurately] that in some states, turf battles [among programs might] overwhelm the performance partnership grant process" (p. 13). Many saw this happening as "state [program] managers accustomed to having a certain amount of funding each year [were] forced to make new justifications for their resources" (p. 13). Still, progress has been made since these shaky beginnings, and managers who ignore these new accountability trends and techniques do so at their agencies' peril.

ECOSYSTEM MANAGEMENT

Ecosystems are characterized by complex relationships among species and considerable natural variability (Rieser, 1991). Eugene Odum (1971), a leading ecosystem ecologist, has defined an ecosystem as a unit of nature in which living and nonliving substances interact, with an exchange of materials between living and nonliving parts (pp. 8–9). "The most common use of [the term] ecosystem by ecologists is in a localized sense, referring to a distinct and coherent ecological community" (Slocombe, 1993, p. 612). In the past, reductionist scientists have viewed humankind as distinct from nature.[2] But the term *ecosystem* as conventionally used today includes systems of varying sizes and includes humans as an integral part.

Managers should understand that the characteristics of ecosystems complicate efforts to manage them. In fact, there is some debate about whether we have enough knowledge to manage ecosystems effectively at all (see, for example, Keiter and Boyce, 1991). Managing on an ecosystem basis, however, is so promising in a theoretical sense for the benefits it can confer that it is a philosophy that will inform environmental debates well into the future. For example, whereas traditional approaches to environmental protection are characterized by fragmentation, ecosystem management is based on recognizing the interconnectedness of the natural world.

Ecosystem management is not a new approach to environmental and natural resources protection (see, for example, Caldwell, 1968). Two decades have passed since the Great Lakes Water Quality Agreement of 1978 included the principles of ecosystem management. More recently, a number of government agencies, including the Department of the Interior and the U.S. Forest Service, have tried to integrate ecosystem-based management into their overall management schemes. A 1995 U.S. Supreme Court decision in the case of *Babbitt* v. *Sweet Home* is important in this regard. The case involved the Endangered Species Act, which makes it unlawful for humans to "take" endangered or threatened species and defines *take* to include harm. The Court upheld a decision by Secretary of the Interior Bruce Babbitt to define *harm* as including significant habitat modification or degradation that actually kills or injures wildlife. This decision provides additional support for applying ecosystem principles to environmental protection.

As we noted earlier, Congress's traditional approaches to resource conservation and environmental protection have been fragmented. The roots of this pathology are both statutory and organizational. Most environmental laws, for example, are differentiated along media lines. For instance, air pollution, water pollution, and land degradation are regulated by distinct federal statutes (such as the Clean Air Act, the Clean Water Act, and the Resource Conservation and Recovery Act).

Reflecting this single-medium focus, separate organizations or management agencies deal with environmental issues that are really interrelated. Most obviously, this balkanization is seen where state and national agencies are managing resources side by side. Separation also exists among a host of federal agencies. For example, agencies that manage federally owned natural resources include the Army Corps of Engineers, the Bureau of Land Management, the Bureau of Reclamation, the Fish and Wildlife Service, the National Park Service, the Natural Resources and Conservation Service, and the U.S. Forest Service. Finally, the single-media statutory focus gets reified within agency structures in the form of separate media offices.

In contrast, ecosystem management is based on the premise that it is important to assess natural systems holistically. In the absence of a holistic approach, managers may simply shift pollution and problems from one medium to another and in the process contribute to the steady deterioration of the environment. Ecosystem management, by recognizing the interconnectedness of the natural world, is an integrated, as opposed to a fragmented, approach to environmental management. Its challenge, of course, is to get programs and agencies to think holistically and work cooperatively as partners when they have a vested interest in dealing only with their parts of the problem.

The Great Lakes region is one area where ecosystem management has taken hold. Efforts to overcome fragmentation in the region date back to the Boundary Waters Treaty of 1909 between Canada and the United States, and the subsequent establishment of the International Joint Commission (IJC). The Great Lakes system is the largest body of freshwater in the world, with its waters washing ashore on a multinational and multistate landscape. As a result, efforts to manage the Great Lakes have taken place at the state, provincial, national, and binational levels.

Since 1973, the IJC's Great Lakes Water Quality Board has identified areas of concern (AOC) within the Great Lakes basin. These areas fail to meet standards specified in the Canada–U.S. Great Lakes Water Quality Agreement. During the 1980s and 1990s, the number of identified AOCs steadily increased. Therefore, in 1985 the IJC's Great Lakes Water Quality Board, in agreement with the eight Great Lakes states and the Province of Ontario, committed to developing and implementing remedial action plans (RAPs) to mitigate these problems (IJC Great Lakes Water Quality Board, 1985). These RAPs are designed to overcome past problems plaguing Great Lakes management. They do so by involving all interests in the process of identifying and dealing with water quality problems in an integrated manner. (For assessments, see Hartig and Hartig, 1992; MacKenzie, 1996.)

Despite the popular currency of ecosystem-based management, however, managers also should understand that it faces a number of serious challenges. First, as long as definitions of ecosystem management compete with one another on equal footing, the concept itself is likely to be attacked as obscure and pseudoscientific. One critic of the ecosystem management concept claims that it "is a meaningless abstraction invoked by bureaucrats who want to exercise national land-use controls, but lack the authority to do it" (Foster, 1994, p. B3).

Second, traditional notions of property and ownership complicate ecosystem management. They do so because they are part of the larger concept of individualism on which liberal political theory is based. The concept of individualism provides a deterrent to policy based on public and transgenerational considerations. To implement ecosystem management successfully, implementers must be able to work cooperatively with property owners individually and with communities collectively.

Third, federal natural resource and environmental management laws complicate efforts to manage ecosystems because they are not applied on the basis of natural boundaries. One ecosystem may therefore be managed according to a variety of legal mandates, some of which may conflict with one another. As a recent General Accounting Office [GAO] report noted, "while ecosystem management will require unparalleled coordination among federal agencies, disparate missions and planning requirements . . . hamper such efforts" (cited in Interagency Ecosystem Management Task Force, 1995, p. 29).

Finally, the political system may impede implementation of ecosystem-based management because the former favors entrenched interests and tends toward conservatism. As future chapters will show, strong, entrenched interest groups benefit from the current system of management. Among others, property rights groups and businesses based on resource extraction will lobby forcefully against adopting ecosystem management. These challenges, of course, need not overwhelm those in a position to adopt practices based on ecosystem management when they are feasible scientifically and politically. They should, however, be recognized and addressed by any manager trying to ensure the long-term viability of any policy or management technique premised on ecosystem principles.

ENVIRONMENTAL JUSTICE

Environmentalists of the 1960s and 1970s focused on developing a national statutory framework in response to environmental and public health risks. For reasons that we will more fully explore in Chapter Six, environmentalists and policymakers at that time were decidedly less concerned than they are today with the inequitable distribution of those threats.[3] In the 1980s, however, a grassroots movement focused on precisely these concerns began to emerge. Specifically, the movement's origins lay in protests against the siting of a polychlorinated biphenyls (PCB) landfill in Warren, North Carolina—a predominantly African-American community. National recognition of the environmental justice movement soon followed, sparked by the release in 1987 of a highly publicized report by the United Church of Christ's Commission for Racial Justice (CRJ).

Environmental justice, according to one leading scholar of environmental law, "focuses on the distributional implications of the way in which our society seeks to manage environmental threats and improve and protect environmental quality" (Been, 1995, p. 1). Other terms used in the past to describe the movement are *environmental racism* and *environmental equity*. Thus, the environmental justice movement, broadly construed, is concerned with unequal distribution of environmental risks based on income, race, or both. Its goals are to identify the existence of distributional inequities of environmental risks, to isolate their causes, and to mitigate them by equalizing exposure to environmental risks.

Reaction to the environmental justice movement has been mixed. Richard Lazarus notes that "the environmental law bar has been surprisingly resistant to environmental justice claims. Much of that resistance derives from basic misapprehension of both the relationship of environmental protection law to distributional concerns and the meaning of environmental justice itself" (Lazarus, 1995, p. 533). Moreover, Lazarus argues, resistance to the environmental justice movement has existed in the past not only in the field of law but also more generally among academics, practitioners, and the polity at large.

Does empirical research have anything to say about the validity of environmental justice claims? Two of the earliest studies conducted to assess the magnitude of problems related to racial injustices were undertaken by Robert Bullard (1983) and the GAO (1983). In the 1970s, Bullard focused on the economic and racial makeup of communities in the Houston, Texas, area that hosted waste disposal facilities. The study, although limited in scope and methodological rigor, found that these sites were located disproportionately in low-income, minority communities. The study thus provided impetus for further policy debate and research in the area of environmental justice. The findings were further corroborated in a more broad-based study done by the GAO in 1983.

Perhaps the two most widely recognized empirical studies of the environmental justice movement to date are the CRJ study mentioned earlier and a study by the Social and Demographic Research Institute at the University of Massachusetts. The CRJ report, issued in 1987, was based on a national survey to determine the socioeconomic characteristics of areas surrounding 415 hazardous waste facilities. The researchers determined the location of the facilities using zip codes, evaluated the racial and socioeconomic characteristics of residents within those zip codes, and then compared the data to information on residents of zip code areas that did not include any such facilities. They found a correlation between hazardous waste sites and both race and income. Sites tended to be located disproportionately in minority and low-income neighborhoods. In 1994, the CRJ updated its study using 1990 census data, and the new findings supported the conclusion that hazardous waste sites are located disproportionately in nonwhite, low-income areas (Goldman and Fitton, 1994).

A report by the Social and Demographic Research Institute at the University of Massachusetts heightened the controversy. As in the CRJ study, researchers found a correlation between the siting of hazardous waste facilities and income. They also found, however, that there was no significant correlation between hazardous waste sites and race (Anderton, Anderson, Oakes, and Fraser, 1994). Methodological differences between the two studies may account for discrepancies between them, including differences in the control population, unit of analysis, and choice of variables. The latter report also reframed the issue in a different way, however. Were disproportionate sitings the result of race or of income?

Upon review of the two studies one researcher contends that the study done by the Social and Demographic Research Institute has a number of weaknesses and errors. He asserts that the conclusions drawn were "simply not credible" (Mohai, 1995, p. 652). Another scholar contends that both studies have methodological flaws and that further empirical research must be done before we have an accurate picture of the nature of the problem (Been, 1995, p. 21).

Toward this end, a more recent study by Tracy Yandle and Dudley Burton (1996) examined ethnic and economic characteristics of communities surrounding hazardous waste sites in metropolitan Texas, both at the time of siting and as of the 1990 census. The authors conclude that at the time of siting, a significant statistical relationship between nonwhite population concentration and hazardous waste facility location did not exist, although poor communities did host a disproportionate number of hazardous waste sites. The obvious inference? Poorer minorities later moved to siting areas to take advantage of the lower rents they produced.

To be sure, comments on the research by Robert Bullard (1996) and Paul Mohai (1996) identify a number of methodological flaws, some of which plague all research in this area. Yandle and Burton, however, have provided one of the few pieces of longitudinal empirical research regarding environmental justice claims and have contributed to the ongoing dialogue. Also, the most statistically sophisticated cross-sectional analysis on Superfund sitings to date has done nothing but further complicate the picture. John Hird (1994) finds a curvilinear relationship: Superfund sites are located disproportionately in both lower and higher income areas. Still, these studies do provide concrete data concerning the existence of distributional inequities in relation to environmental risks. Left unclear, however, are its causes and consequences.

Regardless of who is right, issues such as these are persistently complicating the jobs of environmental managers. Perceptions—real or imagined—are real in their consequences. Managers must therefore, at a minimum, be constantly vigilant about the distributional environmental impacts of their day-to-day decisions. Three primary alternatives exist for vigilant policymakers. First, they may choose to do nothing at this point. After reviewing the evidence regarding problems related to environmental justice, Christopher Boerner and Thomas Lambert (1995) assert that it would be premature to enact regulatory solutions. They conclude this because of the relative lack of empirically rigorous studies that identify the existence and causes of environmental inequities.

A second alternative is to craft regulatory solutions. One possible solution would be to implement an impact assessment test focusing on the racial and economic impact of current and future laws and managerial decisions. The difficulty with regulatory solutions, however, is that they may be ineffective if they do not address the underlying causes of environmental inequities. If Vicki Been (1994) and Yandle and Burton (1996) are correct, once waste disposal facilities are sited in a community, property values drop. The result is described by Boerner and Lambert (1995, p. 77): "Over time, the attractiveness of cheap housing will likely render many host communities low income. A racially skewed income distribution, some degree of housing discrimination, and people's tendency to locate near others who are 'like themselves' often cause these areas to have a larger share of non-white residents. Therefore, changes in the current regulations may not solve the problem."

A final alternative, which is likely to be the most difficult to achieve yet the most effective, is to force communities to internalize the costs that result from resource extraction and consumption. This is the classic "polluter pays principle." Until this is done, some communities are bound to serve as "waste receptacles" for others, and the communities on the receiving end are likely to have insufficient political resources to force the benefiting communities to pay their fair share. Indeed, once they become receptacles, these communities may become progressively weaker (if Yandle and Burton, 1996, and Boerner and Lambert, 1995, are correct). Specifically, as property values decrease, the local tax base declines, leading to further neighborhood deterioration. By forcing communities to deal with their own pollution or to compensate outsiders willing to accept their pollutants, the benefits and burdens of today's economy can be more equitably distributed.

To date, a number of federal and state agencies—including the U.S. Environmental Protection Agency and the Department of the Interior—have developed offices to address environmental justice issues. In addition, President Clinton's Executive Order 12898 established in 1994 an interagency working group on environmental justice chaired by the administrator of the EPA. The order also requires each federal agency to develop an agencywide environmental justice strategy. Inadequate funding for environmental laws undermines these efforts, however, by forcing environmental managers to make trade-offs, and constituencies who lack political clout or resources are not likely to do well when trade-offs are made. Certainly, by fully funding environmental protection laws, by requiring managers to consider the distribution of environmental risks, or both, legislatures may further environmental justice goals. Yet the prospects for this remain minuscule for the foreseeable future.

In the interim, however, managers must pay attention to how their decisions affect equity considerations—or else face the wrath of angry and litigious environmental justice advocates. Risk assessment and communication, as we discuss in Chapter Seven, will become part of astute managers' toolkits under these circumstances. So, too, will their skills in working with these vocal elements in their communities (see Chapter Six). All of this is likely to result in increased conflict in the short term; if managed effectively, however, managers can reap significant long-term benefits (as we discuss in Chapter Eight).

SUSTAINABLE DEVELOPMENT

The term *sustainable development* was first popularized in *Our Common Future,* a 1987 publication of the World Commission on Environment and Development (often referred to as the Brundtland Commission). According to the commission, the goal of sustainable development is "to meet the needs of the present without compromising the ability of future generations to meet their own needs" (p. 43). Used most often in the field of international environmental law and policy, this definition served as the organizing theme for the United Nations Conference on Environment and Development in Rio de Janeiro in 1992. The most significant product of the Rio conference was *Agenda 21,* a global action plan for sustainable development (United Nations Conference on Environment and Development, 1992).

Sustainable development has more recently been applied at national and subnational levels of government. In June 1993 President Clinton established the President's Council on Sustainable Development to develop a set of strategies and policy recommendations for assisting the United States in realizing this goal. The council responded by issuing, in 1996, the report *Sustainable America: A New Consensus.* Its authors take a very broad view of sustainable development. Instead of focusing solely on environmental protection, they emphasize that prosperity requires promoting civic engagement, nurturing social capital, stimulating economic growth, and equitably distributing economic gains.[4]

The concept of sustainable development has drawn widespread criticism for its ambiguity. Nonetheless, the debate over its meaning has forced policymakers to realize that they must consider the environmental impact of human actions not only in the present but also in the future. Thus, central to the notion of sustainable development are two concepts: *intergenerational equity* and the *finite* nature of the Earth's resources. A number of commentators have also adopted an economic interpretation of sustainable development, arguing that the achievement of sustainability involves the maintenance of capital, specifically natural resource capital (such as timber and minerals).

All managers would do well to understand what these concepts mean in practice for their jobs. First, *intragenerational* equity means that managers must try to ensure that the costs and benefits associated with the use of natural resources and with environmental protection are borne evenly among people in the present. One way for managers to think of this term is to consider how their actions affect environmental justice. To the extent that intragenerational equity is not realized, social conflict may result. In contrast, *intergenerational* equity means that managers need to consider how their activities today will affect future generations. Are they stewarding tomorrow's resources, or are they squandering them for today's gain?

Second, and relatedly, sustainable development means that managers must try to conserve biological resources. The United States took a bold step in this direction when the federal government passed the Endangered Species Act (ESA) of 1973. Since that time, and although there has been success in saving some species, more than two hundred of them have become extinct (Brown, 1996). This outcome has resulted partially from the inherently reactive rather than proactive approach that Congress took in the ESA (Tobin, 1990). For example, species achieve protected status only when they are already in danger of becoming extinct. Ecosystem management may yet combine with other efforts to protect species better. But in the interim, managers must deal with another problem. How can they prudently balance the rights of species and those of property owners and workers?

Third, managers need to know how to internalize the costs of environmental degradation in the prices of goods and to alter the way nations measure economic growth. A number of alternative regulatory approaches—such as pollution discharge fees, information provision, and subsidies—may help with the former. These and other nontraditional approaches to regulation may also combine with traditional command-and-control regulations to advance this cause—as we shall see in Chapter Twelve. Changing the way nations measure economic growth requires, in turn, thought in developing systems of national accounts that measure gross domestic product in ways that also depreciate the value of the natural resources consumed to produce it (Van Dieren, 1995).

Fourth, by focusing on organizational processes, managers may be able to reduce humankind's adverse impact on the environment (for example, by reducing ozone-depleting chemicals).[5] Whereas traditional environmental regulations were devised to control pollution, process-oriented changes may prevent pollution. An example of process-oriented change is replacing open-cycle gas turbines with combined-cycle power plants for coal combustion. The combined-cycle process uses both gas and steam turbines, thereby increasing efficiency as much as 45 percent. Combined-cycle power plants can also generate the same amount of energy with less coal and lower emissions. In addition, TQEM, if applied strategically, provides managers with a systematic process-centered approach to moving toward principles of sustainability in their agencies.

Finally, managers can effect sustainable development principles only if they develop and report accurate environmental indicators to chart their progress (see International Institute for Sustainable Development, 1997; Lee and others, 1996; Balaton Group, 1996; Sustainable Seattle, 1995). Lee and his associates metaphorically compare the quest for sustainable development to driving in the fog. For them, indicators can act as little "bumps and guardrails," keeping policymakers and environmental managers on course (if the correct indicators are chosen).

To these ends, Sustainable Seattle (1995) has developed a set of indicators that environmental managers may look to as a starting point. Managers must never forget, however, that indicators are context-dependent (or place-based). Thus, in using "turnkey" indicators like Sustainable Seattle's, they must take into account their own circumstances and adapt the indicators accordingly. Moreover, even when they have done so, managers must ensure that the measures get to the right people in a useable format and in time to affect operating decisions. This in turn requires the use of information management systems that are state-of-the-art and that provide information that has consequences for agency rewards. Strategic environmental information systems (SEIS), analyzed in detail in Chapter Nine, can play a central role in this process.

UNFUNDED MANDATES

No doubt the term *unfunded mandates* is familiar to managers at all levels of government, regardless of their areas of specialization. The term emerged in the late 1970s and early 1980s in response to a number of forces, in particular the growth of federal regulations that either applied to state and local agencies or that they had to implement. As R. Shep Melnick (1983, p. 5) notes, "between 1968 and 1978 Congress passed more regulatory statutes than it had in the nation's previous 179 years." At least a dozen of these intergovernmental regulations were major environmental laws. As we discuss further in Chapters Two, Three, and Six, these laws had a tremendous impact on state and local governments. In most cases, states were encouraged to play a major role in implementing them. But Congress also set minimum criteria that states had to meet before doing so. Moreover, although states and localities were partners in many federal environmental protection efforts, they were partners who could not opt out—whether they were the regulators or the regulatees.

One way in which Congress also attempted to promote environmental protection was through procedural change. For example, the National Environmental Policy Act included a provision that the government consider the environmental impact of proposals for legislation and other major federal actions significantly affecting the quality of the human environment. Another way was by including in environmental laws citizen suit provisions that allow citizens to act as private attorneys general and enforce environmental laws. In the process, as we discuss more thoroughly in later chapters, the judiciary relaxed standing requirements and more vigorously scrutinized agency decision making (Shapiro, 1988; Rabin, 1986; Melnick, 1992; Rabkin, 1989; Rosenbloom and O'Leary, 1997).

The consequences of these actions for states and localities were profound. More precisely, the broader tendency of the courts to urge faster agency action, tighter standards, and more vigorous enforcement also amplified the impact of mandates on states and localities (Melnick, 1983; O'Leary, 1989, 1990a, 1993a; Wenner, 1982, 1994). Melnick (1989, p. 206) has observed that "states receiving small amounts of money from the federal government [find] themselves under court order to follow extensive, detailed requirements spelled out in House and Senate reports and in agency regulations."

Budgetary pressures have also long limited the ability of states and localities to raise revenue sufficient to meet regulatory goals. This is true even when, as recently, state economies are booming. Why? Largely because environmental protection often takes a back seat to funding more immediate pressures for welfare, highway, and prison spending. Managers therefore find fiscal pressures exerted both from the top down by the federal government and from the bottom up by antitax, environment, and "good government" groups.

To understand fully the passions that unfunded mandates spawn, it is useful to trace these pressures over time. During the late 1970s, the federal budget deficit became a concern of the nation as a whole. That concern then spiraled during the 1980s and culminated in the 1995 Balanced Budget Agreement. As a result, the federal government has taken numerous steps to decrease spending. Among these have been efforts to scale back funds appropriated to states and localities for meeting statutory mandates. For example, the amount of grant money available for constructing sewage treatment plants has decreased steadily since the mid-1970s.

Meanwhile, grassroots taxpayer revolts, such as Proposition 13 passed in California in 1978, flourished. These limited the ability of states and localities to generate revenue. In addition to enacting explicit property tax controls, a number of states even limited the total tax collection of their local governments during the 1980s (Swartz and Peck, 1990). Such actions threatened the fiscal base of localities; forced them to use alternative measures, such as user fees, to raise revenue; and meant downsizing workforces that continue to affect their operations in the present. Most recently they have led to major efforts to privatize (through contracting) a host of traditional state and local services (Donahue, 1989), including environmental management functions (discussed more fully in Chapter Eleven).

Upset by the burden that these top-down and bottom-up forces imposed on them, a vocal subset of local government officials helped place the mandate issue on the national political agenda in the early 1990s. A number of cities (such as Anchorage, Alaska; Chicago, Illinois; and Columbus, Ohio) initiated studies of the impact of unfunded mandates. Two national surveys done in 1993 by Price Waterhouse (a private consulting firm) for the U.S. Conference of Mayors and the National Association of Counties received widespread attention in the media and Congress. These studies concluded that mandates have a major impact on local finances, and that they tend to absorb resources that local governments would otherwise allocate among other services (Price Waterhouse, 1993a, 1993b).

Nevertheless, the issue remains an open one. Many see these studies as seriously deficient in a number of ways. First, although they are presented as analyses of the impact of federal mandates on cities and counties, neither accounts for both costs and benefits. Nor did the survey sent to cities provide any opportunity for officials to identify any positive or beneficial aspects of the specified mandates (U.S. Conference of Mayors, 1994).

At the same time, there were even reasons to doubt the validity and ethics of these surveys. Costs were not verified, and the cities and counties participating were informed in advance that the survey would be used to draw attention to the burden posed by unfunded mandates. Consequently, as one report by the staff of the U.S. Senate Committee on Environment and Public Works (1994, p. 9) noted, "tremendous incentives existed for cities and counties to inflate or exaggerate the costs [they] provided to Price Waterhouse." Cities and counties also were asked for only the total costs associated with federal mandates. They were not instructed to account for federal grants associated with mandates. When members of the staff of the U.S. Senate Committee on Environment and Public Works contacted a sample of the survey respondents, they found that only 12 percent had incorporated federal funds into their cost estimates.

When assessing the costs associated with mandates, evaluators should also differentiate total costs from incremental costs. As the committee's staff noted, "many federal mandates are designed to achieve a goal that state and local governments share. Consequently, many state and local governments would take actions toward achieving that goal without a federal mandate. The true cost of the mandate, therefore, is the incremental cost that the mandate imposes on state and local governments" (p. 2). None of the studies just mentioned addressed this key question.

It is also unclear how many cities and counties were sent surveys by Price Waterhouse. We do know that 314 cities and 128 counties responded. But according to the Municipal Year Book, there were 7,175 cities and 3,043 counties in the United States in 1993 (International City/County Management Association, 1993). We also know that because of the limited response rate, costs were extrapolated on the basis of the information gathered. The primary problem with cost estimates like these is that they fail to account for wide variances in state and local conditions. Moreover, the problem is only compounded when an unrepresentative sample is drawn (U.S. Senate Committee on Environment and Public Works, 1994; Conlan, Riggle, and Schwartz, 1995).

Finally, the term *unfunded mandates* is often used inappropriately. This occurs mostly when partially funded mandates (such as the Federal Water Pollution Control Act Amendments and the Safe Drinking Water Act) or voluntary programs (such as the National Environmental Policy Act and the Coastal Zone Management Act) are labeled unfunded. Even if one agrees that unfunded mandates are requirements that impose substantial unreimbursed costs, Michael Hamilton (1990) points out that it is necessary to define *substantial*. For instance, the grant program established under the Federal Water Pollution Control Act Amendments of 1972 to subsidize the construction of municipal sewage treatment plants covered 75 to 85 percent of construction costs (Hamilton, 1990, p. 33). In Illinois this meant that the city of Kankakee, collaborating with a number of neighboring municipalities, was able to construct a $43 million regional sewage treatment facility. Saying that this law was an unfunded mandate because Kankakee had to pay the balance of the costs trivializes the benefits it afforded to citizens in that community.

Although some state and local government officials are outspoken in their opposition to federal mandates, others support them. Paul Posner (1996, p. 141) asserts that "although the general interest group literature suggests that states and localities would be vigilant opponents of mandates, the record [has] actually [been] quite mixed as state and local interest group positions varied across the 12 mandates [studied]." Posner outlines a number of reasons that states and localities may support mandates: because mandates have compelling political appeal, because mandates offer useful political cover, because states and localities face constraining effects of intergovernmental competition, and because the benefits are immediate while the costs are deferred.

Relatedly, Timothy Conlan (1991, p. 47) contends that "a strong federal role can provide state officials with a convenient whipping-boy, and it limits private-sector attempts to play competing jurisdictions against one another in an effort to lessen regulatory burdens." Dewitt John (1994) also suggests that lower levels of government may use the threat of central regulation and intervention to induce environmentally sensitive behavior. An environmental manager from Laguna Beach, interviewed by the authors in 1996, adds, "In some areas it is important for the feds to establish goals." In addition, the deputy mayor of a New Jersey township stated in another 1996 interview that "the costs associated with environmental regulations are not resented, they are needed." These statements are evidence of the multifaceted nature of the impacts of environmental mandates.

Still, environmental mandates do impose significant costs as well as benefits on state and local governments. Consequently, both today's and tomorrow's managers would do well to understand how these mandates affect the metes and bounds of what they can—and cannot—do in meeting the challenges, choices, and opportunities of environmental issues. Mandates can—when prudently applied—realize cost-effective reductions in health, safety, and ecological risks. They may also buttress the capacity of state and local institutions (Hanford and Sokolow, 1987; Weiland, 1996). But prudence also requires that managers appreciate how misguided mandates, unwisely implemented and insufficiently flexible, can be the bane of their existence. In sum, oversimplified characterizations of intergovernmental mandates have the potential to produce ill-informed policies.

CONCLUSION

The environmental policy issues, trends, and trade-offs identified in this chapter are among the most significant concerns facing the United States today. Each issue discussed will shape the nature of environmental management well into the next century. As such, and as we discuss further in Chapter Thirteen, they will affect the abilities of managers to meet their environmental responsibilities as far as the eye can see. But how can managers best come to grips with their options in dealing with these issues? Arguably, the best place to start is with the statutory regime presently framing environmental management in the United States. It is to that regime that we turn next in Chapter Two.

2

WHAT EVERY MANAGER SHOULD KNOW ABOUT ENVIRONMENTAL LAW

There are two laws discrete,
Not reconciled—
Law for man, and law for thing.

—Ralph Waldo Emerson

Perhaps nowhere do the themes of dynamism, adaptation, and communication become more apparent than in the changing demands that lawmakers are placing on both regulators and the regulated community. Indeed, environmental law is changing management in ways and at a pace that is mind-boggling. To name only a few examples, it is altering land-purchase practices, the operation of schools, wastewater collection and treatment, refuse disposal, the operation of hospitals, land-use planning, road maintenance, water supply and delivery, the operation of parks, and the operation of airports. There is scarcely a public, nonprofit, or for-profit organization today that is not affected by environmental regulations.

At the same time, contemporary environmental law is also challenging and superseding our traditional notions of sovereign immunity for public agencies and managers. Historically, a double standard existed by which government entities prosecuted polluters yet were allowed to violate environmental laws with impunity. In 1989, for example, Federal District Court Judge Jim R. Carrigan, in *Colorado* v. *United States*

Department of the Army (1989), called the U.S. Department of Defense's Rocky Mountain Arsenal "the worst hazardous and toxic waste site in America" (p. 1570). In 1988, the U.S. General Accounting Office reported that "federal facilities' rate of noncompliance with [Clean Water Act] priority program requirements is twice that of nonfederal industrial facilities" (U.S. General Accounting Office, 1988b, p. 3). Yet nowhere, it seemed, were these offenders being called to account for their environmental misadventures.

As we discuss more fully in Chapter Three, however, the days of this double standard are numbered (U.S. Environmental Protection Agency, 1994, 1995). Generally, the sovereign no longer has a license to pollute, because environmental law is increasingly imposing significant demands on organizations and their managers. What is more, the courts are increasingly holding them to these new standards.

To appreciate what a dramatic change has occurred for all managers, one has only to look to the history of environmental laws. Indeed, the first 120 years of the United States saw no major environmental legislation (Advisory Commission on Intergovernmental Relations, 1981). The first major U.S. environmental law, the Refuse Act, was promulgated in 1899 as a means of keeping navigable waters clear of refuse that might block ships. It took nearly an additional fifty years before a second major environmental statute, the Water Pollution Control Act (WPCA) of 1948, became law. Following on its heels in the 1950s were the Air Pollution Control Act of 1955 and the 1956 amendments to the WPCA. Still, no mention could be found in any of these statutes of the need to hold public agencies accountable to them (O'Leary, 1993c).

Beginning in the 1960s, this situation started to change as the tide of environmental reform began to swell. Eleven major federal environmental laws were enacted in the 1960s, and seventeen were enacted in the 1970s. By the 1980s the tide had turned into a flood, as an amazing forty-eight environmental bills became law. Then, in 1990, Congress passed significant amendments to the Clean Air Act (CAA), as well as amendments affecting the Federal Water Pollution Control Act. Today Congress continues to fine tune these and other environmental statutes, often trying to increase the liability of managers for organizational misdeeds.

These efforts brought both good and bad news for all concerned. The goods news was that the nation's inordinate focus on economic growth was now increasingly tempered by concerns about the health, safety, and ecological costs of that growth. But this focus also brought bad news that has grown only more pronounced as the years have passed.

Examining the dramatic rise in federal environmental laws in the United States, one author has written, "What we see looking back [on those years] is that pollution control is a new subject. . . . Everything is new—the institutions, the ideas, the rules of law. All have been freshly invented. A large and very complex system has been built over the past 20 years, its separate parts built separately and sometimes without much awareness of the whole structure" (Novick, 1986, p. 12).

In this chapter, we afford synopses of six major sets of environmental laws that managers dealing with this complexity will most commonly encounter in their jobs: statutes involving air pollution, water pollution (both above ground and underground), hazardous waste, pesticides and toxics, and pollution prevention (see Table 2.1 for a summary). Before starting, however, we should note that our aim is not to focus on all aspects of these environmental laws as they evolved. Many of these changes we have saved for subsequent chapters, in which we highlight their implications relative to particular management issues. Moreover, in Chapter Twelve we review the evolution of alternatives to the command-and-control statutory and regulatory structures that we chronicle here and in the intervening chapters. For now, it is useful for readers to get their statutory bearings by reviewing the evolution of the heart of today's regulatory regime and its implications for managers.

AIR QUALITY

The Clean Air Act of 1970 was not the first federal air quality law. But it differed from previous laws (enacted in 1955, 1963, 1965, and 1967) in important ways. First, it defined national goals in the form of ambient standards (levels of air pollution in the surrounding air) that all parts of the country had to meet. Second, it directed the newly created EPA to set national standards for controlling emissions of toxic air pollutants. Third, it set limits for emissions from mobile sources (cars, and later trucks), as "percentage reductions" from existing levels. Fourth, it gave the EPA authority to set national standards for emissions from new sources of pollutants. Finally, it also directed the states to prepare state implementation plans (SIPs) describing how they would reduce emissions from existing sources in areas (air quality districts that are defined in the act) that exceeded the ambient air quality goals.

The cornerstones of the CAA today are the National Ambient Air Quality Standards (NAAQS) the act mandated. Set by the EPA, these standards were to be based solely on the protection of public health and not on economic factors. NAAQS reflect the EPA's best judgment about the maximum concentrations of pollutants that can exist in the

Table 2.1. U.S. Statutory Framework (1969–1993).

	Sources/Problems Addressed	Enacted/Reauthorized	Significant Features
Air quality	Industrial and mobile sources of air pollutants and air toxics	1970 (CAA) 1977 (Reauth.) 1990 (CAAA)	Combines health-based and technology-based rules. State plans are key. Covers conventional and toxic emissions.
Surface water	Industrial and municipal sources; later "nonpoint" sources	1972 (FWPCA) 1977 (CWA) 1987 (WQA)	Uses controls on industrial sources and grants for sewage treatment. Relies on some geographically based programs.
Waste	Current waste generation and disposal Cleanup of abandoned waste sites (CERCLA)	1976 (RCRA) 1980 (CERCLA) 1984 (HSWA) 1986 (SARA)	RCRA/HSWA set comprehensive rules stressing technology controls. CERCLA cleanup based on "polluter pays" and a trust fund.
Toxics/Pesticides	Chemicals used as pesticides (FIFRA) Other chemicals posing "unreasonable risk" (TSCA)	1972 (FIFRA amended) 1976 (TSCA) 1988 (FIFRA amended)	Both employ a risk-benefit or cost-benefit test. FIFRA establishes a national registration program.
Prevention	Pollution Prevention Act (PPA)	1990	Creates a hierarchy of waste management approaches as national policies (reduce, recycle, treatment, and disposal).
Examples of other environmental laws	Safe Drinking Water Act (SDWA) Endangered Species Act (ESA) Oil Pollution Act (OPA) National Environmental Policy Act (NEPA)	1986 (amended) 1973 1990 1969	These address a variety of more specialized problems and issues. EPA is responsible for most but shares responsibility for others (such as NEPA or ESA).

Source: Adapted from Fiorino, D. J. *Making Environmental Policy.* Berkeley: University of California Press, 1995, p. 26. Copyright © 1995 The Regents of the University of California. Used with permission of The Regents of the University of California.

ambient air and not harm the health of the most sensitive parts of the population (such as the elderly or people with respiratory conditions). The law further requires that these ambient standards be set to provide an "adequate margin of safety."

The EPA subsequently issued separate NAAQS for several common air pollutants: sulfur dioxide, ozone, particulate matter, carbon monoxide, nitrogen oxide, and lead. Each state has to show that each of its air quality districts has attained NAAQS or is taking steps through its SIPs to attain them. Any area not meeting the NAAQS is classified as a "nonattainment" area for that pollutant, with subsequent limits placed on the amount of their future growth in the absence of pollution control measures (as we subsequently discuss).

Much of the rest of the law is aimed at meeting the NAAQS. Congress directed reductions in auto emissions of 90 percent for carbon monoxide and hydrocarbons and 82 percent for nitrogen oxide. For stationary sources (such as factories, refineries, and utilities), the law distinguishes new from existing sources. New sources are subject to national, uniform New Source Performance Standards (NSPS). The standards are set according to industrial category and apply uniformly to all new sources of the pollutants covered by the NAAQS. Indeed, they apply even in areas that have met the NAAQS.

The NSPS are technology-based limits; they reflect engineering judgments about what is the best available and most affordable technology per category of industry. The law does not require national emission limits for existing sources. These are set by states as necessary to meet or maintain the NAAQS. That is, if a designated area fails to attain the NAAQS and is considered to be in "nonattainment" with them, it has to set limits on emissions of existing sources or take other measures needed to attain the standards. Finally, the law also requires the EPA to list and regulate several hazardous air pollutants (also known as air toxics), such as benzene and asbestos. These differ from the conventional pollutants covered by the NAAQS, because they can pose more serious and immediate threats to health, even in small quantities.

The Logic of Reform

After years of experience with and mounting criticism of the 1970 CAA, Congress reauthorized the act with some changes in 1977, and later in 1990 after more than a decade of political struggle. Both newer versions largely reaffirmed the earlier command-and-control strategy, but with modifications designed to address several critiques of the implementation of that approach. Environmentalists, for example, excoriated what they called the relaxation of automobile standards since 1970, the paucity of pollution control efforts for acid rain and airborne toxics, and weak enforcement. In contrast, the regulated community— supported by many economists—argued that uniform standards and command-and-control methods were inefficient and ineffective. In effect, it was not enforcement that was lacking but the bases on which enforcement took place. The preferred response of many regulatees and economists: increased use of market incentives and market-based solutions to environmental problems.

Thus, among other things, the 1977 act incorporated an emissions offset policy that the EPA had already adopted administratively. As we discuss more thoroughly in Chapter Twelve, this policy allowed new sources to offset with reductions elsewhere the increases in pollutants that the new sources occasion. It also relaxed standards and rolled back compliance dates for attaining them. Still, critics argued that the act placed southern and western states at a decided disadvantage relative to the rest of the country in terms of economic development and coal production. It did so by requiring new sources of pollution to install expensive scrubber control equipment. Other critics charged that this and other features of the act actually increased sulfur dioxide.

The 1990 version (which we call the CAAA, for Clean Air Act Amendments) tried to deal with some of these criticisms and was a decidedly more important piece of legislation than was the CAA of 1977. Several aspects of the CAAA stand out as especially critical for managers to understand. First, the CAAA revised the provisions for attaining and maintaining the NAAQS for ozone, carbon monoxide, and fine particulates. The most important provision dealt with ozone, for which (based on 1987–1989 data) nearly one hundred areas in the country had not attained the NAAQS. These nonattainment areas were placed in five groups, according to the severity of their ozone pollution. They ranged from marginal (thirty-nine areas) and moderate (thirty-two areas) to serious (sixteen areas), severe (eight areas), and extreme areas (Los Angeles, which was literally in a class by itself). Severe areas were given more time to attain the NAAQS, but they had to meet more stringent and greater numbers of control requirements. SIPs, for example, had to specify how states would attain the ozone NAAQS. Plans for the dirtier areas had to include tighter controls, cover more sources, use economic incentive programs, and require more controls on mobile sources and transportation than did the plans for the other areas. Similarly, areas that failed to attain the NAAQS for carbon monoxide and fine particulates were classified as either moderate or serious. Areas classed as serious had to adopt more stringent controls—such as enhanced auto inspection and maintenance, driving restrictions, and strict industrial controls—than the moderate areas.

Second, the CAAA also expanded the limits on emissions from motor vehicles and set standards for a newer generation of clean fuels. For instance, areas with high ozone levels had to begin using reformulated gasoline and expand the use of fleet vehicles (such as taxis and delivery vans) that can run on these cleaner fuels. Congress also set tighter limits on tailpipe emissions in order to get lower levels of hydrocarbons, carbon monoxide, nitrogen oxide, and particles in the ambient air. In turn, the EPA will have to set even more stringent limits on vehicle emissions by the year 2000, if that appears necessary for achieving the NAAQS.

Third, the 1990 law also adopted strong new provisions for air toxics. The EPA's inability to set more than a handful of standards for toxic air pollutants under the earlier law led Congress to list pollutants and insert deadlines for issuing standards for them. More precisely, the law directs the EPA to set Maximum Available Control Technology (MACT) standards for a list of 189 toxic air pollutants for categories of sources (such as petroleum refineries) that emit those pollutants. The agency has to set MACT standards to reach the maximum emission reductions that it decides are achievable, taking cost and other factors into account. Moreover, these standards must be stricter for new sources than for old sources. In addition, if the EPA determines that significant residual risks remain after these technology-based controls are in place, it must require even stricter controls that protect health with an ample margin of safety.

Fourth, the CAAA dealt with acid rain control. Large industrial sources—mostly utilities in the Midwest—emit sulfur oxide and nitrogen oxide from tall smokestacks. These pollutants are transported long distances, chemically transformed, and fall as acid rain over New England and Canada. Thus, Title IV of the CAAA set a goal for attenuating this problem: reduce annual emissions of sulfur oxide to ten million tons and nitrogen oxide to two million tons below their 1980 levels. Presumably most of these reductions will be achieved through an innovative allowance trading system that we investigate more thoroughly in Chapter Twelve.

The Critique

Managers should understand that the implementation of the 1990 CAAA has not escaped criticism either. For example, the volume of trading in air pollution futures has proven disappointing to date. Also, the CAAA's eight hundred pages (compared to the 1970 CAA's fifty pages) have made it a decidedly complex act to implement. Moreover, not unlike what happened in the hazardous waste policy area (see discussion later in this chapter), Congress's distrust of a Republican administration's implementation of the CAAA caused it to try to limit the discretion of the EPA's managers with tough agency-forcing and "hammer" provisions. For example, the EPA was charged with the incredible burden of writing fifty-five new regulations in two years, and was further prodded to action with one hundred deadlines enforceable in courts of law. Moreover, President Bush's moratorium on all new federal regulations combined with Vice President Quayle's Council of Competitiveness and the scientific complexities of the issues involved to cause the EPA to miss several of these deadlines (such as issuing toxic pollution permit guidelines and standards for reformulated gasoline). Finally, elected officials and managers in several states were outraged when, in late 1992, they were faced with fines for not complying with CAAA regulations that the EPA had not yet produced (Fiorino, 1995; Rosenbaum, 1994).

WATER QUALITY

Managers will find striking similarities to the CAA's regulatory approach in the Federal Water Pollution Control Act (FWPCA) of 1972. Earlier water laws (enacted in 1948, 1956, and 1965) had limited the federal role in this area to guidance, research, investigation, and grants. The 1972 law changed all this. Congress directed the EPA to set uniform, national limits on effluents for all major sources of discharges into water. These limits, known under the law as *effluent guidelines,* are similar to the NSPS in air. They were designed to force industry to adopt the latest available technology. Though states had a role, the FWPCA, like the CAA, set up a centralized program with federal oversight of state activities, at least for point sources of pollution (that is, those with an identifiable discharge point).

The goals of the FWPCA were to eliminate all discharges into navigable waters of the United States by 1985 and to make all water "fishable and swimmable" by the middle of 1983. Both were ambitious goals that still have not been met (and may never be met). The FWPCA also expanded an existing federal program of grants to municipalities for constructing sewage treatment plants, a program that eventually grew into one of the largest public works projects in history. Congress authorized the federal government to pay 75 percent of the cost of these plants. Importantly, there is nothing comparable in the air program, in which nearly all costs are borne by the private sector.

The air and water acts also differ in their use of ambient standards to define goals and set limits on dischargers. Under the water program, there is nothing equivalent to the health-based, nationally uniform NAAQS. Earlier water laws made states set water quality standards for specific bodies of water (lakes or segments of rivers) and then draft plans for meeting them. Consequently, standards varied, depending on each state's decision about the "designated use" of its different water bodies. Based on these standards, state permit officials assigned limits to dischargers as necessary to keep levels of contaminants at or below the standard. The FWPCA continued this program, but with even more federal oversight. States have to review their standards every three years and submit any changes to the EPA for approval. They may set stricter standards based on higher (cleaner) designated uses, but the EPA carefully reviews any proposals to relax standards, and may reject them.

So, although the water act relies on ambient standards, these vary by location and by the designated use prescribed for a water body. As with the air act, a failure to meet a standard can trigger stricter controls. The FWPCA also added a system of technology-based effluent guidelines to the program. Importantly for managers, these guidelines apply to industrial dischargers and municipal sewage treatment plants. They set numerical limits based on the EPA's judgments about "currently available" (by 1977) or "best available" (by 1983) control technologies that dischargers can be expected to meet. The only qualification is that the limits and technologies they are based on must be "economically achievable." Like the NSPS, these effluent guidelines apply to all new sources in defined categories of industrial dischargers, even if the receiving water meets the local quality standard. If by meeting the guidelines a state still does not achieve the standard, the EPA or the state can require still stricter controls.

As they did with the CAA, Congress has reauthorized the water act twice since 1972. The 1977 revisions postponed some deadlines and gave more weight to the control of toxic pollutants. In turn, the Water

Quality Act of 1987 (passed over President Reagan's veto) again put off some of the deadlines and expanded federal programs for nonpoint sources, such as discharges from urban storm sewers. The 1987 act also changed the approach for financing wastewater treatment plants from a system based on grants to local governments to a state revolving-loan fund. In doing so, of course, it further heightened the unfunded mandate rebellion that we noted in Chapter One. Finally, the law also expanded water quality programs for lakes and estuaries, including the special ecosystem programs for the Great Lakes and other areas that we discussed earlier.

Some of the loudest criticisms expressed today about the U.S. water regulatory regime are either shared or scoffed at by public, nonprofit, and for-profit organizations. To begin with, the focus is almost exclusively on point sources of water pollution (that is, pollution from municipal sewage treatment plants and industrial facilities). Yet nearly two-thirds of all pollutants reaching waterways in the nation come from nonpoint sources (such as urban, agricultural, and mining runoff of pollutants). Critics therefore lambaste the regime for failing to regulate waterborne toxic pollutants to the extent required by the FWPCA. For example, charged by the 1972 act to issue toxic pollutant effluent standards for fifty industrial categories, the EPA had issued standards for only half that number by 1992. Finally, many have criticized the slow pace of improvement in many water quality indicators.

In response to some of these complaints, calls for reform—some successful—have mounted. Most popular are proposals for strengthening the discretion of states and localities in choosing ways to prevent nonpoint source pollution, for rolling back deadlines for municipalities trying to meet stormwater runoff regulations, and for making these facilities eligible for federal construction grants. Still, these issues will continue to plague managers into the next century.

A second water statute, the Safe Drinking Water Act (SDWA) needs to be mentioned briefly. Enacted in 1974 and amended in 1986, the SDWA has two principal purposes: to ensure that our drinking water is safe and to prevent the contamination of groundwater, which serves as the principal source of drinking water for 50 percent of the general population and for 95 percent of the rural population in the United States. The most important part of the SDWA is the underground injection control program, which regulates the disposal of liquid wastes underground. A pressing public policy challenge today is that many small public water systems simply cannot afford to monitor and treat the many contaminants that are now regulated pursuant to the SDWA.

HAZARDOUS AND SOLID WASTES

The first significant national law to deal with hazardous and solid wastes came out of Congress in 1976, after the air and water laws were passed. By the end of the 1970s, concerns about the health effects of hazardous wastes rose quickly in salience on the national policy agenda, and by the early 1980s these efforts were among the most important environmental issues facing managers across the nation. What is more, statutory attempts to redress these efforts have become so extensive and complex in the 1990s that managers who remain ignorant of this regulatory regime do so at their peril.

Prospective Waste Regulation

To appreciate this situation, one has to begin with the Resource Conservation and Recovery Act (RCRA) of 1976, an act superseding the Solid Waste Disposal Act of 1965. RCRA set a cradle-to-grave regulatory framework that covered the generation, transportation, treatment, and disposal of hazardous wastes. More precisely, the EPA issued regulations pursuant to RCRA that defined hazardous wastes, tracked wastes from generation to disposal, and set technical standards and rules for issuing permits to facilities that treated, stored, or disposed of wastes.

In this initial version of the law, Congress gave the EPA considerable discretion in meeting these goals. All of this changed, however, when a chagrined Congress reauthorized RCRA as the Hazardous and Solid Waste Amendments (HSWA) of 1984. The EPA's slow pace in issuing RCRA rules, the early Reagan administration's patent assault on RCRA, and public concern about the administration's deeds led Congress to pass one of the most prescriptive laws in its history (Durant, 1993). HSWA directed the EPA to regulate new classes of facilities, including generators of small quantities of hazardous wastes and underground petroleum and chemical storage tanks. To reduce the chance of groundwater contamination, the law also set strict limits on the disposal of wastes on land. In turn, HSWA dealt with facilities that close and leave waste behind by establishing liability, insurance, and corrective-action provisions to cover cleanups.

Even more significant is how Congress wrote the HSWA to force action and severely limit the EPA's discretion. Indeed, many of the more than seventy statutory requirements the act imposed on the EPA look more like regulations than legislation. Because the legislative deadlines under previous laws had been missed, and due to its deep and abiding distrust of the Reagan administration, Congress wrote "hammers" into the HSWA. Under the hammers, if the EPA failed to issue rules by a given date, the statutory requirements automatically fell into place. The most important such provision in the HSWA is a presumptive ban on land disposal of hazardous wastes.

Significantly, Congress gave little attention to the costs and economic impacts of the program it was directing the EPA to implement. And because RCRA does not explicitly allow the EPA to consider costs in setting standards, the HSWA rules are among the most stringent that the EPA has issued. As significant as these problems were, they were but the tip of the iceberg of the challenges that HSWA wrought for managers both regulating and regulated by its strictures. Although we discuss many of these problems in subsequent chapters, three illustrations will suffice presently to give the reader the flavor of these challenges. These illustrations deal with the statute's mandates, regulatory regime, and resource incapacities.

TOO MANY MANDATES, TOO LITTLE TIME In quite rational reaction to HSWA's hammer provisions, the EPA's Office of Solid Waste and Emergency Response (OSWER) had by 1990 issued large numbers of complex regulations faster than any other program office within the agency (U.S. EPA, 1990). Indeed, by 1989 OSWER's mandate-driven regulations had increased by almost 150 percent the number of pages of hazardous waste regulations in the Code of Federal Regulations (CFR). Such regulations took up 209 pages in the July 1, 1981, edition of the CFR, and 509 pages in the 1989 edition.

Moreover, HSWA's congressional mandates had spawned a ninefold increase in the number of waste types and waste management facilities requiring regulation, and the largest portion of the new regulatory universe (approximately 118,000 waste handlers) were small-quantity generators of waste. Finally, the EPA was issuing and implementing rules and regulations affecting 4,700 transportation, storage, and disposal facilities (TSDFs) containing approximately 81,000 waste units, along with an additional 211,000 waste generators (U.S. EPA, 1990, pp. 7, 42–43).

Internally, EPA evaluators were lamenting how President Reagan's budget cuts were interacting with these hammers to undermine both the pruning of cost-ineffective regulations and the establishment of enforcement priorities. More precisely, and in their haste to deter further congressional opprobrium, agency regulators were layering new regulations on preexisting regulations, without either reevaluating the latter or seeing how new and old rules interacted (Durant, 1993).

TOO LITTLE AND TOO CONFUSING DEVOLUTION Originally, Congress envisioned the implementation of RCRA as a federal-state partnership. The EPA therefore moved quickly to authorize states to take over implementation of RCRA's base program (that is, its TSDF component). Authorization involved the EPA certifying that a state had a hazardous waste management program for TSDFs that was "equivalent" to the federal program for implementing RCRA. Congress, of course, failed to define *equivalent,* a situation that considerably complicated the EPA's interpretation of the term (see, for example, Florini, 1982; Schnapf, 1982; and Davis, 1985).

The EPA and the states' problems spiraled exponentially, however, when Congress enacted HSWA. Piqued by the Reagan administration's assault on the EPA, Congress created an even more complex, heavily resource-dependent state authorization process. Specifically, the EPA had to authorize state equivalency across a broad range of activities that went far beyond the cradle-to-grave manifest system developed by RCRA. These activities included such critically important elements as determining corrective actions (such as investigating and determining cleanup needs at a waste facility), developing land disposal restrictions, and promulgating waste minimization regulations.

The result was a regulatory regime that continues today to complicate the jobs of both regulators and regulatees. Not only did states have to get authorization for each task mandated in the early days (they later bundled many together), but they frequently had to acquire additional resources and regulatory authority from their state legislatures to perform these tasks. This was time-consuming for regulators, anxiety provoking for regulatees, and guaranteed to create a maze of different regulatory regimes across the states.

With bottlenecks frequent, with many states authorized for some tasks and not for others, and with Congress still holding the EPA responsible for results, the dismay of both the regulated and regulatory communities grew. For example, many frustrated managers in states and localities began complaining to all who would listen about the EPA's nitpicking second-guessing of state decisions and its immersion in day-to-day decision making at specific sites (U.S. EPA, 1990, p. 14). But it was Congress's agency-forcing in reaction to the Reagan administration's excesses—not the EPA's behavior—that was most responsible for managers' concerns, a fact that many managers fail to appreciate even today. Indeed, the EPA was reacting quite rationally, given the mandates and political pressures it faced.

CUTS TOO DEEP, NONSTRATEGIC, AND ABRUPT Further compounding the angst of regulators and the chagrin of regulatees was an expanding HSWA workload decidedly incommensurate with the EPA's resources. By 1990, for instance, Congress's corrective action mandate meant that a financially strapped EPA shifted resources from its postclosure permitting process (that is, approving plans for cleaning up closed sites). The result was a backlog of about 1,600 facilities awaiting postclosure permits (U.S. EPA, 1990, p. 45). In fact, the EPA estimated that even if all available staff were allocated full-time to issuing only permits—leaving other critical activities undone—it would still need nine years to complete this task.

Meanwhile, the General Accounting Office began attributing poor enforcement performance to inadequately trained inspectors. At the root of these problems for the EPA and the states were high turnover rates as well as inadequate budgets and time for adequate training. Average rates of inspector turnover among state and EPA waste site inspectors for FY 1987, for example, were 19 and 28 percent per year, respectively. These averages masked even more dire circumstances in individual states, such as Texas and Louisiana, which had rates of 30 percent and 70 percent, respectively, in 1989. What is more, the average inspector had less than two years experience, with many splitting their already overburdened time among several other media programs (U.S. EPA, 1990, p. 67).

Again, the implications of these developments were profound, and they continue to confront managers in both the regulatory and regulated communities. In addition, the source of these problems lies largely in congressional rather than bureaucratic decision making. For HSWA regulators at the EPA, perceived shortcomings brought ever more stringent attempts by congressmembers to micromanage the law's implementation. For state regulators, micromanagement wrought ever more frustration with the EPA. And for regulatory targets, these problems incited ever more anger over the EPA's enforcement of all environmental laws, not just HSWA.

Retrospective Waste Regulation

Managers also need to understand that the RCRA-HSWA regulatory regime addressed only risks from *active* waste sites. Its aim was to prevent future Love Canals, not clean up existing ones (Fiorino, 1995;

Landy, Roberts, and Thomas, 1994). To address problems from *inactive* waste sites, however, Congress passed the Comprehensive Environmental Response, Compensation, and Liability Act (CERCLA; also known as Superfund) in 1980. This was the first environmental law designed to remedy problems that were created in the past rather than to reduce pollution as it is created. As such, it presented a whole new set of issues and challenges for managers.

CERCLA directs the EPA to identify sites, rank them according to the hazards they present, and maintain the National Priority List (NPL) for cleanups premised on these rankings. The law then gives the EPA authority to identify the parties responsible for these waste sites and to force them to clean up. Costs are often covered initially by a trust fund (the Superfund) and then the EPA goes after the potentially responsible parties (PRPs) to replenish the funds it expended. It is important to realize, however, that the straightforwardness of these mandates seriously belies their implementation difficulties.

Consider, for example, the plight of the regulatory community as the EPA developed and applied its Hazardous Ranking System (HRS) for listing sites on the NPL. The factors that presumably informed these rankings were the amount and toxicity of waste at a site, how likely it was that waste would migrate from the site, and the threat the site posed to humans living near it. As Douglas Brown (1992) reports, however, the EPA's first HRS was understandably beset by flaws, given its novelty and rush into production. Consequently, it was later replaced with a somewhat more accurate ranking system that was better aligned with evolving pollutant modeling theory. Although the EPA maintained that it never compared original site rankings to revised rankings under the new scoring system, Brown's analysis revealed that the rankings changed by an average of 250 places out of 1,200. Such a discrepancy, if accurately calculated, nearly inverts the rankings of the two systems.

Similarly, the NPL was designed to inform a "worst first" cleanup strategy. That is, sites with the highest scores exceeding 28.5 were to be addressed first. Yet research by C. B. Doty and C. C. Travis (1990) of the Department of Energy's Office of Risk Analysis notes that 88 percent of all sites remediated in 1989 were selected without regard to risk. The researchers reached this conclusion by computing statistical correlations between risk and cost. In effect, remedial costs rather than amount of risk reduced were the primary drivers determining which sites were cleaned up first. Moreover, even when risks were considered, an incredible 70 percent of all Superfund sites remediated in that year had risk levels that the EPA accepted as satisfactory *after* remediation took place at less contaminated sites.

By far the most controversial aspect of the implementation of the Superfund law in the public's mind was the EPA's interpretation that responsible parties would be held to "strict, joint, and several liability." As we discuss in more depth in Chapter Three, this means essentially that each party contributing hazardous waste to a site is responsible in full for the costs of cleaning it up. What is more, this is true regardless of the amount the party contributed, when they did so, and the year the site was created. Consequently, and in the extreme case, a party contributing only a minimal percentage of the waste could be held liable for total cleanup costs—and this could occur despite the party's engaging in the dumping before it was illegal (O'Leary, 1990b).

With the stakes this high for PRPs, time-consuming lawsuits fighting this designation were inevitable. As we have already noted, the EPA applies a "shovels first" policy: it usually pays for a cleanup out of the Superfund and then seeks compensation from the parties involved. Because any one of the parties could be assigned full costs, the parties then begin suing each other to escape personal liability. Those with the deepest pockets—for example, corporations, as well as cities that dumped even minimal levels of hazardous materials from households into landfills—are usually sued first. They in turn sue others.

Because of the dynamics of its concept of strict, joint, and several liability, the CERCLA is known by many as a "full-employment act" for lawyers. Moreover, with actual cleanups proceeding at a snail's pace due to the delays occasioned by these suits, and with studies indicating that nearly one-third of all Superfund expenditures (several billions of dollars) are going to legal fees rather than to cleanup, calls for major overhauls of CERCLA are common (see, for example, Mazmanian and Morell, 1992). Moreover, these calls are heard loudly from hazardous waste generators and municipalities who want to see standards relaxed. Both want to reduce their liability costs, while the latter also want to unlock scores of industrial sites in urban areas for redevelopment. We discuss these topics more thoroughly in Chapter Six.

Still, although many critics wish to amend CERCLA's strictures, a consensus on particular reforms has eluded Congress. Similarly, President Clinton's interagency task force addressing CERCLA's shortcomings has also come up short of agreement. Some experts see the most likely scenario for reform as limiting liability for hazardous waste generated before a given date (such as 1980) and allowing tiered cleanup standards on the basis of future uses of the lands. Agreement on these solutions has not yet been reached, however.

Prior to the 1990s, Congress did react to some of CERCLA's deficiencies. Most importantly, it passed the Superfund Amendments and Reauthorization Act (SARA) of 1986 and added community right-to-know provisions to the law. Among other things, SARA requires firms to maintain and make available data about harmful chemicals that are used or stored on a site, and to report the annual emission of such chemicals. This Toxics Release Inventory (TRI), as we shall see in Chapter Twelve, has become a major source of data on industrial emissions. Moreover, President Clinton's Executive Order 12856 has extended this requirement to federal agencies.

PESTICIDES AND TOXICS

First passed in 1947, the Federal Insecticide, Fungicide, and Rodenticide Act (FIFRA) authorized a national registration program for pesticides. This law stressed the effectiveness of a product as the basis for a decision on registration. Later versions, however, focused more on a chemical's effects on health and the environment. The core of the EPA's regulatory authority is that only EPA-registered products may enter commerce. Thus FIFRA affects the kinds of products that managers in the regulated community can use, the ways they can use them, the strictures under which they may be held liable for harms, and the ways they do their work. At the same time, it sets the metes and bounds of authority to act for managers who are regulators, and expands the regulatory universe they must engage (such as pesticide runoff from farms and other nonpoint sources).

The current standard for registration is that under normal use a chemical will not cause "unreasonable adverse effects on the environment." In making a decision about a particular substance, the EPA must consider "the economic, social, and environmental costs and benefits" of its use. The law directs the EPA to balance risks and benefits (higher economic benefits may offset higher risks).

Like many environmental laws, FIFRA sets higher standards for new products than for existing products. For new products, the burden of proof is on registrants to show that the chemicals are safe. For existing products, the burden is on the EPA to show unreasonable risk before canceling or suspending registration. These parts of the law were defined in the 1972 revisions and amended in 1988. The 1988 changes directed the EPA to reregister six hundred active ingredients in pesti-cides (those with the older registrations) within nine years.

One aspect of pesticides is governed by the Federal Food, Drug, and Cosmetic Act (FFDCA). In accordance with this law, the EPA sets toler-ances, or maximum allowable concentrations, for pesticide residues in food. The law defines one standard for the EPA to use in setting toler-ances on raw agricultural commodities, and another, stricter standard for setting tolerances on processed foods. The differences do not reflect a difference in the risks of the two kinds of products. Rather, they reflect political and legal issues in the passage of the law. This difference in how raw commodities and processed foods are treated is one of the obvious discrepancies in the legal framework. As such, it is a good ex-ample of the kinds of nonscientific pressures affecting risk management that we address in more detail in Chapters Five, Six, and Seven.

Similarly, political factors lie at the heart of frequently heard criti-cisms of the way the EPA has implemented the FIFRA. Of particular concern to environmentalists has been the EPA's inordinately slow pace in registering pesticides, a function, in turn, of its backlog in assessing the health and ecological effects of pesticides. Indeed, by the mid–1980s, the EPA had performed such assessments on only six of more than six hundred active ingredients in pesticides and had not even begun testing a majority of the more than forty thousand pre-1972 pesticides still in use (Ringquist, 1995). Hence, amendments to FIFRA were passed in 1988 (Fiorino, 1995). By that time, however, the slow pace of the EPA's action could no longer be attributed largely to the "cultural" legacy of the original Office of Pesticide Policy (OPP), as many were prone to do. When the EPA was created in 1970, the OPP was brought into the agency from the Department of Agriculture, where unsurprisingly it held a pro-pesticide orientation and a distributive rather than a regulatory mission. Indeed, the primary clients of OPP were farmers and pesticide man-ufacturers, and the office's mission was to promote, not curtail, pesticide use. But after nearly a quarter century, this cultural explanation does not hold as much water as it once did. Changes in tasks, personnel staffing, and clientele have made this predisposition decidedly less powerful among managers (Bosso, 1987).

Consider instead the political forces impeding a reduction in registra-tion backlogs. First, when Congress passed the FIFRA amendments in 1972, it gave the agency the insurmountable task of evaluating more than fifty thousand existing pesticides within four years. Stunned, with-out anywhere near the resources to perform this task, and defensive, the agency adopted a quite rational decision rule in the face of Congress's agency-forcing language in FIFRA: the "rebuttable presumption against registration" rule. If industry could not provide sufficient data or if complaints suggested unreasonable risk, the EPA asked industry to marshal evidence rebutting the presumption of risk. If they could not, the EPA did not register the pesticide. But if industry could provide rebuttal, no formal toxicity testing took place and the EPA registered the pesticide. As well, the EPA privatized some of the testing to private laboratories. This blew up in the agency's face, however, when investigators found that the country's largest testing laboratory and EPA contractor (Industrial Biotest) had falsified tests on more than two hundred pesticides that the EPA had subsequently registered (Fiorino, 1995).

To be sure, the technical complexities of pesticide analysis are also responsible for these delays. Not only does the agency lack needed data on human effects until a pesticide is used, but it takes years to collect and analyze these data once they are available. Nonetheless, other political factors further confound the EPA's efforts in this regard, such as the economic stakes involved for farmers and manufacturers, the media's tendency to focus on crises (see Chapter Five), and the persistently low levels of funding for the pesticide program since its inception.

Because pesticides have been a more than $6 billion per year industry in the 1990s, the EPA experiences strong pressure to keep pesticides in use and little pressure to decertify them. Indeed, with agricultural subsidies often predicated on increasing productivity, heavy pesticide use increases the average profit on an acre of land by approximately $20 (Maney and Hadwiger, 1980). Moreover, the media's focus on crises tends to produce a "pesticide of the month" hysteria, followed by congressional hearings, followed by a diversion of limited resources from long-range plans to respond to these pressures. Finally, and relatedly, the pesticide program at the EPA has experienced a chronic shortage of funding relative to its responsibilities (Fiorino, 1995).

Similar dynamics have plagued the EPA's implementation of the Toxic Substances Control Act (TSCA) of 1976. Congress passed TSCA to cover a range of chemicals currently in production and use that could present health or environmental risks and were not covered by other laws. The TSCA gives the EPA broad authority to collect information on chemical substances and mixtures, to require industry to test chemicals for harmful effects, and to regulate the production or use of any chemicals that pose "an unreasonable risk of injury to health or the environment." The EPA maintains an inventory of existing chemicals (now including some sixty thousand) for which it can require testing or take regulatory action if there is evidence of an unreasonable risk.

Like the FIFRA, the TSCA directs the EPA to balance benefits against risks in regulatory decisions—a task, as we shall see in Chapters Six and Seven, that proves taxing for regulators, regulatees, and stakeholders alike. It suffices presently to note that all three actors are likely to conceptualize health risks quite differently, as do scientists and laypersons. What is more, the balancing of benefits and risks has led of late to a spate of legislative proposals in Congress and in state legislatures to move toward relative risk-based priority setting in regulation. As many—including the members of the EPA's Science Advisory Board—say, inordinate amounts of our environmental dollars are spent on protecting us from threats that pose minimal risks to humans or to ecosystems.

But even as legislators say they want to move in this direction, the political fact of life is this: legislative mandates will also have to be changed drastically to get there (Fiorino, 1995). For example, congressional mandates in effect in the mid-1990s forced the EPA to spend 90 percent of its water budget on point-source pollution even though non-point-source pollution is a decidedly more serious problem. In turn, 80 percent of its budget for groundwater was mandated for aquifer cleanup even though prevention is a more cost-effective strategy. Meanwhile, congressional mandates allocated less than 2 percent of the EPA's budget for ozone depletion, global warming, and critical habitat protection—all considered by scientists to be very serious threats facing humanity (Rosenbaum, 1994).

POLLUTION PREVENTION

With passage of the Pollution Prevention Act (PPA) of 1990, we begin to see a departure from the established first-generation pattern of environmental regulation. This law reflects the recognition—chronicled more extensively in Chapters Three and Four—that the United States has relied too much on end-of-pipe controls and too little on preventing pollution at the source (Burnett, 1996). Prevention is therefore worthy of extensive attention by managers—in terms of both its promise and the obstacles to attaining its goals.

The law defines as national policy the following hierarchy of strategies:

1. When it is feasible, pollution should be prevented or reduced at the source.

2. When prevention is not feasible, pollution should be recycled in an environmentally safe manner.

3. When prevention or recycling is not feasible, pollution should be treated in environmentally safe ways.

4. Only when prevention, recycling, or treatment are not feasible should disposal or releases be used.

Prevention is defined as "source reduction." This includes anything that increases efficiency in the use of raw materials, energy, water, and other resources, or that protects resources through conservation.

What is also notable about the PPA is that—unlike its predecessors— it is not limited to one environmental medium (that is, air, water, or waste) or program. Consequently, managers will find at their disposal the intellectual justification for moving toward results-oriented, priority-based, and multimedia-focused environmental management. Indeed, within the EPA and on Capitol Hill there has been a careful effort not to limit the pollution prevention concept to traditional program boundaries. As we shall see in Chapters Three and Four, however, powerful political, organizational, and implementation obstacles still remain in place that make this transition a Herculean one in many organizations.

Still, many states have been pushed in this direction by the costs savings that some large industries (such as 3M and Monsanto) are accruing from their pollution prevention efforts. Influential as well have been the high costs of complying with a maze of hazardous waste laws and increased reporting requirements. As Chapter Four shows, all states had pollution prevention laws by the early 1990s. Moreover, many states had charged agencies or units of agencies with promoting these efforts, and some either required pollution prevention plans or set goals against which to measure progress.

CONCLUSION

In this chapter, we have reviewed the evolution, implementation, critiques, and problems of six major sets of environmental protection laws that managers frequently confront in their work. We of course hope that managers will cull from this discussion an appreciation for some of the specifics of these statutes. But we also hope that they will see that many of the problems typically cited as bureaucratic in origin have political and legislative roots instead. In particular, we have tried to highlight how legislative agency-forcing and hammer provisions have combined with political realities and persistent resource shortfalls to cause less than optimal performance. At times, agencies implement statutes in ways that are quite rational from their perspective but quite irrational from a societal (or collective) perspective.

This is not to suggest that these environmental protection laws have been unmitigated failures. More accurately, the results are quite mixed. For example, although critics might argue about the effect that command-and-control laws have had on air and water quality relative to other factors (such as changes in industrial output and shifts in fossil fuel use), there is evidence that these laws have improved environmental quality. Over the last quarter-century, concentrations of all criteria air pollutants decreased between 24 percent (nitrogen dioxide and carbon monoxide) and 94 percent (lead). Moreover, Evan Ringquist (1993) found that states with stronger regulatory programs showed greater improvements in air quality than did states with more lax regimes. And while data from the water quality and hazardous waste areas are less impressive, they may result less from invalid causal theories than from what statutes do not permit regulators to do.

But even these problems do not do justice to the new challenges, choices, and opportunities that managers will confront on their jobs for years to come. Indeed, a whole set of evolving issues that cut across all environmental statutes will test both their mettle and their creativity. Not only will the evolution of these issues directly affect public managers as they interact with one another, but they will also affect how public agencies interact with for-profit and nonprofit managers. It is to these issues that we turn next in Chapter Three.

3

SEVEN LEGAL TRENDS THAT EVERY MANAGER SHOULD KNOW

*I recognize the right and duty of this generation to develop
and use the natural resources of our land; but I do not
recognize the right to waste them, or to rob,
by wasteful use, the generations that come after us.*

—Theodore Roosevelt[1]

The responsibilities for implementing Theodore Roosevelt's "rights and duties" and realizing his conservationist agenda are increasingly marbled throughout our country's 83,000 governments, as well as throughout its for-profit and nonprofit sectors. In this chapter we examine seven issues that cut across the rights and responsibilities enunciated in the statutes we discussed in Chapter Two. Importantly, these are issues that promise to complicate even further the realization of Roosevelt's vision.

Although we focus our discussion on trends that most directly affect public managers, it is crucial that for-profit and nonprofit managers also understand the substance and implications of these trends. In some cases, the legal liabilities discussed apply equally to public, for-profit, and nonprofit managers. Moreover, even when they do not it is important for managers to know about these trends. Not only will they better appreciate the regulatory, contracting, and grantmaking regime with which they must deal, but they will also understand better why public managers behave as they do as they pursue the public's environmental business.

Using the evolution of case law as a window for understanding these trends, we begin by discussing at length the single most immediately important trend for public agencies: the erosion of government immunity. Next we discuss two important areas in which this erosion of sovereign immunity has had the most telling impacts on individual managers: their exposure to hazardous waste liabilities, and the extent to which lower- and middle-level government employees are criminally liable for their activities. Next we discuss what case law tells us about the implications of four major trends in the changing environmental responsibilities of government agencies: increased reporting requirements, liability for regulatory takings, the municipality as mini water pollution control agency, and the striking down of flow-control ordinances by the Supreme Court.

THE EROSION OF GOVERNMENT IMMUNITY

Prior to 1970, suits against public administrators and public organizations for harming the environment were rare. Only occasionally did the U.S. Department of Health, Education, and Welfare file suit against a government entity for a water or air pollution violation. In 1971, the newly created U.S. Environmental Protection Agency (EPA), in conjunction with the U.S. Department of Justice, filed its first lawsuit against a government entity, the city of Kansas City, Kansas, for violating the Clean Water Act. Since that time, environmental lawsuits against governments have increased as environmental law has exploded. For example, noncriminal lawsuits against government entities filed by the U.S. government for violations of environmental laws increased nearly 250 percent from 1982 to 1992 (O'Leary, 1993b). Criminal lawsuits for violations of environmental laws, nonexistent prior to 1980, have also skyrocketed ("Defense Attorney Warns. . . ," 1994).

When federal and state entities have been charged with violating laws, the typical defenses that managers have used include sovereign immunity and Eleventh Amendment immunity. The basic principle behind sovereign immunity is that the United States may not be sued without its consent. The basic principle behind Eleventh Amendment immunity is that a citizen of one state may not sue another state in federal court without the consent of the state being sued. Eleventh Amendment immunity has also been interpreted as preventing federal court suits by citizens of the state being sued. We should note, however, that the Eleventh Amendment does not prevent suits against state subdivisions, such as counties and municipalities. Furthermore, state immunity under the Eleventh Amendment does not preclude a federal court from taking jurisdiction over an action against state officers to enjoin them from enforcing an unconstitutional state statute or to recover damages for officers' personal violations of the plaintiff's constitutional rights (see *Ex Parte Young*, 1908).

Rationale

There are many reasons for sovereign immunity. Traditionally, public administrators, as neutral experts, wanted to be insulated from politics and to exercise discretion in their pursuit of the public interest. In a sense they wanted to be responsive to professional values and to their visions of "the good" more than to public demands. The latter could, after all, sometimes be at odds with their expert judgments. At the same time, however, there were less ennobling pressures on managers relative to reducing costs, escaping internal accountability, promoting secrecy, and pursuing convenience that jeopardized the public interest (Durant, 1995a).

In the environmental field, these pressures sometimes stimulated negative practices, such as disposing of toxic and hazardous wastes inappropriately on a massive scale. At other times the U.S. Atomic Energy Commission and its successor, the Nuclear Regulatory Commission, clandestinely ran radiation experiments that poisoned hundreds of people (Ball, 1985). At still other times, less malevolent but nonetheless devastating results occurred when, as Diane Vaughan (1996) suggests, "cultures of deviance" gradually made unacceptable environmental risk taking acceptable. Hence, one major problem with sovereign immunity was that it allowed public administrators to implement policies relatively free from the consequences of their actions. As such, it contributed to popular perceptions that government was incompetent, out of control, and above the law (Durant, 1995b).

Largely because of such injustices and a perceived double standard in the implementation of environmental laws, these defenses are slowly being eroded. Public administrators are now, for the most part, under the rule of environmental law. As a result, the courts are playing a much greater role in controlling, defining, and supervising environmental administrators. The way this has occurred is a story that all managers should know.

Learning to Survive as Regulated Agencies

Historically, the courts have required an explicit waiver of sovereign immunity or Eleventh Amendment immunity by the Congress before exposing agencies to liability for their actions. In the case of sovereign immunity, a federal statute may grant that consent. In the case of Eleventh Amendment immunity, under previous interpretations protection from liability could be afforded by Congress in two ways: through the Commerce Clause (see *Pennsylvania* v. *Union Gas*, 1989, discussed later) or through the section of the Fourteenth Amendment that authorizes Congress to enforce the Eleventh Amendment (*Fitzpatrick* v. *Bitzer*, 1976). The rationale in both instances is that by approving the Constitution and its amendments, the states consented to suits based on these powers. A 1996 Supreme Court case suggests, however, that Congress lacks the power under the Commerce Clause to abridge the states' Eleventh Amendment immunity (*Seminole Tribe of Florida* v. *Florida*, 1996).

Managers should also understand that all major federal antipollution laws waive government immunity in some way, although the specifics differ from statute to statute. The most significant waivers of sovereign immunity include provisions for citizen suits and judicial review. Of the six major environmental statutes implemented by the U.S. Environmental Protection Agency (EPA; see Chapter Two), for example, only the Federal Insecticide, Fungicide, and Rodenticide Act does not contain a citizen suit provision. The other five statutes provide for lawsuits that make citizens, in effect, little attorneys general. All of these statutes provide for judicial review of some sort.

The Clean Air Act (CAA), for example, contains provisions that waive immunity by intending to treat public and private defendants equally. The citizen suit provision of the CAA states that a civil action may be commenced "against any person . . . including the United States and . . . any other governmental instrumentality or agency" alleged to be violating certain sections of the act [42 U.S.C. 7604(a)]. The statute includes in its definition of *person* not only federal agencies operating sources of air pollution, but state and local governments as well.

The Clean Water Act (CWA) also waives sovereign immunity. The citizen suit section of the CWA, for example, states that "any citizen may commence a civil action . . . [for violation of the statute] against any person . . . including . . . the United States and . . . any other governmental instrumentality or agency" [33 U.S.C. Section 1365(a)]. The definition of *person who may be sued* provided by the statute is "an individual, corporation, partnership, association, State, municipality, commission, or political subdivision of a State, or any interstate body" [33 U.S.C. Section 1362 (5)].

The Comprehensive Environmental Response, Compensation, and Liability Act (CERCLA) waives immunity for the United States by defining a person who shall be liable for violating the act as "an individual, firm, corporation, association, partnership, consortium, joint venture, commercial entity, United States Government, State, municipality, commission, political subdivision of a State or any interstate body" [42 U.S.C. Section 9601(D)(21)]. The act further provides that federal agencies are subject to, and must comply with, the statute in the same manner and to the same extent as nongovernmental entities [42 U.S.C. Section 9620(a)(1)]. Similar language is provided in the Resource Conservation and Recovery Act (RCRA), which states that "each department, agency, and instrumentality of the executive, legislative and judicial branches of the Federal Government . . . shall be subject to and shall comply with all federal, state, interstate and local laws concerning waste disposal" [42 U.S.C. Section 6961]. Likewise, the Superfund Amendments and Reauthorization Act (SARA) waives state immunity from suit under the Eleventh Amendment of the Constitution.

The Courts and Congress Enter the Fray

Conflict has arisen, however, among the federal circuit courts concerning whether RCRA and the CWA allow states to sue federal agencies for civil penalties. The conflict arose in part because of the different language and definitions provided in RCRA in several sections (particularly 42 U.S.C. Sections 6961, 6972, and 6928) and in the CWA (particularly 33 U.S.C. sections 1323 and 1365). The issue is especially important to states that are suing federal facilities for noncompliance with environmental laws (see *Colorado v. Idarado Mining Co.*, 1990; *State of Colorado v. United States Department of the Army*, 1989). Efforts to address the split among the appellate courts through congressional legislation succeeded in part, but only after the Supreme Court issued a controversial decision on April 21, 1992.

In *United States Department of Energy v. Ohio* (1992), the state of Ohio sought punitive fines from the Department of Energy (DOE) for violating environmental laws at the DOE's uranium processing plant in Fernald, Ohio. The pivotal issue was whether Congress waived the federal government's immunity from liability for civil fines imposed by a state for past violations of the CWA and the RCRA. The Supreme Court held, in a six-to-three decision, that Congress had not done so in either instance. Examining the full text of both statutes, the justices reasoned in part that because the United States is mentioned in some sections of the laws but not in others, they could not find a "clear and unequivocal waiver" of immunity from liability for civil fines imposed by a state.

Five and a half months later, on October 6, 1992, President Bush significantly increased the EPA's and the states' powers in dealing with the DOE and other federal organizations by signing into law the Federal Facilities Compliance Act. The law expressly waived the sovereign immunity of federal facilities under RCRA, thus making it clear that the EPA and the states may assess fines and penalties against government entities such as the DOE for violations of this law.[2]

The state of Washington lost little time implementing the law: on March 11, 1993, the Washington Department of Ecology assessed fines totaling $100,000 against the DOE for RCRA violations at its Hanford nuclear site ("Washington Fines DOE. . .," 1993, p. 3019). The EPA also did not hesitate to implement the new law: on May 3, 1993, it proposed a $257,600 penalty against El Centro Naval Air Station for hazardous waste law violations. El Centro was the first federal installation to be fined by the EPA pursuant to the Federal Facilities Compliance Act of 1992 ("Navy Air Station Hit. . .," 1993, p. 190).

More recent court decisions have also supported the erosion of government immunity under both federal and state environmental laws. For example, in August 1994, a federal court of appeals upheld New Mexico's right to regulate emissions from the Los Alamos National Laboratory (*U.S. v. New Mexico,* 1994). In December 1993, a federal appeals court ruled that the U.S. Postal Service could be sued for civil penalties by the Pennsylvania Department of Environmental Resources for violations of the state's Clean Streams Law (*Pennsylvania DER v. U.S. Postal Service,* 1993). Interestingly, pivotal factors in the decision were the Postal Service's quasi-independent corporate status and its commercial activities. In July 1994, a federal appeals court ruled that the United States may not claim that sovereign immunity prevents it from being held liable under the federal Superfund law for cleanup costs incurred at a plant used to manufacture critical war material during World War II (*FMC Corporation v. U.S. Dept. of Commerce,* 1994). That same year a district court found that the state of Missouri was not protected from a Superfund suit by sovereign immunity (*Thomas v. FAG Bearings Corporation,* 1994). Meanwhile a federal court found that state RCRA regulations have to be met at federal Superfund sites (*United States* v. *Colorado,* 1993).

Government immunity under environmental laws is not totally dead and still exists, in certain discrete circumstances, as a defense. Moreover, in the aftermath of the 1994 Republican takeover of Congress, some members tried unsuccessfully to exempt Defense Department facilities from all environmental laws. In response, the Clinton administration proposed giving states real authority at federal Superfund sites.

Nonetheless, the trend toward eroding government immunity under environmental laws is real and significant. Governments can no longer assume that a sovereign immunity defense will be available in environmental lawsuits. Managers can therefore increasingly expect to be treated as private parties under environmental laws and in environmental enforcement proceedings. With increased environmental litigation, this trend will be especially challenging and resource intensive as public organizations and employees are forced to put forth greater efforts to defend themselves and their actions. To see how and why this is true, we turn next to liabilities experienced by governments and their agents in a single but critical area: hazardous waste management.

HAZARDOUS WASTE LIABILITIES

Government organizations are increasingly being held liable under federal laws for hazardous waste cleanup costs, primarily because of the critical roles these organizations play. They are generators or transporters of hazardous waste, they arrange for its disposal, and they own or operate facilities that receive hazardous wastes. And to their chagrin, cleanup costs have reached well into the billions of dollars. Moreover, even if they are not liable parties to a cleanup, state and local governments may incur substantial legal and oversight expenses anyway.

Examples of Liability

Consider the following hazardous waste lawsuits involving governments:

• From 1950 through 1973, the state of California had taken an active role in locating, supervising, and regulating an industrial waste facility in the Jarupa Mountains near Glen Avon. In 1974, the state took control of the site to contain wastes that were migrating off it. The EPA and the state then brought suit in 1983 against thirty-one defendants who generated or transported wastes dumped at Stringfellow. During the trial the court determined that the generator-defendants could assert a counterclaim against California for part of the cleanup costs because the state acted as a "quasi-private consultant" in the operation of the landfill. On June 2, 1989, in *United States* v. *Stringfellow,* a jury found the state guilty of negligence in its consultant role. Estimates of the state's liability ranged from $450 million to $750 million (Bingenheimer, 1989).

• In the 1980s, the EPA notified the city of Corvallis, Oregon, that the United Chrome Products plant south of town was Oregon's worst hazardous waste site. Soil and water around the plant had been contaminated with chromium during twenty-eight years of chrome-plating operations. Because the city then owned the land on which the former plant stood, the EPA held the city responsible for cleanup of the site. In 1989, the city filed a $19.7 million lawsuit against United Chrome Products to force the company to pay for the cleanup, an action to be completed by the year 2000 (City of Corvallis, Oregon, 1988).

• When the EPA began cleaning up four Superfund sites on the East Coast in the mid-1980s, 476 parties were sued as generator-defendants in an effort to recoup EPA expenses. The defendants included the town of Barnstable, Massachusetts; the Barnstable High School; the Barnstable Public School System; the Barnstable Water Company; and the Barnstable Dump. Total cleanup costs were estimated at $52 million. One-half of the defendants, including all the Barnstable defendants, were said to fall under the EPA's *de minimis* policy for small-volume generators of hazardous waste. The main concept behind de minimis settlements is proportionality: those who contribute a minimal amount of waste to a site should be assessed for response work, but only on the basis of such factors as the toxicity and amount of waste they actually produced. Together the de minimis parties settled with the EPA for $11 million (53 Fed. Reg. 28, 1988).

• In 1973 and 1974, GAF Corporation dumped industrial wastes in the Colesville municipal landfill, operated by Broome County, New York. Thirteen years later, Broome County and the GAF Corporation agreed, in a $6 million consent agreement, to share the cleanup costs. Upon completion of the cleanup, the state of New York had to reimburse the county for 75 percent of its cleanup costs, as long as the county took the lead in conducting the cleanup ("Current Developments. . .," 1987, p. 15).

These are just a few of the many examples of hazardous waste cleanup suits involving governments and government organizations. A 1991 survey sponsored by the International City/County Management Association concluded that approximately 51 percent of U.S. municipalities and counties own their own landfills (Good, Kissel, Mullins, and O'Leary, 1991). Of the approximately 1,200 Superfund sites on the EPA's National Priority List, 25 percent involve municipalities or municipal wastes. Of these, about one in five sites is a municipal land-fill. The EPA expects the number of such sites to increase in the future. The current average cost of cleaning up a Superfund site is more than $25 million, and the EPA projects that this amount will eventually exceed $40 million.

Meanwhile, at the federal level, a 1990 study conducted by the Congressional Budget Office concluded that more than 2,300 facilities owned by federal agencies handle hazardous wastes or contain hazardous waste contamination. The same report found that more than 7,100 properties formerly owned by federal agencies may incur financial liabilities from contamination problems. This could occur because the United States owns one-third of the nation's land, making it a major "potentially responsible party," or PRP, under hazardous waste law. Already there were more than 1,000 federal facilities on the EPA's Federal Agency Hazardous Waste Compliance Docket. Many of these sites were—and remain—old mining, oil, and gas sites owned by the U.S. Department of the Interior and the U.S. Department of Agriculture.

As we noted, DOE and Department of Defense installations have also been cited for hazardous waste contamination. By 1994 (the most recent summary data available), the EPA's Office of Enforcement and Compliance Assurance (OECA) reported that the number of federal facilities on the nation's Hazardous Waste Compliance Docket had nearly doubled since 1988. More precisely, as greater numbers of facilities were inspected, the number of sites on the docket went from 1094 to 2070 (U.S. Environmental Protection Agency, 1995, p. ES–18). Moreover, the OECA reported that only 62 percent of all federal facilities were in compliance with the RCRA (p. ES–5).

Terms of Liability

As mentioned previously, CERCLA authorized the EPA to commence legal action forcing the abatement of hazardous waste pollution at Superfund sites that pose an "imminent and substantial" threat to public health or the environment.[3] Importantly, the courts have interpreted CERCLA as imposing strict liability on regulatory targets. This means that waste generators, such as a city or state, may be subject to liability even if they have not departed in any way from the standard of reasonable care and have not violated any environmental laws.[4] Additionally, the courts have ruled that where injury is indivisible (that is, where it is not clear whose wastes caused what damage), liability is joint and several.[5] This means, as we noted in Chapter Two, that the federal government can proceed against any one party or a group of potentially liable parties for the total costs of any cleanup. If these parties are found liable, defendants have tended to sue other potential PRPs for contributions, if these PRPs can be found.[6]

Importantly, the federal government (or any other plaintiff) need not prove that a potential PRP's actions were the cause of the environmental threat or harm in question. Courts have held that CERCLA requires no more proof than showing that a generator sent out hazardous wastes for disposal, that the wastes ended up at a site where a hazardous response action was necessary, and that wastes of the type the generator disposed of were present at the site.

But are government agencies "persons" liable for redress under hazardous waste laws? Although CERCLA initially defined a person subject to hazardous waste cleanup liability as including the "United States Government, [a] State, municipality, commission, political subdivision of a State or interstate body," Congress further clarified this definition in 1986. In SARA, it added a section clarifying that a state "shall be subject to the provisions of this Act in the same manner and [to] the same extent" as any nongovernmental entity. The courts also have found local governments not to be immune from suit.[7]

Managers will also find no respite from liability as "persons" when RCRA is involved. Pursuant to RCRA, when EPA has evidence that the past or present handling, storage, treatment, transportation, or disposal of any waste presents an "imminent and substantial endangerment," the agency may bring suit against any entity that has contributed to the situation. Possible defendants include those who—like many governments—are past or present generators, transporters, or owners or operators of treatment, storage, or disposal facilities.

In such a situation, the EPA may order a government agency to desist from specific activities, may order the government to take specific actions that EPA deems necessary, or both. The EPA may also take appropriate administrative actions [42 U.S.C. 6973(a)]. Any state or local government that violates a court order under these circumstances may be subject to fines of up to $5,000 for each day that the violation or noncompliance continues [42 U.S.C. 6973(b)].

If convicted of violating any other applicable requirements of RCRA, a state or local government may face civil penalties of up to $25,000 per day [42 U.S.C. 3008(g)]. Criminal penalties can be as high as

$50,000 a day [42 U.S.C. 3008(d)(7)(A)]. Upon a second criminal conviction, the fine is doubled [42 U.S.C. 3008(d)(7)(A)]. Additionally, the act contains penalties for the offense of "knowing endangerment." In this instance, an organization may be fined up to $1 million [42 U.S.C. 3008(e)].

Life in Limbo?

Aside from the substantive implications of increasing liability for hazardous waste violations, these kinds of court suits also introduce tremendous levels of uncertainty as they wend their way through the judicial system. For managers, this can mean life in virtual limbo if the suit directly affects them or if they are seeking to take cues from it. We address how, why, and with what consequences this is true in more detail in Chapter Six. Presently, however, it is useful to acquire a flavor for these problems (as well as for the substance of the law) by examining two recent cases in depth.

PENNSYLVANIA V. UNION GAS The pivotal issue in *Pennsylvania* v. *Union Gas* (1989) was whether a private party could sue a state to recoup portions of its cleanup costs as a PRP. Pennsylvania asked the U.S. Supreme Court to interpret the 1986 Superfund amendment when it appealed a lower court decision permitting private parties to bring such a suit. The case began in 1980 when the Commonwealth of Pennsylvania, carrying out flood control measures, excavated at a site formerly owned by Union Gas Company. The state had held an easement on the property. During excavation, workers struck a large deposit of coal tar that began to seep into a nearby creek. The EPA immediately ordered a cleanup, which the Pennsylvania and United States governments jointly carried out. The U.S. government spent an estimated $1.4 million on the cleanup, which included reimbursing Pennsylvania for its costs.

As is typical in such a case, the federal government then sued Union Gas in district court to recoup costs incurred in cleaning up the spill. Union Gas responded by denying liability and filing a complaint against Pennsylvania. In that complaint the company alleged that the Commonwealth had "negligently caused, or contributed to, the discharge" and should therefore share a portion of the cleanup costs.

Pennsylvania defended itself by asserting that the courts long had interpreted the Eleventh Amendment of the Constitution as granting sovereign immunity to the states in federal court. The district court agreed, and dismissed that portion of the lawsuit. Later, the EPA and

Union Gas settled the primary portion of the suit, and the district court also dismissed the action. Union Gas, however, appealed the district court's dismissal of Pennsylvania as a defendant in the case. In a divided opinion, the court of appeals for the third circuit affirmed the lower court. Reasoning that "Congress must express its intention to abrogate the eleventh amendment in unmistakable language in the statute itself," the court found no such expression of intent in CERCLA (*United States* v. *Union Gas,* 1987, p. 1345).

On October 8, 1986, Union Gas appealed the decision to the U.S. Supreme Court. Nine days later, the president signed SARA into law in an attempt to clarify whether a state could be sued under CERCLA. The Supreme Court responded by remanding the case to the appellate court with orders to consider whether the new changes in the law would affect the outcome of the case.

In its second examination of the case, the third circuit reversed itself and held that SARA provided the clear language the court previously found lacking in CERCLA. Thus, under the act Pennsylvania could be sued by private parties as well as by the federal government. Pennsylvania immediately appealed to the Supreme Court, arguing among other things that the court of appeals erred because the Superfund amendments never explicitly referred to the Eleventh Amendment. Pennsylvania also argued that even if the lower court's interpretation of the statutory change was correct, the court erred by applying the law retroactively. So high were this case's stakes for all governments that Pennsylvania was joined by a coalition of seventeen other states when oral arguments were heard on November 31, 1988. Coalition members maintained that the decision placed an improper and inordinate burden on state treasuries.

On June 15, 1989, the Supreme Court issued a decision affirming the court of appeals. Unpersuaded by Pennsylvania's arguments, the Court agreed with Union Gas that Congress had unmistakably provided clear language rendering states liable for monetary damages for hazardous waste cleanup. Moreover, it was within Congress's power to do so. This five-to-four decision seemed to force Pennsylvania to defend itself against a Union Gas lawsuit seeking to recover cleanup costs.

The decision was reversed, however, in 1996 when the Supreme Court held to the contrary: Congress did not have the power under the commerce clause to override the states' Eleventh Amendment immunity from suit for violations of federal laws (*Seminole Tribe of Florida* v. *Florida,* 1996). The 1996 case concerned the Indian Gaming Regulatory Act, but it raised the question of whether the federal courts may now hear suits against states to enforce federal environmental laws. Thus, seventeen years after the issue was first raised, aspects of this important question remain open.

CITY OF CHICAGO V. ENVIRONMENTAL DEFENSE FUND Similarly disconcerting for public managers has been the uncertainty occasioned by the courts in the hottest hazardous waste challenge facing local governments today: the release of ash from municipal incinerators. In *City of Chicago* v. *Environmental Defense Fund* (1994), the Supreme Court held that if the ash resulting from incinerating municipal waste was itself hazardous, it must be treated as hazardous waste. In this decision, the Court overruled an EPA interpretation of RCRA that was beneficial to local governments, posing in the process monumental challenges for those using trash incinerators.

Fourteen years earlier, in 1980, the EPA had excluded household wastes from the definition of hazardous waste, even if those wastes contained toxins (such as batteries). In 1984, the Hazardous and Solid Waste Amendments further convinced the EPA that Congress intended to exempt household waste from hazardous waste regulations. One outcome was less stringent requirements for those local governments that provided trash disposal service to their residents.

The Environmental Defense Fund (EDF) sued. It argued in part that the clear language of the statute demonstrates that Congress intended to exclude a recovery facility's management activities but not its generation of toxic ash from the burning of household wastes. Defending itself, the city of Chicago pointed to a Senate report that states that solid waste incineration should not be considered generation, transportation, treatment, storage, or disposal of hazardous waste if it burns only household and nonhazardous waste. Further, the city argued that it would be an economic hardship if it had to comply with hazardous waste regulations every time it burned solid waste.

Ultimately the Supreme Court agreed with the EDF's arguments. In a seven-to-two decision, the Court held that although the management activities of a resource recovery facility are excluded from Subtitle C regulation, generating toxic ash is not. The implications of this decision are potentially quite dramatic for managers. Whenever they burn solid waste that is tested and found hazardous, they must follow more stringent and costly hazardous waste regulations. Moreover, local governments as well as private parties have incurred substantial expense in complying with this ruling. Managers must either separate this waste before burning it, or treat its ash as hazardous. They also have had to retrofit incinerators in order to separate bottom ash that is hazardous from less hazardous fly ash.

As important as the uncertainties created by the judicial labyrinth are in complicating how managers do their jobs, they also can change what they do. For example, liability for hazardous waste cleanup may severely curtail important governmental functions. This may occur as officials prune or slash programs in order to fund additional hazardous waste cleanup. Further, local governments may be reluctant to provide traditional services, such as refuse control and landfill space, fearing liability. Finally, any liabilities incurred may be considered in bond ratings that evaluate government solvency. Thus they may raise the costs, or even cripple the ability, of state and local governments to borrow funds for other projects and services.

CRIMINAL LIABILITY OF LOWER- AND MIDDLE-LEVEL GOVERNMENT EMPLOYEES

Our review of legal trends would be disastrously incomplete were we to ignore what the courts have said about the personal liability of managers. Prior to 1980, there were no felony penalties for criminal conduct under federal environmental statutes. What is more, after Congress enacted felony penalties for criminal conduct in the major federal environmental laws,[8] the primary targets of prosecutors were private sector employees and businesses who were "midnight dumpers." This is, of course, quite curious, because most federal environmental statutes make no distinction between public and private violations. Recently, however, government employees increasingly are becoming the targets of criminal lawsuits when they violate environmental laws. Indeed, today there are several former public administrators who are convicted felons because they violated these laws. What is more, felony penalties can reach as high as one million dollars and fifteen years in prison.

The first thing that managers need to know about their criminal liability is this: judges have adhered to the old idea that ignorance of the law is no excuse. Judges and juries determine on a case-by-case basis whether public administrators acted knowingly. This, generally, involves deciding one of two things: did the person "generally intend" to take the action that prompted the violation in question, or did he do nothing to prevent harm when he had the chance?

Significantly, federal environmental statutes do not specify who within an organization should be held liable for environmental crimes.

Consequently, responsibility tends to vary from case to case, with prosecutors, judges, and juries assigning blame. In private-sector cases, the courts have found low-level employees, middle-level managers, top-level corporate officers, and even corporations themselves liable. This has not been the case, however, in criminal litigation when environmental laws are broken by public administrators. Instead, federal prosecutors, judges, and juries have tended largely to target lower- and middle-level government employees. With only a few exceptions, top decision makers have escaped prosecution.

The following examples of lower- and middle-level public administrators found criminally liable for violating environmental laws are both eye opening and sobering.

• The fuels division director at the Adak Naval Air Station in Alaska was held criminally liable for his actions under the CWA. In 1988 and 1989, this employee ordered jet fuel pumped through pipes he knew would leak fuel into a creek that flowed into the Bering Sea. He was convicted of knowingly discharging a pollutant into surface waters and for negligently discharging pollutants. In its decision, the court wrote that federal employees are subject to all federal requirements concerning water pollution (*United States* v. *Curtis,* 1993).

• Three civilian engineers employed by the Army to work on chemical warfare systems are now convicted felons. They each were found personally liable for illegally storing, treating, and disposing of hazardous wastes on Army property. Neither the Army nor the commanding officers at the Aberdeen Proving Ground in Maryland were cited as defendants. This happened, moreover, even though such practices were widespread in the Defense Department and the engineers were not acting on their own behalf (*United States* v. *Dee,* 1990).

• The former director of public works for Ocean Shores, Washington, became a convicted felon when he was found guilty of aiding and abetting the illegal disposal of hazardous wastes. The wastes included paint left over from road maintenance and grease sludge removed from the kitchen of the city's golf course. On the director's orders, another employee buried both sets of wastes near the city's sewage treatment plant. No one else in the city's hierarchy was held liable for this violation (*United States* v. *Hoflin,* 1989).

• A civilian maintenance employee at Fort Drum, an Army camp in upstate New York, is today a convicted felon. He was found guilty of failing to report the release of hazardous substances. The maintenance worker, who was supervised by Army officers, directed a work crew to dispose of waste cans of paint in an improper manner and failed to notify state or federal environmental authorities when the buried cans leaked. The public employee maintained in court that he was too low in the chain of command to be liable since he was not in charge of the facility. The judge in this case gave the following instructions to the jury:

> The paint waste was released from a truck assigned to the workers by the Defendant. . . . The truck, individually[,] and the area of the disposal[,] constitute facilities within the meaning of . . . [the statute]. So long as the Defendant had supervisory control or was otherwise in charge of the truck or the area in question, he is responsible under this law. The Defendant is not, however, required to be the sole person in charge of the area or the vehicle. If you find that he had *any authority* [emphasis added] over either the vehicle or the area, this is sufficient regardless of whether others also exercised control [880 F. 2d at 1550].

Moreover, a court of appeals had already confirmed that any person "in a position to detect, prevent, and abate a release of hazardous substances" could be considered in charge, and so be found liable for such an environmental crime (*United States v. Carr,* 1989).

Certainly the implications of targeting lower- and middle-level government workers in environmental crime prosecutions are several. First, for managers there is a decline in hierarchical authority that is quite positive. When an individual who buries paint knows she will be held personally responsible, she is much less likely to bury it, whether independently or on orders from above. In contrast to this, however, there is an issue of fairness. How fair is it to prosecute a lower-level career bureaucrat when his or her supervisor knew or should have known of the actions that triggered the violation? Relatedly, if higher-level government executives are not held to the same standard as lower-level employees, they simply may grow even more unconcerned about environmental issues. Finally, attracting and retaining managers of high quality may become more difficult for organizations. In this era of tight resources and growing demands, the threat of a felony conviction for violating environmental laws may be enough to push valuable career public servants out the door and discourage others from entering.

INCREASED REPORTING REQUIREMENTS

Accompanying this trend toward personal liability has been another trend that places managers squarely within the crosshairs of liability for environmental actions or inactions. Specifically, environmental statutes and regulations increasingly are demanding a greater amount of information from organizations and their contractors. Personnel, for example, must file "manifest" forms with the EPA whenever they transport or dispose hazardous waste. The CWA and the CAA both require extensive self-monitoring and reporting by organizations. Relatedly, the Occupational Safety and Health Act has more than one hundred record-keeping and training requirements, many concerning environmental practices.

Consider the following cases in which managers have been found guilty of violating the reporting requirements of environmental laws:

• In Enid, Oklahoma, a court found a former superintendent of the public utilities department guilty of eighteen felony violations and two misdemeanor violations of the CWA. Regulators charged the superintendent primarily with falsifying reports concerning the discharge of raw sewage into a stream. Each felony conviction carried a maximum penalty of five years in prison and a $25,000 fine, while each misdemeanor conviction brought a maximum penalty of one year in prison and a $10,000 fine (*United States* v. *Brittain*, 1990).

• In Big Springs, Texas, a court found the superintendent of utilities guilty of knowingly making false statements on wastewater treatment plant discharge reports. He had filed these reports on behalf of the city. He was sentenced to one month in prison for each of five counts of violating the CWA (*United States* v. *Windham*, 1989).

• In Pennsylvania, a court convicted a former superintendent of a local government sewage treatment plant of filing false laboratory reports with the state's Department of Environmental Resources. It fined this person $1,000 and put him on probation for three years (*Pennsylvania* v. *Frey*, 1989).

• In Cleveland, Ohio, a court found a former commissioner of the Hopkins International Airport guilty of failing to report the release of hazardous substances and making false statements to the EPA. This person had to perform one thousand hours of community service, was sentenced to 180 days of home detention, and was given four years of probation. His conviction was part of a prosecution centering on the illegal burial of 148 barrels of hazardous wastes. After burial, these barrels were crushed by a bulldozer, causing them to leak (*United States* v. *Bogas*, 1990).

Although each of these cases concerns atypical instances of lying or falsifying reports to other government entities, even the most scrupulously honest manager may get caught in the legal quagmire surrounding federal and state environmental reporting and record-keeping requirements. Environmental laws are complex, sometimes difficult to understand, and expensive to comply with or implement. It is not hard to imagine a busy manager who is a nonspecialist in environmental matters failing to keep up with these reporting requirements, being unaware of changes in environmental laws, or having unavailable the funds to comply adequately with environmental regulations. Yet such individuals may find themselves imprisoned or fined heavily for their shortcomings. To be sure, the EPA, Congress, and President Clinton have sought to streamline environmental data reporting requirements ("Consolidated Environmental Data," 1995, p. 1998). Yet, those requirements that remain are sizeable, labor intensive, and time-consuming. As such, they will continue to challenge managers everywhere (O'Leary, 1993b, 1994a).

LIABILITY FOR REGULATORY TAKINGS

Also changing the face of public management is the courts' evolving interpretation of what constitutes regulatory takings by government. The idea of regulatory takings is not new. The Fifth Amendment of the Constitution clearly states that private property shall not be taken for public use without just compensation. In 1922, Justice Holmes wrote, "while property may be regulated to a certain extent, if regulation goes too far it will be recognized as a taking" (*Pennsylvania Coal Co.* v. *Mahon*, 1922, at 415).

Although the concept was there, the federal courts hardly ever found that a regulation went too far. Thus, until recently regulators proceeded with little concern about federal courts' involvement in the actual operation of land-use regulation. Two Supreme Court cases decided in 1986 and 1987 involving state and local governments demonstrated the more serious operational entry of the federal courts into land-use regulation and convinced regulators that the Supreme Court's regulatory taking doctrine would indeed apply to them. The cases were *Nollan* v. *California Coastal Commission* and *First English Evangelical Lutheran*

Church of Glendale v. *County of Los Angeles.* In *Nollan,* the Court held that a state agency must be prepared to prove in court that a "legitimate state interest" is "substantially advanced" by a state regulation, and that an "essential nexus" exists between the "end advanced" (or the enunciated purpose of the regulation) and the "condition imposed by the application of the regulation" to the property which restricted the owner's use of it. In *First English,* the Court held that invalidation of the offending regulation is not an adequate remedy for a regulatory taking and that just compensation for a temporary taking must also be provided.

Hence, in deciding whether a government regulation or decision is a taking of property without just compensation, the courts examine two aspects of a case. First, judges look at whether or not the regulation substantially fails to advance a legitimate governmental interest. Second, the courts look at whether implementing the regulation deprives the owner of all economically viable uses of the property. The following cases are illustrative of these two tests.

Whitney Benefits v. United States

In 1991, a federal court of appeals held that the mere passage of the Surface Mining Control and Reclamation Act (SMCRA) of 1977 effected a regulatory taking without just compensation for property owned by the Whitney Benefits Company. The Court reasoned that the passing of the SMCRA prevented the mining of hundreds of acres containing coal. This deprived the mining company of all economic use of its property, even though the company had not applied for a mining permit. The court ordered the U.S. government to pay the company approximately $60.3 million, plus prejudgment interest from August 3, 1977.

Loveladies Harbor, Inc. v. United States

In a case decided in 1990, a court found that New Jersey and the federal government were preventing the residential and commercial development of twelve-and-a-half acres on Long Beach Island, New Jersey. They were doing so when, respectively, they passed the New Jersey Wetlands Act and the wetlands provisions in the CWA. Finding this a regulatory taking without just compensation, the court ordered the federal government to pay the developer more than $2.6 million plus interest from the date of the taking, May 5, 1982.

Florida Rock Industries, Inc. v. United States

In a third case, decided in 1990, a court found that denying a permit to Florida Rock Industries to mine ninety-eight acres protected under the CWA constituted a regulatory taking without just compensation by the Army Corps of Engineers. The court reasoned that denying the permit deprived Florida Rock Industries of all economically viable uses of its land. The court ordered the federal government to pay approximately $1 million plus interest from the date of the taking, October 2, 1980.

Lucas v. South Carolina Coastal Council

On June 29, 1992, the U.S. Supreme Court announced its decision in the case of *Lucas* v. *South Carolina Coastal Council*. The pivotal issue was whether implementing the South Carolina Beachfront Management Act (BMA) was a regulatory taking of property. The decision, while narrowly drafted, has implications for the future of all U.S. environmental and natural resource laws. As such, it deserves more detailed treatment than the previous cases.

David H. Lucas, the petitioner, purchased two vacant oceanfront lots on the Isle of Palms in Charleston County, South Carolina, for $975,000. He intended to build single-family residences on the lots, but in 1988 the South Carolina Legislature enacted the BMA [S.C. Code Ann. Sections 48–39–10 *et seq.* (1989 Cum. Supp.)]. The act prohibited Lucas from constructing on the property any permanent structure (including a dwelling) except for a small deck or walkway. Lucas filed suit in the Court of Common Pleas, asserting that the restrictions on the use of his lots amounted to government taking his property without justly compensating him. The lower court agreed with Lucas, maintaining that the BMA rendered the land "valueless," and awarded him more than $1.2 million for the regulatory taking. Upon appeal, the Supreme Court of South Carolina reversed the lower court's decision. The judges maintained that the regulation under attack prevented a use that seriously harmed the public. Consequently, they argued, no regulatory taking occurred.

The U.S. Supreme Court, however, in a six-to-three decision, reversed the holding of the highest court in South Carolina and remanded the case to it for further action. In its decision, the Court articulated several pivotal principles that constitute a test for takings that all managers should know. First, the justices emphasized that regulations denying a property owner all "economically viable use of his land" require compensation, regardless of the public interest advanced in support of the restraint. As such, even when a regulation addresses or prevents a "harmful or noxious use," government must compensate owners when their property is rendered economically useless to them.

At the same time, however, the Court threw the issue of whether a taking occurred in Lucas' case back to the South Carolina courts. The lower courts now had to examine Lucas's understanding of the content of the state's power over the "bundle of rights" he acquired when he took title to his property. Put differently, the pivotal question for all state regulators today is this: Do state environmental regulations merely make explicit what already was implicit in any property title (that is, the right to regulate its use), or are they decisions that come after a person acquires title that were not originally implied. If the latter, they are takings that governments must compensate.

Equally important in *Lucas* was what the Court did not discuss in its narrowly worded opinion. First, the Court did not say that Lucas was entitled to compensation. Rather, it implied that the South Carolina Supreme Court was hasty in concluding that Lucas was not entitled to recompense. Second, the Court did not address the issue of property that is merely diminished in value—a far more common occurrence. Instead, it only addressed the issue of property that was rendered valueless. Finally, in pushing the regulatory takings issue back onto the state, the Court did not say that state laws may never change. Indeed, the majority held that "changed circumstances or new knowledge may make what was previously permissible no longer so." Hence, the Court left the door open for some regulation of newly discovered environmental harms after title to a property changes hands. Still, Lucas did prevail. Upon remand, the South Carolina Supreme Court reversed its earlier decision and awarded Lucas more than $1.5 million (Wise and Emerson, 1994).

Dolan v. Tigard

A few years after *Lucas,* the Supreme Court continued to develop the area of regulatory takings in a local government planning and zoning case that also is having profound effects for managers at all levels of government. In *Dolan* v. *Tigard* (1994), the owner of a plumbing and electrical supply store applied to the city of Tigard, Oregon, for a permit to redevelop a site. The plaintiff wanted to expand the size of her store and to pave the parking lot.

The city, pursuant to a state-required land-use program, had adopted a comprehensive plan, a plan for pedestrian and bicycle pathways, and a master drainage plan. The city's planning commission conditioned Dolan's permit on her doing two things. First, she had to dedicate (that is, convey title) to the city the portion of her property lying within a one-hundred-year floodplain so it could improve a storm drainage system for the area. Second, she had to dedicate an additional fifteen-foot strip of land adjacent to the floodplain as a pedestrian and bicycle pathway. The planning commission argued that its conditions regarding the floodplain were "reasonably related" to the owner's request to intensify use of the site, given its impervious surface. Likewise, the commission claimed that creating the pedestrian and bicycle pathway system could lessen or offset the increased traffic congestion that the permit would cause.

As mentioned earlier, in *Nollan* (1987, p. 825), the Court had ruled that an agency must be prepared to prove in court that a "legitimate state interest" is "substantially advanced" by any regulation affecting property rights. This decision required agencies to show that an "essential nexus" exists between the "end advanced" (that is, the enunciated purpose of the regulation) and the "condition imposed" by applying the regulation. The Court was silent, however, about how judges should interpret these terms.

After reviewing various doctrines that state courts had used to guide such analyses, the Court in *Dolan* enunciated its own test of "rough proportionality." It stated, "No precise mathematical calculation is required, but the city must make some sort of individualized determination that the required dedication is related both in nature and extent to the impact of the proposed development." If there is rough proportionality, then there is no taking. In *Dolan,* the Court decided that the city had not made any such determination and concluded that the city's findings did not show a relationship between the floodplain easement and the owner's proposed new building. Put more directly, the city had failed to quantify precisely how much the pedestrian and bicycle pathway would proportionately offset some of the demand generated.

The implications of the Court's doctrine in this case are profound for public agencies. The facts are hardly unique and represent the types of zoning decisions that local governments make daily. What is more, its logic potentially extends to all local government regulatory activities. Finally, the decision means that the federal courts can become even more involved than they already are in reviewing and judging the adequacy—

the dissent in *Dolan* said the "micromanaging"—of local regulatory decisions (Wise and O'Leary, 1997).

With the burden of proof now falling on the government, considerable litigation is an inevitability. Local governments will thus have to do more individualized analysis of the expected impacts of land-use changes and the conditions they impose on them. Not only will this be more costly, but it will also likely have a chilling effect on regulatory activity at that level. Finally, no one knows what constitutes "rough proportionality," so local regulators should expect continuing litigation in different regulatory contexts. Lower and appellate courts will have to begin operationalizing this test for them, a decidedly time-, labor-, and uncertainty-intensive exercise.

Consider, for example, what has happened to date in this regard. At any one time, more than two hundred takings cases have been pending in the court of claims. Moreover, the majority of these cases on any given day are likely to concern environmental and natural resource regulations. The statutes most affected, to date, are the CWA, the Endangered Species Act, and the Wilderness Act. Nor are the stakes Lilliputian. Environmental groups charge that if takings suits are successful, the trend will destroy years of hard-fought incremental progress in protecting the environment. Government regulators agree, adding that the trend could devastate already ailing government budgets. This will be true especially if proposed federal legislation is enacted that would take compensation payments from the coffers of the agency that issued such regulations. As we discuss in Chapter Six, the property rights movement sees no problem with this. They argue in part that payment is merely fair compensation for years of losses triggered by environmental regulations.

Thus, regulatory takings cases are being watched closely by all stakeholders. Indeed, several of them have already appealed new cases to the Supreme Court. Public managers must therefore continue to await the definitive word on takings. But resolved or not, the regulatory takings issue will be part of the dynamic environmental leitmotiv facing them for years to come.

THE MUNICIPALITY AS MINIATURE WATER POLLUTION CONTROL AGENCY

Yet another area of environmental law that affects thousands of public administrators is the growing responsibilities of municipalities as miniature water pollution control agencies. Incredibly, some environmental laws are in effect trying to turn regulated agencies partially into regulatory agencies. In the past, municipalities needed only to concern themselves with their own water pollution. Today these local government entities are responsible not only for their own wastes but also for that of other parties as well. Specifically, they must control industrial discharges to all "publicly owned treatment works" (or POTWs) and prohibit illegal discharges into separate municipal storm sewer systems. To do any less means that they too will meet litigants in court.

Pursuant to the CWA, municipalities that discharge wastewater from POTWs must apply for and adhere to a National Pollutant Discharge Elimination System permit. To obtain this permit, large municipality POTWs (that is, those that treat more than five million gallons per day) must accept and implement a number of new regulatory responsibilities. These include identifying and educating industrial users about all pertinent regulations, inspecting industrial users and monitoring their actions, investigating industrial users' violations of pretreatment standards, and prosecuting any violations by industrial users (O'Leary, 1993b).

Further, Congress and the EPA have increased the chances that a municipality will be sued if they fail to do these things. First, the EPA, states, and citizens can all file suits against a municipality for noncompliance with the CWA. Second, they can do so whenever a municipality does not enforce the law as stringently as the EPA or a state thinks it should. Additionally, this highly subjective determination may be made after the fact, with little prior guidance given to the municipality.

Managers also should understand that if a municipality acting as a water pollution control agency is the subject of an enforcement action, sanctions vary. They can range from a phone call for minor violations to three years in prison and fines of $50,000 per day for criminal violations (33 U.S.C. Section 1319). Also, a municipality may have to agree to take certain actions to remedy these problems and to prevent them from recurring, including filing suits against industrial violators, making all who discharge into the POTWs comply by certain deadlines, or even trying to shut down violating industries.

Obviously the implications for managers of such a dramatic role reversal are stunning. So too are the implications associated with the cultural challenges involved in being simultaneously a regulator and a regulatee. First, becoming a water pollution control agency can be costly and resource intensive, depending on the size of and environmental challenges facing the municipality. In many instances, new ordinances must also be passed that give the local government the necessary legal enforcement powers. Such efforts require legal expertise initially, and engineers, inspectors, and additional clerical staff later (O'Leary, 1993b).

Second, by imposing more, unfamiliar, and unfunded demands upon municipalities, Congress is reducing citizen discretion, managers' options, and agency capacities to perform their primary missions. Moreover, as local choices narrow and mandates grow, the chances increase of taking action that might prompt lawsuits. This creates a difficult environment in which to work, especially for local government managers whose regulatory actions are being evaluated with twenty/twenty hindsight (O'Leary, 1994b). Such an environment also does not help for-profit and nonprofit organizations seeking judgments from local public managers.

Finally, should a municipality be found liable for violating the CWA, monetary penalties may be more than city coffers can bear. Special taxes or fees may be needed to support such sanctions, or other programs may have to be curtailed to pay penalties. As of this writing, Congress and President Clinton are considering changes to the CWA that would lessen the burden on local governments and address the problem of unfunded environmental mandates. As yet, however, the metes and bounds of reform are unclear.

FLOW CONTROL

As we noted in Chapter One, transjurisdictional environmental problems are real, widely recognized, and difficult to handle. They also are not novel. Indeed, for years one of the biggest controversies in environmental management has been whether states and local governments may keep trash out of their districts. In 1994, however, the Supreme Court decided a case that reflects a new cutting-edge issue in environmental management: keeping trash within a specific state or local government boundary and not allowing it to be shipped out for economic reasons.

In *C & A Carbone, Inc. et al.* v. *Clarkstown, New York* (1994), the town of Clarkstown agreed to allow a private contractor to construct a solid waste transfer station within the town's limits and to operate the facility for five years. At the end of the five years, the town planned to buy the facility for one dollar. To finance the transfer station's cost, the town guaranteed a minimum waste flow to the facility, for which the contractor charged a tipping fee. In turn, and in order to meet the waste flow guarantee, the town adopted a flow-control ordinance that required all nonhazardous solid wastes generated within the town to be deposited at the transfer station. Forbidden was the shipping of nonrecyclable wastes out of the city's limits to locations charging a lesser tipping fee.

After discovering that the Carbone company and other haulers were shipping their wastes to out-of-state locations, Clarkstown filed suit in state court. The city sought an injunction requiring Carbone to ship its wastes to the town's transfer station. The lower court granted summary judgment to the town, and the appellate court affirmed. Carbone and other haulers appealed to the U.S. Supreme Court, arguing, among other things, that the flow-control ordinance violated the Commerce Clause of the U.S. Constitution.

In a six-to-three decision, the Supreme Court reversed the decisions of the lower courts, holding that the ordinance did indeed violate the Commerce Clause. The Court reasoned that although the ordinance was a local one, its economic effects were interstate in nature. The justices also reasoned that the article of commerce involved was not so much the waste itself but the service of processing and disposing of it. Moreover, they found that the ordinance unfairly favored certain operators who provided these services, disfavored others, and squelched competition. Finally, the Court maintained that the town had other avenues for addressing its local interests. For example, it could issue health and safety regulations to address environmental safety concerns. Alternatively, taxes or municipal bonds could subsidize the costs of the facility.

Like *Dolan* and *Lucas,* the implications of *Clarkstown* are widespread and profound for managers. Hundreds of local governments have entered into similar arrangements involving not only transfer stations but also the financing of landfills and incinerators. In Onondaga County, New York, for example, the county has spent more than $175 million to build a trash incinerator. Moreover, all these arrangements involve local governments agreeing to dispose of their trash at the sites in question. The *Clarkstown* case may jeopardize the future of the Onondaga County incinerator, as well as the future of other incinerators around the country.

Consider what *Clarkstown* has already occasioned across the nation. Municipalities have issued more than $10 billion in bonds to finance trash-burning plants around the country, and more than one-half of the states have enacted laws allowing flow-control ordinances. Many haulers are now trying to use the Court's decision to obtain releases from prior agreements. Most county officials contend, of course, that the agreements are contract based, not ordinance based. But local haulers maintain that the contracts were coercive in nature. Moreover, the end product—a violation of the Commerce Clause—is the same. To be sure, several local government associations are trying to persuade Congress to overturn the Supreme Court's decision. Yet managers who are attempting to cope in the interim find themselves in legal limbo when it comes to anticipating change in this dynamic legal environment.

IMPLICATIONS FOR MANAGERS

The developments we have chronicled in this chapter are prompting nothing less than a fundamental change in environmental management practices. Positive changes in operating procedures that are necessary but sometimes wrenching are occurring in order to make public employees more aware of the legal implications of their actions. Also, with more variables to consider, decision making in many public, for-profit, and nonprofit organizations is becoming slower and potentially more costly. Especially salient to public agencies is the issue of how they will pay for the staff and resources needed to meet these increased environmental responsibilities, for the court suits that these legal developments are likely to spawn, and for any monetary penalties assessed by the courts for violating the statutes.

Aside from pay issues, the difficulties of attracting and retaining public employees are spiraling apace with these changes. Doing more with less—whether a laudable goal or not—is already a stressful challenge for most government workers. So too is their need to understand new technical environmental information, with threats of felony convictions and large liability judgments if they fail to do so. Will many quality workers opt out of a public service career in environmental management? Maintaining a reasonable level of morale and a service ethic in such an atmosphere is daily becoming a tougher challenge for managers. Thus public managers need to stress to their employees that they will not escape scrutiny by fleeing to the private sector.

More positively, there are several ameliorative steps related to this dynamic legal environment that managers can take, regardless of which sector they work in. Those who are currently in the field can retool periodically to become aware of the environmental responsibilities and liabilities facing them. They can gain this knowledge from regular degree programs, certificate programs, and continuing education courses in colleges and universities. They can also try to educate their employees routinely about environmental law changes, choices, and challenges. Once employees grasp the basics of environmental law, managers have to help them keep abreast of statutory changes and new case law that may affect the operations of their organizations.

Within their organizations, managers can ensure that environmental assessments are done periodically. In an environmental assessment, an organization completely examines its operations to pinpoint areas needing attention. For example, an environmental assessment can help a manager identify and find ways to control hazardous substances at her facility. Environmental assessments are important for both ongoing operations and facility closure and restoration.

Managers can further minimize their liabilities by working in tandem with their federal, state, and local regulatory communities to address environmental problems. Cooperation from the very beginning is not only wise, it is the law. Yet many regulatory targets worry that the sharing of problems with regulators will only lead to penalties. Meanwhile, many regulators worry that they will be accused of being captured by the polluters they regulate. What managers in regulatory targets should know, however, is that EPA guidance documents set out three mitigating factors that may lessen penalties for violating environmental laws: voluntarily disclosing environmental violations, cooperating with the government's investigations, and implementing preventive measures and compliance programs. Meanwhile, managers in regulatory agencies should know—and are learning (as we shall see in Chapters Five through Eight)—that strategic engagement with the media and all stakeholders is usually better than court suits.

One author suggests eight minimum requirements for an effective compliance program (Woodrow, 1994). Agencies—in both the regulated and the regulatory communities—should be sure that

- Line managers monitor compliance with environmental laws
- Environmental policies are integrated into the daily work environment
- Self-auditing procedures are adopted
- Employees are trained in how to comply with environmental laws
- Incentives for complying are offered to them
- Employees who violate environmental policies are disciplined

- Improving compliance is continually stressed as a goal
- Alternative approaches—such as minimizing wastes, preventing pollution, and involving employees in agency environmental decision making—are adopted

Finally, managers should also be sure that all actions they take to address and prevent environmental problems are documented. Included in this record should be *what* they did, *why* they did it, and *who* they consulted. Efforts to train employees are also appropriate to document. Records must be exact and comply with appropriate requirements. Proper records can be invaluable in defending an organization's or employee's actions in a subsequent lawsuit. From a regulator's perspective, what gets measured in organizations is usually what gets done.

CONCLUSION

Familiarity with the potential legal liability under which managers, their agencies, or their companies labor is a necessary but hardly sufficient condition for successful environmental management. As we noted in the Introduction, those seeking either reactively to avoid liability or proactively to reconcile their organization's mission or missions with emerging environmental concerns will find that they also must communicate effectively to skeptics the value that environmental management can add to ongoing and future operations.

Typically, however, even the most self-interestedly sympathetic or most environmentally zealous converts to environmental management will find change difficult. Prevalent within many agencies is an administrative orthodoxy of hierarchy, rules and regulations, and functional bases of organization. These can stifle continuous process improvements, effective communication, and organizational learning. Yet overcoming these barriers is vital for adapting prudently, effectively, and in timely ways to environmental challenges, choices, and opportunities. Consequently, we turn in Chapter Four to the sources of this resistance, to one important means touted for overcoming it (total quality environmental management), and to the promise versus the performance of that approach.

PART TWO

WORKING WITH STAKEHOLDERS TO PRODUCE ENVIRONMENTAL VALUES

4

DESIGNING EFFECTIVE ENVIRONMENTAL MANAGEMENT SYSTEMS

You cannot build a Staff as you build a house,
from the bottom upwards, and then when it is all finished
put the Chief of Staff on top of it like a chimney.

—Winston Churchill[1]

Several years ago, a total quality environmental management (TQEM) training seminar for federal regional employees took place in Albuquerque, New Mexico. The organization's leaders were vigorously pursuing a major TQEM effort. Their goals were multiple and geared toward many of the managerial challenges posed in Part One of this book. The organization's leaders wanted to make their associates more sensitive to the environmental concerns and needs of their customers. They wanted to alleviate through teamwork the functional balkanization that got in the way of meeting those needs in efficient and cost-effective ways. They wanted to create among employees an attitude of taking personal responsibility for continuously improving their work. Paramount in this regard was getting them to consider the environmental impacts of their efforts systematically and to attenuate them. Finally, they wanted to reduce employee and organizational liability for environmental concerns.

Following a lecture on TQEM principles, an audience member asked a question that at first glance seemed facetious: Was learning from the local newspapers that you are fired consistent with TQEM principles regarding the empowerment of frontline workers? As the lecturer prepared to demur vigorously, other audience members turned away from the podium and began peppering with barbed questions a defensive regional official sitting in the audience.

The organization's leaders, it seemed, had talked of empowering employees, of focusing on outcomes rather than inputs, and of building cross-program work teams. Yet the organization's budget, accounting, and employee reward systems spoke otherwise. They remained geared toward individual rather than team program performance, toward measuring inputs rather than outcomes, and toward centralizing rather than decentralizing authority. In sum, too broad a gulf had developed between the TQEM principles that the organization's leaders touted and its day-to-day operations.

To say that this has been a common problem with TQEM initiatives is not to suggest that many TQEM successes do not exist at all levels of government in the United States. Although some might worry that focusing on TQEM—or on Total Quality Management (TQM) more generally—means giving too much attention to a "fad" that is waning in popularity, we feel that the opposite is true, for several reasons. First, because much of what TQEM addresses in public organizations relates to issues that are central to classical management theory, TQEM's diagnoses of the problems that conventional bureaucracies spawn for environmental protection are timeless. Consequently, examining through this lens the organizational barriers that managers face in building an environmental ethic in their organizations has much to offer.

Second, ours is an uncommon focus on what researchers and practitioners have found to be the conditions under which TQEM is more or less likely to succeed (for a more extended treatment, see Durant, 1998b). Thus, like the Planning, Programming, and Budgeting Systems of the 1960s, TQEM may be a fad that takes root and has long-term beneficial effects in certain situations and not in others. Managers will benefit from knowing when—and under what strategically savvy ways of application—success is more likely to occur.

Third, even as TQEM appropriately loses much of its early boosterism, it is becoming increasingly clear that its focus on cross-functional and (less often) interorganizational process improvements will be with managers for a long time. To be sure, TQM's focus on "doing it right the first time" has been superseded in change-adept organizations by a focus on "doing it better the second and third times" (Kanter, 1997; Hammer, 1996). But process-centered organizations are increasingly the model for organizations seeking to deal with turbulent and fast-paced environments like those that managers encounter in the environmental policy arena (Hammer, 1996).

Finally, the utility of TQEM as a construct for simplifying the implementation of global metastandards for environmental management developed by the International Standardization Organization (ISO) may yet revive its appeal among cynics. As we shall discuss, the ISO—a worldwide federation of 119 member countries—has developed auditable conformance standards that are designed to enhance product quality (the ISO 9000 series) and environmental quality (the ISO 14000 series). Both series are premised directly on W. Edward Deming's "plan-do-check-act" cycle for TQM initiatives (discussed in greater detail later in this chapter). Additionally, the ISO 14000 series has many elements consistent with the Malcolm Baldrige Award's broader TQM criteria for evaluation of total systems. Finally, both series hold the promise of breaking down barriers to effective interorganizational partnerships, given their focus on creating boundaryless organizations.

Thus some managers may eventually use these quality-centered metastandards as criteria for contractors who wish to do business with them; others may use them as management models for their own operations; and still others may find their costs too steep to meet and simply fall back on TQEM principles for themselves and their contractors. But as researchers and consultants agree, managers in organizations that have ISO 9000-based systems like TQEM already in place will find implementing ISO 14000 principles much easier than those who do not already have such systems. Resuscitated in the process will be ossified bureaucratic structures and processes and environmentally reactive cultures in organizational units and programs, if not throughout the organization.

Pointing out the gap between TQEM aspirations and implementation *does* say, however, that successfully inculcating such an ethic is tough. Research has consistently chronicled how career managers who think otherwise are quickly set straight as they try to convert quality management principles into practice. Nor should organization heads pursue TQEM efforts with their eyes closed. To paraphrase Churchill, the chances of building organization-wide commitments to TQEM principles from the bottom up, and placing leaders astride them like chimneys as afterthoughts, are negligible. A TQEM paradox often exists: the greater the degree of customer focus and employee empowerment an organization seeks, the greater is its need for strong, resolute, and committed leadership.

To date, research has not charted a precise course for anyone trying to navigate the turbulent waters of TQEM interventions. Nonetheless, it does afford guidance for doing so without beaching on the shoals of unrealistic expectations, premature initiatives, and strategic or tactical missteps. In today's era of fiscal stress, managers are routinely confronted with the risks and opportunities of meeting environmental management goals in new ways. They therefore cannot afford to ignore how promising TQEM principles can be for innovatively and cost-effectively attaining their environmental management goals.

What is more, if TQEM can simplify the implementation of ISO 14000 principles in organizations and among their contractors, this technique holds the potential to alter fundamentally the relationship between organizations and their stakeholders. As Uzumeii (1997) suggests, "Management system meta-standards [like ISO 9000 and 14000] are not simply another management fad. They represent a new management technology that may have a profound impact on the near term evolution of management practice. It is now clear, for example, that metastandards are technically feasible, that they can affect management theory, and that they have the potential to fundamentally change the power relationship between organizations and key stakeholders" (p. 1).

WHY TQEM?

As noted in previous chapters, the existing statutory framework for environmental protection that managers will encounter is decidedly out of sync with the nature of the problems it seeks to confront. Environmental problems cut across different media (such as air, water, and land); dealing with these problems means partnering multiple organizations in different sectors that are not used to working together; environmental risks and impacts are interactive, cumulative, and substitutable; and toxic dangers have multiple pathways. Yet Congress—and in turn federal, state, and local regulators—has consistently approached environmental protection one medium, one risk, and one pathway at a time. Moreover, although most single-medium environmental statutes make passing nods toward reducing and preventing pollution, their overwhelming focus has been on end-of-pipe solutions rather than on upstream source reductions.

Rationale for a Regulatory Morass

How did such a regulatory regime come into existence and survive despite its obvious and costly shortcomings? Primarily, the regime is a function of the order in which environmental problems attained salience, were addressed legislatively, and were studied scientifically (such as the Clean Air Act, followed by the Federal Water Pollution Control Act). Moreover, whenever pressures mount to redress the problems this regulatory regime affords by creating a single "organic" (that is, integrated multimedia) statute, critics denounce the implementation dilemmas that reform would create. As we discuss more fully in Chapters Five and Seven, scientists are frequently unsure of precisely how various risk factors interact, what their cumulative effects are, and how to rank them in priority across media.

Even if this were not true, however, the existing regime provides political and regulatory benefits that make reform difficult. To begin with, legislators find it easier to think in terms of single-medium problems and become expert in them. What is more, legislators' electoral needs make them only selectively attentive to media problems; the different parts of the country they represent are faced with different types of dominant issues (Fiorino, 1995). Also, no one wants to diminish the electoral credit that single-medium-focused grantsmanship presently affords legislators in these areas.

Meanwhile, the environmental and business constituencies that have formed around specific media programs and largesse are loath to endure change. They fear losing power, access, and regulatory continuity if the system changes (Moe, 1989). Thus, despite their lamentations, many of these constituencies are more comfortable with the "devil" they know than with the one that multimedia regulation may create.

Managerial Consequences

These rationales aside, however, the present regulatory regime wreaks havoc for even the most environmentally committed managers. They must learn to function effectively in an excessively balkanized, cost-ineffective, and complex system that often creates perverse incentives for doing so. Moreover, this is true whether one is a regulator or a regulatory target in the system.

The sequencing of single-medium statutes, for example, has encouraged both regulators and the regulated community to "media-shift" problems. Regulatees historically have shifted their waste streams sequentially from air to water to land as they have tried to stay one step ahead of federal statutes. Likewise, regulatory program managers have often tried to shift responsibility for dealing with environmental problems to the budgets of other program offices ("that's an air problem, not a water problem"). At best, these actions mean that only pieces of environmental problems are effectively addressed. At worst, they stymie significant progress on more cost-effective, risk-predicated, and outcomes-oriented environmental management.

The nation's single-medium focus has also further exacerbated the bureaucratic pluralism that plagues all conventionally organized bureaucracies (Knott and Miller, 1987). Reflecting this focus, single-medium program offices now populate regulatory organizations throughout the land. These offices routinely are pitted against one another in a zero-sum competition for power, resources, and prestige in organizations. Diminished in the process is cooperation across media programs in the absence of extraordinary effort and commitment by an organization's leaders, managers, and employees.

Witness, for example, the candid comments of one Environmental Protection Agency (EPA) staffer in Washington: "I can't be worried about organization-wide issues; I get my priorities from the Clean Air Act." Another staffer adds, "I was selected by the administrator, nominated by the president, and confirmed by the Senate to run the [X] program, not to think broadly about the environment" (National Academy of Public Administration, 1995, p. 127). Managers affected by these statutes do not, of course, have this luxury. They are charged with "portfolio" management, stretching precious resources across competing requirements in ways that will satisfy regulators, taxpayers, and public health and safety experts.

Managers trying to ascertain what constitutes compliance for their organizations or to set cost-effective priorities for addressing environmental problems are faced with multiple and frustrating obstacles. In these tasks, they have to expend precious resources preparing for separate inspection teams from different media offices. Each team demands different information, insists on compliance with the team's standards, and has no incentive to consider what other inspection teams are asking for, finding, and requiring for redress. Why? Because their activities are evaluated, rewarded, or punished by oversight committees focused on single-medium performance.

In sum, managers, their contractors, and third-party partners often face a perplexing dilemma when dealing with regulators. As managers try to coordinate, gain consistency of approach, or set environmental priorities, they repeatedly face a system that is ill-conducive to these efforts. As the National Academy of Public Administration (1995, p. 127) points out:

Power flows from the congressional authorizing committees to the assistant administrators who head the media programs, and then to their staff members. These staff set national standards, write and defend regulations, design the programs that implement the regulations, and approve program delegations to states. Power then flows to the regional offices' division directors and their staffs, and then to the managers and staff operating the programs in delegated states. The barriers between programs are further reinforced by corresponding fragmentation in the environmental community, in industry, and in professional and technical associations.

Meanwhile, within the regulated community, environmental health and safety units tend too frequently to be isolated from, rather than integrated with, line operations and decisions. Consonant with that status, career rewards for those in environmental units are sometimes sparse, topping out at ranks and salaries considerably lower than those of their colleagues. Nor does it help that organizational leaders have traditionally seen environmental management programs as tangential, if not anathema, to their primary missions.

Recently, however, the confluence of several developments has raised the plausibility to organizations of TQEM as a new environmental management paradigm. This approach values cost-effective environmental management initiatives that are multimedia-focused, conducive to but not requiring an emphasis on pollution prevention rather than control, and dependent on continuous environmental quality improvements that get hardwired into management and operating decisions. TQEM's allure has risen as the costs, complexity, legal liability, and anger of regulatory targets dealing with today's system have mounted.

The Push from Government

According to environmental scholars, the dominant legislative predisposition of the 1990s has been to shift from pollution abatement to pollution prevention (Rosenbaum, 1995; Vig and Kraft, 1994; and Ringquist, 1993). As alluded to briefly in Chapters One and Two, the penultimate expression of this shift in philosophy occurred at the federal level when Congress enacted the Pollution Prevention Act of 1990. This act created a priority system for waste disposal options. From most-preferred to least-preferred, these options were reducing, reusing, treating, and disposing of hazardous waste.

Likewise, under Title III of the Emergency Planning and Community Right-to-Know Act (part of the Superfund Amendments and Reauthorization Act of 1986), various classes of the regulated community must publish the types and amounts of their discharges in the Toxics Release Inventory. Premised on an informational approach to regulation (see Chapter Twelve), public disclosure of waste-stream contents and volumes has proven to be a mighty public relations problem for many firms. As such, it has simply become good business for the regulated community to reduce the quantity of its waste streams and to purge the most toxic effluents from them.

Meanwhile, President Clinton's Executive Orders (EOs) 12856, 12780, and 12873 have further focused the attention of federal managers on pollution prevention. The first of these EOs requires all federal facilities to have pollution prevention plans in operation and to reduce their output of toxic pollutants 50 percent by 1999. The latter two EOs require them to develop affirmative procurement programs to reduce their purchase of toxic substances. More recently, the EPA's Project XL, Common Sense, and Sectoral initiatives have stressed pollution prevention while giving the regulated community more flexibility in meeting diverse regulatory standards. In turn, all states have some type of hazardous waste pollution prevention program, twenty-nine of which have statutes establishing pollution prevention offices.

Finally, the United States—through its representative, the American National Standards Institute (ANSI)—has itself been involved in developing ISO 14000 metastandards. Among other things, these standards have further encouraged pollution prevention as part of continuous process improvement. The genesis of these standards was the 1972 United Nations Conference on Human Environment, which ultimately led to the report, *Our Common Future* (World Commission on Environment and Development, 1987). As we noted, this report contains the first formal reference to the virtues of sustainable development, and it calls on polluting industries worldwide to develop effective environmental management systems. Within one year, fifty nations took up the challenge, creating a movement that led directly to the 1992 United Nations Conference on Environment and Development—the Earth Summit—in Rio de Janeiro.

Partially to prepare for that conference, the ISO set up the Strategic Advisory Group on the Environment to recommend international standards. By 1995, an EPA official was elected vice chair of the U.S.

Technical Advisory Group (TAG). Created by ANSI to represent U.S. interests in negotiations over standards, the TAG—and its Sub-Technical Advisory Groups—consists today of more than six hundred individuals representing three hundred organizations. These include government organizations, major industries' environmental auditors and standards bodies, consumer groups, and environmental organizations.

Although compliance with ISO standards is voluntary, they are designed to create a single, generic, and internationally recognized set of environmental management system (EMS) process and product criteria. These criteria help organizations operating in the global economy to avoid duplicative or inconsistent regulatory regimes, and to afford a common baseline against which consumers can evaluate the competing claims of "greening" industries. Organizations can apply for certification (or registration) by licensed third-party auditors that they are in conformity with criteria for EMSs defined in ISO 14001. Published in September 1996, these standards also allow self-certification by organizations.

The ISO 14001 standards identify key principles for managers to use when implementing an EMS, including commitment to continuous process improvement, pollution prevention, waste minimization, and compliance with environmental legislation and regulation. The standards also show managers how to measure, monitor, and evaluate the performance of the EMS on these factors. As such, they try to help managers build "learning organizations" that are capable of assessing accurately, persistently, and in a timely fashion the impacts of their activities on the environment and the progress they are making in reducing or preventing pollution. Also focusing managers' minds on these techniques are other ISO 14000 series product guideline standards. These emphasize such things as life-cycle costing (discussed later), environmental labeling, and environmental product standards.

As noted earlier, no company has to adopt EMS process or product standards. Yet powerful informal pressures to do so can develop. First, the marketing pressures to conform can become overwhelming as competitors, whole industries, nations, and regional bodies (such as the European Union) adopt them as either requirements or commitments for doing business. Second, adopting the ISO 14000 series can help managers demonstrate a commitment to environmental compliance. Such a commitment can in turn constitute a mitigating factor should regulators assess liabilities for noncompliance.

The Pull from the Business Community

Still, the single most compelling motive driving interest in pollution prevention comes from the cost savings touted by, and demonstrated in, leading corporations. Importantly, these results were occurring long before ISO 14000 standards were nudging organizations into getting "greener." Together, however, the push of government legislation and ISO standards as well as the pull of demonstrated cost savings now prompt many to say that environmental standards are good for industry, public agencies, and contractors as long as they prod them into waste minimization efficiencies that they might not otherwise recognize or pursue (Porter and van der Linde, 1995; Cairncross, 1992; Fischer and Schot, 1993; and Schmidheiny, 1992). Moreover, as Dean Telego (1993, p. 1) writes, "Central to protecting and preserving corporate assets, net income, and public image from potential environmental loss exposures and liabilities is designing and implementing [a TQEM] risk management program that has as its centerpiece an integrated pollution prevention program."

Today, such titans of industry as the 3M Corporation, Kraft General Foods, Reynolds Metals, Texaco, and DuPont embrace pollution prevention, and with it, TQEM principles. At these corporations, such concepts as full-cost environmental accounting, total cost assessment, and life-cycle costing are mantras of program managers. Full-cost environmental accounting allows users to allocate their total costs (that is, both the direct and indirect costs of labor, capital, and environmental cleanup) to specific products, product lines, or operations. In contrast, total cost assessment allows users to integrate environmental costs into capital budgeting analyses to show the comprehensive and long-term costs and savings associated with a given investment. Finally, life-cycle costing permits users to assign a monetary value to the total environmental consequences associated with a product, process, facility, or system over its lifetime (from raw material acquisition to disposal).

The litany of savings spawned in industry by TQEM principles is now legendary. At 3M, for example, corporate officers attribute nearly a half-billion dollars in cost savings over fifteen years to their Pollution Prevention Pays program. Similarly, programs at DuPont reduced waste chemicals by approximately one billion pounds between 1985 and 1992, saving the company nearly $50 million annually.

These savings did not necessarily entail massively disrupting organizational operations. For example, a DuPont plant in Texas that was spewing out 110 million pounds of waste per year initially eschewed pollution prevention plans. Its engineers argued that they were too expensive. After a second review, however, managers found that they could reduce waste by two-thirds and save $1 million annually by eliminating only one toxic chemical from the plant's production processes.

Evidence from Government

Are the same benefits realizable in public organizations? The EPA (1995) argues that pollution prevention efforts will flourish only when its own (and state) programs become more multimedia oriented, when more flexibility is allowed in remedy selection, and when a source reduction mind-set permeates all phases of regulatory activities (permitting, compliance, and enforcement). Accomplishing these goals requires an epiphany from legislative and judicial sovereigns predisposed toward single-medium problems, end-of-pipe solutions, and "gotcha" regulatory mind-sets. And alas, funding to meet statutory deadlines and court consent decree milestones will continue to push pollution prevention projects into the background at many organizations (see Chapters Two, Three, and Six).

Still, the results of TQEM efforts have been encouraging in certain situations. For example, the Department of Energy's defense program recycling effort at Los Alamos National Laboratory alone saves the department approximately $140,000 per year. Likewise, the Navy has reduced its plastic waste by 70 percent. So impressive has this effort been that the Navy has begun developing technology to eliminate buoyant plastic discharges from naval vessels. One also cannot dismiss lightly the savings that pollution prevention efforts have afforded in terms of court costs avoided, liability exposure limited, and employee health and safety improved. Finally, estimates that 80 percent of the cost of complying with each regulation goes into documenting polluting actions show the potential monetary savings that TQEM approaches can generate.

Likewise, a review of the quality management literature focusing on efficiency improvement finds a wealth of positive results in qualitative case studies across a range of policy areas (see, for example, Cohen and Brand, 1993; Cohen and Eimicke, 1994; Gore, 1993; Koehler and Pankowski, 1996). Decidedly less impressive, however, are the results of the few studies applying bivariate, multivariate, and time-series statistical analyses to assess productivity improvements. Two things are striking about these disparate findings. First, the positive results are nowhere near as significant in scope and impact as the early advocacy literature predicted (Durant and Wilson-Gentry, 1993). Neither, however, are they as minimal in effect as skeptics thought they would be.

At the Internal Revenue Service (IRS), for example, various project teams in the Ogden and Fresno service centers produced savings of $3.7 million and $12 million, respectively (Mani, 1995). Likewise, the Air Force Logistics Command reports that the mission capability of its fleet improved from 40 percent to 76 percent, while its delinquent purchase deliveries decreased by 83 percent (Cohen and Brand, 1993). Meanwhile, the IRS found that its accuracy in answering taxpayer questions improved nearly 25 percent.

Similarly promising are improvements claimed by several states and localities applying quality principles. For example, city managers and organization directors responding to Evan Berman and Jonathan West's (1995) national survey exhibited modest, albeit positive, impressions of the technique's material (productivity enhancing), solidarity (teamwork), and purposive (quality improvement) benefits. Using a five-point scale ranging from 2 (very negative) to +2 (very positive), respondents rated gains in efficiency at .98, cost reductions at .84, and ability to cope with resource constraints at .88. Solidarity gains related to empowerment and team building garnered ratings ranging from .77 (delegating responsibility) to .92 (improving group decision making) to 1.01 (improving unit communication). Finally, respondents saw the greatest gains in purposive rewards: they rated service quality improvement at 1.04.

Noteworthy as well are Theodore Poister and Richard Harris's (1997) findings regarding the impact of long-standing quality improvement efforts by the Pennsylvania Department of Transportation. In the most statistically sophisticated and theoretically grounded assessment of such efforts to date, path analysis reveals that the department substantially reduced its maintenance backlogs. Moreover, these benefits exceeded the quality program costs associated with it by one-third. Admittedly, the absence of experimental controls in this study (and most others) means that these researchers could not eliminate rival explanations for efficiency gains. Nonetheless, Poister and Harris's findings are important and encouraging to those contemplating TQEM initiatives in their organizations.

Granted, an organization can collect and make available baseline emissions data for pollution prevention without committing to TQEM principles. It can also build program-based information resource management systems capable of meeting these needs. Indeed, it can even reduce source emissions in individual programs without TQEM. What an organization cannot do without TQEM, however, is take full advantage of the organization-wide budgetary, political, and environmental promise that customer-oriented, risk-prioritized, and outcomes-oriented pollution prevention strategies offer.

Still, success is not guaranteed. Indeed, a review of the literature suggests that there are conditions under which TQEM initiatives are more or less likely to succeed within public organizations and among their contractors. Before discussing these conditions, however, we turn first to the ends and means of attaining a TQEM ethic in public organizations.

A TOTAL QUALITY MANAGEMENT ETHIC

In deconstructing the terms of TQM, Steven Cohen and William Eimicke (1994) have afforded a most concise yet cogent definition of TQM principles: "*Total* means applying to every aspect of work, from identifying customer needs to aggressively evaluating whether the customer is satisfied. *Quality* means meeting and exceeding customer expectations. *Management* means developing and maintaining the organizational capacity to constantly improve quality" (p. 450). In essence, organizations focus in unprecedented ways on critical self-evaluation, on acquiring and interpreting data sufficiently to inform that evaluation, on constant process improvement, and on customer satisfaction. A quality culture also debureaucratizes organizations. It dissuades their members from seeing management as "control," from seeing "doers" (subordinates) as separate from "thinkers" (managers), and from seeing work tasks as isolated functions. Promoted instead is an ethic that embraces "teamwork, coaching, listening, and leading" (Bowman, 1994, p. 134). This ethic also focuses employees on end products or services that meet or exceed customer rather than bureaucratic expectations.

Finally, a quality culture presses managers and their associates to think beyond their individual programs, units, and organizations. They begin seeing themselves as "coproducing" organizational missions with associates and organizational stakeholders. Within their organizations, employees come to appreciate that they are customers of other units who supply things they need. What is more, they come to understand how they in turn have customers—associates in other units who depend on their actions. In essence, employees learn to think of their organizations as part of an assembly line of producers and consumers (the organization, its contractors, third-sector actors, and organizational stakeholders). These internal and external actors must coordinate and cooperate as partners if citizens and stakeholders are to receive (or perceive) improvements in service quality.

How does an organization become a learning organization? Proponents of TQM approaches proffer a set of principles and a grab bag of tools for effecting them (see especially Deming, 1986, and Juran, 1988). The principles are straightforward. First, managers and their associates must see their work as continually needing improvement. Second, they must see themselves as cross-functional team members responsible, and meaningfully rewarded, for constantly improving their work processes. Third, managers must understand that frontline workers, their suppliers, and their customers frequently know better than managers what constitutes quality, how to get it, and how to assess it. Fourth, frontline employees must appreciate that improving quality means anticipating and correcting problems before they occur. Finally, an organization's political appointees must understand that success depends on their being committed to, modeling, and rewarding these behaviors in persistent and compelling ways.

Proponents of applying TQM in public organizations offer a variety of "hard" and "soft" techniques for improving quality (for more in-depth treatments of these techniques, see, for example, Milakovich, 1995; Koehler and Pankowski, 1996; Lawler and others, 1992; Carr and Littman, 1990; and Carnevale, 1995). Among the former are such tools as flowcharts, process analysis worksheets, tree diagrams, and root-cause analyses. These can help employees determine what the flow-of-work process really is and improve it. Likewise, they offer such tools as cause-and-effect diagrams and fishbone charts to link outcomes with production processes.

In turn, surveys of suppliers, employees, and customers help provide data necessary to inform the decisions that these techniques suggest. Organizations can supplement these surveys with flow, trend, control, and Pareto charts; with statistical process controls (both control charts and process capability); and with political force-field analyses. Framing all these methods are reengineering principles that break down functional departmentation. Departments are replaced, where possible, with flow-of-work structures that promote cooperation, added value, and customer satisfaction.

Contributing to these efforts on the "soft" side of the quality prescription ledger are several techniques. TQM relies on team building to unfreeze entrenched attitudes and to refreeze quality cultures. As such, employees must receive the training that true empowerment requires. Toward this end, a "nested" team-building approach is most often prescribed. Using brainstorming, multivoting, and selection-grid decision techniques, TQM has organizational leaders working with key resource suppliers and customers to develop a strategic vision or plan. In turn, process improvement teams composed of lower-level managerial and line employees use the "hard" analytical techniques discussed earlier to link the goals of their plan to day-to-day operating decisions, processes, and emphases.

Establishing a TQEM Ethic

Applying these principles to environmental concerns, a TQEM ethic requires an organization to focus unflinchingly on integrating environmental values into everyday operating decisions. At the core of this philosophy are source reduction and pollution prevention as ways to enhance continually the quality of the goods or services the organization produces. In the process, an organization begins coproducing both process improvements and definitions of what constitutes quality by remaining focused on customer (internal and external) perceptions.

As management experts routinely counsel, however, structure must follow strategy (Thompson, 1967). Thus, success in this endeavor depends on how well managers link their TQEM goals to three sets of organization structures: administrative, responsibility, and account (or control) structures (see Hall, Rosenthal, and Wade, 1993; West, Berman, and Milakovich, 1994; Poister and Harris, 1997). Respectively, these structures tell what different parts of an organization do, who personally is responsible for achieving what with available resources, and who measures the organization's performance in what ways. Ideally, planning, budgeting, and accountability structures are integrated in mutually reinforcing ways—an approach that some have dubbed a "balanced scorecard" model of strategic management (Kaplan and Norton, 1996).

To the extent that these structures send signals or create incentives that are inconsistent with one another and with environmental sensitivity, the less likely it will be that an organization will successfully inculcate a TQEM ethic in its employees. In turn, for this adroit meshing to occur, managers must pay sustained attention to—and assess their progress on—four critical sets of activities. Should they ignore any of these, TQEM efforts will die aborning.

First, they must prompt, exhibit, and widely tout the commitment of their leaders to multimedia-based, results-oriented, and bottom-line-enhancing environmental management initiatives. Second, and toward these ends, managers must maintain robust and up-to-date process-oriented and results-oriented environmental databases. (We refer to these in Chapter Nine as strategic environmental information systems.) In turn, they must link these databases directly to their organization's planning and operating decisions. Third, managers must painstakingly develop and reward employee understanding of the environmental implications of the employees' work. Concomitantly, they must convey to all workers how both employees and the organization can prosper by considering environmental quality before they act. Finally, they must infuse their environmental management efforts with an intense commitment to determining and understanding stakeholder perceptions, needs, and values.

In Chapter Six we refer to these efforts as building a "coproduction environmental ethic" in an organization. For now, however, we only need to mention how ISO 14001 standards for certification require that managers use "holistic proactive management" and "total employee involvement" in "defining environmental roles from the bottom up." They also require "top management backing, resources, and visibility to support" this bottom-up process (CEEM, 1998). Finally, present plans call for making ISO 9000 total quality standards more compatible with ISO 14000 broader environmental quality standards by the years 2000 and 2001. TQEM principles may thus become even more important in the years ahead as managers oversee their contractors who comply with ISO 14000 standards or adapt similar EMS or product standards to their own operations.

Building Leadership Support for TQEM

Gaining support for TQEM initiatives from an organization's political leaders and career employees can be a challenging, even daunting task. One of the most effective ways to get superiors—whether appointed, administrative, or legislative—to pay attention to TQEM principles is to provide them with information related to the costs of doing nothing. Documenting the savings of private and public organizations that have employed TQEM can be quite useful. So too are best-in-class benchmarking exercises that compare existing organizational practices and performances with the TQEM practices of top performers. Finally, it does not hurt to emphasize the insurance, liability, and operating costs saved by organizations and their contractors when applying these principles.

One does not have to rely exclusively on these comparisons, however. Using successes garnered from small TQEM pilot projects as levers for selling TQEM to superiors can also be effective (Cohen and Eimicke, 1995). These efforts can be focused on projects where the potential for and rewards of success are greatest (see discussion of these conditions later in this chapter). Moreover, in looking for cost savings from these efforts, managers should canvass all the components of the assembly line of activities involved in meeting their environmental management priorities. Finally, selling others on the value of applying TQEM principles also works by identifying, mobilizing, and involving other champions of the process. These actors—within an organization, among its contractors, or in legislatures—can make compelling appeals on both normative and instrumental grounds. Normatively, they can tap into the public's well-established concerns about public health, safety, and environmental values (see Chapters Five through Seven). Instrumentally, they can cite the benefits they have seen accrue from the better community, employee, and legislative relations that a demonstrable focus on environmental management can provide (see, for example, Cohen and Brand, 1993; Berman and West, 1995; and Carnavale, 1995).

If energized, organizational leaders will then have to play strategic, tactical, and symbolic roles in fostering TQEM. Because we will discuss many of these roles momentarily, it suffices presently to speak in general terms. Most critically, leaders must be prepared to articulate, demonstrate, and model the behaviors necessary to sell internal and external stakeholders on the value that environmental management adds to the organization's primary mission. In the process they must envision, promote, and institutionalize environmental management thinking and values both within and outside of the organization.

For starters, focusing on customers is, by itself, a most powerful lever for cultural change. As business consultants Gene Hall, Jim Rosenthal, and Judy Wade (1993) note, a crucial way to change organizations is to alter their vocabularies. The words employees use in daily organizational life pattern the way they think and act. Thus, if terms like *customer satisfaction, environmental quality,* and *environmental value-addedness* become part of everyday speech in an organization, its employees will acquire new understandings about what is valued and what is not. Moreover, if these approaches are institutionalized and rewarded in responsibility, accounting, and budget structures, significant behavioral shifts in environmental management can occur.

By the same token, however, focusing on the environmental quality perceptions and needs of external customers can initially threaten organizational members. Customer surveys may reveal inadequate performance, misidentified goals and objectives, and skill or technology needs that an organization presently cannot meet. To be sure, the potential exists to let these data help contribute to a strategic plan that addresses these shortcomings. But as Deborah Cook (1996) notes, even change of the most positive kind can leave managers and their associates temporarily grieving for old ways.

A period of defensiveness is typical as well. After all, TQEM's emphasis on continuous process improvement means that employees must identify previous or ongoing errors they may have made or let pass. The angst produced may manifest itself in anger, missing TQEM deadlines and meetings, or even outright sabotage of the process.

Consequently, researchers have suggested a variety of unfreezing strategies. Included prominently among these are "positive reminiscence" (Hall, Rosenthal, and Wade, 1993); "creating a sense of urgency" (Goss, Pascale, and Athos, 1993); creating an "amnesty" policy (Cohen and Brand, 1990); and confronting resisters directly after a reasonable period of adjustment (Cohen and Eimicke, 1996). Perhaps the only nonobvious strategy among these is positive reminiscence. In this approach, every meeting opens by encouraging employees to talk about what they did right in the past and to relive past successes—if any—in dealing with environmental management questions. Researchers find that talk soon transitions into participants recognizing how they could have done better, what obstacles they faced, and how they might now redress them.

While this is going on, however, leaders should begin institutionalizing their TQEM vision. To this end, five tactics are useful:

- Setting up headquarter-level environmental management committees that include political appointees and program managers. These can set a strategic direction for TQEM values and ensure that they are incorporated into any organization-wide strategic planning efforts that exist.

- Assigning cross-functional responsibilities to teams of employees. These teams in turn should focus on both process reform and results.

- Creating information networks among teams that stress timely sharing of process and quality data in user-friendly formats.

- Introducing outcomes-based performance evaluation measures that are clear, that stress collaborative and quality values, and that are consequence-laden.

- Creating customer satisfaction milestones, holding meetings to assess progress toward them, and including members from all relevant functions in these meetings.

TOWARD DATA-INFORMED TQEM DECISIONS

A second major aspect—and arguably the linchpin—of any TQEM effort involves data collection, management, and analysis. In Chapter Nine we cover the kinds of obstacles that managers may face in this endeavor and how they might create strategic information resource management systems that compensate for them. Presently, however, we focus only on the kinds of data that are crucial to any TQEM effort. Critical, as well, is managers' appreciation of the ways in which they must link these data to operating decisions, and how TQEM analytical techniques can assist them in doing so. The conventional wisdom is, as we noted, abundantly true in the case of TQEM initiatives: what gets measured is what gets done in organizations.

Not surprisingly, given TQEM precepts, and when applying ISO 14000 series standards and models, any data collection effort begins and ends with anticipating, understanding, and coping with customer and stakeholder needs and values. As we shall see in the chapters on community relations (Chapter Six) and risk communication (Chapter Seven), an organization's perception of its environmental management efforts may differ appreciably from the perceptions held by observers. Still, working with communities to develop environmental management measures that all will accept as laudatory is a promising way to deal with this dilemma.

In essence, organizations should collect four general types of measures in any serious TQEM effort: lagging, leading, outcome, and stakeholder feedback indicators. *Lagging indicators* are data indicating the results that existing processes will produce. These provide managers with baseline information against which they can measure such things as reductions in hazardous waste streams, lost work time from injuries, or regulatory violations avoided from process changes. Useful measures might include the amount of emissions avoided (such as energy units-to-product ratios), travel miles reduced, waste toxicity minimized, waste materials recovered (takebacks), and disposal costs avoided.

In contrast, *leading indicators* are management steps taken that should later produce better environmental outcomes for the organization. These include training, documentation, the timeliness of corrective actions, resources committed to environmental management-related capital investments, and environmental audits (both self-audits and external reviews). In essence, these measures are useful in assessing and exhibiting an organization's environmental management commitment to legislators, regulatory organizations, the media, and the general public. At the same time, they help determine how consistent short-term environmental management tactics are with an organization's long-term strategic environmental management goals.

Outcome measures tabulate the impacts that an organization's environmental management initiatives actually have on community health, safety, and the environment. They link shortcomings in this regard to specific gaps in an organization's activities, and they provide comprehensive data for continuous process improvement. No doubt they are also the most difficult measures to acquire. For instance, assigning responsibility for improvements or reductions in environmental quality to specific organizations can be difficult. What is possible, however, is to link an organization's waste generation and procurement decisions with environmental stewardship. Measures of the former might include tons of waste recycled, reclaimed, or sold per year. Measures of the latter include the amounts of recycled versus "virgin" materials used per year in operations, as well as the ratio of renewable to nonrenewable product purchases per year.

Finally, internal and external *stakeholder feedback measures* link an organization's actions to existing perceptions, concerns, preferences, and needs. On the basis of these measures, managers can determine what their customers think they are doing right, what needs improvement, and what opportunities exist to alter perceptions. We discuss various techniques for actively listening to both internal and external stakeholders in our chapters on working with communities (Chapter Six) and communicating risk (Chapter Seven). Presently we note only that any outreach effort worth its salt does four things: anticipates concerns, incorporates internal and external feedback into operations, educates the public about existing TQEM efforts and constraints, and disabuses stakeholders of any misperceptions they may harbor.

ASSESSING EXISTING STRUCTURAL CAPACITY

How can managers assess the present or evolving capacity of their organization, its contractors and grantees, and its third sector partners to move toward establishing a TQEM ethic? Any worthwhile assessment has to consider what we have already identified as critical: how well integrated are environmental concerns and measures with line operations and planning. In turn, a commitment to continually improving this relationship is recognizable most clearly when all elements of Deming's plan-do-check-act cycle are in place and working well. To plan means to establish needs and priorities, to do means designing and implementing environmental management initiatives that are aligned with strategic goals, to check means monitoring these initiatives for consequences, and to act means revamping initiatives based on this feedback.

Managers know that in this circular process TQEM problems exist in planning and doing if

- Only minimal assessment of internal and external customer, stakeholder, and network needs and priorities takes place
- Data analysis is not used to determine problems and identify improvement priorities
- Cross-functional work teams do not exist to identify problems
- Environmental management initiatives remain misaligned with organizational goals, objectives, and action plans
- Environmental management initiatives lack sufficient resources for implementation
- Cross-functional implementation teams do not monitor and verify progress toward environmental management goals
- Monitoring information is not shared with decision makers in timely and useful ways to prioritize and make corrections in processes

No longer allowed are balkanizing of functions or marginalizing or isolating of environmental management planning processes from an organization's core activities. If an organization is already involved in a larger TQM effort with empowered work teams, environmental management staff should be fully integrated into these teams to represent these values. If not, managers should inaugurate cross-functional and multidisciplinary teams. Included on these teams should be environmental, financial, operations, program personnel, media relations, and (when possible) community representatives. Only in these ways, and with a reward structure reinforcing such efforts, can environmental management concerns get mainstreamed in an organization.

To help themselves set priorities, these teams can take advantage of such techniques as cause-and-effect (or fishbone) diagrams and Pareto analyses. Using the former allows team members to look at the environmental management implications of four primary features of organizational operations—materials, methods, manpower, and machines—and to rank them accordingly for redress. Using the latter helps them to see problem frequencies by constructing histograms for each area. Team members can then determine, for example, what actions will generate the highest rates of return on organizational investments in environmental quality (see also Chapter Nine).

In these types of priority-setting exercises, participants should consider a variety of environmental management tactical options. As Grace Wever (1996) notes, these include opportunities to engage in pollution prevention efforts; reduce risk and toxicity exposure; identify, factor in, or work to change regulatory drivers standing in the way of risk-based priority setting (such as enforcement orders and milestones agreed to before adequate information was available); enhance project acceptability to the public; and reduce off-site exposure potential (such as groundwater migration plumes).

The checking and acting phases, in turn, require team members to focus on two priority items. First, managers should limit reporting formats, make them easy for generalists at higher levels in an organization to understand, and ensure that they are amenable to regulatory reporting requirements. If political appointees, corporate executives, and senior managers are overwhelmed by reams of obtuse technical and risk information, if they do not understand it, and if that information is tangential to meeting the organization's mission or regulatory needs, they will not take TQEM seriously.

Second, the team should strive to ensure that program managers have easy access to cost analyses. Continuing, up-to-date, and accurate analyses—whether predicated on life-cycle costing or not—are important for many source reduction activities. After all, prices fluctuate for recycled products, procured parts or chemicals, and administrative overhead. Moreover, for many cities, moving beyond 25 to 35 percent recycling targets has proven financially disadvantageous.

BUILDING CAPACITY AND COMMITMENT

The path to successful TQEM initiatives is strewn with good intentions beached on the shoals of employee and contractor or grantee insensitivity, indifference, or intentional sabotage. The epitome of what implementation scholars call a bottom-heavy process, TQEM depends on subordinates exercising largely unsupervised discretion in environmentally conscious and protective ways. This in turn often requires a dramatic cultural shift on their part.

Thus, in addition to the substantive, structural, and symbolic tactics described earlier, organization leaders must do four additional things for employees (and for contractors and grantees where noted):

- *Expend considerable and targeted resources on environmental management training.* With resources dear, these efforts might begin by focusing on employees with high-risk jobs (either to themselves, public health, or ecosystems) and then gradually expand training to others. Moreover, because meeting regulatory compliance mandates is the most immediate challenge, training should probably start here. Stressed as well should be general awareness of the organization's environmental management goals, job-specific training related to them, and new environmental management techniques or procedures.

- *Directly or indirectly involve subordinates and contractors in environmental management decision making.* Leaders should focus on including members of both formal and informal organizational networks. Useful in plumbing their perceptions are focus groups, internal longitudinal surveys of employees, and protection for whistle-blowers.

- *Rotate environmental management, program management, operating personnel, and technical or scientific staff through one another's offices for periods of time* (see Chapter Ten). This can help foster perspective, mutual understanding, and (it is hoped) more prudent and realistic environmental management decisions. Many private corporations now require employees to have cross-training experience in both program operations and environmental management before they promote them.

- *Be sure that employees, contractors, and third sector partners understand that managers are scrutinizing their environmental management actions.* These actors must perceive that what monitors find will have consequences for their careers. To this end, leaders must tangibly and intangibly reward the championing and implementing of environmental values (see also Chapter Ten for a list of such rewards). These might include gain sharing for units cutting costs through pollution prevention or source reduction and formally rating environmental management actions in employee performance appraisals.

TOWARD A CONTINGENCY-BASED APPROACH TO TQEM

As should be evident by now, implementing TQEM principles successfully in any organization requires tenacity, patience, and cunning. Indeed, all of the pathologies of conventional bureaucracies that classical organization theory identifies come into play in these situations. Consider as illustrative what William Rago (1996) describes in his analysis of a TQM initiative at the Texas Department of Mental Health and Mental Retardation. He found that the organizational and personal barriers to conveying purpose were protean and their sources were mundane. Lack of ownership of values, the absence of consensus about them, and teamwork problems were rampant among employees. These in turn were attributable to three factors: lack of time to participate in meetings, discomfiture with debate, and perceptions that TQM activities were not as important as other responsibilities.

Similarly stubborn were the obstacles to improving cross-functional coordination, communication, and empowerment. The personal discipline necessary for making decisions consonant with strategic plans was missing, as was an organizational commitment to consensus decision making. Likewise shackled were policy communication and empowerment initiatives. The most critical psychological barriers to success were managers not feeling responsible for carrying out TQM policies, their fear that associates might make incorrect decisions, their perception that they were losing power, and their inability (or unwillingness) to think beyond their own self-interest. In turn, organizational factors exacerbating these problems included an inability to define purpose, lack of understanding about how empowerment should work, and poor policy integration within the organization.

All is not lost, however. Taken together, prior research suggests that managers should expect TQEM initiatives to vary in difficulty and levels of success. Several factors seem critical here. Be wary of proceeding, for example, until a resource commitment exists that is commensurate with training needs (Berman and West, 1995); personnel and performance appraisal systems support team-based TQM philosophies (Bowman, 1994; Berman, 1996); the personnel department has expertise in TQM (Berman, 1996); and managers are prepared to gather broad-based understanding and support from senior management, public officials, professional associations, political groups, and community leaders (Loveless and Bozeman, 1983).

All this in turn offers the broad outlines of a framework suitable for defining the conditions under which such efforts are more or less likely to be difficult or to succeed (Durant and Wilson-Gentry, 1993; Wilson-Gentry and Durant, 1994). First, managers should start with the rebuttable presumption that TQEM efforts are more easily established and sustained when

- Initiatives target discrete production tasks or projects
- Initiatives have noncontroversial means and ends
- Initiatives are carried out at the operating (or production process) levels of a single organization
- The production processes involved are noncontroversial, have inputs that are easily monitored and compared to outputs, and have agreed-upon measures of success that are easily identified
- Employee performance awards are related to TQEM precepts
- Standard operating procedures (SOPs), bureaucratic routines, and regulations are consonant with TQEM values
- SOPs, bureaucratic routines, and regulations are changed quickly to reflect these values

Second, managers can anticipate that TQEM initiatives are likely to be more successful when organization leaders afford TQM training that is linked to employees' work rather than to abstract TQEM principles, is aggressively conveyed to departmental personnel by the human resource department, and is consistently and broadly applied to the human resource department's own activities.

Finally, managers can expect more difficulty institutionalizing TQEM initiatives when the changes they entail or the results they may produce are not trumpeted, modeled, and institutionalized by organizational leaders; when they involve massive shifts in goals and mission; when they will result in nonincremental shifts in operations that affect many units; when they will result in internal or external redistribution of power, resources, or services; when they will require legislative approval; when they are not accompanied by broadly participative planning and management; when they are attempted by organizations with weak, unsupportive, or divided clienteles; and when they require high levels of trust among employees and managers where none exists.

CONCLUSION

As this chapter has chronicled, one of the most important things for managers to do when creating an environmental ethic in an organization or among their contractors and partners is to sell it internally to colleagues and externally to the organization's stakeholders. Thus far we have focused largely on the protean obstacles of resistance typically encountered within organizations and implementation networks, and we have offered a contingency approach to meeting that resistance. But whether managers are bent on selling a TQEM ethic or ISO 14000 principles to their associates or contractors, or whether they are merely trying to improve environmental management processes piecemeal to meet environmental regulations, actors outside of the organization must also see the value of TQEM principles. Here again, however, the obstacles faced can be substantial. For starters, an organization's experts might view environmental problems quite differently than citizens do. To begin understanding why this happens, we turn next to the media's role in defining environmental challenges, and how to deal strategically with these dynamics.

5

WORKING WITH THE MEDIA

Accustom yourself to give careful attention to what others are saying, and try your best to enter into the mind of the speaker.

—Marcus Aurelius[1]

A wealth of research has shown precisely how important the media can be in affecting public opinion. Consequently, only the most foolhardy manager dealing with environmental management issues would think it unimportant to understand how, why, and with what managerial consequences the print and electronic media help frame environmental issues today. Nor would she underestimate how important media coverage of the environment and her organization's related activities can be to destroying, maintaining, or rebuilding the public's trust in her organization.

We argue therefore that managers must positively and strategically engage the press on environmental management issues. Moreover, in doing so, they must take Marcus Aurelius' advice to heart: they must listen attentively and enter into reporters' minds. Such a strategy in turn requires managers to understand the environmental management opinion climate within which they operate today, to appreciate how the media affects that climate, and to learn what they can do about it. To do any less is to let others define an organization's environmental management image in the community.

PUNDITS, PUBLIC OPINION, AND ENVIRONMENTAL PROTECTION

What are the nature, depth, and breadth of the public's commitment to environmental protection? Nearly a quarter century's worth of survey research is quite revealing. Indeed, this literature offers lessons for managers who are either agnostic, cynical, or committed to effective environmental management.

Lessons for Environmental Agnostics and Skeptics

For starters, if managers see environmental concerns as faddish, limited to elite yuppies, and flouted without substantial consequences for their organizations, they are seriously mistaken. Americans have exhibited a broad-based, sustained, and growing normative (or consensual) commitment to environmental protection since the 1970s (Hays, 1992; Kempton, Boster, and Hartley, 1995). Indeed, they have joined citizens worldwide in expressing what researchers variously term the *new environmental paradigm* (Dunlap and Van Liere, 1978; Milbrath, 1984), the *postindustrial worldview* (Olsen, Lodwick, and Dunlap, 1992), and *postmaterial values* (Inglehart, 1977).

Basically, managers can expect to encounter a baby-boom generation with its immediate needs relatively satisfied that now has the time and luxury to worry about nonmaterial concerns such as the environment (Mohai and Twight, 1987). Some observers, of course, see the trend toward environmentalism as more interest group than generationally driven (Douglas and Wildavsky, 1982; Tucker, 1982; Hays, 1987). But whether concern for the environment is driven by forces that are sinister (namely, anticapitalist), utilitarian (such as the self-interested pursuit of quality of life at the expense of lost jobs for others), or public interest oriented (that is, concerned about public health generally), the results are the same.

Survey research reveals that anywhere from 58 to 73 percent of all Americans consider themselves to be environmentalists. What is more, survey data collected over the past two decades reveal that the public's attachment to environmental values has grown gradually, persistently, and significantly. This is true whether considering voting preferences, willingness to pay for environmental improvements, or preferred trade-offs between environmental protection and economic growth (Rosenbaum, 1995; Kempton, Boster, and Hartley, 1995).

Nor should managers think that environmental concerns are limited to socioeconomic elites in their communities. Survey research consistently shows a much more broad-based commitment than that. As Willett Kempton, James Boster, and Jennifer Hartley (1995, p. 7) note, environmental concerns are not limited to citizens who are "educated, wealthy, white, and liberal." As was mentioned in Chapter One, and as is discussed in more detail in Chapter Six, the environmental justice movement is vibrant in many communities. Meanwhile, the Black Caucus in Washington, D.C., has been among the strongest and most persistent supporters of environmental protection laws in Congress. Finally, toxic populist groups active in many localities are often begun and led by individuals from lower-income neighborhoods where polluting facilities are located.

Lessons for True Believers

By the same token, however, if managers are true believers about greening their organizations, they should not count on the public's general normative consensus about environmental values to help advance their aims. As public opinion scholar Riley Dunlap (1989) points out, consensus regarding environmental values is best characterized as passive. By this, he means that support for environmental values is "widespread, but not terribly intense" (p. 131).

Relatedly, the environmental management choices facing managers today involve more complex value trade-offs than questions tap when they ask respondents to choose between environmental and efficiency goals. Hazardous waste cleanup, for example, does not typically call upon managers to make "go" or "no go" decisions framed in these terms. Instead, they must grapple with such multidimensional issues as how clean is clean enough to protect human health? At what pace and in what priority should cleanup occur? What impact is acceptable on persons of color or of low income? A passive consensus on environmental values cannot help managers weigh and make trade-offs among these competing values. Only the more site-specific community relations and risk communication techniques outlined in Chapters Six and Seven, respectively, can assist them in these situations.

Most likely, managers will also find that the relative importance that citizens assign to various environmental issues varies significantly across time (Downs, 1972). So too does the relative priority they give to environmental issues relative to other concerns. Thus, citizens may not support particular environmental management priorities at any given time, even though they are generally supportive of environmental management initiatives overall. Indeed, even interest groups mobilizing to support these efforts may fall short at times of creating sustained interest in environmental issues. Consider, for example, the angst, outcry, and countermobilizing efforts of environmentalists during the Reagan presidency. By 1989, however, respondents to Gallup surveys persistently ranked environmental spending a distant eighth in priority relative to other spending possibilities (Rosenbaum, 1995).

Finally, the more that environmental regulations impinge on citizens' lifestyles, the less managers may be able to count on public support (Rosenbaum, 1995). Indeed, recent debates over particulate standards, catalytic converters on gas power mowers, and mandatory car inspections are quite revealing. They demonstrate vividly that citizens and their elected representatives are willing to go only so far when personal cost, inconvenience, or lifestyle changes are involved in environmental protection.

The Battle in the Press for Public Support

Given this passive consensus on environmental values, managers can ill afford to take public opinion for granted. And given the critical role the press plays in opinion formulation, it behooves managers to understand the print and electronic media's role in this enterprise. Otherwise they will be at a decided disadvantage relative to other stakeholders in the environmental protection arena. Both proponents and opponents of environmental regulation have long understood that the "medium is the message" (McLuhan, 1970).

As detailed in the next chapter (Chapter Six), on working with communities, managers are very likely to run into toxic populist groups during their careers. These groups may ply with virtuosity what members call the "victimage ritual" to get and maintain the media's attention. With the goal of combating the sizable financial and political advantages that the regulated industry enjoys, toxic populists deliberately try to create a "tidal wave of frightening speculation" by "turn[ing the regulated industry] into demons" (D'Antonio, 1993). In turn, they try to reframe the debate as one of "morality, not science." They do so in order to offset the resource disparity (legal, technical, scientific, and otherwise) that the regulated industry typically enjoys over them.

As we also discuss more fully in the next chapter, managers also can expect to run into formidable opponents of aggressive environmental protection. To promote their aims, for example, some in industry will use media "greenwashing." Other opponents at the grass roots will use direct confrontations with public servants (as well as court suits) to grab the media's attention. Greenwashing involves advertising and public relations campaigns that make positive but deceptive claims about a company's or industry's environmental sensitivity and commitment. These opponents may also not be above planting fictitious stories in the press to discredit environmental regulation. Used at times are, for example, outlandish and inaccurate anecdotes about the way regulators are implementing environmental policy. Moreover, opponents continue to repeat these stories—and the media often continues to print them—long after environmental proponents have discredited them.

Meanwhile, members of the property rights (or "wise use") movement will use the press to dismiss as unconstitutional and un-American the health, safety, and environmental concerns of national environmental groups, toxic populists, and community activists. They portray these groups as countercultural "monkey wrenchers" determined to stymie capitalism and destroy individuals' freedom to use property as they see fit. By restraining certain land use, regulations allegedly constitute takings of the value of land by government without properly compensating owners (recall the discussion of this issue in Chapter Three). Property rights proponents also mimic the tactics of more mainstream opponents of environmentalism. For example, they try to marginalize all environmentalists' arguments by disingenuously touting extremist views or regulatory snafus as typical of the environmentalist agenda.

Do these tactics really manipulate or take in the media? Hardly, but journalists are captives of their respective mediums (print and electronic). What toxic populists understand—as do managers who hope to be successful in dealing with environmental issues—is that their morality-play tactics fit nicely into the crisis-emergency-resolution format of contemporary print and electronic journalism (Weaver, 1994; Reilly, 1994). Within this soap-opera-like plot structure, someone is in grave danger, someone heroically intervenes, and someone gets saved. Meanwhile, antiregulatory extremists understand that if they repeat stories often enough, they find their way into "boilerplate" passages in wire service stories. The initial accuracy of these stories is often beside the point. Initially, reporters rush to beat competitors to the scoop; later they quote them indiscriminately as context for new stories.

Additionally, both groups appreciate how television images can overpower words in shaping people's opinions. After CBS correspondent Leslie Stahl presented a film report negatively contrasting excerpts of President Reagan's speeches with his proposed budget cuts (including cuts to environmental programs), a White House official thanked her profusely. Puzzled, Stahl asked, "Did you hear what I said? I killed you"—to which the official chortled, you "still don't get it. . . . No one heard what you said. . . . The picture is all that counts. . . . A powerful picture [of a confident and assertive President] drives out the words" (Fallows, 1996, p. 62).

In sum, managers are very likely to deal with public opinions regarding the environment that are mischievously informed by what Richard Harwood (1992) calls "commercially correct" journalism. Put most succinctly, the protagonists in environmental battles understand that bad news attracts more readers and viewers than does good or positive news. In turn, the more emotionally charged and negative the bad news is, the better it is for sales and advertising revenues. A manager's dilemma—and the dilemma for deliberative democracy more generally—is profound. The more persistent the message and the more vivid the account of threatening or titillating environmental events, the more likely readers or viewers are to react emotionally rather than cerebrally to the news they read or hear (Durant, 1995a).

Nor should anyone think that environmental moderates do not either resort to or at least try to benefit from these tactics. To the contrary, mainstream environmentalists use these tactics to advance the "precautionary principle" to counteract competing claims—for example, to urge that the benefits of acting now (such as on global warming) outweigh the costs of delaying action. Their opponents retort with the "cautionary principle"—that the opportunity costs of acting under conditions of uncertainty outweigh the benefits.

Increasingly, thoughtful observers both inside and outside the media have concluded that television and newspapers "dominate the conversations of democracy" in deleterious ways (Harwood, 1992; see also Fallows, 1996; Kurtz, 1994; Weaver, 1994; Moyers, 1990; for a contrary opinion, see Page, 1996). As the preceding suggests, however, this certainly does not happen for want of conveying information. Rather, the problem arises from the nature, quality, and interpretative tenor of the information that the print and electronic media convey. What television news does best is convey emotions to mass audiences. What it does worst is deal well with complexity. In contrast, newspapers and magazines convey complexity quite well. Their audience, however, is decidedly more limited to attentive readers and specialists (Jamieson, 1992).

Among the most distressing of these tendencies that managers encounter when dealing with environmental management issues are the industry's repeated focus on

- Cynical interpretations of events
- Conflict, titillation, and emotion
- Who wins and who loses, who is ahead and who is behind, or why personal advantages rather than principled beliefs drive decision making
- Style, strategy, and tactics over policy or program substance and implications
- Personality or celebrity rather than context and understanding of issues
- Objectivity rather than discriminating judgments about the merits of various arguments (also known as the "dueling expert" format)
- Interviewing the "available" rather than the most expert sources on a topic
- Favoring as interviewees those who speak succinctly, colorfully, combatively, in sound bites, and without qualifying their remarks
- Treating interviewees as equals, despite differences in stature and consensus judgments about the positions they take
- Reporting non-peer-reviewed research as good science
- Being intolerant of uncertainty or ambiguity when experts comment on unfolding or controversial events

As media expert Stephen Hess (1994) argues so persuasively, the media's jaundiced, personalized, and conflict-driven eye is attributable to a variety of changing market realities (see also Underwood, 1995). These include pressures by new corporate owners to cut back news operations, the growing segmentation of news markets, the declining influence of news bureaus relative to corporate home offices, and the blurring of what news is with the advent of tabloid journalism (see also Postman and Powers, 1992). But regardless of their causes, examples abound at all levels of how the "new news" is crimping deliberative processes regarding environmental management issues.

MEDIA COVERAGE OF THE ENVIRONMENT

To the extent that managers suspect that appeals to "good science" will automatically carry the day with the general public, they will be sadly disappointed (see, for example, Burnham, 1991; Lichter, Lichter, and Rothman, 1994, especially pp. 259–263). According to the National

Science Foundation, media news coverage tends largely to highlight the exotic and dangerous aspects of science (Gerbner, Gross, Morgan, and Signorelli, 1980).

Life Imitating Art?

Take, for example, the way that environmental biotechnology for waste treatment has been portrayed by major network news, by the popular press, and by specialized publications. Amy McCabe and Michael Fitzgerald's (1991) content analysis of news sources between 1987 and 1990 found a striking lack of reporting on bioremediating hazardous waste, despite that many experts viewed this approach quite favorably. Waste disposal applications appeared in only 7 percent of all biotechnology stories reported (N = 463).

Instead, the brunt of news coverage went to applying biotechnology in the medical field (39.5 percent) and to the legal, ethical, and regulatory issues involved with it (35.2 percent). The former had a very personalized, crisis-oriented, and dramatic bent—such as the life-or-death race against time of biotechnological breakthroughs for combating AIDS. The latter stories adapted the familiar conflictual lens and morality play format, with a heavy component of protests against biotechnology.

What is more, the content of these reports by network news organizations revealed a disturbing trend. They either hyped biotechnology as salvation (such as that it will solve the problem of oil spills, salt marshes, and estuaries) or fear-mongered it as damnation. Conveyed mostly was an "unmistakable, and extremely dramatic, sense of dread, uncertainty, and fear [about] unknown risks" (McCabe and Fitzgerald, 1991, p. 20). Moreover, citizens seeking to use the reputations of sources to assess the credibility or biases of the claims presented on television could not do so. Typically these stories used only generic labels (such as "experts," "scientists," "oil spill managers") to describe interviewees.

Some managers might infer that narrow choice of sources, as well as skewed and incomplete reporting of environmental issues, is to their organization's advantage. But as this book's chapter on risk communication (Chapter Seven) reports, citizens are more likely to fear things when they do not understand them or when they feel they cannot exert control over the risks involved. Skewed, noncontextualized, and incomplete reporting only heighten misunderstandings or fears that things are beyond citizens' control. When this happens, it is more likely that they will balk or question an organization's environmental management activities.

Nor do these developments affect only the way that the electronic media report on environmental issues. During 1989, for example, *Media Monitor* reported that fully 40 percent of all environmental stories published in either the print or electronic media (238 out of 595 stories) dealt with oil spills (189 of which focused on the Exxon *Valdez* incident). The next most popular environmental topics were animal rights and species protection. Not surprisingly, reporters covered the former as protest movements and focused on charismatic megafauna (such as the condor, the bald eagle, or pandas) in the latter. Meanwhile, during the Alar pesticide scare, only 15 percent of all print and electronic media stories reported any risk figure that might have helped citizens put the threat into broader perspective (Friedman, 1991).

Note, however, that this reporting slant plays into the hands of neither environmental extremists nor those trying to develop a strong environmental ethic. For example, in both small and large cities, local newspapers may be reluctant to raise environmental issues at all (other than in "greenmail"). They fear alienating major advertisers. They may also wish not to put citizens at risk of losing their jobs by focusing on pollution problems, or to highlight activities that reflect badly on elected officials with ties to powerful people and advertisers in the community.

To be sure, many editors will claim that they are sensitive to environmental issues. Yet the economic pressures of the news business can make even the most committed editors backpedal on this commitment. As media commentator Everette Dennis (1991) points out, environmental issues typically compete at a severe disadvantage with a range of sensationalist, personality-driven, and celebrity-focused articles and stories. "The environment," he writes, quoting a practitioner, "just isn't sexy enough" (p. 60). And even if it were, the complexity of environmental issues means that reporters covering them must have an uncommon combination of scientific, technical, economic, and political literacies. With the supply of this kind of talent so limited, most media outlets find hiring science reporters too expensive to justify. Certainly there are affordable personnel willing to take full-time environmental assignments, but they are conspicuously absent in most media markets.

A Mixed Bag

Readers should not infer from all this that media coverage of the environment is as strikingly wanting today as it was two decades ago. With the *New York Times* taking the lead, the quantity of environmental coverage in both the print and electronic media dwarfs that of the 1970s. So too does the knowledge level of reporters in large media markets, as the establishment of the Society for Environmental Journalists attests. What is more, recent empirical research regarding local newsrooms indicates that career systems increasingly militate against biased or "soft" news reporting of any kind (Goodwin, 1997). Seriousness and credibility are increasingly the ways to move up into major media markets.

None of this, however, has yet attenuated significantly the career disincentives that historically have driven environmental reporting. The stature of environmental reporters within newsrooms remains that of second-class citizens (Dennis, 1991). As such, they get less respect, get less attractive assignments, and get less front-page or top-of-the-newscast treatment for their stories. In turn, this makes the environmental "beat" distinctly less attractive to ambitious reporters.

So what are managers dealing with environmental issues to do? We argue that they should make every effort to work with the media, but without rose-colored glasses. Doing so means they must understand not only the business aspects driving environmental coverage, but also the pressures motivating reporters to write environmental management stories the way they do. On this basis they can devise a mutually beneficial relationship with the media, one predicated on conditional cooperation with reporters.

WHAT JOURNALISTS NEED

Although many managers view the media with trepidation, they should understand that they have several things that reporters need quite badly. These include access to environmental management information, legitimacy and sourcing, hooks and color, and context. Knowing how these factors come into play and how managers can deal with and use them to advance their environmental management goals is central to developing a conditional cooperation strategy. The tactics and strategies we relate are culled from the observations of practitioners, participant observers, reporters, and scholars doing research in this area (see, for example, Fitzwater, 1995; Moore, 1995; Cohen and Eimicke, 1995; Chase and Reveal, 1983; Garnett, 1992; Larkin, 1992; Pearce, 1995; LaMay and Dennis, 1991; Hansen, 1991; Johnson, 1987; Boynton, 1989; and Linsky, 1986).

Access

Reporters covering any beat need access to information, to decision makers, and to street-level bureaucrats delivering services. These needs become especially apparent in the environmental policy arena. As noted earlier, environmental beats may be growing, but they are typically staffed by individuals with low levels of scientific literacy. Moreover, these reporters have little time to get technical advice, given the filing deadlines they face. Also, even if they have time, they seldom know where to go for environmental information (Friedman, 1991). So where do journalists get their information? Repeated surveys suggest that managers—for better or worse—are their most frequent sources (Jackson, 1991).

Still, if managers are looking to buttress their organization's expertise and actions in good science arguments provided by outside scientific experts, they will need to proactively marshal these forces. Studies typically find that environmental and toxic populist groups are the next most frequent sources of information. Scientists or risk experts lag far behind in terms of frequency of contact (Sandman, Sachsman, Greenberg, and Gochfeld, 1987). What is more, the press—seeking to put faces on or personalize stories and to frame them in terms of conflict or threat—will often focus on the most dire possibilities that toxic populists conjure up.

Clearly, if managers want the perspectives of scientists or risk experts covered, they must facilitate access to them for reporters. This also allows managers to build bridges to reporters by extending them a professional hand in an area in which journalists are typically quite weak or pressed by deadlines. Better still, organizations can cultivate goodwill by institutionalizing ways for reporters to tap scientific, technical, and governmental expertise for their stories. New Jersey, for example, has for years used a Mobile Environmental Risk Information Team (MERIT) to do this. Staffed by public health specialists, MERIT rushes to the scene of breaking environmental stories and affords background information to reporters.

Ranging from most to least labor intensive and costly for organizations to budget (or cobudget with others), additional alternatives include

- *Twenty-four-hour hotlines.* These may be staffed by public health experts and answer reporters' questions.

- *Wire services*. These are fact sheets on environmental risk data and situations that can be faxed or telexed to newsrooms for background information and graphics.
- *Environmental risk press kits*. These are written in laypersons' language and include names, telephone numbers, and e-mail addresses for experts from various environmental fields; glossaries of technical terms; and essays by experts on various topics.

But whether personalized or institutionalized, the access that managers grant to or facilitate for reporters should be put into perspective. Neither means that managers are creating friends in the process. Former Reagan and Bush press secretary Marlin Fitzwater's (1995, p. 11) advice should inform all relationships with the press: "Treat them [reporters] like professionals and they will be your friends[;] treat them like friends and they will betray you every time. . . . It offends their [professional] principles."

Legitimacy

Reporters also depend partially on managers for the legitimacy of their stories. After all, they need the comments of authoritative sources to give their stories credibility. Moreover, they must have these interviews in formats and in ways that are useful and timely enough to meet their story deadlines. Such pressures are rife with tactical opportunities for managers to advance their environmental management agendas. Furthering these ends, however, also involves learning the mechanics of newsrooms and proactively using this information to advance one's cause.

BE PROACTIVE Knowing how precious access to legitimate sources is to reporters, smart managers take the initiative themselves. First they get to know reporters' deadlines (these will vary from medium to medium; see later discussion). They then try assiduously to schedule interviews and get in touch with reporters in time to meet these deadlines. Developing a reputation among journalists for dependability, accessibility, and good faith effort in these matters is immensely helpful to managers.

In the process, managers can accomplish things that might otherwise prove difficult. For example, they can contact reporters to communicate environmental management information indirectly to other organizations (that is, through their stories). Relatedly, managers can also use these stories as trial balloons or calls for help for particular environmental management initiatives. Less manipulatively, planting stories can let key actors in other organizations know what another organization is doing (or thinking of doing). Finally, if they give this information without attribution, managers can have "plausible deniability" if others react negatively to it.

In doing all this, however, managers must be smart. Environmental management items, for example, have to really be newsworthy. Otherwise, managers will quickly wear out their welcome with reporters. Lost as well will be opportunities to act strategically when managers really do have important stories to tell, reframe, or rebut.

Likewise anathema is showing favoritism in granting or facilitating access to particular reporters, papers, or stations. All have long memories about scoops or inside information not being made available to them but being given to others. A reputation for dealing fairly with reporters is critical if one has any hope of receiving the same treatment from them. As such, a good rule of thumb for managers is this: never tell any one reporter or media outlet what you are not prepared to tell everyone.

Also, as soon on the job as possible, managers should learn and understand the personalities, styles, ambitions, reputations, and ongoing rivalries of reporters covering their organizations. By doing so, they can avert serious mistakes in granting access (or in preparing for an interview). Moreover, there is no excuse for not knowing these things about reporters. Information on their traits is readily available from colleagues, from reporter bylines on stories, and from personal interaction.

LEARN THE MECHANICS OF THE BUSINESS Savvy managers dealing strategically with reporters' legitimacy needs will also learn the larger ebb and flow of production schedules at the newspapers and stations they deal with most. For example, some managers with controversial news to release have timed their announcements to fall into the "Friday night news hole" or around holidays at most newspapers and television stations. As television consolidated its hold on evening news audiences, evening newspaper sales fell from 57 to 33 percent of total sales between 1975 and 1990. Concomitantly, Saturday readership is extremely low relative to weekday readership. Indeed, falloffs in readership are as dramatic as 50 percent in most newspapers' circulations (Pearce, 1995).

The Clinton administration has also honed to perfection another set of useful tactics related to timing the release of unfavorable news. During Whitewater hearings, Clinton officials did two things: they combined a preemption strategy with timed and disjointed release of information.

Both actions made it difficult for readers to connect the dots among events (Mintz, 1997). For example, on slow news days the White House routinely preempted the release of unfavorable news before turning it over to Whitewater committee members. More precisely, it announced this news itself. In this fashion, the administration "dull[ed] its edge" (Mintz, 1997). When committee members later released the same information, it sounded like old news to many readers or listeners. The lesson for managers: release unflattering information before "it [is] selectively leaked or used by" antagonistic individuals. Moreover, by releasing this information "in context and surrounded by facts," the administration jousted effectively with opponents trying to release information in the most uncomplimentary ways possible (Mintz, 1997).

Equally effective was releasing reams of information while at the same time calling reporters' attention to certain aspects of it. By doing this, the White House used to its advantage the deadline pressures under which the press labors. More precisely, it saved reporters the time necessary to cull important tidbits before reporting deadlines. Finally, in a tactic designed to "avoid the aura of a major news event," the White House released information confidentially to one or two selected reporters for "private placements" in the press (Mintz, 1997; see also Kurtz, 1998).

In contrast, Thursday is typically critical in the production cycles of weekly newsmagazines. Reporters have to write and file by that day, and editors close down stories by late Friday. They then produce and distribute copies over the weekend so the public can buy the magazine at newsstands on Monday. Thus, any offers that managers might give to newsmagazine reporters on Friday have little value to the reporters. Still, managers should be responsive to any requests received on that day to verify facts or answer questions that editors or staff researchers have raised about the reporter's initial story.

It is also wise to understand what weekly (or monthly) magazine reporters need most. Because they are repackaging information already available in daily press reports, reporters' reputations depend on their skill in delivering such things as context (capsule summaries of history are most appreciated), meaning, body language, facial expressions, and anecdotes from the events as they unfolded (Pearce, 1995).

To an extent, of course, the Internet has made manipulating reporting and production deadlines inherently more difficult for managers. If an organization does not already have a Web page with an environmental host, hypertext links, and chat rooms, managers should consider starting one. In fact, an "E-newsletter" site for Web browsers can effectively put an organization into the news and counter disinformation about its activities. What is more, making an organization's environmental management officials (and others) available to chat groups can further help to get an unfiltered environmental management message out to the public. Relatedly, we recommend that part of someone's job should be to monitor the Internet. This person can correct any misperceptions, inaccuracies, or malicious falsehoods he comes across.

Sourcing

Once they have decided to grant access to a newsperson reporting on environmental management issues and initiatives, managers must determine the best formats and approaches for doing so. Before addressing personal sourcing relationships with reporters, however, we want to offer a few words about organizing and staffing for media relations.

ORGANIZING FOR SUCCESS Many organizations find it useful to designate a single media spokesperson to handle environmental management issues. Some organizations use such a person to represent the organization as a whole, others designate such a person for each program, and others do neither or both. If resources or organizational politics preclude selecting such a representative on a permanent basis, experience indicates that organizations should be sure to designate a single spokesperson if environmental management crises break. In any event, however, understanding the advantages and disadvantages of doing so is important.

An environmental management spokesperson can serve several functions that will advance an image to reporters and citizens of an organization's environmental sensitivity and commitment. Most notably, an environmental management spokesperson affords (1) an institutionalized point of contact for reporters and a conduit to program managers within an organization; (2) a full-time, media-savvy person focusing on environmental management issues; and (3) a single voice on the environment when crises or emergencies occur. As such, this spokesperson should, if needed, have direct access to an organization's leaders and participate in any strategic planning or environmental management decision-making exercises that they undertake. Keeping environmental management spokespersons in the dark will cause reporters to discount them as valuable sources. Worse yet, misrepresentations by them will come back to haunt the organization in future reporting (Pearce, 1995).

To be sure, any person selected as spokesperson must have expertise in environmental issues, must understand media relations, and must pay full-time attention to cultivating and maintaining reportorial rapport. But environmental management and media expertise are not the only things an organization must look for in an environmental management spokesperson. This individual must also be able to communicate environmental management information to reporters in ways that facilitate a key need they have: to take environmental management complexities and arcana and translate them for readers and listeners.

Some organizations that have a single environmental management spokesperson also designate environmental media liaisons (EMLs) in each of their programs. These liaisons act either formally or informally as rapporteurs to and conduits of information from the organization's environmental management spokesperson. In this role, EMLs can perform several important functions. First, they can funnel information regarding newsworthy items to environmental management spokespersons and give a "heads up" if they think environmental troubles are brewing. Toward these ends, EMLs can filter program actions through the prism of how they will look to and be covered by the media. In the process, they can become an organizational head's eyes and ears regarding program and operating-level commitment to environmental values. Finally, EMLs—by their very presence—persistently remind subordinates about environmental values as day-to-day operations proceed apace.

SETTING THE RULES OF THE GAME Whether or not organizations choose to designate single or program-specific spokespersons (or EMLs), managers still have direct contact with reporters regarding environmental management issues. Prudence dictates that they respect one inviolable principle: explicitly agree with reporters about the ground rules (or mix of ground rules) for any interview. Assuming that reporters will automatically treat comments as off the record is a mistake. Unless this is explicitly stipulated, reporters will not do so unless they are particularly worried about losing future access to the interviewee.

This said, a second principle emerges: managers must become well acquainted with the following four basic sourcing ground rules for interviews:

- *On the record.* Any information given is fair game to be quoted directly and attributed to the interviewee. Certainly the downside stakes or risks involved can be high in putting one's organization officially on record. This is especially true when ambiguity is high, controversy is swirling, or insufficient vetting of positions or information has occurred. Many departments or organizations thus limit going on the record to (in descending order) their press secretary (speaking for top leaders), their environmental management spokesperson or spokespersons, and their most senior level officials (such as the deputy assistant secretary and up in federal organizations).

• *On background.* Reporters may paraphrase or directly quote anything said, but they cannot attribute the comments to the interviewee. Instead, comments are attributed to generic sources, such as "organizational officials" or "administration officials." Some public affairs staffers will only go on background. If reporters challenge these terms, managers need pay no mind. The choice is theirs, not the reporters'.

• *Deep background.* Reporters cannot attribute anything said to either the interviewee or her organization. Thus they must attribute any information acquired during the interview to their own research or interpretations. As such, savvy reporters will try to negotiate an upgrade of this information to on-background status. They do this to protect their own reputations if the information later proves inaccurate. Again, however, this choice rests with the source, not with the reporter.

• *Off the record.* Reporters cannot use the information they acquire in any way or in any other story. Instead, they agree to use the information solely to put things into context for their own planning or strategic purposes.

These rules may or may not all be invoked in one interview or press briefing.

Knowing these ground rules leads in turn to a third principle: these guidelines offer strategic opportunities for managers to get out (or stymie) the environmental messages they wish (or do not wish) to convey. For example, they can go on background to gain a reputation for being forthcoming with reporters but without risk to themselves or to their organization. After all, those interviewed are still helping reporters to tell the interviewee's story and are aiding them in understanding the issues involved.

This so-called Brand X sourcing technique is also useful whenever managers are unsure how the environmental management information imparted will be used by the journalist. Sources may be embarrassed, for example, if reporters combine their comments with information from other sources that are less credible, inaccurate, or at odds with official organization or management policy. By the same token, backgrounding also affords protection to a manager's own sources of information. Finally, Brand X sourcing is a useful tool for building trust when the information involved is extremely sensitive or when interviewees are unsure that something (procedurally or substantively) will occur.

How can managers be sure that reporters will live up to whatever sourcing ground rules they agree to? To begin with, no reporter can afford a reputation for reneging on these commitments. Their sources for stories in a whole host of policy areas will dry up accordingly. What is more, managers can explicitly state that this will be the case if the reporter breaks any of the ground rules set.

Hooks, Color, and Tick-Tocks

Managers also need to appreciate how much reporters look to them to validate and enliven their prose, interpretations, and electronic images. Both print and electronic reporters consistently vie with their colleagues over whose stories will get the ever-shrinking space or airtime available. Managers can leverage this situation to their advantage by understanding the pyramid style of writing that reporters use to make their stories stand out.

Reporters are taught to write their stories to allow editors, page layout personnel, and network news producers pressed for space and time to cut them from the bottom. Consequently, they try to "needle" a story; that is, they try to grab their editors' and readers' attention by providing dramatic, eye-catching information in the first paragraph. Following this "flaming lead" are subsequent paragraphs of decreasing importance. Any context given tends to occur by the end of the third or fourth paragraphs. Finally, a chronology of prior events (a *tick-tock*), which typically trails the story, is viewed by all as most expendable for cutting.

A reporter's dependency on this technique, known among journalists as "angling" a story, is something that managers can exploit to get out their organization's environmental management story. The keys for doing so are deciding how they want a story's lead to read and then angling press releases, interview lines, and briefing information that can catch editors' and readers' attention. And they need not stop there. In the second and third paragraphs of stories, reporters need direct quotes to legitimate their story. They will look repeatedly to anyone who can consistently provide these in timely ways. Managers can thus gain strategic leverage by thinking ahead about ten-word-or-less quotes or phrases that will help frame any environmental management story in terms of the organization's message. Advantageous as well is always being available to reporters seeking last-minute checks on the accuracy of their tick-tocks.

At the same time, however, managers need to be wary of environmental management "quote shoppers." These are reporters who already know what they are going to write and who have a reputation for sticking to it—no matter what new information they acquire. These journalists tend only to fish for quotes that will support their preconceptions and will not use those that do not. At the same time, managers must also be cautious about what they do not say to reporters, especially when assumptions (implicit or explicit) underlying questions are incorrect. When assumptions are faulty, managers do well to refute them and provide clearer background information to place their responses in context. Otherwise, reporters are likely to write the story as if all assumptions are accurate. Finally, it is important to pay attention as well to the tone and body language accompanying one's responses to environmental management questions. Both are fair game for reporting, and are especially attractive to newsmagazine reporters trying to freshen up or put a new spin on relatively old news.

Getting Reluctants to Talk

As noted earlier, journalists must enliven their stories if they are to get news time. But coaxing these kinds of statements from reluctant interviewees can prove difficult. Reporters have therefore developed a variety of tricks of the trade for loosening tongues. Smart managers are not only wary of the following traps that reporters set (Pearce, 1995), but are also able to turn them to their organization's advantage.

FIRING POINT BLANK This tactic is a disarmingly "quick, bold, straight shot" (Pearce, p. 107) that stuns people, catches them unprepared, and may evoke images of defensiveness. This happens because the reporter's provocative premise asks for only a yes or no response. The rub, of course, is that environmental management issues are seldom amenable (technically, instrumentally, or politically) to binary responses.

"Is the Secretary planning to sue Company X for noncompliance with SO_2 standards?" "If Congress fails to appropriate sufficient funds for water testing, will you challenge EPA's trichloroethylene (TCE) standards in court?" "Is the state EPA making you do this because of a personal vendetta between your boss and Administrator Smith?" In these circumstances, managers should pause before answering and ask themselves three questions. First, would any answer given be informed by the facts? Second, is it within the manager's authority to give an answer? Finally, would the response be consistent with any instructions or understandings the manager has with organizational leaders or the administration presently in power? If the answer to any of these questions is no or "I'm not sure," managers are wise to demur from answering the question directly. One might respond with a "no comment," by referring reporters to previous positions or statements given, or by suggesting that nothing is served by speculating.

LEVERAGING AND BACKHAND TECHNIQUES These two tactics are reportorial strategies built on slight of hand. Leveraging occurs when reporters imply that they know more than they really do about an organization's environmental management situation. They take a couple of things they do know, repeat them, and hope that interviewees will tell them the whole story after inferring incorrectly that they already know it. If this works, an unwary interviewee then becomes the source of the information in a subsequent article or piece. A related trick is for reporters to use the information they have to construct their own version of events, and then get interviewees to appear to affirm or disaffirm them. For example, a reporter might say, "I've learned from the governor's office that you've decided to fight on for this project, despite a lot of NIMBY [not in my backyard] resistance in the neighborhood. How will you do this?"

Backhanding, in contrast, involves a reporter saying that she is trying to confirm "minor details" of a story. In fact, however, she is trying to nail down major aspects that still elude her. Examples might include a reporter saying, "I'm just calling to clear up a few minor details related to the wastewater treatment plant in Rutledge," or "I wanted to be sure I had these details correct before I printed this story."

Ways for managers to combat these techniques are multiple and involve turning the tables on the reporter. First, managers should always be alert when reporters approach them in these ways. Second, when they suspect backhanding or leveraging, they can do a few things: decline to respond, or say that they are neither confirming nor denying the entire story. Finally, they can ask reporters to recount their total understanding of the situation. If accurate, a thoughtful statement on the record might be useful. Moreover, reporters may provide information not already known by the interviewee (discussed further shortly).

RED HERRING, SILENCE, AND BLUSTERING These three tactics are reportorial strategies designed to let emotions rather than intellect drive what interviewees say about environmental management issues. *Red herrings* are typically couched in commiserations that either begin or end in phrases like, "Don't you think . . ."—for example, "Boy, those Mothers Against Toxic Pollution in our Neighborhoods [MATPN] are really not negotiating in good faith. Don't you think they should get real?"

Should a manager either let this statement pass, try to get around it by changing the subject, or shrug and grimace, he leaves himself quite vulnerable. The article's headline the next day might well read, "Frustrated Organization Official to MATPN: 'Get Real.'" Again, prudent things to do in such situations are to be careful of one's body language, to examine the premises of the questions, and to openly contest them if they are inaccurate or embarrassing.

Likewise, the *silence* tactic seeks to exploit any uncomfortableness that interviewees might have with gaps in conversations. Reporters who want additional environmental management information will sometimes sit silently after an initial response, hoping that managers will blather on to fill the silence. This may give reporters facts not previously known or further leads to pursue. In response, managers can turn the tables on reporters by waiting out the silence, asking if there are any other questions, posing some of their own, and then thanking journalists for the interview.

Finally, some reporters use *blustering* to make interviewees feel that dire reportorial consequences will occur if they do not answer environmental management questions. Because of the obvious dangers to access that it creates, blustering is seldom used. Still, when invoked, it takes a variety of forms. Reporters may threaten to print an embarrassing story, to report that an organization is stonewalling, or to show a closed door with a manager's nameplate on it should she refuse to comment.

In the first two tactics, some managers quite effectively play hardball with reporters: if a reporter proceeds, he will have zero access in the future. Moreover, in the case of the closed door tactic a manager may actually be better off using this strategy than doing a television interview with a hostile reporter. For example, if one suspects that editing will either twist details or leave much of the organization's environmental management story on the cutting-room floor, pictures of a closed door may actually be preferable. This is especially true if managers provide instead a tightly worded written statement in place of the interview.

EGO AND INSIDER STRATEGIES Not unlike the previous three strategies, ego and insider tactics also appeal to human nature. In both cases, reporters try to lower an interviewee's guard by appealing to his or her vanity. Included here are appeals to any predisposition the manager might have for self-promotion, for avoiding blame, or for crafting or maintaining reputations that they are in the loop on environmental management issues. Questions might go like this: "I know that you want to do the right thing when it comes to reducing airborne toxics, so who's opposing it and what are they saying?" Another tack might be, "You really inherited a mess in the water quality program. How did you go about cleaning it up?" To be sure, reporters are trying to understand what is happening. But they are also fishing for the color, conflict, and "racehorse" qualities of an emerging environmental management story that can catch their editors', readers', and viewers' attention.

As tempting as these opportunities might appear, they are largely fraught with personal, organizational, and political risk. In general, seasoned media veterans (see, for example, Fitzwater, 1995) find it better to eschew such opportunities. Articles incorporating such responses frequently refer to organizations as "in disarray," "engaging in backbiting," or "adrift." Worse yet, their titles may convey the sense of conflict on which the media thrives: "Agency at Odds with Administration's Position on Solid Waste Treatment Facility." Moreover, if managers' responses are unflattering to others, they violate another fundamental press relations principle: never denigrate colleagues in the executive branch; they may "pee on you with greater skill than you can pee on them" (Pearce, 1995, p. 104).

Two corollaries of this principle are useful as well. First, managers should never run down their organization's policies, no matter how much those policies differ from the managers' personal preferences or how heavily the managers dissented from the policies privately. Second, there is no such thing as expressing a personal opinion when one is an environmental manager. Unless backgrounding rules explicitly preclude this, managers should assume that whatever they say gets reported as their organization's official position.

BAITING THE BRIEFER This technique is premised on the same principle as the firing-point-blank tactic already discussed. Nonetheless, its purpose differs: reporters are trying to incite the kind of anger that editors relish publishing. This tactic is especially prevalent when the press smells an environmental management scandal—real or imagined. A typical question in this genre involves getting managers to react to another person's comments—accurate, misquoted, misleading, or taken out of context. For example, "Councilwoman Jarvis has just accused you of deliberate deceit in regard to TCE releases, just another incident in a pattern of misrepresentation and cover-up. Does she know what she's talking about?"

The substance of questions like these is quite serious, whether true or not. Therefore, managers must deal with them openly, credibly, and honestly. In the short run, however, these questions are posed to make respondents angry and to make their anger the story's needle. In these situations, the image that managers project is oftentimes as critical as what they say. Consequently, depersonalizing and disinflaming the situation are prudent tactics: maintain a calm demeanor, look confident, and remain assertive. Assuring everyone that the organization will get to the bottom of these charges is also paramount (Fitzwater, 1995). Thus, prudent responses might include, "I'm not sure Councilwoman Jarvis actually said that," "We're doing everything we can to check the validity of those statistics," and "We will not be satisfied until every child's health is protected."

Equally important in these situations is not to assume the integrity of the information coming in from others—even from the mayor's or governor's office. Information is often unavoidably missing in the case of fast-breaking environmental management events. In addition, it gets garbled quite easily (either intentionally or unintentionally) as it flows from within and from outside an organization. Seasoned interviewees or briefers therefore always try to leave a way out for themselves and their organizations in case contradictory information later becomes available.

One strategy, of course, is to admit ignorance. Another is a simple "no comment," especially when an organization or its administrator is still debating the answer to the question raised. Still other managers find that obfuscating helps, as long as one appears authoritative while uncertainties or ambiguities get resolved. Thus, answers are given but then qualified so much that even more uncertainty develops (Fitzwater, 1995).

Still, evidence suggests that managers risk their credibility by taking this tack too often. To temper this possibility, many "source" the information they give: "Yes, the administrator's January 15th statement on nitrogen oxide standards and enforcement is still operative." As in all interview or briefing settings, however, lying, bluffing, or misrepresenting facts is both unethical and counterproductive. The old saw from Watergate is definitely true: problems lie not so much in the act itself but in the cover-up.

PREPARING FOR THE MEDIA EVENT

To be sure, knowing reporters' needs and tactics can work to a manager's advantage in environmental management interview situations. So too can knowing exactly what one wants out of any interview or briefing. Managers who do not know what they want are by default letting the media define or shape their organization's environmental management message. Thus we cannot overstate the importance of preparing for any media event, be it a one-on-one interview, a news conference, or a photo opportunity. As former Secretary of State James Baker once put it, so profanely, "poor preparation leads to piss-poor performance."

Getting Out Your Message

Savvy managers start by having an environmental management agenda that they want to convey to reporters. An environmental management theme or message of the day, week, or month is essential. So too are talking points for everyone dealing with the media, interest groups, and organizations. Foremost in mind should be images of how these themes will, or should, translate into headlines and news stories. This is true whether dealing with the print or the electronic media. Thus managers should try to marble sound bites into their comments. Ideally, these are brief, catchy phrases that colorfully, metaphorically, or wittily condense the heart of the organization's environmental message. The electronic media thrive on these.

Examples of this technique abound. Consider several culled directly from recent environmental stories in the *Washington Post*: "We are losing wetlands at the rate of losing one Rhode Island every three years"; "Lifeboat Earth has a leak"; five years after the Rio Earth Summit, "the planet has grown broader of girth [more populated], shorter of breath [has dirtier air], and increasingly addicted to bad habits [carbon-based fuel usage] that threaten its survival" (Warrick, 1997, p. A06).

Colorful or personalizing statements at the beginning or end of presentations are particularly important when presenting complex data (such as on health or ecological risk reduction or deforestation). It always helps to frame these data in ways that put a human face on organizational accomplishments. Typical leads might include, "What these data mean for preschool children is . . . for the taxpayers of this city are . . . for backpackers and birders in our town are. . . ." If a human-face approach does not work, common reference points may.

For example, "Worldwide, we are losing the equivalent of Nepal every year to logging or slash-and-burn agriculture."

Intelligence Giving and Gathering

A second thing managers can do in preparing for any interview or briefing is figure out what information they want to learn or disseminate during the meeting. To do so, they must first anticipate the kinds of environmental management questions that reporters are likely to ask, develop responses to them, and craft these in terms of intelligence giving and gathering needs. To some extent, of course, the events that prompted an interview hint at the kinds of questions to anticipate. If an organization provides regular briefings to reporters, other good predictors are the kinds of environmental management questions asked previously. Indeed, if a talking-points strategy has been working effectively over preceding weeks and months, anticipating reporters' questions will be easy.

We cannot emphasize enough that any briefing with significant stakes for environmental management programs should see staffers prebriefing interviewees. During prebriefings, participants should engage in a freewheeling question-and-answer session. Moreover, even when the stakes appear much smaller, an awkward or maladroit response can sometimes raise the stakes considerably. Therefore, before any briefing managers should at least discuss with politically and media-savvy associates what they think reporters are likely to ask and then try out responses on them.

As we noted earlier, effective managers also use interviews to acquire information they lack and to plant seeds of inquiry in reporters' minds. Reporters, after all, talk to many people and know what they are thinking, reacting to, and planning (both officially and on background). Moreover, reporters understand that sharing such information is part of the long-term reciprocal relationship they are trying to cultivate with their sources. A good rule of thumb for managers dealing with environmental management issues is to try to learn more from reporters than reporters learn from them (Pearce, 1995).

This of course takes additional preparation. Managers should always learn from reporters where they have been, who they have interviewed already, and what future interviews they are planning. In terms of the first two items of information, a reporter may have toured areas (such as wetlands or sewage treatment plants) in other jurisdictions that managers have not toured, or met with neighborhood groups that managers need to know more about. Also, a reporter may have interviewed nemeses or supporters of particular initiatives, and if managers are trying to inculcate a strong environmental ethic in their organization, they may cull information from the reporter about the tactics and successful strategies of other proponents.

Regarding who else a reporter intends to interview, managers can take two strategic tacks, either individually or in combination. First, they can suggest future areas of inquiry that will either reveal or convey information they need to mobilize support for their environmental management agendas (for example, "You might ask the senator about. . . ."). Second, they can identify other interviewees from whom they might gain perspective, meaning, or support for the environmental themes and discussion points they are emphasizing (for example, "You really need to talk to . . . about this").

Finally, a variety of ways also exist to leak positive and negative information to the press during interviews. To be sure, organizational leaders often rail against leakers who provide embarassing information to the press. They also excoriate, ostracize, and make life generally miserable for those who are caught doing the leaking, seeing them as untrustworthy whistleblowers. Thus, managers contemplating this tactic must understand that leaking can cost their careers dearly. If they see no other alternative (especially morally) to leaking, they may engage in it knowing fully that in doing so they might have to fall on their own swords (O'Leary, 1994a).

Protecting Your Organization's Image

A third aim that managers should have going into any interview is to cultivate among reporters an image of honesty, professionalism, forthrightness, and prudent responsiveness. Key parts of doing this are enhancing the public's understanding of the organization's environmental management effort, presenting organization positions in accessible ways, and responding directly and quickly to misperceptions. As noted earlier in this chapter, many citizens (as well as reporters) are "policy challenged." They do not understand the arcana of environmental issues, science, and politics. Neither do all citizens or reporters understand how environmental management decisions are made in agencies, within communities, and intergovernmentally. As a consequence, an organization's environmental management image may suffer from things over which its leaders and managers have little or no control.

Thus, when interviewed, savvy managers explain who does what and why, who makes what decisions, and who allocates resources for environmental management in their organization. Relatedly, candor over what their organization can and cannot do or influence can reap dividends.

The chapters on working with communities (Chapter Six) and communicating risk (Chapter Seven) offer a variety of suggestions about how organizations can deal with this deficit in understanding. For now, however, our focus is on how overestimating a reporter's control over story content can inadvertently undermine an organization's environmental image. Reporters, for example, cannot guarantee that anything said will or will not appear in a story. Nor can they guarantee that managers' comments will appear in proper context, with accurate attribution, or with flattering photography.

As noted, the pyramid style of reporting and the limited time slots for news stories on television and radio mean that editors and newsroom directors ultimately decide what gets included in a story, how, when, and with what pictures. For example, with local television newsrooms dependent on satellite feeds (from CNN and other broadcasters) and file footage for pictures, reporters can never be sure what pictures will accompany their stories. Snippets of original quotes may appear out of context in stories, be used as voice-overs accompanying pictures of billowing smokestacks, or end up as clippings on the cutting-room floor.

For these reasons, managers have learned to take precautions. Many are careful not to give long, rambling, taped interviews to television reporters. These may be cut substantially or spliced together creatively to fit reporters' story lines. Lost in the process can be much of what an interviewee thought she was communicating so cogently. In contrast, while live interviews may be steeped in perils of their own, they at least give managers more control over content.

Finally, experience suggests that anyone doing live environmental management interviews should stay away from hit-and-run formats in the streets or in corridors. There are too many factors (including bumping, intermittent shouting, or loud and persistent background noise) in these settings that managers cannot control and that can garble their message. Moreover, these situations offer too many opportunities to fall prey to point-blank and red herring reportorial strategies. If backed into these circumstances, however, managers can turn to many of the coping strategies presented earlier in this chapter to limit the damage.

CONCLUSION

This chapter has recounted the formidable obstacles and opportunities that press relations can afford managers dealing with environmental issues. Premised on understanding the needs of reporters in all media, the chapter has offered some strategies and tactics for managers wishing to become more media savvy as they pursue such an agenda. But being media savvy is only one dimension of effective environmental communication, let alone of effective TQEM programs predicated on a strong environmental ethic. A second critical component is working smartly with the communities who are reading and listening to these media and are affected by the organization's operations. It is to this topic that we turn next in Chapter Six.

6

WORKING WITH COMMUNITIES

*The problem is not in what we do, but in
what we become by doing it.*

—Oscar Wilde[1]

Certainly there are important normative reasons in a democracy for involving communities in the decision making of public organizations, for responding to their concerns, and for incorporating their thinking into organizational actions. Indeed, on these grounds alone such a commitment seems de rigueur for today's and tomorrow's managers—whatever their specialty, program responsibilities, or areas of jurisdiction. What is more, the benefits of doing so without compulsion are increasingly becoming clear: "comanagement," "costewardship," or "collaborative planning" of the environment by public managers, regulatory targets, and citizens working together appear to be promising trends in the 1990s. Finally, if the place-based (or geographically based) decision-making processes recommended by the U.S. Council on Environmental Quality in 1997 take root in organizations such as the Bureau of Land Management, the Forest Service, and the Environmental Protection Agency (EPA), working adroitly with communities will become essential in the twenty-first century (Harwood and Williams, 1998; Freemuth, 1998; Cawley, 1998).

These rationales aside, however, progress on this front is hardly a given. Historically, as we have noted, public managers have been no more nor less likely than private industries to change or modify their behavior to meet their communities' environmental concerns (Wilson and Rachal, 1977; Durant, 1985; Paehlke, 1991). Viewed at best as costly nuisances tangential to the primary missions of organizations and at worst as antithetical to them, environmental concerns and regulations often have aroused strong negative reactions among such managers.

Aside from unfunded mandates, statutory provisions for citizen participation and citizen lawsuits have traditionally been among the greatest challenges to many managers. But if anything, these requirements are today more vibrant than ever. Not only are they increasingly detailed, but they also are the foundation for more comprehensive community relations activities enumerated by the EPA and the states.

We thus hope that more noble reasons for working closely with communities will inspire public managers to do just that. Moreover, we are sure that many managers do not need external prodding. But for those who are uninspired by these values, or who see them only as tangential to their primary missions, there are very practical and hard-nosed reasons for rethinking this position. Indeed, in light of the political, fiscal, and legal exigencies under which managers labor, we argue that the advantages of developing a *coproduction environmental ethic* within their organizations far outweigh the costs of doing so.

A coproduction environmental ethic imbues an organization's members with an abiding awareness of the five issues with which we began this book. Employees are cognizant of how their activities and operations affect present and future generations in the communities they serve (such as how they affect sustainable development locally, nationally, and globally). They are also sensitive to how the benefits and burdens produced by these activities impact historically disadvantaged members of these communities (that is, they are sensitive to environmental justice issues). At the same time, employees have a sense for the efficiency and effectiveness gains that are possible in an era of unfunded mandates by focusing on pollution reduction and prevention, on ecosystems, and on prioritized risks. Finally, they understand that meeting each of these objectives starts with, and ultimately depends for success on, mutually defining with their communities a sense of the issues, trends, and trade-offs involved in their work (that is, they have a new sense of accountability for the actions they take).

Consequently, a coproduction environmental ethic is predicated on creating a prudently open, early, and meaningful stakeholder participation process. Operationally, a coproduction environmental ethic affords community stakeholder involvement that is early, direct, and diverse in perspective; that affords stakeholders adequate access to all relevant information; that permits routinized face-to-face discussions by stakeholders with organizational personnel; and that provides an equal distribution of power in collective decision making (Fiorino, 1990c).

What a coproduction environmental ethic is not, however, is a prescription for abdicating leadership. In fact, like TQEM, there is a paradox involved in developing such an ethic: the greater the amount of community stakeholder involvement pursued, the more important becomes strong, resolute, and strategic leadership. Thus, before embracing a coproduction ethic as valuable to working with communities, public managers need to understand its rationale, its realpolitik, and its prospects for success. So, too, do for-profit and nonprofit managers who will be asked to participate in, or who will themselves decide to develop in their own organizations, a coproduction approach to environmental management.

LISTENING TO COMMUNITY STAKEHOLDERS

Historically, many managers have seen community participation requirements as time-consuming, frustrating, and eroding their professional discretion and autonomy. Quite frankly, they are correct. But this is precisely what legislators intended to do. Left to their own devices, managers at public and private pollution sources have tended to consider inadequately the impact of their operations on the public health, safety, and environment of local communities (Wilson and Rachal, 1977; Durant, 1985; Durant, Thomas, Brown, and McClellen, 1986). Consequently, many managers have become part of the nation's environmental problem rather than the answers to it. In turn, they have contributed to a widespread, dysfunctional, and alarming sense of "anomic democracy" in America (Crozier, Huntington, and Watanuki, 1975): government is seen as incompetent, unresponsive, out of control, and above the law. Meanwhile, industries are seen as arrogant, uncaring, and similarly above the law.

But the reality today is that managers have two choices when it comes to working with local communities. They can either try to work cooperatively and strategically with them or they can meet them adversarially in court. The latter, of course, can produce costly, time-consuming, managerially disruptive, and even mission-threatening results (Wilson, 1989; O'Leary, 1993a, 1993b, 1993c; Luton, 1997). Thus, even disgruntled managers often concede that ignoring or circumventing community concerns can come at a very high price. Consider, for example, the direct or vicarious experiences that many elected officials and public managers had during the 1980s as they tried to site hazardous waste facilities in neighborhoods across the United States. So effective was grassroots neighborhood opposition (known as the "not in my backyard" or NIMBY syndrome) that only eleven new hazardous waste sites were permitted to be built across the country between 1980 and 1986 (Mazmanian and Morell, 1992).

From these and other more recent experiences with local opposition to facility sitings, managers learned that a variety of factors diminish their chances of success: the complexity of government regulations, the use of untried technologies, differing perceptions of risk, perceptions of inequities in risk exposure, and fundamental distrust of business and government officials (Morell and Magorian, 1982; Kraft and Clary, 1991; Andrews, 1988; Bingham and Mealey, 1988; Mazmanian and Morell, 1992; and Luton, 1997). In turn, and in line with these factors, one of the most consistent lessons they learned was this: "a broader community consensus on long-range and broad strategies for regional economic growth and environmental protection, arrived at through a legitimate and open community decision making process" is critical for success (Mazmanian and Morell, 1992, p. 180).

To be sure, environmental statutes have long had community participation requirements that organizations have had to observe. But in truth, unenthusiastic managers have frequently finessed them. After all, some mandates are vague and leave it up to managers from the regulatory and regulated communities to determine what constitutes adequacy. Thus, what really motivates managers who are otherwise wary, unsympathetic, or overtly hostile to community involvement or environmental management values are the strong citizen suit provisions in environmental statutes. As noted in Chapters Two and Three, these provisions make public stakeholders "little attorneys general" in enforcing their strictures.

The Rise of Adversarial Legalism

Most environmental laws are what Donald Schoenbrod (1983) calls *goals statutes*. These are laws that ordain open-ended outcomes (such as clean air or clean water) to which citizens have a right—sometimes regardless of cost, competing values, existing knowledge, or organizational resources. Part of the "rights revolution" identified by R. Shep Melnick (1995), these laws have helped foster a major development for managers that sorely complicates their efforts to reconcile environmental goals with their organizations' primary missions: the rise of adversarial legalism (Schuck, 1995). More precisely, stakeholders are increasingly prone to try securing through the courts the rights that the environmental statutes summarized in Chapter Two give them grounds to pursue, expand, and protect.

As such, rights-based adversarial legalism has had a profound effect on organizations. First, it helps define the kinds of stakeholders with whom organizations have to deal. Second, adversarial legalism helps determine the strategies that these stakeholders use and the leverage they can exert over an organization's environmental management initiatives. Finally, it highlights the extent to which early, timely, and meaningful stakeholder participation in environmental management decisions becomes a most rational strategy for managers.

How does it accomplish these things? Once a public good is labeled a right, it attains an elevated claim on public resources. Rights, after all, cannot be compromised facilely. Hence they will be upheld in court if elected officials or agencies deny them without sufficient cause. Under these circumstances, regulators and regulatees worry, quite rationally, about what constitutes compliance with such open-ended claims. What is more, and as was noted in Chapter Two, most environmental statutes have three features that make escaping responsibility for real or perceived shortcomings almost impossible. These include citizen suit provisions, "organization-forcing" and "hammer provisions," and timetables for meeting statutory goals. Citizen suit provisions grant automatic standing-to-sue to citizens, a normally substantial and difficult legal impediment to overcome. In turn, organization-forcing and hammer provisions provide bases, respectively, for court challenges and congressional rulemaking if an organization fails to take specific actions. Finally, timetables (often unrealistic) force routine monitoring of organizations' actions and reviews of the progress managers have made toward meeting these goals. Afforded in the process are periodic opportunities for environmental groups to sue laggard or noncomplying public or private managers (Melnick, 1995).

Meanwhile, polluters have learned to take advantage of what Martin Shapiro (1988) calls the "technology forcing" and "fudge factors" in environmental statutes to pursue their version of adversarial legalism. Although rights are typically found in the "aspirational" preambles of laws, technology-forcing language (such as Best Available Control Technology) typically follows. As noted in Chapter Two, this language is precise in terms of requiring particular technology fixes for problems. There is room, however, for the regulated community, for example, to dispute what constitutes best available or best achievable in particular instances. Finally, fudge factors are those aspects of statutes that allow balancing of different considerations (such as costs and benefits) at the local level or that allow tailoring of decisions to local circumstances. Obviously these too enable, and have been seized upon as opportunities for, polluters to ply their brand of adversarial legalism.

Other Implications for Managers

Former EPA administrator William Ruckelshaus (1993) argues that the quest for perfectionism that drives Congress's embrace of the rights revolution in environmental policy has come at a high price. Promising results that are politically, scientifically, or financially impractical ensures trust-eroding failure for both regulators and regulatory targets. But whether one agrees or not with Ruckelshaus's assessment (and many do not), it is hard to dispute that adversarial legalism (as practiced by environmentalists and the regulated community alike) and the rights revolution have had at least three managerially challenging features (Kagan, 1995). First, environmental groups invoke legal rights and procedural requirements backed by threats of judicial review. Second, deliberation gives way to disputation in court when these implicit threats do not provoke the changes that critics wish. Finally, the results of these legal decisions vary, lack predictability, and sometimes get reversed. Consequently, they tax the nerves, steadfastness, and patience of managers, even those with high tolerances for ambiguity and commitments to integrating environmental management values into their organizations' operations.

For managers, turbulent and ambiguous task environments such as these can wreak havoc on day-to-day operations. What is more, they can sorely complicate any attempt at long-term comprehensive strategic thinking, a framework that legislative overseers are increasingly expecting (such as the Government Performance and Results Act of 1993 requires). As Robert Kagan (1995) puts it, these problems start with one basic reality: community stakeholder involvement through adversarial legalism "can be invoked by the misguided, the mendacious, and the malevolent as well as by the mistreated" (p. 93). Moreover, when deadlines are unrealistic, when organizations fail to meet them, and when managers are excoriated in court for real or imagined failures to do so, citizen mistrust is not confined to the environmental grievance in question.

Another, more mundane, major implication for managers of community participation through adversarial legalism is that it can be highly disruptive of an organization's mission, managerial prerogatives, and program priorities. Consider, for example, Melnick's (1983) critique: judges can become embroiled in complex policymaking issues, render decisions that exceed their expertise, and stymie policy innovation in public organizations.

Researchers have found that typical responses by public organizations to court decisions include reprogramming funds and personnel from program to program within offices, or from program office to program office (O'Leary, 1993a). Equally disruptive are court decisions that are either vague or insufficiently tailored to the problem addressed. These decisions tend to have repercussions that go far beyond the remedy they decree for specific programs. Indeed, they frequently cascade throughout an organization to affect other programs in unintended ways.

Community participation through court suits also enhances the relative power of attorneys while simultaneously diminishing that of technical and scientific professionals (O'Leary, 1993a). This occurs as surviving judicial scrutiny becomes a paramount consideration when organizations act (Wilson, 1989). In the extreme, an organization can become overly cautious, even to the point of paralysis. In the end, court suits create winners and losers both inside courtrooms and within organizations that carry out environmental programs.

Thus, contrary to commentators who worry about "judicial imperialism," the rub is not so much that judges are substituting their expertise for that of scientific and administrative experts. Granted, this happens, and it shows the high stakes gambled by managers who find themselves airing disputes in courts. More commonly, however, judicial decisions can interrupt or fundamentally alter organizational deliberative processes. This occurs as court decrees mandate actions that professionals either lack the capacity to fulfill, must shift precious resources to complete, or have to skip necessary steps in their deliberative processes to accommodate (O'Leary, 1993a).

The results of enforcement-driven priority setting can be stunningly pernicious. Court decisions do not always reflect objective or relative threats to public health, safety, or the environment. Consent decree milestones often have little to do with relative-risk rankings in communities, and they are not helpful when judges fundamentally misunderstand organizational cultures, decision rules, and missions (Wilson, 1989). In these instances, prescribed legal ends go unmet, beached on the shoals of organizational diffidence or outright opposition.

Positive Aspects of Adversarial Legalism for Managers

All this is not to suggest that court suits do not also offer benefits to society, as well as to organizationally disadvantaged program managers. Indeed, their results can be normatively praiseworthy and instrumentally needed. Hence we would err egregiously if we failed to mention how the threat of adversarial legalism can also be useful to program managers bent on fostering effective environmental management programs in organizations that lack them.

Consider the following benefits. Environmental management programs that might not otherwise receive attention because of internal organizational politics, prejudices, or inertia can rise in priority. Resources may then get reprogrammed from privileged environmental management program offices to those that are less privileged but deserving. These same programs can also gain leverage over central budgeting offices when the latter want to cut program resources (O'Leary, 1993a). Moreover, managers bent on "greening" their programs or organizations may find that threats or actual environmental lawsuits are their greatest allies, because they can buttress, if not give priority to, their claims for organizational attention, resources, and commitments.

No one can guarantee such results, however. Hence, risk-averse public managers throughout our federal system have begun to understand the preemptive virtues of a coproduction environmental ethic of involving stakeholders in their operations in meaningful ways as early as possible. First, being attentive up front to community stakeholder concerns affords opportunities for an organization to maintain, establish, or rebuild public trust within their communities (Berman, 1996). When citizens feel that managers are listening to, considering, and responding to their concerns in good faith ways, their sense of efficacy increases. This can in turn translate into a higher regard for the organization's environmental management actions. What is more, this trust can carry over to programs that are not directly related to environmental issues.

The second advantage of pursuing a coproduction environmental ethic relates to an organization's bottom line. When focused on such things as preventing pollution, minimizing waste, or selecting hazardous waste remedies, a coproduction environmental ethic can cut organizational costs in several ways. Daily operations can become more efficient and effective when managers consider community viewpoints early in policy or program design. Moreover, the legal exposure of the organization's members can be minimized, as can an organization's court costs and delays, when stakeholders feel that their views are valued.

Third, astute managers also understand the practical programmatic considerations that make a coproduction environmental ethic eminently sensible today. To redress second- and third-generation environmental problems, organizations will often need the acquiescence of individual or group stakeholders. For example, multiple decisions made by independent actors performing opaque tasks in nonhierarchical situations are what produce some nonpoint source pollution. Similarly disaggregated and immune to constant supervision are many pollution prevention, energy conservation, and waste management activities.

In Chapter Twelve, on alternatives to traditional regulatory schemes, we review how command-and-control, hierarchically based regulatory regimes are disastrously ineffective under these circumstances. Individuals co-degrade the environment; hence they must willingly coproduce the solutions desired for these problems. An organization's job may sometimes be to show or persuade them of the virtues of doing so.

WHAT MANAGERS NEED TO KNOW ABOUT A COPRODUCTION ENVIRONMENTAL ETHIC

Managers intrigued about developing a coproduction environmental ethic in their organization must understand that doing so is not an easy task. Those accustomed to dispensing their expertise to, and pursuing their primary missions amid, a homogeneous, passive, and nonlitigious citizenry will be especially challenged. Chagrined as well will be anyone who expects that clearer lines of communication will solve their environmental management problems.

Most frustrated will be managers used to a traditional, public-relations-premised, professional-technocratic model of community participation. As we will show momentarily, the environmental community in general, and grassroots community groups in particular, are long past docilely accepting one-way flows of communication from "experts" to citizens. But even when managers pursue a coproduction environmental ethic premised on the idea of expertise-based solutions to mutually defined problems, progress can be a turbulent, frustrating, and problematic experience.

Extensive delay is common. Managers should expect stalled negotiations, breakdowns in trust, and outcomes into which not everyone will buy. Indeed, disgruntled stakeholders may walk out of the process or still go to court over the outcome. But compare these possibilities to the higher potential of lengthy litigation delays should an organization eschew meaningful stakeholder participation altogether.

Managers should also heed the lessons that the Bureau of Land Management (BLM) is learning as it pursues collaborative planning with communities (Harwood and Williams, 1998). These lessons are summarized in Table 6.1. Perhaps the most serious obstacle the BLM has faced in moving in this direction is the objection from critics both within and outside the agency that it is abdicating its legal responsibilities. Most likely any manager pursuing such a strategy will be similarly challenged. As Peggy Harwood and David Williams (1998) of the BLM argue, however, "federal law is quite specific on the decisions that only public land managers can make. . . . BLM has options in how it carries out these responsibilities, but it is still liable for the outcomes, even when it has agreements with others" (p. 7). Thus, as we further emphasize shortly, managers must make these legal constraints clear to stakeholders at the outset of any collaborative effort.

Research suggests that given the realpolitik of using coproduction techniques, managers must have three sets of literacies to be successful. First, they must have a broad understanding of what motivates the disparate, politically savvy, and litigious "publics" who are operating nationally. Given the vibrant networks of national groups that exist today, and their propensity for getting involved in local actions, managers should know well the disparate environmental management philosophies and tactics of these groups. Second, managers should be able to identify stakeholders in their organization's immediate environmental management task environment, anticipate their concerns, and deal strategically with them. Finally, managers must understand how their organization's approach to structuring community involvement in environmental management programs will affect what happens as a result of that approach.

A MISCELLANY OF ENVIRONMENTAL STAKEHOLDERS

The number, diversity, and tactical jujitsu of environmental stakeholders can seem overwhelming at first. Certainly any attempt to offer a complete and up-to-date listing of environmental groups, motives, and tactics in a book such as ours is doomed to fail. Many such groups spring up and die overnight; others are unique to different communities and their problems. Indeed, experts compute that more than ten thousand national, state, and local environmental groups exist today (Kriz, 1993). What is possible to convey, however, is a sense of the four major types of environmental stakeholder groups that managers

Table 6.1. Collaboration as a Tool for Improving the Management of Public Lands: BLM Workshop, Missoula, Montana, April 1997.

Collaborative relationships over time build trust and a capacity to work together. Collaboration has a lot in common with Jeffersonian democracy: a belief that an informed and involved citizenry will make better choices and decisions.

Collaborative efforts work best when they are community led. Even though federal land managers may initiate collaboration, they must know when to let go; they must participate but remain open and willing to share power and responsibility with local communities and institutions.

Communities organize on different scales and must include national and local interests. Collaborative planning represents a shift of power from the agency to the stakeholders, not a shift of power from the agency to only local communities.

The entire community must agree on protocols for monitoring what people care about. Monitoring results of management actions is key. Achieving a common vision using a collaborative approach will work only if undertaken as a shared responsibility.

Success hinges on collecting and sharing a common base of science and information. New information technology has become less costly and more widely used by all stakeholders. This situation lends itself to data swapping and the compilation of information from multiple sources.

Launch collaborative planning only when "ready for prime time." Community maturity is important. It is much easier to participate in a collaborative community effort when there is a willingness to work together to develop a common vision.

Deep institutional and legal barriers to collaboration may exist. Recognize and avoid as many land mines and barriers as possible. It is a mistake to think that a new era has dawned everywhere. There are some places where collaboration will not work.

Leadership is important. Learn to take risks. Adopt new roles and new attitudes. Focus on building all kinds of relationships with both formal and informal networks of community opinion leaders. Federal land management agencies cannot be good stewards by standing behind federal boundaries.

Source: Harwood and Williams, 1998, p. 5. Used with permission of the authors.

typically encounter: the "Group of Ten," the toxic populists, the environmental justice movement, and alternative biocentric and anthropocentric groups.

The Group of Ten

Through the early 1980s, a passive approach to community involvement in decision making was a relatively safe strategy. Despite the local impacts of environmental detritus, few grassroots environmental groups existed in most communities. Dominant instead were the so-called Group of Ten, which consisted of ten national environmental groups located in Washington, D.C. With memberships exceeding eight million persons, this informal and often collaborative alliance of mainline groups consisted of the Sierra Club, the Wilderness Society, Friends of the Earth, the Environmental Defense Fund, the Izaak Walton League, the National Wildlife Federation, the National Audubon Society, the National Parks and Conservation Association, the Natural Resources Defense Council, and the Environmental Policy Institute.

These organizations had little incentive during the 1970s to develop the deliberative capacity of community stakeholders. Given the rather woeful regulatory efforts of state and local governments, these groups saw their immediate task as building a national regulatory regime. Grassroots community organizing took time, effort, and resources away from their work of shaping the metes and bounds of congressional legislation. What time remained went into affecting how national statutes were implemented. Thus, lobbying, giving technical advice, and filing court suits were their primary focus during this era.

Granted, several national organizations (such as the Sierra Club, the Environmental Defense Fund, and the League of Women Voters) made some effort to develop grassroots organizations and the capacity for affecting community decision making. But they did so only sporadically, without intensity, and by focusing on adversarial rather than collaborative mechanisms for community participation. Moreover, even when they did focus on developing grassroots participation, their efforts reflected the stress that federal environmental statutes put on end-of-pipe technical solutions to first-generation pollution problems. In sum, they offered technical assistance when local actors requested it, but stayed away from grassroots mobilizing.

Second, and relatedly, the rulemaking process that implemented these laws diverted attention away from grassroots organizing by anyone. Especially undercut by this "procedural republic" (Sandel, 1996) was local group participation in environmental rulemaking. Reflecting national statutes, rulemaking focused primarily on general problems rather than on local contingencies. What is more, anyone hoping to intervene and parry effectively in this adversarial rulemaking process needed both sufficient funding and substantial technical, scientific, and legal expertise (West, 1985; Kerwin, 1994).

Third, local groups could not plausibly claim that they represented broad segments of the nation. They lacked the financial wherewithal from membership dues and foundations to be major players in rulemaking. Unaffordable were prominent public interest law firms to represent them in hearings, to marshal technical expertise on their behalf, or to show how important their views could be to deliberations.

All this, of course, did not mean that organized community groups did not exist or that they were quiescent. To the contrary, many began developing their own grassroots capacities—often with grants, technical support, and mobilizing efforts from various EPA program offices. For example, as early as the Carter administration, the EPA's Community Relations program set up across the country twenty-one rather effective civic education project sites related to the Water Quality Act. Later, during President Reagan's second term, thirty-one community groups from twenty-two Superfund sites convened by the Environmental Defense Fund actually developed a set of citizen participation guidelines for the EPA.

Yet even with these efforts, citizen participation programs were always among the first and most substantially cut whenever fiscal exigencies arose. And in most instances the few in-house staff that these citizen participation programs had integrated into existing media programs were not spared the knife. Meanwhile, consultants hired to enhance community participation were unable to affect significantly existing ways of doing business in public programs (Sarianni and Friedland, 1995). Moreover, they could not overcome systematic efforts to do two things during Reagan's first term: withhold information from the public, and present whatever was released in unnecessarily complex technical terms.

By the same token, there were few advocates of coproduction processes within state and local regulatory organizations until well into the late 1980s (Sarianni and Friedland, 1995). Most of these organizations saw stakeholder involvement as threats to their existing programs and routines, to meeting federal deadlines, and to bringing to fruition public works projects that legislators wanted. Moreover, whatever community participation did occur at any level of government was adversarial rather than collaborative. As noted earlier, the procedural republic encouraged such strategies, and old habits die hard. Consequently, some managers can still expect to find an enduring residue of these strategies—as well as the distrust they occasioned—whenever dealing with some mainstream environmental groups.

One area in which managers are likely to confront this distrust most directly is in the skepticism that many Group of Ten members harbor toward quantitative risk management (QRM) approaches to ranking environmental problems. To proponents, the QRM paradigm is compelling, powerful, and critical to rational priority setting in an era of fiscal constraints. Who, after all, could argue with using "good science" to inform risk-based priority setting that compares risks and risk trade-offs in terms of economic costs and benefits to public and ecosystem health? Moreover, what better way to rectify what proponents feel is inordinate regulatory attention to minor risks (such as hazardous waste sites) rather than to major ones (such as indoor air pollution and global warming)(Graham and Hartwell, 1997)? And politically, what better way exists for public organizations to combat the Office of Management and Budget's emphasis on only cost-benefit analysis than to introduce health and ecosystem criteria into rulemaking deliberations?

Many mainstream environmentalists, however, see QRM in a very different light. Its technical complexity, they argue, marginalizes citizens (Commoner, 1994). QRM also permits some harm to persons or ecosystems when risks are presumed small or costs too high to address (Doniger, 1989). Moreover, these calculations exaggerate our existing scientific knowledge, especially when it comes to ecological risk. As such, opponents argue that a "better safe than sorry" regulatory approach makes more sense than one predicated on the twin illusions of complete knowledge and quantitative precision. Finally, many mainline environmentalists fear that QRM will produce decidedly less effort to minimize waste than our present technologically based standards afford (Prendergrass, Locke, and McElfish, 1995). Thus, managers expecting that QRM-based arguments will automatically carry the day with environmental groups should think again.

The Toxic Populist Backlash

The substantive disconnection between community concern for local environmental problems and the Big Ten's focus on national (and then global) issues caused a serious rift in the environmental movement. As

the 1980s progressed, many community activists grew increasingly convinced that the Big Ten's shift toward third-generation problems such
as global warming resulted in local concerns getting short shrift. Other
activists worried that Big Ten organizations had lost their independence
by becoming too dependent on corporate and foundation funding. Still
others worried that the Big Ten had merely grown too comfortable
with nibbling at the margins of environmental laws.

Into this void soared an angry, vocal, and community-based environmental movement. Led in many instances by concerned working- or
middle-class mothers fearing for their families' health and safety, the
toxic populist movement was born, and it remains vitally alive today.
Some in the movement commence battle armed only with anecdotal
knowledge of alarming rates of maladies (such as asthma) in their
neighborhoods. They associate these maladies with the pollution they
see, feel, smell, or ingest from nearby pollution sources or that may
arise if waste facilities are located in their neighborhoods. They or their
allies then collect more systematic evidence of "case clusters" of maladies (such as birth defects) suffered by present or past residents of
their neighborhoods, or evidence of what might happen if a polluting
plant is put in their area. Later they may introduce as evidence more
formal epidemiological studies of their neighborhoods (or of other
neighborhoods), provided that others with greater resources and expertise take up their cause.

By no means should managers dismiss these groups as too amateur-
ish to cause them problems. If they do, they may find lying in wait a
cadre of lawyers flush with victories over those who similarly underes-
timated the talents of toxic populist groups. Indeed, this movement
has grown so much in numbers, networking, and formidability that
managers who do not understand its perspectives and tactics do so at
their own peril. So successful, institutionalized, and professionalized
has this movement become in today's information age that many of
these groups have now established national legal and technical support
networks.

Among the most active and well known of these groups have been
the National Toxics Campaign, the Citizen's Clearinghouse for Hazardous Wastes, the Military Production Network, Nader's Public Interest
Research Groups and the affiliated National Environmental Law
Center, the Southwest Research and Information Center, Critical Mass
(for nuclear power issues), Clean Water Action, Physicians for Social
Responsibility, and Citizens for a Better Environment. (For more extensive listings of these types of groups, their respective agendas, and their

tactics at all levels of government, managers should consult the Internet sites listed in Table 6.2.)

Anyone jousting with these groups needs to be aware of three things in order to understand and work with them effectively. Namely, toxic populists tend to distrust scientific enterprise, give little deference to public health agencies, and may try to frame issues in morality-play terms. In Chapter Seven we discuss how these factors combine to make risk communication strategies critical to effective environmental management. Presently, however, we will limit ourselves to portraying the worldview that animates the actions of these groups.

Toxic populists tend to be inherently suspicious of, if not hostile toward, traditional scientific methods. Thus, managers expecting statis-

Table 6.2. Surfing the Green Net:
A List of Selected Sites to Get You Started.

http://www.epa.gov	Web site of the U.S. Environmental Protection Agency
http://www.doi.gov	Web site of the U.S. Department of Interior
http://www.doe.gov	Web site of the U.S. Department of Energy
http://ecosys.drdr.virginia.edu/Environment.html	University of Virginia WWW Virtual Library–Environment
http://envirolink.org/envirowebs.html	EnviroLink Environmental Library
http://www.econet.apc.org/econet/	Econet
http://www.envirosw.com	Directory of Environmental Resources
http://www.enn.com:80	Environmental News Network (ENN)
http://www.essential.org/monitor/monitor.html	Essential Information (Ralph Nader)
http://planetark.org/news	Reuters Environment News
http://www.sej.org/	Environmental Journalism Home Page
http://www.webdirectory.com	Environmental Organization
http://http2.sils.umich.edu/~cbriggs/environ_murphybriggs2.html	Guide to Environmental Resources on the Internet
http://www.gene.com/ae/RC/conservation.html	Access Excellence: Conservation and Environment

tical risk studies alone to persuade these groups that they are wrong will be sadly mistaken. Toxic populists place much more credence on lay experiential knowledge. As such, they demand decidedly less evidence than scientists do to prove that any adverse health effects are attributable to nearby pollution sources (Brown, 1993). In effect, they assume causality until proven otherwise, while scientists assume precisely the opposite.

Regardless of how unscientific an organization's risk experts may feel these claims are, however, managers cannot afford to cavalierly dismiss them as erroneous. There are too many examples of toxic populists being correct (see, for example, Harr, 1996). Indeed, even very small case clusters have correctly led to identifying carcinogenic linkages before scientists have confirmed them. Illustrative are the accuracy of their concerns regarding scrotal cancer among chimney sweeps, occupational exposure to vinyl chloride, and carcinogenicity of diethylstilbestrol (DES) to unborn fetuses (Lave, 1982).

Toxic populists also feel that scientists focus inordinately on the effects of single agents rather than on the interactive (or synergistic) and cumulative effects of multiple agents over time. They also complain that the scientific community is too focused on direct (or primary) risks to today's citizenry. This focus, they feel, myopically deemphasizes the indirect risks and costs to that generation, while totally ignoring threats of all kinds to future generations. Finally, toxic populists—along with members of the Group of Ten and environmental justice groups (discussed shortly)—feel that scientifically informed risk management focuses inordinately on cancer risks. Relatively ignored until recently are risks related to the immune, reproductive, developmental, and neurological systems (Silbergeld, 1993).

Also excoriated is risk assessment as toxic populists see it practiced traditionally. They deride its focus on single rather than multiple pathways for toxic agents to enter the body, and they criticize it for too readily downplaying statistically insignificant low-level exposure to pollutants. For example, while pathogens such as dioxin from incinerators directly enter the lungs, they also enter the body by bioaccumulating in food supplies. Yet risk assessments too often deemphasize the latter. In effect, toxic activists substitute health significance for statistical significance as their criterion for alarm. As noted in Chapter Five, some activists may then rush to the press to announce their findings and begin the drumbeat for alarm, redress, and compensation.

Importantly, recent events indicate that toxic populist arguments regarding the need for cumulative and integrated risk management approaches are gaining ground. During 1997, for example, Congress's Commission on Risk Assessment and Risk Management urged an integrated approach to risk management: "Creative, integrated strategies that address multiple environmental media and multiple sources of risks are needed if we are to sustain and strengthen the environmental improvements of risk reduction our nation has attained over the last 25 years" ("Risk Commission Stresses . . . ," 1997, p. 3). Later the same year, the EPA issued a cumulative risk guidance document prodding its members to "account for risk from multiple sources, stressors, routes of exposure, and [identify] the impacts of those multiple risks on different subpopulations" ("EPA Cummulative Risk Guide . . . ," 1997, p. 3). Still, the challenge remains immense. As one environmental consultant put it at the time, the guidance document is "an enormously complex and ambitious project that will strain the seams of science" (p. 3).

The Rise of the Environmental Justice Movement

As noted in Chapter One, a third set of organized community interests that managers are likely to encounter today are those associated with the environmental justice movement (EJM). In many ways, this movement revives a long-neglected connection between ethnicity, race, and public health issues enunciated first in early twentieth-century urban America (Gottlieb, 1993). For decades hence, however, the conventional wisdom was that only the white middle class and upscale yuppie recreationists were interested in contemporary environmental issues. Working class and ethnic voters were thought to worry more about preserving the jobs that polluters produced than about the toxics that polluters emitted disproportionately upon them.

But during the last fifteen years, low-income minority groups and their representatives in Congress, state legislatures, and city councils have become among the nation's strongest and most vigorous pollution watchdogs (Mohai, 1996). This began, you will recall, as distressing data became public during the 1980s. For example, there were charges that the life expectancy of migrant workers was twenty years below the national average, that women of color were especially at risk for health problems given racial and gender segmentation in labor markets, and that significantly more blacks than whites lived in air quality nonattainment areas. It was also claimed that commercial hazardous waste sites were disproportionately located in low-income black neighborhoods, and that economically distraught Native American reservations were courted disproportionately as future solid or hazardous waste sites (Higgins, 1993).

Thus, managers who automatically assume that persons of color or of low- to lower-middle-class means prefer jobs over environmental quality can make a politically and managerially costly misjudgment. So too can those who propose marginalizing these groups as politically, technically, and economically impotent. Increasingly, loosely knit networks of umbrella groups are beginning to redress this situation by affording political, economic, and technical sophistication to grassroots workers. Included among these groups are the NAACP Legal Defense and Education Fund, the United Church of Christ Commission for Racial Justice, the African American Environmental Association, the American Association of Blacks in Energy, La Raza, and Native Americans for a Clean Environment.

EJM groups share with toxic populists the philosophy that traditional environmentalism has systematically hurt rather than helped their cause (Bullard, 1983, 1996). Thus, as with toxic populists, a key word in the EJM lexicon is *elitism*. It is not, however, the elitism of the scientific community that most animates EJM concerns. As Robert Bullard (1994) explains, it is an elitism with three primary components: compositional elitism, ideological elitism, and impact elitism. *Compositional elitism* is the movement's belief that environmentalists come largely from privileged classes. *Ideological elitism* posits that environmentalists from these classes consciously or unconsciously pursue reforms that distribute benefits to themselves and impose costs on low-income persons of color. Finally, and relatedly, *impact elitism* purports that these reforms place minorities and low-income persons at unparalleled and disproportionate risk from toxic pollutants.

A key component of all this for EJM groups is the role that public officials and agencies play in affecting business-location decisions within local communities. Particularly obnoxious to movement members are public zoning decisions and tax subsidies that encourage polluting industries to stay or locate in low-income areas. Excoriated as well are exclusionary zoning, redlining, and facility sitings that perpetuate racially segregated neighborhoods that are environmentally toxic and in which regulation is lax.

To counter these threats to their communities, EJM groups have often adopted the nonviolent protest tactics of the civil rights movement. They have also copied the successful tactics of more well-to-do citizens pursuing NIMBY or LULU (locally unwanted land use) campaigns. Spurred by the seminal report *Toxic Wastes and Race in the*

United States (United Church of Christ Commission for Racial Justice, 1987) and by successor studies, they have taken to the streets, to legislatures, and to courtrooms. Still, many operate on shoestring budgets that historically have disadvantaged them in long-term battles, deficient as they also often are in legal, toxicological, hydrological, and engineering skills.

Help, however, is increasingly at hand for EJM groups. More mainline elements of the environmental movement—such as the Sierra Club, the Environmental Defense Fund, the National Wildlife Federation, and the Natural Resources Defense Council—are reaching out to them across the country. The hope of these mainline groups is to bridge the racial, class, and ideological chasms that have historically diverted EJM and Group of Ten members from profitable partnerships. In turn, civil rights groups such as the American Civil Liberties Union have also entered the fray on behalf of environmental justice groups. Meanwhile, the Clinton administration has mounted a serious campaign to improve the knowledge base and capacities of EJM groups nationally and in particular cities.

Part and parcel of this effort, although much broader in its informational scope, is the administration's initiative to profile on the World Wide Web the environmental records of factories in five industrial sectors: the automobile, metals, oil refining, paper mill, and steel industries. Among the components of the profiles (which will include the number of inspections, the compliance status, the penalties imposed, toxics release inventory data, weighted pollution releases, and pollution-to-production ratios) will be racial and income breakdowns within three miles of each plant.

Perhaps most sobering for managers is how environmental groups plan to use this information. As Ryan Clark (1997) of the Natural Resources Defense Council suggests, environmentalists are likely to use these profiles to target for lawsuits organizations that appear not to be enforcing or complying with pollution laws. Thus it is not surprising that the Environmental Council of the States has joined with private industry in urging the EPA to delay the project until the accuracy of all data is verified.

Important as well is the Clinton administration's touted Brownfields Initiative, a program emulated by many state legislatures. It is designed to attract businesses back into abandoned, idle, or underused urban industrial and commercial sites (Maas, 1997). In these areas, business expansion and redevelopment are complicated by real or perceived environmental contamination. Worried about the liabilities for toxicity they may incur should they locate or relocate in these areas, companies tend to pass them over in favor of suburban locations.

Make no mistake: EJM groups are not opposed to the jobs that such efforts might bring into their areas. What they are cautious about is watering down environmental regulations, other regulatory standards, and enforcement as a price for attracting these jobs. Sensitive to these concerns, the administration created the 1995 Brownfields Action Agenda, which sought to ensure that partnerships between EJM groups and other Brownfields stakeholders (such as banks, real estate developers, and government organizations) would inform deliberations about how best to proceed.

Finally, managers should not underestimate the potency of the street demonstrations, pickets, and other direct action tactics that EJM groups have historically employed. These groups can quickly put regulatory and regulated organizations on the defensive, reframe debates in ways that are unflattering to the organizations, and cause managers to lose the battle for public opinion. Indeed, one has only to look to the worldwide success of such groups as Greenpeace to see how effective these tactics can be.

The Rise of Alternative Movements, Paradigms, and Tactics

Greenpeace is only one of a host of alternative and more radically "biocentric" groups (such as the Clamshell Alliance, the Seals, and the People for the Ethical Treatment of Animals) that managers may confront in their communities. Groups with this philosophy emphasize that humans must accommodate themselves to nature rather than vice versa. In the process they urge us to see nature—both animate and inanimate—as having intrinsic value and rights (Nash, 1989). Associated with the "deep ecology" movement, this decidedly nonanthropocentric worldview says that humankind's needs (for economic development or a healthy existence, for example) have no inherent right to trump the needs of nature. As a consequence, the goal of these biocentric groups is straightforward, albeit grandiose: "to reverse the course of the urban and industrial order and to challenge and ultimately eliminate or unmake a technology-based industrial civilization" (Gottlieb, 1993).

Consider, for example, the exploits of Greenpeace. Formed in 1971 as a multinational, direct-action organization, Greenpeace initially focused on antitoxic, antimilitary, antinuclear, and species protection causes. Its leaders' tactics were simple: engage in high-risk, media-savvy, guerrilla theater to get the public to pay attention to these issues. Thus, to this day Greenpeace is associated in people's minds with obstruction-ist confrontations involving whaling ships, nuclear vessels, and toxic polluters. Recently, however, Greenpeace has also exhibited a growing emphasis on publishing research reports that support its positions. In addition, members have begun working with local communities, a development of central import to any organization trying to build a coproduction environmental ethic.

Its actions and direct mail appeals during the late 1980s were so suc-cessful that Greenpeace had offices in 150 countries and a larger mem-bership than any of the other Group of Ten environmental organizations. Recently, however, Greenpeace's fortunes in America have floundered. After the organization's staunch opposition to the Persian Gulf War, U.S. membership plummeted from nearly 1.2 million in 1991 to approxi-mately 400,000 in 1997. In response, Greenpeace has closed its ten re-gional offices, slashed its U.S. staff from four hundred to sixty-five employees, and cut its budget from $29 million to $21 million. In the process, it has narrowed its focus to two primary issues that managers are most likely to find drawing the attention of group members: global warming and old-growth timber logging.

In their focus on logging, Greenpeace joins the remnants of what was once the most radical organization in philosophy and tactics that managers (largely in the West) encountered: Earth First! The organi-zation pursued its prowilderness and anticapitalist goals by such "eco-tage" or "ecomarauding" tactics as "monkey wrenching." Sometimes dangerous and illegal, monkey wrenching involves tactics such as tree spiking and the disabling of vehicles to halt timber production in old-growth forests. Moreover, any of these tactics can provoke outright violence at any time.

After an FBI sting operation involving the blowing up of power lines brought conspiracy charges against the leader of Earth First!, a major-ity faction split from it. Rejecting the antihuman welfare aspects of founder David Forman, this splinter faction began exploring a more expansive social agenda. Most significantly for managers, its leaders began to build alliances with toxic populist and environmental justice groups. In the end, Earth First! retreated from the more extreme philo-sophical and tactical eccentricities it had practiced in the past. Thus, although it is decidedly less visible in the national media today, in some communities it still poses challenges and opportunities to managers seeking to build consensus over environmental issues.

For example, today managers may find working with Earth First! members much like working with another set of organizations from this alternative movement: public interest research groups (or PIRGs). Differentiating his PIRG movement from most mainstream environmental groups are Ralph Nader's unabashedly anticorporatist philosophy and his emphasis on local citizen empowerment. Working to foster the latter is a coterie of professional experts financed by membership fees. These experts perform research and initiate specific campaigns (such as bottle bills and asbestos bans) led by student and community volunteers.

Managers err, however, if they assume that anticapitalist, countercultural environmental groups are the only groups afoot in their communities. As we noted in Chapter Five, on the media, radical property rights and state's rights groups may also be active in some places. In the extreme, and located in the West, groups affiliated with the county rights movement have taken to confronting managers directly. Some of these skirmishes have been illegal and have been cast steeply in civil disobedience terms akin to those used by Earth First! More moderate in their tactics are groups who use the same court suit strategies that have proven so effective for mainstream and toxic populist groups across the country.

These more anti-environmental factions are increasingly finding themselves at odds in western states with members of the *free-market environmentalist movement*. This movement seeks to end user preferences and subsidies on public lands by competing with prodevelopment interests for leases on public lands (Kenworthy, 1997). Taking to the courts, these environmentalists have successfully forced at least one state's (Arizona's) land management department to allow greater competition for these leases.

BUILDING A LEARNING ORGANIZATION

Certainly managers need to know the agendas and tactics of these four general types of environmental groups, because they may be active in their communities. But managers also need the answers to three interrelated questions as they pursue a coproduction environmental ethic: How do managers anticipate precisely which stakeholders in their community—environmental or otherwise—should be included in their deliberations? How can they stay abreast of developments in the concerns, strategies, and tactics of these environmental stakeholders? Finally, how can they keep up with what has, and has not, worked previously in dealing with stakeholders? We argue that success in these endeavors leaves managers no alternative but to create a "learning organization" that is attuned to them.

Learning organizations are continually open to the lessons of history. They routinely collect, analyze, benchmark, and widely share the environmental management experiences of their employees, programs, and stakeholders. Additionally, they scour the Internet systematically for environmental management politics, strategies, and innovations worldwide. They persistently institutionalize "reconnaissance" systems within their organizations. Indeed, as was noted in Chapter Four, the environmental management system standards of ISO 14001 are designed explicitly to help managers develop learning organizations of this kind. These organizations thus advance the idea of a coproduction environmental ethic in public, for-profit, and nonprofit organizations.

As noted, statutes such as CERCLA and RCRA, along with the Clinton administration's Brownfields Initiative, enumerate extensive community relations mandates (including the development of plans). The EPA, in turn, adds to these requirements. These mandates certainly produce reconnaissance of sorts, but alas, often after problems arise. In contrast, the coproduction environmental ethic we tout is a preemptive attempt to acquire two-way communication before problems arise.

Internal Reconnaissance

Two ways to combine actual and virtual learning about working with environmental stakeholders in communities have already taken root in the private sector. The first method involves building *lessons-learned databases*. The second is known as *knowledge mapping*. Organizations can readily adapt both approaches in order to become more environmentally sensitive, strategic, and attuned to local community groups.

Lessons-learned databases employ group software such as Lotus Notes to create virtual chat rooms among otherwise isolated employees. Managers use these intranetting devices to share environmental knowledge about community actors and experiences with environmental problems. Importantly, this information includes lessons about how others have identified, involved, and strategically used community groups in the past. Similarly, organization-wide knowledge mapping occurs when lists of individuals who have dealt with particular environmental issues are available in either hard copy or (better yet) computer files. These individuals are listed as contact or resource persons who can share their expertise with others who are dealing with the community for the first time, in new ways, or under unusual circumstances.

Certainly there is no guarantee that anyone will take advantage of these databases. Consequently, managers bent on encouraging their use must ensure that resources are adequately allocated to keep the databases current and, hence, attractive to use. Wise, as well, is ensuring that employee performance ratings are linked partially to their use. Finally, and most critically, they must ensure that their information management systems can get these data in usable formats, to the right persons, and in a timely enough way to inform future actions (see Chapter Nine for details).

External Reconnaissance

The potential contributions of the information age do not stop within organizations. Managers can gain a sense for the evolving concerns, issues, and tactics of the environmental community by routinely consulting the Internet. Again, Table 6.2 lists several useful sites that offer a wealth of additional environmental links. Many of these sites also allow managers to disseminate information about their organization's environmental activities.

But "virtual" information sources go only so far. Learning organizations often turn to permanent advisory boards composed of community stakeholders. Advisory boards are hardly unique to learning organizations. As we have noted, some are required by statute or regulation. Other organizations opt to build them defensively or under external pressure (such as Superfund site-specific advisory boards and technical advisory groups at the Department of Defense and the Department of Energy). Meanwhile, administrator Carol Browner's *place-based* or *community-based* environmental management initiatives necessarily incorporate advisory boards.

What differentiates the use of such boards by learning organizations, however, are the proactive, rather than reactive, ways that managers use them. Learning organizations consistently tap these boards for advice that helps to anticipate, define, alleviate, or cope with the environmental consequences of organizational operations. Learning organizations also differ in terms of when they use these boards. Unlike conventional bureaucracies, they involve board members at the beginning of organizational deliberations, not late in the process. They also make extensive efforts to consult routinely with representatives of that board through periodic meetings, by e-mail, by phone, and by newsletter. Finally, learning organizations hold informal briefings with key stakeholders long before formal news releases are issued. This is particularly true when stakeholders express moderate to high levels of concern about an organization's activities.

Another way that learning organizations acquire firsthand information about citizen concerns and about the degree of citizen involvement they will need is through *community interviews*. In these interviews, twenty-five to thirty unaffiliated citizens or group representatives in an affected geographic area are randomly or reputationally queried about their concerns. To identify these people, managers contact community organizations (such as churches and schools). They then typically schedule interviews during weekend or nonwork hours during the week. And if citizens are disgruntled already, learning organizations canvass door-to-door and give advance notice to residents about future meetings.

Many learning organizations also establish and widely publicize telephone hot lines as well as Internet home pages that provide managers' e-mail addresses for comments. Through these media they simultaneously dispense environmental management information and solicit input from citizens and stakeholders (see, for example, the Chesapeake Bay Program's Web site at http://www.epa.gov/r3chespk/index.html). If an organization provides these interfaces, however, care and constant updating are critical lest information become outdated and further arouse citizen cynicism or ire.

Potentially effective as well are the full-scale environmental management public forums or town meetings that some learning organizations hold. These meetings can be double-edged swords, however. On the positive side, they can help managers understand what most concerns stakeholders about an organization's environmental management activities. But if conflict is already intensified, if forums are treated only as public relations or media events, or if stakeholders perceive previous forums as such, organizations risk further inflaming the situation. In these cases, small group informal meetings that preclude public posturing are safer and more worthwhile. What is more, learning organizations understand that even when times are serene, managers should never enter public forums without understanding what they want to accomplish in them.

Finally, some regulatory agencies (such as those in Arizona) have incorporated random surveys of citizens into their deliberations. Known as *public value assessments,* these surveys tap general opinions about risk priorities. But unless they are subsequently used to disabuse the public of misunderstandings, such plebiscitary approaches risk taking uninformed opinions as givens. As we discuss shortly, one important role of managers is to improve citizens' understanding of complex issues, not merely to react to their sometimes uninformed preferences or prejudices.

Ensuring Adequate Stakeholder Representation

Despite how widely these approaches to organization learning appear on the surface to cast the net, they are insufficient. Many affected interests may not come to meetings, use hot lines or the Internet, or have attitudes that are sufficiently formed or condensable into survey-question categories. This would be less of a problem were it not for one of the greatest pitfalls that organizations face in pursuing such efforts: creating disgruntled stakeholders who feel that they have been left out of the process.

We argue that *scenario writing* exercises (Bardach, 1977) can help managers to diminish significantly the chances of this occurring. Scenario writing requires managers to take a sober and "dirty-minded" political assessment of their organization's operations. Participants in such exercises ask (Levin and Ferman, 1985)

- What environmental problems or risks may result from our actions?
- Who may these problems affect?
- How might those affected react?
- Who has the ability to help our organization avoid or mitigate these problems?

To discover answers to these questions, an organization starts with a series of brainstorming sessions with program managers, information resource management and environmental management directors and their staffs, and environmental management media specialists. Asked and answered are a set of related subquestions that inform the ones just listed. These include, but are not limited to, the following:

- What are the likely environmental consequences (positive and negative) of given organizational operations?
- Who in the community might be especially helpful in anticipating the metes and bounds of potential problems, in setting priorities for addressing them, and in explaining what transpires to the general public?
- How might the media most negatively and most positively portray these activities and the environmental management issues they raise?

- Who in the community might be helpful in offering ways to ameliorate or eliminate entirely the negative consequences of these operations?

- Who among the organization's traditional constituencies, legislative sovereigns, and regulators has the ability to affect whatever operating decisions are made?

- Who in the larger community might be affected positively or negatively by these actions?

- Who in the community has the resources and predisposition to oppose or support the environmental consequences that these actions may incur—whether or not they are directly affected?

- How likely is it that these supporters or opponents will work actively for or against particular environmental management options?

- Are there ways to involve these individuals or groups in order to create bandwagon effects supporting environmental management choices and other operating decisions?

- Who will speak for future generations in any deliberations that take place?

DOS AND DON'TS

As noted earlier, managers who think that better communication alone will solve their environmental management problems will be sadly disappointed. Indeed, under certain circumstances, outlined in this section, so-called better communication may actually compound an organization's problems. Our argument, instead, is that managers must be strategic in anticipating, structuring, and coping with the community participation that inevitably arises when choices have to be made in an era of civic environmentalism, proceduralism, and adversarial legalism.

Nor are we suggesting that managers need totally and always to open up their organizations to citizen participation, or to respond automatically to public demands under all circumstances. Citizens and other stakeholders are not always "customers" who know best, or "owners" to whom managers must pander. What communities dealing with environmental management issues often need most from managers and outside experts is tutoring in the intricacies of public problems (Gawthrop, 1984).

Finally, we are not arguing that tutoring citizens in these complexities involves either selectively marshaling evidence in an organization's favor or engaging in one-way flows of communication to the public. Our position, instead, is that the role of managers in a democracy—especially public managers and their surrogates in the for-profit and nonprofit sectors—is to enhance, not diminish, the quality of deliberation on these important issues. To these ends, we advance five general principles for managers working with communities when specific policy choices must be made: vary the scope; foster two-way communication; foster procedural fairness; avoid misinformation, demonizing, and conflicts of interest; and be candid about constraints.

Vary the Scope

As John Clayton Thomas (1995) avers, smart managers tailor the extent of any formally structured participation on specific decisions in their organizations to the situations they face. Of course, to an extent this assumes that they *can* control these parameters—a premise we doubt. Where we do agree wholeheartedly, however, is with Thomas's advice to take a contingency approach to community participation. Striving for full-scale, formally structured, and procedurally unassailable coproduction on all decisions is infeasible, unnecessary, and potentially dangerous. Rather, we join Thomas in arguing that managers should match coproduction styles to environmental management situations when contemplating the breadth and formality that are needed and prudent on specific decisions. What is more, we feel that such a strategy is decidedly less risky when managers have routinized the other means of internal and external reconnaissance we have discussed.

Fully explicating Thomas's arguments in this chapter is impractical. We can say, however, that he offers several rebuttable presumptions worth thinking about when structuring community relations. His basic premise is that formally structured involvement in particular decisions should expand in scope commensurate with an organization's time and its need for more information and to gain public acceptance. Ranging from least to broadest in scope, Thomas identifies five styles of participation:

- *Autonomous decision making.* Managers have no need or time to involve the public at all. Except when time constraints preclude, we feel that managers should use this approach quite sparingly. Again, institutionalizing the suggestions we have offered about public outreach should diminish the need to use this approach anyway.

- *Modified decision making.* Managers need to cull information from segments of the population but still make final decisions themselves to meet their needs.

- *Segmented public consultation.* Managers need to engage a segment of the public in defining the problem, get that segment's ideas about solutions, and incorporate them in a final decision.

- *Unitary public consultation.* Managers need to involve the public as a whole in doing the same things as in the segmented consultation.

- *Public decision.* Managers and the public codetermine the choice made.

Foster Ongoing Two-Way Communication

Once key stakeholders have been scoped and identified, the ongoing two-way communication process envisioned by a coproduction environmental ethic requires careful preparation. Prior experiences suggest that a useful way for managers to organize their approach to such matters is to think in terms of the eight primary steps of any two-way decision-making process (Juanillo and Scherer, 1995).

The first step is *problem identification.* Here managers must take care to schedule enough time into their work plans to ensure that any recommendations made in stakeholder meetings occur in time to inform operating decisions. They must also identify very early the kinds of information they will need to inform these decisions. Often a long and tedious process, information gathering should begin—according to our earlier reconnaissance methods—well in advance of when managers need the information. What is more, managers should collate and present any technical and scientific information they have in ways that laypersons can understand. An already jaded public will not treat obfuscation kindly.

In *eliciting* (step 2) and *validating* (step 3) *values,* managers also need to provide sufficient time for brainstorming as wide a variety of values as possible at two levels. For the first, or general values, level, organizational brainstorming sessions might consider environmental, social and human, long-term management, economic, and general use impacts. To ensure that participants systematically consider these values, the use of a matrix is often helpful. On one axis, array relevant options; on the other, display consensus values that emerge from deliberations.

At a second, more detailed level, managers and stakeholders in these sessions might break down the consensus values selected into the precise activities that will operationalize those values. For example, they might incorporate economic values into the choice of future uses of land parcels (such as industrial versus residential use), or they might operationalize environmental values in terms of off-site or on-site storage of waste produced. Finally, participants might use these environmental management subvalues to derive *discrete criteria* (step 4) for evaluating the options generated. These criteria might include such factors as long-term safety, organizational costs, community benefits and costs, and on-site disposal requirements.

As they move through the *option generation, evaluation, scoping,* and *final judgment* phases of the decision process (steps 5 through 8), participants do not merely examine discrete environmental management alternatives. Instead, they constantly frame and reframe the consideration of these alternatives in terms of the consensus environmental management values and decision criteria developed earlier. This in turn makes it extremely difficult for participants to retreat later into purely self-interested environmental management positions. Doing so can mean losing face and credibility.

Foster Procedural Fairness

Differences, of course, over ends and means are endemic to any deliberative process involving disparate stakeholders. Thus all participants will not agree on the decisions made in their collective name. Thus, the only way to keep all stakeholders at the table and for them to buy into these decisions is to establish a consensus-based decision rule. To be sure, this gives each stakeholder a veto, even in the face of overwhelming support for a particular option. But participation is voluntary, and managers cannot coerce anyone into agreeing to abide with decisions.

Still, a *working consensus* that includes 80 to 90 percent of stakeholders can be achieved. What is more, it can be a powerful force in exerting peer group pressures on those who are reluctant to acquiesce in any decisions made. Thus, managers must establish decision rules early and develop procedures that incorporate everyone's concerns. In the end, progress depends on participants believing that the rules of the game are not stacked against them.

Avoid Misinformation, Demonizing, and Conflicts of Interest

Stakeholders will bring both overt and latent agendas to any deliberative forum they attend. Consequently, managers should not allow misinformation, demonizing of opponents, and conflicts of interest to mar organizational deliberations. Most helpful might be the professional services of a skilled, neutral (but not indifferent), and knowledgeable third-party facilitator.

As we discuss in more detail in Chapter Twelve, trained facilitators are useful for breaking the ice among distrustful stakeholders and in translating complex issues and concepts into language that everyone understands. In addition, they can steer deliberations around the posturing or dilatory tactics of those who do not have adequate support for their positions. Facilitators are also skilled in developing and enforcing decision rules that outlaw the demonizing of opponents during deliberations. Finally, if they pursue their work professionally, they can advance an organization's reputation for impartiality.

Before hiring facilitators, managers should again weigh the stakes involved and decide accordingly. How serious are missteps stemming from information gaps, stakeholder pique, and low levels of public acceptance? If these stakes are sufficiently high, a variety of individuals who specialize in mediation techniques in general and in environmental matters in particular can be employed. In the end, the expenses that an organization incurs by hiring facilitators may look relatively small compared to the costs of breakdowns in talks or in public trust.

Be Candid About Constraints

When doing all this, however, managers need to be careful not to raise stakeholder expectations unduly. At the outset, they should make clear to participants the bounds (wide or circumscribed) of their legal authority to act unilaterally. Participants should also understand up front the extent to which their input will drive decision making (see Thomas's typology of styles, discussed earlier). Successful environmental management deliberations also depend acutely on all stakeholders understanding that managers have to balance a variety of factors in their decision making. Unless all these constraints are initially made clear to stakeholders, they may grow angry and later file suit challenging any decisions made.

An organization's success in working with communities also depends on foreshadowing for participants the methodological difficulties that may arise during deliberations. For example, nothing can sour talks quicker than perceptions that relevant data have been selectively withheld, tampered with, or "massaged." Certainly these perceptions can be real and part of a deliberate strategy to deceive or slant information to someone's advantage. But they can also result inadvertently from inconsistencies in data collection, processing, and storage within organizations. The best that managers can ensure is a good faith effort to anticipate, make known, and redress these problems as talks proceed.

CONCLUSION

This chapter has argued that managers would do well to anticipate the kinds of environmental problems that can arise as a result of their organization's operations. Most useful in anticipating the legal, managerial, and political vulnerabilities and options available to them in such matters is developing a coproduction environmental ethic within their organization. In the process, and consonant with the epigram introducing this chapter, what organizations do (that is, learn) will be what they become (learning organizations). But two-way communication about environmental management issues is a difficult process. This is especially true when shared understandings about health, safety, or ecological risk do not exist. Why this occurs, and how to cope with it, are the subjects of Chapter Seven.

7

COMMUNICATING RISK

Nature never deceives us; it is always we who deceive ourselves.

—Jean Jacques Rousseau

What is risk communication? Consider the following examples taken from real-life experiences with this process:

• A large chemical producer in Louisiana issues the information required annually under the federal Toxics Release Inventory, listing the volumes of toxic chemicals it has discharged into the air, water, or on land. Meanwhile, the Department of Environmental Quality is busy responding to questions about chemical releases. Environmental advocates use the information to call attention to the need for stricter controls on the chemical industry.

• The EPA administrator holds a press conference to assure people that a pesticide known as EDB (ethylene dibromide), widely used as a fumigant on citrus and grain, does not present an immediate health threat, despite fears to the contrary. He cannot say definitively what the long-term risks of the chemical are, but he promises a thorough study. He feels it is necessary to reassure the public in the wake of media reports that he thinks overstated the risk.

• A national newspaper publishes a story about a neighborhood in central California where an unusually high number of children have been diagnosed with cancer. Despite careful investigation by health and environmental agencies, no environmental cause has been found. Some residents support the government's decision to conduct more studies; others view the illnesses as a statistical oddity and fear the local economic effects of more negative publicity.

• The EPA begins a public information campaign to make the public aware of the risks they may face from concentrations of radon in their homes. The goal is to get people to test for radon and to take corrective action if the radon exceeds recommended levels. Government experts debate whether the campaign should be designed simply to inform people of the risks or to persuade them to test for radon and take corrective action if needed.

• A scientist employed by a waste management firm speaks at a community meeting to share the results of a quantitative risk assessment conducted by the firm. According to the expert, the risk assessment demonstrates that a waste incinerator the firm wants to build will not pose unacceptable risks. The community is divided. Some residents want the incinerator for the jobs it will bring; others do not trust the company and fear adverse health effects.

These examples present risk communication as a combination of messages, processes, and political situations. In the first example, a chemical company releases information required under federal law. The information provokes a debate about the health effects of the entire industry.

In the second example, the most visible environmental official in the country tells people that his agency does not know exactly how risky the use of a chemical is in the long run but fears of immediate harm are unfounded. His statements are half risk communication and half candid communication of uncertainty.

The third example describes a genuine puzzle in the town of McFarland, California. Officials cannot explain a disturbing cluster of cancer among the town's children with any apparent environmental cause, despite extensive study by experts. Residents debate the causes of the illnesses while government experts try to find an explanation.

The fourth example refers to what probably was the largest and most systematic public information campaign in the EPA's history. Much of what is known today about communicating risk came from the radon experience and the research studies associated with it. Whether the purpose of the government's radon campaign should have been to inform or influence illustrates fundamental issues in risk communication.

Finally, the situation in the last example is common; people across the country have opposed the siting of incinerators and other unwanted facilities in their communities. Research on risk perception shows that there is more at issue in these disputes than a debate over statistical risk, as experts define it. Distrust and skepticism about expert claims are also factors.

Risk communication has been defined in various ways. An early approach defined it as "an intentional transfer of information designed to respond to public concerns or public needs related to real or perceived hazards" (Plough and Krimsky, 1990, p. 226). A broader definition describes it as "any public or private communication that informs individuals about the existence, nature, form, severity, or acceptability of risks" (p. 226). The National Academy of Sciences (1989, p. 21) uses an even broader approach, defining risk communication as "an interactive process of exchange of information and opinion among individuals, groups, and institutions." It involves "multiple messages about the nature of risk and other messages, not strictly about risk, that express concerns, opinions, or reactions to risk messages or to legal and institutional arrangements for risk management." In this chapter, risk communication is discussed more in terms of the second and third definitions than the first, but the first definition has shaped the development of the field.

Why dedicate a chapter in a book on environmental management to the subject of risk communication? After all, we communicate or respond to information about risk all the time. "Be careful crossing the street," the parent warns the child. "Watch out for that loose brick," the nervous homeowner tells the visitor walking on the aging patio. Visual warnings of risk are everywhere, including traffic signs, advertisements for investment funds, signs on escalators in shopping malls, and labels on bottles of aspirin, wine bottles, paint cans, and packs of cigarettes.

Of course, people do not always respond to warnings about risk. They jaywalk, cross against the light, trip on loose bricks, take medicines they should not, drink alcohol, smoke cigarettes, and invest foolishly. In one of the earliest alleged cases of risk communication in history, Eve ignored the warnings and ate the apple. People often ignore information about risk. More importantly, they often take a risk even after they have been warned; they decide that the benefits of their acts will likely outweigh the risks.

Thus, as we noted in Chapter Six, risk communication—in concept and in practice—is not as simple as it first appears. In fact, among policymakers, scholars, environmental managers in industry, and environmental activists there has been a great deal of debate. What is risk communication? How seriously should it be studied? What should its purpose be? Why does it not always influence people? What should its role be in a democratic society?

We begin this chapter by discussing the foundations of risk communication: the concept of risk, its role in environmental management, and research on risk perception. Next we consider the risk communication process, broken down into the source of a risk message, the design of the message, the channels for delivering risk information, and the audience for risk communication. Following this discussion we look at what is known about risk communication at a practical level and how managers can improve it. Finally, we conclude by considering the role and appropriate uses of risk communication in a democratic society, and we discuss general issues regarding risk perception and communication for managers.

THE DEVELOPMENT OF RISK COMMUNICATION

Two leading scholars on risk communication, Alonzo Plough and Sheldon Krimsky, noted in a 1990 article (p. 223) that "prior to 1986 there were only a few essays in the scholarly and policy literature with 'risk communication' in their titles." In the second half of that decade, however, the study and practice of risk communication expanded rapidly. Indeed, most of the references cited in this chapter were published in the late 1980s, an era best known as the risk communication decade (see, for example, Covello, Sandman, and Slovic, 1988; National Academy of Sciences, 1989; Zimmerman, 1987; Slovic, 1986).

Why the sudden interest in a tool and a process that now seem so central to environmental management? After all, people have been debating and warning about the risks of technologies (nuclear power), chemicals (asbestos and lead), and practices (genetic engineering) for years. What happened to make risk communication the subject of systematic study, research, and training?

One thing that happened was that the public became aware of various kinds of risk and started to demand a voice in social and political decisions about them (Fiorino, 1989). A particular source of controversy was nuclear power, which became an issue in the United States and an even larger source of controversy in western Europe (Nelkin, 1977). Indeed, the origins of risk perception and communication research grew out of the nuclear power industry's pragmatic and self-interested efforts to understand why the lay public was so suspicious of their industry. After all, the probabilistic risk assessments conducted by the industry had shown that nuclear power was a relatively safe technology in which the chances of a serious accident were for all practical purposes zero. Why did the lay public not see the world through the same "rational" eyes as the experts?

From these origins, the field of risk communication grew and flowered. But this flowering did not occur along one simple, straight path. Baruch Fischhoff (1995) offers a history of risk communication from the perspective of the technical expert and government officials who have been the principal risk communicators. His history is organized around seven developmental stages that managers should appreciate. Each stage builds on its predecessors, but does not necessarily replace them.

The first stage was prerisk communication, or the view that "all we have to do is get the numbers right." The task of assessing risks was left to experts, who saw no need to share their assumptions, methods, or even a detailed review of their results with the public. This rationale, however, failed to satisfy popular qualms, in part because of its reliance on technical methods that were inaccessible to a lay audience. The experts then moved to a second stage of primitive risk communication based on the notion that "all we have to do is tell them the numbers." The problem, as the nuclear industry learned, was that the public usually did not understand or accept the experts' numbers as the final word on the risks they would have to bear.

The next three stages reflect the rapid maturation of the field, although within the limited confines of helping the public understand and deal with risk more "rationally." In the third stage, "All we have to do is explain what we mean by the numbers," researchers and other risk professionals applied themselves to the task of helping people understand probability distributions and the other fine points of risk assessment. From there it was a natural progression to the fourth stage, that is, "All we have to do is show them that they've accepted similar risks in the past." If people could not be convinced of the logic of accepting relatively trivial statistical risks, then they should be presented with comparisons to the more common risks they tolerate every day. If you accept the greater risks of driving, smoking, or eating some naturally occurring carcinogen, the risk communicator might say, then why not accept the smaller risk of a waste incinerator down the street? "The anecdotal experience of many risk communicators," according to Fischhoff (1995, p. 141), "is that such comparisons are as unpopular in practice as they are disingenuous in principle."

In the fifth stage, "All we have to do is show them that it's a good deal," risk communicators tried to persuade people of the social and economic benefits of the risks they were being asked to accept. One problem with this approach was that often some people enjoyed the benefits while others bore the risks. The last two stages then brought risk communication to a more appropriate level for a democratic society. Risk communication expanded to encompass two-way information flows—from the lay public to government and experts and back (Fiorino, 1990c). Thus, a sixth stage, "All we have to do is treat them nice," reflected a willingness to acknowledge the public's concerns and the importance of treating them with respect.

Finally, in the seventh stage, "All we have to do is make them partners," the field of risk communication reached a new level of maturity. It became part of a larger concern with public participation. Many researchers and practitioners now see their major goal as involving the public in risk decisions. They view risk communication as a process in which government educates people about sources of risk and their effects while learning about public concerns and perceptions. They thus envision a process highly consonant with our emphasis on developing a coproduction environmental ethic in agencies.

Given the rapid growth in the popularity of risk communication and the dynamics of its development, it should not be surprising that people do not always agree on what risk communication is and what its goals should be. The organizers of a 1994 national conference of risk communication experts put it this way (Chess, Salomone, Hance, and Saville, 1995, p. 115):

- Is successful risk communication persuasion, transfer of information, public participation, or empowerment of citizens to make decisions?

- Should it produce an informed citizenry, a compliant citizenry, an alert citizenry, or an empowered citizenry?

- Should the goal be better decisions, fairer decisions, more consistent decisions, or in the throes of environmental gridlock, any decisions at all?

At different times, each of these definitions could describe risk communication. There are situations in which a transfer of information is enough and the goal of an informed citizenry is sufficient. There are other times when government should aim not just to inform people but to influence their behavior. Issues involving clear health risks, such as lead, radon, or asbestos, typically meet this test. Finally, there are times when risk communication is an essential part of a democratic process, with success defined as effective public participation and empowerment of citizens to affect policy choices.

THE FOUNDATIONS OF RISK COMMUNICATION

Today, risk communication is central to environmental management. Yet as recently as the 1970s, when the principal laws authorizing the national environmental programs were passed, the idea of risk as an organizing concept and metric for comparing problems was missing from the environmental policy lexicon. Thus, it is fair to say that there would have been no such thing as risk communication without the efforts of risk perception researchers over the last twenty years. Their work has built an analytical and empirical foundation for risk communication. It has helped risk communicators understand how to inform people about risk. Moreover, as we just noted, it has supported the growth of risk communication from a narrow process of moving information from experts to the public, to a broader process of debate and participation. In short, risk perception research has helped to make public concerns and judgments legitimate. With this view, we begin by defining the concept of risk and describing its role in environmental policy. We then turn to the field of risk perception and address its significance for the study and practice of environmental risk communication (Cohrssen and Covello, 1989; Glickman and Gough, 1990).

The Concept of Risk in Environmental Policy

Risk may be seen most simply as the possibility of suffering harm. All of us engage everyday in activities that expose us to the possibility of harm. These include crossing a busy intersection, breathing polluted air, eating certain foods, undergoing medical tests (such as X-rays), and playing sports. Moreover, we make intuitive risk-benefit comparisons all the time.

But how do we make these decisions when environmental risks are involved? We need to start by considering two dimensions associated with risk. The first is the *probability* of harm. Of the people who engage in a given activity or who are exposed to a technology or substance, what proportion are likely to suffer harmful effects? The second dimension of risk is the *severity* of harm—its magnitude or significance. Activities that lead to death or irreversible injury are taken far more seriously than those that lead to a minor injury and warrant, at worst, a trip to the emergency room. Thus, risk may be defined as the probability times the severity of harm.

The probability of harm is a fairly straightforward concept. It is usually expressed as the number of adverse effects expected to occur either for every number of exposures or per the total population. For example, the risk of any of us dying in a car accident in the United States in any year is about two in ten thousand. This number does not account for how many trips each of us might make by car, our driving habits, or where we live—all factors that could affect our individual risk. It simply gives an average risk of death that is spread over the entire population.

The EPA estimated in the late 1980s that exposures to radon gas seeping into homes caused between seven thousand and thirty thousand excess cases of lung cancer annually (those beyond what would have been expected without the radon exposures), with fourteen thousand the most likely midpoint estimate (Cole, 1993). Again, these numbers do not distinguish among geological formations, kinds of construction, and occupancy patterns of buildings, or whether people smoke—all of which substantially affect the individual risks of lung cancer. As in the auto example, they give an estimate of the average risk across the population.

Policymakers also distinguish between two broad categories of risk. The first category is the risk of harm to human health—anything from eye irritation caused by air pollution to death due to high levels of exposure to a toxic substance. The object of concern is people and their well-being. Health risk may be described along several dimensions: Are effects acute (immediate) or chronic (long-term)? How serious are they? Are they irreversible? How many and what kinds of people are affected?

The other major category of risk is harm to ecological resources. The possibility of harm to endangered species, impaired visibility in a national park, lost wetland acreage with a consequent loss in biological diversity—all of these are examples of ecological risk. The field of risk communication has developed almost entirely as a means of warning or otherwise interacting with people about health risks. Although there has been initial work on using risk communication in responding to ecological risks, our focus in this chapter is, of necessity, on communication regarding health risks. The field of ecological risk communication is still in its infancy.

Precisely how did environmental risk to humans eventually come to seize a central place on the agenda of policymakers? Tracing its evolution from the 1960s, one finds both technical and political reasons. The technical reason was the emergence of quantitative risk assessment in the 1960s, a development made possible by the growth of operations research and decision analysis during and after World War II. Plough and Krimsky (1990, p. 225) describe it in these terms: "The methods first used in mathematics, economics, and statistics slowly diffused into the social and health sciences and gave rise to a number of hybrid approaches for calculating risks and quantifying decision making. By the late 1960s the decision methodologies brought promise of a systems science that could provide a rational basis for complex policy decisions concerning technological risks."

Coinciding with the evolution of these methodologies was the emergence of the environmental movement and the creation of the EPA, the Occupational Safety and Health Administration, and other environmental health agencies in the 1970s. In addition to technical capability, there was also now a political need to assess and quantify risk. The demand for risk assessment increased in the late 1970s and early 1980s, as government regulators looked for ways to set priorities, establish regulatory standards, and justify policy choices.

One major sign of the importance and maturity of the field of risk assessment was the 1983 publication of the National Academy of Sciences' (NAS) report, *Risk Assessment in the Federal Government: Managing the Process*. The report reviewed risk assessment and its use at several agencies, considered methodological issues, and urged federal agencies to use risk assessment. It also distinguished *risk assessment* (the more neutral scientific process of describing the probability and degree of harm) from *risk management* (the more political, value-based process of deciding when, how, and to what degree to control or reduce health and environmental harm).

The EPA embraced the NAS recommendations and took steps to increase the agency's capacities for risk assessment. Indeed, not only were these recommendations seen as powerful technical tools, but they also gave the EPA a source of potential leverage when fighting with the OMB over budget cuts during the Reagan years. The agency also adopted the distinction between risk assessment and risk management, largely as a way to insulate the technical process of risk assessment from the more political aspects of risk management. Although this distinction is not nearly as clear as it has often been presented (see, for example, Whittemore, 1983), it has served this political purpose quite well to date. Finally, the field of risk communication emerged as the third element in the nation's risk triad, becoming the subject of its own NAS report in 1989.

Perceptions of Risk

As we noted in Chapter Five, one of the most important findings to emerge from the research on risk in the last twenty years is that risk means different things to different people. The early, somewhat awkward attempts at risk communication were based on the assumption that everyone—experts, government officials, and the lay public alike—views environmental risk in similar terms. Public fears about technologies such as nuclear power or genetic engineering were attributed to a lack of knowledge about the sources of risk and about the methods used by technical experts to assess such risks. If only the lay public could be taught to think as rationally as experts, they could be persuaded to accept "safe" technologies.

These views on the "irrationality" of the lay public's evaluations of risk gradually changed through the 1980s, largely due to the work of such researchers as Paul Slovic, Baruch Fischhoff, and Sarah Lichtenstein on the topic of *risk perception.* Working from the perspective of cognitive psychology, they studied attitudes toward risk, the evaluation of different kinds of risk, and the factors that affect evaluations of the acceptability of risk (see Table 7.1). Much of their research focused on psychological factors. But other researchers studied social and cultural influences on risk perceptions as well, factors of critical import to public policymakers. These social and cultural factors helped to explain the differences, first noted in Chapter Six, between the lay public's intuitive evaluations of risk and the formal, quantitative evaluations made by experts (Douglas, 1985; Douglas and Wildavsky, 1982; Fischhoff, Slovic, and Lichtenstein, 1982; Rayner and Cantor, 1987; Slovic, 1987).

For managers, the bottom line on risk perception research as it affects the practice of risk communication is reducible to the following propositions: risk means different things to different people; people tend to ignore or discount discrete, familiar, voluntary, and low-probability risks; feelings of control and opportunities for participation influence evaluations of the acceptability of risk; people evaluate risk as members of a community; and trust is an important influence on risk perceptions.

Table 7.1. Qualitative Factors Affecting Risk Perception and Evaluation.

Factor	Conditions Associated with Increased Public Concern	Conditions Associated with Decreased Public Concern
Catastrophic potential	Fatalities and injuries grouped in time and space	Fatalities and injuries scattered and random
Familiarity	Unfamiliar	Familiar
Understanding	Mechanisms or process not understood	Mechanisms or process understood
Controllability (personal)	Uncontrollable	Controllable
Voluntariness of exposure	Involuntary	Voluntary
Effects on children	Children specifically at risk	Children not specifically at risk
Effects manifestation	Delayed effects	Immediate effects
Effects on future generations	Risk to future generations	No risk to future generations
Victim identity	Identifiable victims	Statistical victims
Dread	Effects dreaded	Effects not dreaded
Trust in institutions	Lack of trust in responsible institutions	Trust in responsible institutions
Media attention	Much media attention	Little media attention
Accident history	Major and sometimes minor accidents	No major or minor accidents
Equity	Inequitable distribution of risks and benefits	Equitable distribution of risks and benefits
Benefits	Unclear benefits	Clear benefits
Reversibility	Effects irreversible	Effects reversible
Origin	Caused by human actions or failures	Caused by acts of nature or God

Source: Covello, V. T., McMallum, D. B., and Pavlova, M. Effective Risk Communication: The Role and Responsibility of Government and Nongovernmental Organizations. New York: Plenum Press, 1989. Used with permission of Plenum Press.

• *Risk means different things to different people.* Expert risk assessments measure only one dimension of risk. Experts rely on formal assessments of risk as a statement of probability times magnitude, with the results stated in measurable terms such as expected fatalities. The lay public thinks more intuitively about risk, on the basis of a more complex set of social and cultural differences.

• *People tend to ignore or discount discrete, familiar, voluntary, and low-probability risks.* Unknown, dreaded, or catastrophic events, and those posing consequences for future generations, inspire higher levels of public concern. People seem to conclude intuitively that the sum of damage spread across society from familiar events poses less of a threat to society than even a small number of unusual or catastrophic events. For instance, the Three Mile Island nuclear accident caused no immediate deaths and perhaps no long-term physical illness, but it had a major effect on public attitudes toward nuclear power due to its "signal potential" (Slovic, 1987, p. 284).

• *Feelings of control and opportunities for participation influence evaluations of the acceptability of risk.* Psychological researchers have concluded that "a generalized expectation of being in control reduces the experience of stress" (Douglas, 1985, p. 34). The American political culture reinforces this psychological tendency, because participation and consent are central values. Regarding themselves as citizens more than as subjects, Americans expect to be able to participate in and consent to decisions that affect them directly. People are especially likely to react negatively to risks that are imposed on them by outside forces over whom or which they lack control.

• *People evaluate risk as members of a community.* Risks are not perceived and evaluated in a state of social and cultural isolation. Research has shown that people react to risk as part of a community, where norms about the acceptability of different kinds of risk "are debated and socially established" (Douglas, 1985, p. 69). The lay public intuitively recognizes what the experts' analyses fail to appreciate: a catastrophic event that affects the very survival of the community (such as a core meltdown at a nuclear power plant) is a far greater risk than a series of discrete events whose consequences may be absorbed by the community as a whole. Included in this notion of community are the effects of risks on future generations.

• *Trust is an important influence on risk perceptions.* People's perceptions of risk cannot be separated from their attitudes toward the social and political institutions that manage those risks. Much of the skepticism the lay public has shown about attempts by public officials and industry to explain and justify risk reflects a distrust of the sources of the risk information (Kasperson, 1986; Slovic, 1993). Environmental managers must face the fact that public confidence in social and political institutions has declined steadily since the 1960s (Lipset and Schneider, 1983, 1987). Trust, moreover, is asymmetrical; it is easier for managers to lose the public trust than to regain it.

THE RISK COMMUNICATION PROCESS

Initial thinking on risk communication focused mostly on what was being communicated—the content of the message. How should technical information be presented? To what extent should graphics or comparisons to other risks be used? As the field developed, however, policymakers and scholars gave more attention to the overall process for communicating risk. Most treatments came to distinguish among four elements in the risk communication process that managers need to understand: the source of the message, the design of the message, the channel for delivering the message, and the target or recipients of the message (Covello, von Winterfeldt, and Slovic, 1987). These four elements provide a framework for managers to understand what is known about the risk communication process.

The Source of the Message

The most common sources of risk communication messages are government agencies and industry. Risk communication is not restricted to these sources, however. As we noted in Chapters Five and Six, environmental advocates, community groups, scientific organizations, and the media play important roles. Government may communicate risk information to fulfill its responsibility to protect public health, to inform the public of an issue that requires action, to stimulate public debate and discussion, or to respond to claims made by other groups. When industry communicates risk information, it may be to respond to public fears, to ensure that it is taking steps to minimize risk, to fulfill a legal mandate, or to advocate particular positions that advance its interests. Community groups often draw attention to a risk in order to mobilize public opinion.

Perceptions of these sources affect public assessments of and reactions to risks. For example, a nonprofit agency with a long-standing and positive relationship with a community will have more credibility than one that is new to the area or that has a record of difficult relations. The perceived competence of a source is also an important factor. The EPA's mistakes in its initial assessments of possible chromosomal damage at the Love Canal hazardous waste site in the late 1970s affected its credibility on that issue (and others). The Department of Energy's false statements about the possible health effects of atomic testing in the 1950s undermined its credibility for decades to come. "One year of being honest with the public is not enough" (National Academy of Sciences, 1989, p. 120). Finally, credibility problems may extend well beyond a particular organization. The steady decline in public confidence in government over the last thirty years has affected the credibility of individual agencies, even though the agencies themselves may have done nothing to earn the public's distrust (Lipset and Schneider, 1983, 1987).

Thus, for managers dealing with environmental concerns, trust is a central issue and a major challenge in risk communication. Where should they focus their attention to build trust? As Roger Kasperson (1986, p. 278) suggests, four kinds of perception affect public trust and confidence in organizations, particularly public organizations: the organization is competent, the organization is unbiased, the organization cares about who it serves, and the organization gives people a fair opportunity to make their views known. It thus seems wise to focus on these perceptions of the organizations that communicate about risk.

The Design of the Message

How best to design risk messages has been one of the central challenges risk communicators have had to face. The challenge is this: How can managers take information based on highly technical, quantitative analyses and put it in a form that is understandable to the lay public? Government and industry, among others, have had to walk a fine line. They need to convey the technical complexity and uncertainty behind their analyses, both as a matter of honesty and to maintain the public's trust. At the same time, they have to present risk information in terms that a typical citizen untrained in toxicology, risk assessment, or statistics may use and act on.

In dealing with this challenge, risk communicators have gone through some painful experiences. In the early years, before they learned many of the practical lessons of risk communication, experts and government officials would go before an audience and present risk information pretty much as they would explain it to each other. Their explanations were full of technical jargon and references that had little meaning to the lay public. They were perceived as cold, uncaring technicians who talked down to people and worried little about people's needs and concerns. Recognizing this problem, the EPA prepared a pamphlet in 1988 that warned risk communicators: "Technical language and jargon are useful as professional shorthand. But they are barriers to successful communication with the public" (U.S. Environmental Protection Agency, 1988).

Still, experts in risk communication formulated the problem in different ways. To some, the problem was the inadequacies in the public's scientific understanding and their inability to think in terms of probabilities or other key aspects of risk. These risk communicators advocated efforts to improve public education in scientific and environmental fields. To other experts, the problem was the limits of technical analysts in conveying information clearly. Their solution was to train government officials and experts to present information effectively before a lay audience. To still others, the problem was a lack of knowledge about how best to convey technical information and uncertainty. For example, should graphs or other visuals be used? Or should environmental risks be compared to other risks that are better known to the public, such as the risks of driving or flying on a commercial airliner?

This last perspective has influenced much risk communication research. Risk professionals typically state their findings in terms of statistical probabilities. They may conclude, for example, that the risk of cancer from exposure to an air pollutant ranges from 4×10^{-4} (four excess cases for every ten thousand people exposed) to 1×10^{-6} (one excess case for every million people exposed). These statements, on their own, lack meaning for most people, so risk assessors have turned to risk comparisons for analogies. For example, a one-in-a-million risk means that in ten cities with a population of 100,000 each, one inhabitant of one city is likely to develop cancer due to exposure.

The EPA's efforts to communicate information about radon exposure in homes illustrate the use of risk comparisons. One widely distributed brochure compares the health effects of each of several average annual radon levels to other, better-known activities that also pose a risk of lung cancer (Cole, 1993, p. 218). For example, according to the brochure, an average annual radon level of four picocuries per liter (the EPA's recommended action level) poses a lung cancer risk comparable to smoking half a pack of cigarettes a day. At an average annual level of ten picocuries, the risk of lung cancer is roughly similar to having five hundred chest X-rays each year. The same listing tried to give a sense of probabilities by listing how many in a community of one hundred exposed people were likely to die from radon at different levels: two out of one hundred at four picocuries, five at ten picocuries, seventeen at forty picocuries, and so on.

A variety of other techniques are available to managers who are trying to enhance the design of risk messages so that they better inform laypersons. For example, they can design messages to frame information or decisions by presenting the same numerical results in different ways. Presenting risk estimates in terms of lives lost rather than lives saved, for example, may influence how people evaluate risks. Appeals to authority ("nine out of ten scientists support this view") and emotion ("children are especially vulnerable to these risks") also affect public reactions to information. Such techniques may help managers to improve public understanding and influence behavior, but they also open the door to manipulation if managers (or stakeholders and the media) use them inappropriately (National Academy of Sciences, 1989, pp. 88–93).

The Delivery Channel

Another element in the risk communication process is the channel used to deliver the message. Early efforts tended to assume that people received information in a state of isolation from other influences. Researchers soon found, however, that the social, political, and cultural contexts in which risk information is conveyed are important (see, for example, Douglas, 1985; Krimsky and Plough, 1988; Rayner and Cantor, 1987; Johnson and Covello, 1987). In turn, this research has several implications for managers involved today in the risk communication process. First, these findings underscore the emphasis in Chapter Six on knowing the community. How are citizens likely to perceive government or industry officials? Who are the opinion leaders in a community? What organizations or people are likely to have credibility in warning people of risks and influencing their behavior in ways that reduce risks? Which of the conventional media do people in the community rely on: mass circulation newspapers, community newsletters, radio, television? What role do schools, religious organizations, and other community groups play in transmitting information and shaping opinion?

Managers also need to tailor the delivery of messages to community characteristics. What may be effective in an affluent, white community in suburban Chicago may be ineffective in a rural, black, Mississippi community. Higher educational levels and socioeconomic status, better access to political elites, greater political power, and easier access to technical experts describe the Chicago community's context for responding to risk messages. Characteristics of the Mississippi community are less formal education, less economic and political power, a distrust of traditional political elites, and a lack of access to independent technical experts.

One lesson that risk communicators have learned in poorer, minority communities is the important role that religious institutions and leaders play in communicating information and influencing public opinion. With health risks such as lead exposure—which affect mostly poor, inner-city, minority children—religious leaders are an essential part of the system for delivering risk messages. Nor can managers ignore their potential for identifying and reacting to environmental justice concerns.

That professionals now take community characteristics seriously is confirmed by a 1994 survey of risk communication researchers and practitioners. One of three topics that participants recommended as a research priority was learning how to communicate with communities of different races, ethnic backgrounds, and incomes (Chess, Salomone, and Hance, 1995; Vaughan, 1995). "Because social and cultural differences may affect how people see both risk and public institutions, symposium participants stressed the importance of developing needs assessment methods that are sufficiently sensitive to the concerns of diverse communities and situations" (Chess, Salomone, Hance, and Saville, 1995, p. 117). Respondents urged that "models and resource materials that help communicators understand diverse cultures . . . [should] be developed and made available to agency practitioners" (p. 122).

The Target or Recipients

As noted previously, early efforts at communicating risk are best described as *expert-centered*. The objective was to convince people of the validity and rationality of the experts' risk assessments. Problems were attributed to the lay public's inadequacies: an inability to understand probabilities, difficulties in comprehending the technical language of risk, unrealistic demands for scientific certainty, unreasonable comparisons of technological to naturally occurring risks, and an unwillingness to change opinions when confronted with new information.

Largely on the basis of the findings of risk perception research, today's risk communicators have adopted a more positive view of laypersons that managers should understand. First, and consonant with the coproduction model of decision making, most risk communicators now see risk communication as a two-way street (National Academy of Sciences, 1989, p. 10). As we noted earlier, the lay public has important information of its own to communicate to agencies, industry, and other risk communicators. Most especially, the public is now viewed more as a source of values and preferences to be consulted than as a problem to be solved. Second, risk communication is now defined more broadly (along the lines of Fischhoff's seventh development stage) as a participatory process, not just as a process of transmitting messages from experts. Indeed, many risk professionals urge moving beyond the two-way street to the image of risk communication as a kind of mixing bowl in which information is exchanged, issues about risks are debated, and the public participates with government officials and technical experts in making decisions (see, for example, Fiorino, 1990c; Kasperson, 1986; Otway, 1987; Reich, 1985; Ruckelshaus, 1985). This would take the coproduction ethic to its ultimate height.

Perceiving the public as partners in decision making transforms risk communication. Not only is it a tool for reducing individual risk (by informing people about risk and influencing their behavior to reduce risk), but it is also a mechanism for enhancing public participation in the political and social processes of making decisions about collective risk. This broader conception of the public as citizens as well as subjects of risk messages is more consistent with the American political culture than the narrow conception of risk communication (Almond and Verba, 1963). Moreover, to the extent that this view leavens trust in their agencies, managers will be advantaged as well.

LESSONS LEARNED

Research on risk perception and communication today has found its way into a myriad of popular outlets, including training courses, brochures, and technical assistance. Indeed, there are more guidelines and lessons in print than we can possibly cover in this chapter. Consequently, this section offers only a sampling of that advice and suggests sources for additional guidance. Although much of this advice is culled from risk perception research, some of it is the product of practical, hard-earned experience with risk communication in the field. Moreover, although written largely from the perspective of environmental regulators, the logic of many of the recommendations offered is useful to regulatory targets as well.

At times these materials express what many would regard as common sense. For example, in 1988, at the peak of the risk communication decade, the EPA published its brochure *Seven Cardinal Rules of Risk Communication.* "Although many of the rules may seem obvious," the introduction states, "they are continually and consistently violated in practice." These rules offer practical and much-needed advice. "Accept and involve the public as a legitimate partner," is the brochure's first rule. It also urges risk communicators to show respect for the public and to "underscore the sincerity of your effort" with early public involvement. Stressed as well is the goal of producing "a public that is involved, interested, reasonable, thoughtful, solution-oriented, and collaborative; [the goal] should not be to diffuse public concerns or replace action."

The second rule urges risk communicators to "plan carefully and evaluate your efforts," to begin with clear objectives such as "providing information to the public, motivating individuals to act, stimulating response to emergencies, or contributing to the resolution of conflict." It stresses, among other things, the need to pretest risk messages, to consider different strategies for different audiences, and to aim the communications at specific subgroups in the target audience.

The third rule in the brochure stresses the need to "listen to the public's specific concerns." Find out what people are thinking, let different parties be heard, and recognize underlying agendas. In an especially useful piece of advice that reflects key findings of the risk perception research, this rule also stresses that people are "often more concerned about such issues as trust, credibility, competence, control, voluntariness, fairness, caring, and compassion, than about mortality statistics and the details of quantitative risk assessment."

Rule five recognizes the importance of understanding the organizational and community contexts for risk communication. It urges risk communicators to "coordinate and collaborate with other credible sources." They can accomplish this by building bridges with key organizations, working through influential intermediaries, and issuing messages jointly with "other trustworthy sources (for example, credible university scientists, physicians, or trusted local officials)."

Rule seven responds to criticism of government risk communication efforts as apparently cold, uncaring, and overly technical. "Speak clearly and with compassion," is the advice. Guidelines reminiscent of those emphasized for media relations in Chapter Five include such core lessons as the following:

- Use simple, nontechnical language.
- Use vivid, concrete images that communicate on a personal level.
- Use examples and anecdotes that make technical data come alive.
- Avoid distant, abstract, unfeeling language about deaths, injuries, and illnesses.
- Acknowledge and respond to fears that people express, such as anxiety, fear, and outrage.
- Use comparisons to put risks in perspective.
- Include a discussion of actions that are under way or that can be taken.
- Tell people what you cannot do.

Rule seven also cautions that no matter "how well you communicate risk information, some people will not be satisfied." It adds, more optimistically, that if "people are sufficiently motivated, they are quite capable of understanding complex risk information, even if they may not agree with you."

Publications such as *Seven Cardinal Rules* provide straightforward yet important advice to risk communicators. Although the critics of these efforts are correct in asserting that the advice often reflects little more than common sense, it is obvious that a lack of common sense plagued many early efforts at risk communication. Moreover, some of the advice may *not* be obvious to people who are highly trained in technical fields. Even today, many experts lack training or experience in explaining technical issues to nonspecialists, in dealing with public fear and frustration, and in representing institutions whose credibility and sometimes competence are doubted by the public.

Two other practical guides for managers are worth mentioning. Although they were published independently, both are available as appendixes in *Effective Risk Communication* (Covello, McMallum, and Pavlova, 1988). Commissioned by the Chemical Manufacturers Association, *Risk Communication, Risk Statistics, and Risk Comparisons* (Covello, Sandman, and Slovic, 1988) offers risk communication advice for plant managers. "A basic assumption of the manual," the authors write in the introduction, "is that risk communication, when done properly, is always better than stonewalling" (p. 1). The guide's five parts cover how to present risk information, guidelines for explaining risk-related numbers and statistics, guidelines for providing and explaining risk comparisons, examples of risk comparisons, and lessons for anticipating objections to explanations of risks. Although prepared for the chemical industry, it is a useful guide for public and nonprofit managers, as well as for community activists interested in viewing risk as industry managers see and explain it.

Relatedly, a second manual aimed at government risk communicators is *Improving Dialogue with Communities: A Risk Communication Manual for Government* (Hance, Chess, and Sandman, 1988). Prepared for the New Jersey Department of Environmental Protection, it too is a practical and accessible guide for government officials who deal with communities that face known environmental risks. The manual is designed to help agencies communicate these risks more effectively, to enable them to understand public perceptions better, and to help them predict community responses to agency actions. It also seeks to increase the effectiveness of decisions by involving concerned publics, improving dialogue, and reducing unwarranted tensions between agencies and communities. It explains risks more effectively and alerts communities to risk in productive ways. What makes *Improving Dialogue* especially useful for managers is that it draws so effectively on the lessons learned by experienced risk communicators. Each chapter includes an introduction explaining the topic, a list of guidelines with explanations that draw on interviews with experienced communicators, and brief responses to commonly asked questions. The sections on explaining environmental risks and comparing environmental risks to other risks are especially valuable.

For managers who want to explore risk communication in more depth than brochures provide, the National Academy of Sciences' aforementioned *Improving Risk Communication* (1989) is an outstanding source. Issued by the Committee on Risk Perception and Communication of the National Research Council, it offers a comprehensive, readable treatment of the field. Fischhoff's appendix, "Risk: A Guide to Controversy," is an excellent overall guide to risk perception and communication from the perspective of a leading researcher. The many sources listed in the references for this appendix provide additional in-depth information on risk perception and communication.

Finally, an explicitly more case-based source of practical advice for managers is the EPA's *Citizen's Guide to Radon,* published first in 1986, followed by a second edition in 1992. Between the release of these editions, the EPA conducted research that vastly improved the 1992 edition of this brochure (Cole, 1993, pp. 226–230). More precisely, the 1992 *Citizen's Guide* urges the following:

- *Be prescriptive as well as informative.* People will be more likely to respond to the radon threat—to test their homes and take corrective action if necessary—if the brochure tells them what they should do rather than just informs them about the possible risk. The 1992 version gives clear, easy-to-follow directions for how to test and when to mitigate through corrective action.

- *Streamline guidelines on testing and mitigation to minimize barriers to public action.* Research shows that too much emphasis on long-term testing and action means that many people do not continue or follow up on their efforts to test and reduce radon levels. The newer version of the radon guide streamlines the testing process in the hope of encouraging more people to follow up (although at the cost of possibly reducing the accuracy and validity of the tests that are conducted).

- *Overcome public denial through the use of persuasive appeals such as concern for the family.* Research finds, as we also recommended for dealing with the media, that people are more likely to act when the risk is presented in terms of the effects on children. Thus, this approach would be more effective than appeals based only on adult effects.

- *Provide an appropriate level of radon information, because too much or too little information may result in an undesired effect.* Presenting homeowners with too much information, researchers find, may allow them to create excuses for inaction. Conversely, giving too little information could place too great a burden on government agencies that would have to respond to requests for more assistance. The 1992 version of the brochure is based on a decision to balance these factors.

- *Personalize the radon threat with tangible, relevant comparisons to familiar risk.* In the revised document, the EPA increases the use of comparisons to risks that are more familiar to people. It provides separate risk charts for smokers and nonsmokers and compares radon to other risks, such as drunk driving, drowning, fires, and airline and auto crashes. The two risk charts are reproduced in Tables 7.2 and 7.3.

- *Stress that radon problems can be corrected, but do not overstate the ease of fixing them.* The new version of the radon guide stresses in practical terms what people can do to reduce radon levels and provides realistic estimates of remediation costs so people can make informed choices.

THE FUTURE OF RISK COMMUNICATION

So what can we say about the future of risk communication? Both its narrow and broad views meet important needs; what matters is knowing when each view is appropriate, being explicit about the objectives,

Table 7.2. EPA Radon Risk Chart: Radon Risk If You Smoke.

Radon Level	If 1,000 people who smoked were exposed to this level over a lifetime ...	The risk of cancer from radon exposure compares to ...	What to do: stop smoking and ...
20 pCi/L	About 135 people could get lung cancer	100 times the risk of drowning	Fix your home
10 pCi/L	About 71 people could get lung cancer	100 times the risk of dying in a home fire	Fix your home
8 pCi/L	About 57 people could get lung cancer		Fix your home
4 pCi/L	About 29 people could get lung cancer	100 times the risk of dying in an airplane crash	Fix your home (consider fixing between 2 & 4 pCi/L
2 pCi/L	About 15 people could get lung cancer	2 times the risk of dying in a car crash	
1.3 pCi/L	About 9 people could get lung cancer	(Average indoor radon level)	(Reducing radon levels below 2 pCi/L is difficult)
0.4 pCi/L	About 3 people could get lung cancer	(Average outdoor radon level)	

Note: If you are a former smoker, your risk may be lower.
Source: U.S. Environmental Protection Agency, 1992.

Table 7.3. EPA Radon Risk Chart: Radon Risk If You've Never Smoked.

Radon Level	If 1,000 people who never smoked were exposed to this level over a lifetime . . .	The risk of cancer from radon exposure compares to . . .	What to do
20 pCi/L	About 8 people could get lung cancer	The risk of being killed in a violent crime	Fix your home
10 pCi/L	About 4 people could get lung cancer		Fix your home
8 pCi/L	About 3 people could get lung cancer	10 times the risk of dying in an airplane crash	Fix your home
4 pCi/L	About 2 people could get lung cancer	The risk of drowning	Fix your home (consider fixing between 2 & 4 pCi/L)
2 pCi/L	About 1 person could get lung cancer	The risk of dying in a home fire	
1.3 pCi/L	Less than 1 person could get lung cancer	(Average indoor radon level)	(Reducing radon levels below 2 pCi/L is difficult)
0.4 pCi/L	Less than 1 person could get lung cancer	(Average outdoor radon level)	

Note: If you are a former smoker, your risk may be higher.
Source: U.S. Environmental Protection Agency, 1992.

and using risk communication responsibly in varied situations. Thus we conclude this chapter with a brief assessment of risk communication in light of these objectives.

Risk Communication as a Policy Instrument

In Chapter Twelve we explore more robustly the range of policy tools open to environmental policymakers. It suffices presently to note that one leading analysis of policy instruments identifies three different approaches: "carrots, sticks, and sermons" (Bemelmans-Videc, Rist, and Vedung, 1997). *Carrots* offer economic inducements, through subsidies, tax benefits, or other economic incentives. *Sticks* rely on a strategy of regulation, in which the state issues binding rules, and noncompliers are subject to sanctions. *Sermons* use information to persuade people to act in a desired way.

As we have repeatedly noted, among the three strategies, environmental policymakers have drawn largely on sticks, emphasizing command-and-control regulation (see, for example, Bardach and Kagan, 1982). Carrots have been less prominent, although strategies based on market incentives have expanded recently. Meanwhile, although sermons are one of the oldest policy instruments, they have until recently drawn less attention in the field. As the growing importance of risk communication demonstrates, however, the centrality to regulators of the latter is increasingly apparent and likely to rise.

At times risk communication will be the primary strategy, as it has been in the radon case. At other times it will provide an important complement to regulatory, economic incentive, or other strategies. Here the case of lead is illustrative. Federal and state governments have implemented a number of regulatory actions regarding lead, including banning it in gasoline, tightening drinking water standards, and requiring site cleanup wherever it is present. In addition, however, government agencies have provided information on possible lead risks, especially those to children, and advised people of ways to reduce their risks from exposure (see, for example, U.S. Environmental Protection Agency, 1991). Similarly, for problems that are widely dispersed or that occur in people's homes (such as radon), a regulatory strategy is, respectively, too expensive and too intrusive. A strategy based on warnings to people of potential risk and suggestions for when and how to take corrective action is eminently more practical and appropriate.

As we also noted in prior chapters, community right-to-know laws in several states during the 1980s and the federal Emergency Planning and Community Right-to-Know Act in 1986 also have used information effectively as a policy tool. In addition to requiring government to provide risk information directly to the public, such laws now require polluters to provide risk information to citizens as well. As Susan Hadden (1989a) has noted, these laws have "occasioned groundswells of interest" in risk communication by all affected parties. "Industry representatives were especially concerned about the effect that data about large-scale emissions would have without complementary information about exposure on actual health effects" (p. 145). In sum, the study of risk communication is a necessary part of government's efforts to inform people about risk, to set priorities for allocating scarce resources in cost-effective ways, and to influence polluters and citizens to change their risky behaviors.

Risk Communication as an Element in Public Participation

Whatever its value as a regulatory approach for reducing individual risk, risk communication also has a normative value: it supports public participation in collective decision making by both regulators and regulatees. Indeed, participants from both communities in a 1994 national symposium on risk communication called for "new models for public participation, evaluations of the strengths and limitations of existing models, and development of a typology of approaches" (Chess, Salomone, Hance, and Saville, 1995, p. 117).

Thus, for all intents and purposes, the study of risk communication and public participation have converged—and will continue to do so in the future—in a symbiotic relationship. As Fiorino has noted elsewhere, "Clearly, if people are going to take part in decisions about risk, they need information on issues, positions, and choices. [And to] the extent that risk communication research is directed toward participation in policy deliberations, it can contribute to citizen participation" (Fiorino, 1989, p. 515). Risk communication thus may help solve a larger dilemma in American society—the need for better mechanisms for citizen participation in government decisions.

For decades, research by political scientists has documented the value that the American political culture places on participation, consent, and fairness (see, for example, Almond and Verba, 1963). We are entering what perhaps is a new era in environmental management, one in which communication and interaction (Glasbergen, 1996) will play more important roles in the policy process. Risk communication provides a valuable set of tools, methods, and experiences to heighten the quality of participation for all involved.

Risk Communication as Technically Superior

We bring this discussion to a close on an unabashedly assertive note: without a doubt, environmental management is far better off with the study of risk communication than it is without it. Environmental risk presents modern society, its leaders, and its managers with many choices, most of which involve technical information and scientific uncertainty. To present this information competently yet sympathetically, to engage the public in responsible debates about risk, and to appreciate the basis for public concern and the limits as well as the strengths of technical analysis requires an understanding of risk perception and communication. This is the front line of environmental management, and it is no place for amateurs.

Perhaps Fischhoff (1995, p. 144) made the best case yet for risk communication when he wrote a few years ago

> Risk communication has to be taken seriously. One cannot rely on undisciplined speculation about the beliefs or motivations of other people. One cannot expect to quiet a raging controversy with a few hastily prepared messages. One cannot assume that expensively produced communications will work without technically competent evaluations. Those who ignore these issues may be the problem, as much as the risk is. The price of their ignorance is borne by everyone concerned. The public is demeaned by the experts as being hysterical, while the experts are vilified as being evil.

CONCLUSION

As we argued in Chapter Six, inculcating a strong environmental ethic in organizations requires personnel to work actively, effectively, and strategically with a variety of community stakeholders with diverse interests. This in turn requires effective two-way communication, with the ideal product being a coproduction environmental ethic stressing expertise-based solutions to mutually defined problems. Complicating the success of these efforts while taxing the patience of managers who are implementing them, however, is a persistent gap between how scientists and citizens perceive risk to public health and the environment.

The field of risk communication offers valuable lessons and tools for managers dealing with environmental issues. It first emerged as a way to communicate technical information to the lay public about environmental risk, often with the less than laudable goal of minimizing public concerns. Since then, it has matured into a field of research and practice involving not only the communication of information about risk among government, industry, experts, and the public, but also the larger process of making collective decisions about societal risk. Research on risk perception was an essential part of this maturing and broadening of the field, and it provides the analytical foundation for the practice of risk communication today. Managers dealing in any role with environmental management issues may benefit from the study of risk communication. This is especially true if they interact in their communities with the various stakeholders and publics reviewed in Chapter Six.

Thus, without question the increasing emphasis within environmental policy and management on consultation, partnerships, and interaction makes risk communication knowledge and skills important commodities for managers in the years to come. Indeed, adapting to tomorrow's dynamic environmental challenges requires managers who are trying to cope with any conflicts posed by these issues to persistently hone these talents. Evidence, argument, and persuasion are the key constants facing today's and tomorrow's public, nonprofit, and for-profit managers. Importantly, however, an emerging alternative to traditional venues for resolving any conflicts that do emerge over environmental and natural resource management involves alternative dispute resolution techniques. Known by advocates as environmental dispute resolution, this technique's origins and logic, its strengths and weaknesses, and its dos and don'ts are the topics of Chapter Eight.

8

RESOLVING ENVIRONMENTAL DISPUTES

We must work to usher in a new era in the history
of the environment . . . by the resolve to listen and
to work out our differences.

—William K. Reilly, former EPA administrator[1]

The eminent political scientist Harold Lasswell (1958) once defined politics as a process of deciding "who gets what, when, how." This definition fits environmental politics as well as any. Whatever notions we have about a convergence of interests under the goal of sustainability in the long run, in the short run environmental politics is a process of deciding who gets what, when, and how. As such, it has social and economic consequences that inevitably involve political conflict.

Consider how these competing interests and values manifest themselves in concrete situations:

- A local government needs additional space for its municipal landfill, but the community around the landfill objects because of the added traffic, noise, odors, and adverse effects on property values.

- People who want to preserve a wetland for its aesthetic and resource value oppose a developer proposing to build a shopping mall that would destroy part of it.

- The owners of a smelting operation want to continue to operate, but cannot afford the latest emission control technology; this sparks a dispute between those who want jobs and those who fear the health effects of continued emissions.

- A public or nonprofit agency that uses toxics faces community demands for closer regulatory oversight; the agency resists because it worries about the need to protect confidential data.

- Some people in a community feel that oil and other resources exist to improve human material well being and thus favor their development; others fear the catastrophic effects of an oil spill on local ecosystems.

As we have noted throughout this book, controversies like these have traditionally been resolved through formal adversarial processes. More precisely, parties to a controversy often turn to the courts or to the legislature in the hope of resolving a dispute in their favor. At the other extreme, parties may press their issues outside the formal political process through demonstrations, boycotts, or other direct action. Because both sets of alternatives have their costs for managers, in previous chapters we have offered ways to ameliorate those costs (for example, by developing a coproduction environmental ethic and better community relations). But sometimes conflicts are unavoidable and get out of hand. Thus our concern in this chapter is with another path, one in which parties who have reached a stalemate do not go to court. Instead, they try to resolve their differences through negotiation and mediation, an approach known as alternative dispute resolution (ADR). Because our focus is on the use of ADR to resolve environmental conflicts, we call this approach environmental dispute resolution (EDR).

ENVIRONMENTAL DISPUTE RESOLUTION DEFINED

EDR consists of a set of techniques, processes, and roles that enable parties to a dispute to reach agreement with the help of a neutral third party known as a mediator. Importantly, these mediation techniques of EDR have been used successfully in cases related to the use and management of natural resources, the siting of industrial and other large facilities, land use, pollution control, and other related issues (Bacow and Wheeler, 1984; Susskind and Weinstein, 1980–81). Still, writers discussing EDR have offered many definitions for it over the years.

In their book on community organizations and environmental disputes, James Crowfoot and Julia Wondolleck (1990, p. 19) propose three characteristics of an EDR process: "voluntary participation by the parties involved in the dispute; . . . direct or 'face-to-face' group interaction among the representatives of these parties; and . . . mutual agreement or consensus decisions among the parties on the process to be used and any settlement that may emerge." In her analysis of the first decade of experience with EDR, Gail Bingham (1986, p. 5) uses EDR "to refer collectively to a variety of approaches that allow the parties to meet face to face in an effort to reach a mutually acceptable resolution of the issues in a dispute or potentially controversial situation." Although there are differences among the various EDR approaches, she adds, "all are voluntary processes that involve some form of consensus building, joint problem solving, or negotiation" (p. 5).

George Cormick and Leah Patton (1980), who mediated two early EDR processes (the Snoqualmie and I–90 disputes in Washington state, discussed later in this chapter), offer an "operational" definition of EDR. They define mediation as "a voluntary process in which those involved in a dispute jointly explore and reconcile their differences." The mediator "has no authority to impose settlement." The mediator's strength "lies in the ability to assist the parties in resolving their own differences." The test at the end is agreement: "The mediated dispute is settled when the parties themselves reach what they consider to be a workable solution" (p. 78). Cormick and Patton's definition corresponds with the key elements of the Crowfoot and Wondolleck and Bingham definitions: voluntary involvement of the parties; joint, face-to-face interactions and negotiations among the parties; and consent of the parties as the essential conditions for settling the dispute.

Based on these views of EDR, we define it as follows:

• *The parties must agree to participate in the EDR process.* Participation is voluntary. The parties to the dispute must have concluded that their chances of achieving an acceptable outcome with EDR are better than with litigation or any other route. If participation is involuntary, it is not EDR.

• *The parties or their representatives participate directly.* If the parties to a dispute are to maintain control over the result, they must be able to participate in the process. They may participate directly, or they may organize to select someone else on their behalf. If they are excluded from the discussions, it is not EDR. And except for subcommittees or one-on-one negotiations on some issues, it is also not EDR if they are represented by someone they did not select.

- *The third-party mediator has no independent, formal authority to impose an outcome.* The role of the mediator is to help the parties reach agreement. His authority derives from the willingness of the parties to participate and agree to an outcome. If the mediator has the legal authority to impose a result on the parties without their consent, it is not EDR.
- *The parties must be able to agree on the outcome.* The consent of the affected parties is the final test of success for an EDR process. The objective of the process is to reach agreement on a decision or recommendation. If parties can be compelled to support an outcome that is favored by some but not by all (as they might be in a judicial proceeding), it is not EDR.
- *Any participant may withdraw and seek resolution through a more formal process.* A corollary of the parties' rights to consent to an outcome are their rights to withdraw from the process and seek to resolve the dispute in another forum, such as the courts. EDR is not so much an alternative to traditional conflict resolution as it is a complement.

In sum, managers need to understand that EDR attempts to resolve a dispute or potentially controversial situation by using an impartial, third-party mediator before formal legal or political alternatives are pursued. We discuss different forms of EDR in a later section of this chapter. First, however, we must consider two important questions: What are the sources of environmental conflict that make EDR an attractive dispute resolution alternative? and Why has there been such interest in EDR in the last twenty-five years?

THE SOURCES OF ENVIRONMENTAL CONFLICT

There have generally been two views about the conflicts that create a need for EDR. From one perspective, environmental conflicts are the product more of psychological and social factors than of underlying conflicts in values or interests. The goal of the EDR process (and the task of the mediator) is to overcome the heated emotions, historical distrust, negative stereotyping, and traditional biases of the parties that we noted in Chapters Five and Six. Once the parties understand each other's point of view, see one another as people trying to solve a problem, and work through their traditional hostilities and distrust of the others, they will be able to resolve their differences. Thus, in this view conflict is more a result of perceptions of the parties than of any objective differences they need to overcome.

The other view, however, is that environmental conflicts are more a product of disagreements over values, interests, or facts than a product of psychological or social factors. Although social and psychological factors may increase the level of hostility, cloud the underlying basis for the dispute, and make agreement difficult to achieve, they are not the primary cause of conflict. In this view, environmental disputes arise from different views of the world, contrasting expectations about who wins and who loses, and factual uncertainties behind the dispute. Thus, the mediator's task is more to accommodate values and reconcile interests than to overcome social and emotional barriers among the parties.

This chapter is based more on the second view than on the first. Although psychological and social perceptions are important in nearly any environmental dispute and need to be addressed by the mediator and the group as a whole, most environmental disputes derive from more than just misunderstandings or emotional biases. Therefore we focus on those disputes in which somebody gains and somebody else loses, or in which differing visions of the future conflict. Certainly there is much for managers to learn from books that focus primarily on the psychological and social sources of conflict and how best to overcome them (for example, Maser, 1996). After all, these factors are important in any dispute settlement process. But the reality is that most environmental disputes that managers face reflect natural and inevitable conflicts in modern society (see Amy, 1987), conflicts that EDR can, and must, resolve in order to be effective.

Taking this perspective, we find that environmental conflicts are traceable to three sources, each of which may be present in a complex dispute. The first source is *differences in values and worldviews*. Crowfoot and Wondolleck (1990) describe these differences nicely: "Some individuals perceive an intrinsic value in things that are wild and natural while others do not. Some see a societal obligation to protect species and preserve habitat while others do not. Some place priority on maintaining biological diversity and environmental integrity for future generations while others place priority on harnessing nature's resources to service the needs of today's society" (pp. 6–7). Several studies over the years (such as Inglehart, 1977; Dunlap, 1989; Milbrath, 1984) have empirically corroborated these findings by documenting differences in worldviews and values that shape attitudes on environmental choices. (For a summary of opposing views on the malleability of these attitudes, see Gabel, 1998.)

The second source of environmental disputes is *conflicting interests*. Questions of who gets what, when, and how are at the core of most disputes; hence our earlier insistence that managers should engage in extensive and strategic stakeholder analyses under the conditions identified by Thomas (1995). Who are the likely winners and losers? The waste management company that wants to build an incinerator in a community may face opposition from residents who fear declines in property values and a disruption of their serenity. The interests of a public advocacy group that advocates a ban on a chemical because of its possible health effects will conflict with those of the for-profit, public, and nonprofit agencies that manufacture or use the chemical. To be sure, these disputes can also reflect differences in values held by different groups, but there are usually material stakes at risk as well.

A third source of environmental disputes is the technical *uncertainty* that surrounds various courses of action. As we noted in Chapters One and Six, many environmental issues are contentious because they raise issues at the boundaries of scientific knowledge (Ozawa, 1991). Policymakers and experts simply do not know in many cases what the risks of various courses of action will be. For a pollutant such as dioxin, for example, which is released from municipal waste incinerators and many kinds of industrial and agency operations, competing experts hold different points of view. Even the official U.S. government position on the risks of dioxin has changed over the years. Thus, although debates over scientific issues reflect underlying value differences and interest conflicts, scientific uncertainties contribute an independent dimension to many disputes as well.

Is the conflict produced by these factors necessarily a bad thing? To the contrary. As Michael Hamilton (1991) avers, conflict "is a necessary condition in a pluralistic democratic society, serving [as it does] as an instrument of social integration and economic change" (p. 166). As we suggested in Chapter Six, managers should understand the benefits that accrue from early and meaningful participation of diverse stakeholders pursuing their competing interests in organizational decision-making processes. Moreover, the environmental movement itself, and the shift in public values that supported the proliferation of national environmental laws in the 1970s and 1980s, were themselves the product of conflict among elements in American society. Consequently, not only is some degree of conflict inevitable, it is how a complex society evolves. What EDR offers, however, is help in trying to keep these conflicts manageable, proportionate, and ultimately resolvable through creative solutions.

THE RISE OF EDR

"Don't litigate, mediate" has been one of the slogans of environmental politics in the United States over the last twenty years. This has occurred as the downsides of the adversarial legalism we discussed in Chapter Six have grown patently more obvious. Frustrated with the costs, delay, and feelings of loss of control that often accompany litigation, many people in both the regulatory and regulated communities have turned to mediation and negotiation to resolve environmental policy disputes. Proponents of EDR have seen it as a faster, less costly, more accessible, and more certain way than lawsuits to resolve their disputes (Folberg and Taylor, 1984).

As we noted earlier, a principal frustration with litigation is *delay*. Litigation is a highly structured process designed to protect individual rights through elaborate procedural guarantees. What the lay public views as technicalities of legal proceedings are in fact a series of safeguards against abuse, oversights, or factual errors. But safeguards or not, the picture that Charles Dickens paints in his novel *Bleak House,* of complex litigation that stretches on endlessly, is the image most people have of litigation.

Another perceived weakness of litigation that we have discussed is its *costs*—financial, administrative, and image. One obvious reason for financial and administrative expenses is the length and complexity of legal proceedings. Another is the need for access to professional expertise. Litigation requires lawyers who charge substantial fees. At the same time, preparing for and conducting a trial often requires not only legal expertise but various kinds of costly in-house or contracted scientific and technical expertise as well. Concomitantly, administrative uncertainties about outcomes increase, as do public perceptions that defendants are bad actors. As these costs have mounted, regulators, regulatory targets, and other critics of litigation have sought a way to reduce them dramatically.

Finally, once parties turn to the courts to resolve a dispute, they experience a major *loss of control* over the outcome. Indeed, a judge or jury—not the parties—determines their fate. Of course, the litigants can decide to withdraw from the judicial process and settle the dispute by negotiation, but this simply strengthens the arguments in favor of EDR. Why not design a process in which the parties set out from the start to resolve issues to their mutual satisfaction?

If these problems are not enough, court cases also may not resolve the issues involved (Kagan, 1995). Yes, litigation is a way of forcing a decision from an authoritative third party. However, managers must understand that it is not necessarily a way of resolving issues that divide the parties. Judges, for example, may not rule on the issues at stake; indeed, they may remand them for reexamination by the parties involved. Alternatively, judges may render decisions that appear to settle the issues for the moment. But the dispute may continue in another forum, if any of the parties continue the fray in the legislature, appeal to administrative authority, or file additional litigation. Thus, proponents of EDR see it as a way of truly resolving issues at the root of the disputes among parties.

Critics of environmental litigation have not had to look far for a way to adapt to what has become an untenable legal quagmire. The techniques of alternative dispute resolution (ADR) had already been applied with success to other areas of social and political conflict in the 1960s and 1970s. Indeed, this approach itself arose in such areas as family law, landlord-tenant disputes, commercial disagreements, consumer issues, and labor-management conflicts (Administrative Conference of the United States, 1987; Mills, 1991).

Folberg and Taylor (1984) make the case for EDR comprehensively, yet succinctly: "Mediation can provide conflict resolution for environmental disputes far less expensively, in terms of time and money, than can litigation. Moreover, it can provide all participants a greater sense of satisfaction because of their active role. It allows the participants to maintain a degree of control. It allows the consideration of more creative environmental options than does litigation. Most important, mediation promotes cooperation" (p. 220).

The discussion in this chapter reflects this view of ADR. We think that when they are well-designed and used appropriately, ADR methods and processes offer not only an effective means of resolving disputes, but also a way to improve relationships and build a better foundation for problem-solving. We should point out, however, that our conclusions about the advantages and disadvantages of ADR when applied to environmental disputes are based on the experiences of mediators and participants, as revealed largely through case studies. As O'Leary (1995) found in her review of the literature on environmental dispute resolution, there is little systematic, empirical research on its benefits and weaknesses. Managers should pay careful attention to the circumstances and the relationships among parties in determining whether or not ADR is appropriate for a specific dispute.

The first generally recognized application of EDR to a major environmental controversy occurred in 1973. In that instance, the Governor of

Washington asked two professional mediators to help resolve a dispute over a proposed flood control dam on the Snoqualmie River. Gail Bingham (1986, p. 14) notes that this dispute "contained two elements essential to mediation attempts—the issues were seemingly intractable, and the parties were willing to try something new."

The same mediation team was asked a few years later to help resolve a long-standing dispute over the widening of an interstate highway into Seattle (a case considered in more detail shortly). The parties eventually reached an agreement that was implemented over the next several years (Cormick and Patton, 1980). Importantly, these initial applications of EDR laid the groundwork for its use in other situations. Supported by foundations (such as Ford and Hewlitt), and fueled by growth in the dispute settlement professions, EDR expanded rapidly in the late 1970s and 1980s. More precisely, from a few cases in 1975–76, its use soared to thirty-five cases in 1984 alone (Bingham, 1986, p. 29).

What types of disputes was EDR used to resolve? In her 1986 assessment of the state of EDR, Bingham profiled more than 160 cases of environmental dispute resolution. The issues in these disputes fell into six categories. Well over half (eighty-six cases) involved disputes of *land use,* such as commercial development, housing, facility siting, and transportation. Another thirty-three involved *natural resource use or management* issues—for example, fisheries, timber, and mining. Of the remaining disputes, seventeen dealt with *water resources* issues (such as water quality, flood protection, and water use), thirteen involved *energy* issues (such as the siting of small-scale hydroelectric plants and geothermal development), thirteen dealt with *air quality* issues (such as odor, acid rain, and local air pollution), and the remaining six involved *toxics* (such as chemical regulation, asbestos removal, and waste cleanup policies).

Among these cases, about three-fourths were what Bingham calls *site-specific* disputes; the remainder were considered *policy-level* disputes. A dispute was considered site-specific "if it concerned a specific natural resource such as a river, lake, or island or a site that was defined by its proposed use" (p. 10). A policy-level dispute was one in which "the area affected was designated by political boundaries, such as a city, county, state, or the nation as a whole, or if it involved a type of natural resource that occurs in many locations, such as all rivers" (p. 10). This is an important distinction, as we shall see later when we offer a framework for classifying applications of EDR.

Presently, however, it suffices to note that site-specific disputes turn on a particular geographical location and situation and begin as disputes among specific parties. The outcome of the EDR process is typically limited to that site, situation, and set of facts. In contrast, the outcomes of EDR processes in policy-level disputes apply more generally to similar situations across a political jurisdiction. Moreover, they are prospective in their orientation, in that they usually define a framework for resolving future disputes. Unlike site-specific disputes, policy-level disputes do not begin as disagreements among specific parties. Instead, they "are shaped gradually as public concern brings issues to the attention of policy makers or scientists[,] or as policy makers and scientists themselves raise issues" (Bingham, 1986, p. 77).

By the early 1980s, successes with EDR in resolving site-specific disputes hiked people's interest in applying its methods, techniques, and roles to broader policy controversies. Instead of allowing a dispute to fester and reach an impasse, at which point the disputing parties might decide to seek the assistance of a mediator, why not bring the mediator into the process at an early stage, with the goal of developing general policy frameworks for resolving future disputes?

Since then, efforts to apply EDR to policy-level issues have taken two principal forms. One is federal agency efforts to apply EDR to the administrative rulemaking process, in what generally has been termed *regulatory negotiation* or *negotiated rulemaking* (Harter, 1982; Perritt, 1986). Instead of issuing a rule that the parties will challenge later with a lawsuit, the reasoning went, why not bring them together early in the process of developing the rule so that they might reach agreement before it is issued? Thus, the interest in regulatory negotiation is driven by the same impulse that stimulated earlier interest in EDR: the desire to bring people together in face-to-face discussions to agree on an outcome (Fiorino, 1988). The outcome in this instance, however, is a proposed regulation that the parties agree to comply with later. Note, however, that although the term negotiation is used, there is a third party mediating the process.

The second way in which EDR is applied to policy-level disputes is less to resolve them than to narrow the range of disagreement, clarify positions, generate new options, or generally to inform policymakers. Referred to as *policy dialogues, policy forums,* or *consensus-based dialogues,* these applications convene a broad range of interests—government, industry, advocacy groups, academic experts, trade associations, local activists—in an effort to agree on principles or make recommendations to policymakers. These dialogues or forums, which have grown in number in recent years, are now seen as valuable variations of EDR processes. Federal agencies such as the Environmental Protection

Agency and the Department of the Interior, as well as many of their state-level counterparts, frequently use these dialogues to set out areas of consensus and reduce conflict.

Positive experiences with EDR stimulated efforts to institutionalize it in the 1980s through statutes and administrative procedures. Among the first states to pass statutes authorizing EDR were Massachusetts, Rhode Island, Texas, Virginia, and Wisconsin. They required applicants for solid or hazardous waste siting permits to negotiate an agreement with the affected communities (Bingham, 1986, pp. 51–52). Meanwhile, at the federal level, Congress passed the Negotiated Rulemaking Act of 1990. It encouraged federal agencies to use negotiation in their rulemaking processes and formalized many of the practices that EPA and other agencies had adopted. Several states have since used this regulatory negotiation model as well (Administrative Conference of the United States, 1995, pp. 369–374).

FORMS OF EDR

Although EDR has built on experience with alternative dispute resolution processes that had been developed in other policy areas, it differs in many important respects from these applications. The contrasts are especially visible in labor-management disputes, in which many ADR methods and techniques were pioneered and many dispute-resolution professionals cut their teeth (Cormick and Patton, 1980). For example, labor-management disputes typically involve two parties of roughly equal status and power in a highly institutionalized process (in law and practice), with issues such as pay and benefits the resolutions of which are reversible. In contrast, managers will find that environmental disputes typically involve several parties of varying status and power, ranging from state or national government representatives to major corporations to local citizen groups made up of volunteers. Also, the outcomes in many EDR disputes (survival of a species, preservation of an old-growth forest, introduction of genetically engineered materials) may prove to be irreversible, with long-term effects on future generations.

EDR approaches not only differ substantially from their predecessors, however. They also vary in focus among themselves. Consequently, we think that managers would do well to understand EDR applications as differing along two dimensions: their *scope* and their *objectives*. The former dimension refers to a concept we discussed earlier: *the scope of the dispute.* Is the dispute limited to a particular resource, location, or situation (is it site-specific)? Or does it apply more generally to a class of resources, locations, or situations (policy-level) within a political jurisdiction?

Recall that in site-specific disputes the relevant interests usually are easily identifiable, the parties typically have reached an impasse, and the pressures to resolve issues force the parties to seek the services of a third party. In policy-level disputes, the parties anticipate future differences among interests and attempt to establish a policy framework for resolving them. The resolution applies generally to future disputes. Put differently, site-specific dispute resolution resembles the judicial process (resolution of a concrete dispute among specific parties), whereas policy-level dispute resolution is more akin to the legislative process (resolution of general issues in anticipation of future disputes).

The second dimension of classifying EDR applications relates to their principal *objective*. As we noted earlier, sometimes the objective is to *reach a formal decision* that will be implemented. The key in these instances is whether any of the parties at the table have the legal and political authority to make and implement the decision. If they do, participants can make a binding decision. At other times, however, everyone understands that the authoritative decision makers are not part of the process. In these instances, their objective is to *make a recommendation* to decision makers. Recall, again, that the intention in these cases is less to resolve issues than to shape them in some way by narrowing differences among the parties, building a shared understanding of issues, and clarifying areas of agreement and disagreement.

How often, and with what significance, are these different types of EDR used in practice? In the cases of EDR she analyzed, Bingham (1986, p. 77) found a relationship between the scope of the dispute and the objective of the dispute resolution process. In 56 percent of the site-specific cases, the objective was to reach a formal decision. This was the objective in only 9 percent of the policy-level cases. The latter is, of course, not surprising. Policy-level dispute resolution addresses issues that are still taking form; it involves identifiable interests but less easily identifiable parties; and it aims more to narrow than resolve a dispute. Consequently, the objective is usually more limited than it is in cases of site-specific disputes.

Certainly there are many other ways for managers to differentiate among EDR applications: according to the parties to the dispute, the role of the third-party mediator (or even whether a third party is involved), the levels of government involved, the kinds of issues raised (such as whether they pose scientific or technical issues), the time constraints that the parties face (such as a legislative or court deadline for agreement), or the number of parties involved (O'Leary, 1995). Each of these distinctions is important. But we feel that the scope of the dispute and the stated objective of the process are the most useful ways for managers to classify, compare, and develop strategies for using EDR applications.

Figure 8.1 presents the interaction patterns of the two dimensions, with examples of EDR applications in each dimension. In the upper left quadrant of the figure are cases in which the parties attempt to resolve site-specific disputes with the objective of reaching a formal decision. Many of the better-known cases of EDR fall into this category, including three early, relatively successful applications: the previously mentioned Snoqualmie dispute in Washington State, the Storm King controversy on the Hudson River in New York, and the I-90 highway dispute in the Seattle area. In the lower left quadrant are cases in which the parties seek to make a formal decision on a policy-level rather than site-specific dispute. Federal agency efforts with regulatory negotiation are a good example. Disputes are policy level, with the parties trying to resolve general issues and establish a policy for settling future controversies.

On the right side of the figure are disputes in which the parties are trying to make a recommendation to decision makers, not reach agreement on a formal decision. The reason could be that the interests with

Figure 8.1. Classifying EDR Applications.

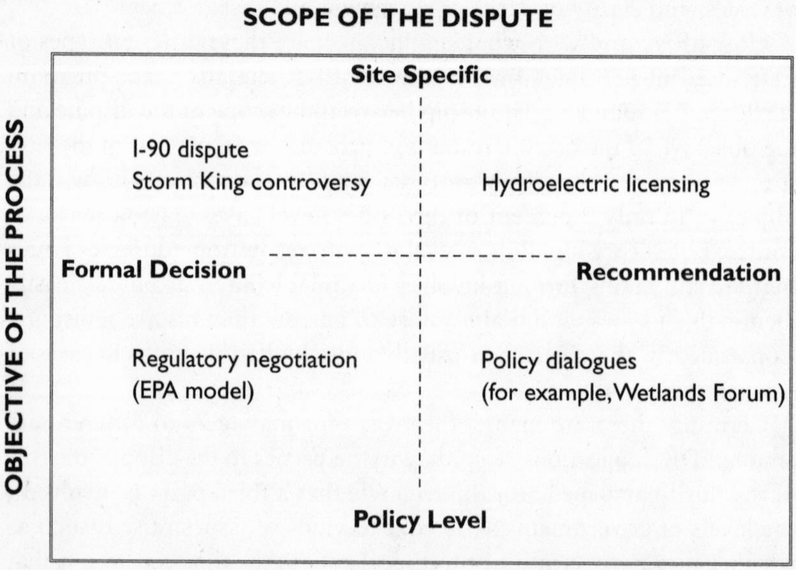

SCOPE OF THE DISPUTE

the power to make and implement a decision are not at the table. In this instance, the purpose of the consensus process might be to influence decision makers. Or the issues could be such that even if the decision-making body is represented at the table, the parties see a need to clarify issues, develop new options, or narrow the differences in order to influence a later decision.

The upper right quadrant represents situations in which parties offer these recommendations in a site-specific dispute. An illustration is the use of mediators to recommend actions on small-scale hydroelectric licensing to the Federal Energy Regulatory Commission. The lower right quadrant includes such policy dialogues as the Wetlands Forum, convened for the EPA by the Conservation Foundation in the 1980s to achieve consensus among diverse recommendations for a national wetlands policy. The membership included three governors, state legislators and agency directors, environmental groups (such as the National Audubon Society and the Nature Conservancy), businesses (such as ARCO and Weyerhauser), farmers and ranchers, and academic experts. The stated objective was not to agree on a national wetlands policy that would be binding on all the participants; that was beyond the scope of the discussions and beyond the ability of the parties to implement. Rather, the objective was to discover common ground among disparate interests, to clarify areas of dispute, to generate options, and to narrow the range of disagreement in the hope of promoting a consensus on wetlands issues.

To this end, the group reached a consensus on the interim goal of "no net loss of the nation's remaining wetlands base" and on the long-term goal of increasing "the quantity and quality of the nation's wetland resource base" (Conservation Foundation, 1988, p. 3). At times, regulatory negotiation fits this type of dispute as well. In negotiations that the Occupational Safety and Health Administration (OSHA) held in the 1980s, for example, it chose (unlike the EPA) not to participate as a party-at-interest. It allowed the other parties to negotiate a proposal that they then recommended to OSHA for consideration (Susskind and MacMahon, 1985).

Another variant in this quadrant is the use of policy dialogues to resolve broad technical issues. For example, in the early 1990s, the EPA asked Resolve (a Washington, D.C., mediation group formerly affiliated with the World Wildlife Fund) to convene a dialogue recommending revisions in the tests used to evaluate pesticides for their effects on aquatic life. The Aquatic Effects Dialogue Group (AEDG) met monthly over a sixteen-month period. Its membership included (in addition to the mediator) technical experts from the EPA, the Fish and Wildlife Service, the Department of Agriculture, pesticide manufacturers, testing labs, universities, and environmental groups. The AEDG addressed four issues: the adequacy of current aquatic testing tiers, methods for modeling and estimating environmental concentrations, methodology and design of mesocosm (natural water bodies, such as ponds, used to conduct tests), and issues of interpreting and extrapolating from mesocosm studies. The group came up with a list of fifteen implementation activities for the EPA, industry, and other regulatory targets (Resolve, 1992).

HOW EDR WORKS IN PRACTICE

To see how EDR works in practice, we turn next to in-depth case studies of two heralded applications of the process. The first case examines an early site-specific dispute, involving the construction of I–90 into Seattle from its eastern suburbs. The objective of the process was to make a decision that was binding on the parties—an objective that was achieved. The second case is the EPA's use of regulatory negotiations. This case also illustrates the use of EDR to make a binding decision, but in policy-level rather than site-specific disputes.

Making Formal Decisions on Site-Specific Disputes: The I–90 Mediation in Seattle

The I–90 dispute began with a proposal in 1964 to build a ten-lane freeway and bridge to connect I–405 in Bellevue (east of Seattle) with north-south I–5 in Seattle. The seven-mile I–90 freeway was designed to remedy traffic congestion on a bridge over Lake Washington, across Mercer Island, and into eastern Seattle. The communities most affected by the congestion, and the strongest supporters of the new freeway, were the residents of Bellevue and Mercer Island who had to make the daily commute along the current road. In the original proposal, a new ten-lane bridge would replace the bridge then in use; the old bridge would be reserved for Mercer Island vehicles.

The principal opposition to I–90 came from residents of eastern Seattle where the new freeway would enter the city and connect with I–5. They saw the new road as a source of noise, pollution, and aesthetic harm. Opposition to the freeway also came from several people and groups who opposed using any new money for highway construction, arguing instead that any funding used ought to improve and expand mass transit. The latter prospect became available in 1974 when Congress passed a law that allowed states to reassign some federal highway funds from urban freeways to mass transit. The position of the Washington Environmental Council, a coalition of environmental organizations in the state, was that "improvements in the I–90 corridor must increase public-transit capacity, not car capacity" (Talbot, 1983, p. 28). The opposition to I–90 included stakeholders with immediate, short-term, quality-of-life concerns and less immediate, long-term, environmental and transportation-planning concerns.

The controversy dragged on until, in 1975, the state highway department modified the design to try and reduce adverse environmental effects. It proposed to decrease the number of new lanes that would be constructed from ten to six, to upgrade the existing bridge over Lake Washington (which would have been scrapped) by adding four more lanes, and to reserve two of the ten lanes for buses and car pools. The department also redesigned the Seattle part of the road to make it more environmentally acceptable.

These changes did not mollify opponents, however, and the controversy continued. The 1974 law that we just mentioned not only allowed states to reallocate funds for mass transit but also created new pressures for resolving the controversy. In 1975, Governor Dan Evans persuaded the state legislature to pass a law requiring the jurisdictions of Seattle, Mercer Island, Bellevue, and Kings County (which encompassed the other three jurisdictions) to vote for or against a reallocation of highway funds for mass transit. As expected, Bellevue and Mercer Island voted against a reallocation. Seattle, however, also voted against it at that time. The city, it seems, was divided between neighborhoods that opposed the freeway and business interests that favored it on commercial grounds. Kings County voted against the reallocation, and thus for the freeway, but stated that it was flexible on the number of lanes. Meanwhile, in voting for the freeway the Seattle City Council also stated that it would support an eight-lane rather than ten-lane road, with three lanes in and out of the city and two for mass transit.

By now the state highway department probably had enough political support to proceed without concessions, but officials still were concerned about subsequent legal challenges from residential opponents in Seattle. This led them to seek agreement among all parties on the number of lanes and their use. To these ends, they turned to Gerald Cormick of the University of Washington's Mediation Institute to assess the prospects for mediation. A leader in EDR, Cormick matched the dispute against four preconditions for mediated settlement that managers would do well to appreciate: the presence of an impartial mediator, a well-defined dispute with some urgency about resolving it, a balance of power among participants, and the willingness and ability of participants to negotiate. After three weeks of interviews, he decided it was worth trying.

Why did the parties agree to EDR? The highway department saw it as a way to achieve some level of consensus on the design of the project. Meanwhile, opponents knew that they would not be able to stop the highway but would have an opportunity to influence the design. One Seattle official noted at the time that "I–90 was going to get rammed through one way or another. We saw mediation as the only practical way of influencing the highway design" (Talbot, 1983, p. 32). The governor was also pushing for a negotiation. However, he "cast mediation as an experiment to get the jurisdictions to agree on how the highway would be designed, and not as a process that would determine whether the highway would be built" (p. 33). The only active interest group that did not participate was the environmentalists, because they would not commit to be bound by any agreements reached. Still, even they participated indirectly by applying pressure to Seattle officials.

The final negotiating group included two representatives each from Seattle, Bellevue, and Mercer Island; representatives from Metro (the regional transit authority, which wanted the two mass transit lanes); participants from Kings County; and officials from the state highway department. The process began in March 1976 and extended through the summer and into the fall. In the initial phase, Cormick and his colleague Leah Patton (also of the Mediation Institute) met separately with the parties to discuss their positions and objectives. The full group met only once during the summer. Most of the discussions took place between the mediators and individual parties, often through informal phone conversations and breakfast meetings.

In August, after the Seattle City Council voted against totally reassigning the federal highway funds to mass transit (ensuring the money for I–90) but indicated some flexibility on lane use, the discussions focused on the number of lanes. Bellevue and Mercer Island favored ten lanes; Seattle wanted no more than eight. The parties considered several alternatives and compromises throughout the fall. These alternatives focused on the number of lanes, on reserved lanes for Mercer Island drivers, and on dedicating two lanes for mass transit.

None of these alternatives was acceptable to all the parties. Consequently, by October the talks deadlocked. Yet, just before a November meeting that most people thought would end the process without an agreement, the Seattle City Council suggested a compromise. Mercer

Island drivers could use one of the transit lanes, as long as the design ensured that the extra cars would not slow bus and carpool traffic. The highway department came up with these design changes. At the final November meeting, the mediators were asked to write a draft of an agreement in a working session that became a final negotiating meeting. They produced a draft "that everyone agreed to take back to their respective councils for ratification" (Talbot, 1983, p. 37). Within a few weeks, all of the participants signed the agreement.

Although federal funding cutbacks delayed construction for some time, Allan Talbot (1983, p. 95) judges that the I–90 mediation was "successful within the specific objectives of the mediation effort" (to craft a binding decision). But how well do EDR site-specific efforts do more generally? Of the other five cases of EDR (all site-specific) that he profiles in his book, Talbot ranks three as "clearly successful" and two others as less than successful in that they did not lead to the results anticipated. More broadly, Bingham's analysis of 132 cases of site-specific EDR that took place before mid-1984 found that 103 (78 percent) resulted in some form of agreement acceptable to the parties.

Making Decisions on Policy-Level Disputes: Regulatory Negotiation

The EPA's efforts with regulatory negotiation illustrate the use of EDR to make decisions that are national in scope and prospective in objective. In these instances, the deciding body (EPA) is at the table. Moreover, the agency commits to issuing any consensus that emerges as a proposed rule (so long as it is consistent with the EPA's legal authority). Thus the objective is to *make* rather than *recommend* a decision.

As we noted in Chapter Six when discussing the procedural republic, rulemaking is the process by which administrative agencies take statutory instructions and turn them into legally binding regulations that agencies implement and enforce (Fiorino, 1995; Kerwin, 1994). Recall that at the federal level, rulemaking is carried out within the procedural framework of the Administrative Procedures Act (APA) of 1946, as amended. Equivalent laws also exist at the state level. The APA requires that agencies provide affected parties with an opportunity to comment on proposed rules, that they respond to those comments, and that they give fair warning to regulated entities before rules become binding. Both the courts and the Congress have expanded these minimal requirements over the years. Finally, the APA also provides that affected parties may challenge rules in the federal courts once the agency issues them as final, a privilege the affected parties commonly use to the chagrin of public managers.

The EPA's interest in regulatory negotiation in the early 1980s reflected its accumulated frustration with what Philip Harter (1982) terms the "malaise" of conventional rulemaking. Like other critics, the EPA saw the process as slow and subject to delay, with some rulemakings stretching on for years. Information demands on the agency to write and justify requirements were also substantial. Moreover, when agencies heard from parties during a rulemaking, it was usually either one interest at a time or as part of a formal written comment period that became highly adversarial. More precisely, and anticipating lawsuits, parties used this opportunity for dialogue (Shapiro, 1988) with the agencies to stake out, for the record, hardened positions that judges would later review. Thoughts of developing an effective and workable regulation premised on compromise entered few minds at this juncture.

To combat these tendencies, regulatory negotiation applies the principles and techniques of EDR to rulemaking. The agency convenes a negotiating committee of representatives from all interests affected by a rule, typically including federal agencies, regulated firms, environmental advocates, state and local officials, and trade associations. The committee also selects a neutral facilitator to serve as process manager for the negotiations, usually a professional in the EDR field. The objective of the negotiation is to reach agreement on the content and language of a proposed rule. With EPA participating as a party-at-interest, the committee protocols enable any party to withdraw from the negotiation at any time without prejudice to its legal rights. In turn, the negotiating protocols provide that the process will end only when the committee fails to reach agreement by a fixed date, or when it agrees that it has reached an impasse. If either of these happens, the EPA reverts to a conventional rulemaking process in which the parties still may participate.

The negotiation of New Source Performance Standards for woodstoves illustrates what the process may accomplish (Funk, 1987). Begun in March 1986, this was the fourth of the EPA's early experiences with regulatory negotiations. The committee's purpose was to agree on technology-based emission standards and to implement rules for regulating newly manufactured woodstoves. Such stoves are major sources of particulate emissions. In addition to the EPA, the parties at the table included the states of Colorado, New York, Oregon, and Vermont; the Natural Resources Defense Council; a national air quality control association; the Wood Heating Alliance (an industry group); two woodstove manufacturers; and the Consumer Federation of America. The committee completed its negotiations in August 1986, having reached agreement on the core issues. The EPA then published a proposed rule in February 1987 that reflected the agreement.

In the end, the process enabled the parties to negotiate outcomes to their mutual benefit. Consider the interests of the different sides regarding the timing of new limits. EPA, state, and environmental representatives wanted emission limits in place quickly to reduce air pollution and help meet proposed ambient air standards for small particulates. The woodstove manufacturers wanted assurances of sufficient time to test, certify, and market new models before the compliance date. Eventually, the negotiating committee agreed to a one-year delay in compliance for small manufacturers, to a two-phase standard that became more stringent in the second stage, and to alternative certification provisions that allowed temporary default certification. The latter kicked in when there were backlogs in laboratory testing or in EPA's application processing. As a result of these agreements, the first phase of the new emission limits took effect much earlier than it might have, as per the wishes of the regulatory community. This was accomplished, however, by taking the industry's practical concerns into account up front, rather than waiting to resolve them in court later.

How did participants assess this EDR experience? Most stressed EDR's benefits over conventional approaches as a deliberative process (Fiorino, 1988). For many, it was their first opportunity to engage representatives of other interests in face-to-face policy discussions. Participants also appreciated the chance to make their case and to try bringing the other parties around to their point of view. For industry representatives, the process enabled them to bring their detailed technical knowledge and practical implementation concerns into the process of writing a regulation. Meanwhile, environmental groups found that by taking into account the industry's implementation issues—concerns about timing, agency capacity for issuing permits, preparing for model changeovers, or process redesigns—industry was more willing to consider more stringent standards for environmental performance. Finally, all parties thought that the process yielded a more effective, workable rule with a higher rate of compliance from the industry than was typical in conventional rulemaking (Fiorino, 1988).

There were also downsides, however, that managers would do well to appreciate. One weakness that most participants cited was the time required to conduct a successful negotiation. During the six to eight months of the negotiations, they had to put in considerable time, especially in the final drive for consensus. Yet they also recognized that the length of the conventional rulemaking process and the likelihood of litigation at its end meant that they might have actually saved time with EDR. Other potential weaknesses noted in the process reflect dilemmas associated with using EDR for general policy-level disputes (Amy, 1987). Troubles tend to occur if all of the affected interests are not at the table, if nonindustry or nonagency parties do not have the resources and technical knowledge to participate effectively, if the consensus of participants does not reflect the best interests of society as a whole, and if the process does not ensure the validity of needed data.

How typical is the EPA's experience with using EDR in policy-level disputes? In her analysis of thirty-three policy-level disputes mediated before 1984, Bingham found that parties reached agreement in three-quarters of the cases. In most of them, however, the objective was only to make recommendations rather than binding decisions. Since then, most EPA efforts using EDR to make binding decisions have led to consensus on proposed rules. Finally, some agencies, such as OSHA, have successfully sponsored EDR negotiations, but without participating as a party-at-interest in the process. Under these circumstances, agreements become recommendations to decision makers (such as those at OSHA) that they may accept, reject, or modify.

MAKING EDR WORK FOR YOU

In this final section, we take up two remaining issues regarding EDR that managers need to consider. First, under what circumstances, and for what kinds of disputes, is EDR most likely to be successful? Second, what are some strategies and techniques that effective EDR negotiators have used successfully?

When EDR Is Most Likely to Succeed

Not all situations are suitable for EDR. For instance, there may be too many parties to a dispute to make negotiation feasible. At other times, issues may be so complex and so laden with scientific uncertainties that the parties cannot make headway. At still other times, the long-term implications of any agreement reached may be so profound for future generations that EDR may not be seen as legitimate. Finally, the levels of distrust and emotional dislike among parties may be so high in some cases that a political or judicial process with an authoritative third party is the only viable path to take.

Sometimes all of these adverse conditions exist in the context of a given environmental dispute. If they do, the prospects for using EDR successfully are slim at best. If some but not all of these conditions exist, a manager should assess the situation and talk informally with the parties to the dispute before deciding whether or not to commit to a full EDR process. If none of these conditions exists, then experience so far suggests that the prospects for success through EDR are excellent.

Thus managers need to understand that EDR is most likely to work when

- There are a manageable number of identifiable interests
- There are no major issues that involve scientific uncertainty
- The core dispute raises no fundamental value or symbolic issues
- The parties are able to achieve a level of trust and a sense of shared purpose
- There exists a rough parity in relative power among the participants

There are a manageable number of identifiable interests. If too many interests need to be represented or representatives of those interests cannot be identified, EDR is unlikely to succeed (Blackburn, 1991, pp. 134–135). Most site-specific disputes present a limited and identifiable set of interests: the developers who want to build a housing development against the conservationists who want to protect the wetland; the refinery that wants to expand its operations against the community that fears higher levels of pollution, traffic, and noise; the haulers contracted by a municipality who want to transport hazardous wastes through an area against the residents who want them to find an alternative route. Wisely, as we noted, EDR was first applied to site-specific disputes in which a manageable number of identifiable parties were present.

This condition is harder to meet, however, when managers try to apply EDR to prospective policymaking, such as a negotiated rulemaking. Because the objective of the negotiation is to agree on policies of general applicability and future effect, the list of interests potentially affected may be very long. A rule of thumb for managers is this: if twenty to twenty-five members on a committee cannot represent the range of affected interests, then there are probably more interests than the process can accommodate. Thus EDR probably is not the approach to take.

There are no major issues that involve scientific uncertainty. EDR is most likely to succeed for managers when there is general agreement on the factual premises of the negotiation. Consider, for example, the prospects if the EPA had tried in 1997 to achieve consensus on a proposed tightening of the National Ambient Air Quality Standards (NAAQS) for ozone and particulates. Under the Clean Air Act, the NAAQS must be set at a level that will protect the most sensitive parts of the population from adverse health effects. The proposal was the subject of considerable debate over the adequacy of the scientific evidence supporting the tighter standards. Proponents argued that they reflected "sound" science, while opponents bridled that they were based on "junk" science. Under these circumstances, it is hard to imagine an EDR negotiation process having any chance of success. Thus, managers should be wary about using EDR whenever disagreement exists at these levels.

The core dispute raises no fundamental value or symbolic issues. It is a simple fact of political life that some issues are more negotiable than others. The chances for success in EDR are highest for managers when there are issues in which the parties feel comfortable trading off preferences, rather than taking an either/or position on one or two major issues. Importantly, most parties to a dispute are decidedly unlikely to make concessions when issues involve—or are defined in ways that require—compromises in their environmental core belief systems (Sabatier and Jenkins-Smith, 1993). Thus, any attempt to, for example, negotiate the public's health is not likely to gain the support of many constituencies. The greater the range of issues on which parties may compromise, the more likely it is that participants will get something they want out of the negotiation. This typically occurs when the means to ends are at issue rather than the ends themselves (Sabatier and Jenkins-Smith, 1993). Thus managers should understand that EDR is far more difficult to use when major value or symbolic conflicts are involved.

The parties are able to achieve a level of trust and a sense of shared purpose. As we noted in Chapter Six in regard to community relations, successful negotiation requires that the parties hold, or be able to achieve, a minimal level of trust among themselves. This is often difficult for managers to predict initially. Given the controversy that surrounds most environmental issues and the history of adversarial relationships among contending parties, trust building is usually an uphill battle, to say the least. Indeed, this recognition prompted our recommendations in Chapters Four, Six, and Nine for managers to build a coproduction service ethic within their agencies.

Experience has also shown, however, that face-to-face negotiations held over a period of time, with parties committed to good-faith participation, can reap dividends (Stoker, 1989). They may enable people to overcome previous distrust, discover shared interests and goals, and build constructive working relationships that lead to successful outcomes (Mansbridge, 1994). Consequently, where distrust exists in the short term, managers might also see EDR as a long-term remedy for it. In this case, regulatory negotiations afford opportunities to interact directly with diverse parties, to build relationships, and to understand the different points of view that determine positions on issues. Moreover, whenever actors see that they will have to interact together on a regular basis, they are less likely to balk at or abandon decisions made (Stoker, 1989).

Still, some situations and patterns of relationships do not bode well for EDR. One of the EPA's conspicuous failures in regulatory negotiation was an attempt in the mid–1990s to negotiate revised farmworker protection standards for pesticide use. Besides the EPA and state agricultural agencies (who regulate pesticide use in most states), the principals in the negotiations were representatives of farmworker unions and growers' associations. It turned out that the history of relations among farmworker and grower interests was so bitter and the commitment to good-faith negotiation so weak that the process terminated after less than a year. The contending parties were more interested in using the negotiating process to strengthen their relative political positions and to score points against the other side than to agree on a mutually acceptable result. Thus, managers should try to see whether these kinds of problems are likely before turning to EDR. If they are, success is highly unlikely.

There exists a rough parity in relative power among the participants. This condition is important for managers in two ways. First, if parties are to commit to good-faith negotiations, they need to believe they can accomplish more from participating than they can from pursuing their goals through the courts, legislatures, or alternative processes. If one party has disproportionate power, it is unlikely to give up that advantage by participating in an EDR process. In both the Hudson River and I–90 disputes, for example, the parties turned to mediated EDR only when they realized that they were at an impasse. No party was in a position to achieve what it wanted without entering into negotiations with the others. Second, a rough power parity is necessary for the parties to believe that any agreement reached will be carried out.

Thus managers need to understand that prospects for implementation are best when each party has something to hold over the others. To be sure, they can try to overcome these disparities by using such techniques as bandwagon strategies (inducing major players to agree, thus creating momentum and motivation for others to compromise), packaging (redefining issues in ways to create new supporting coalitions), disaggregating problems (breaking up big decisions into smaller, more politically palatable ones), and linkage strategies (logrolling) (Bowen, 1982). But unless opportunities for these tactics exist, managers do well to stay away from EDR under these circumstances.

Strategies and Techniques for Successful Negotiations

Once EDR begins, managers must be able to negotiate effectively. One of the most influential books on negotiating strategies and techniques is Fisher, Ury, and Patton's *Getting to Yes* (1983). Using the concept of *principled negotiation* developed as part of the Harvard Negotiation Project, they propose four principles for successful negotiation on which all managers should focus:

> *People*: separate the people from the problem.
>
> *Interests*: focus on interests, not positions.
>
> *Options*: generate a wide variety of options for reconciling interests.
>
> *Criteria*: insist that the results be based on objective criteria.

Separate the people from the problem. Negotiations are not just about substance. People and relationships matter as well. As Ury and Fisher put it, "the basic approach is to deal with the people as human beings and with the problem on its merits" (p. 40). Moreover, successful negotiators separate people issues from substantive issues by giving attention to *perceptions* (What are people thinking and why?), *emotion* (What are people feeling and why?), and *communication* (Are people speaking to be understood and with a purpose? Are they actively listening?). Effective negotiators also avoid problems by helping participants to build relations based on trust and by getting them to commit to participating in good faith. Finally, they understand the role of personal relationships in EDR processes and use them to promote progress toward agreement.

Focus on interests, not positions. This is also a central element in principled EDR negotiations. As Fisher, Ury, and Patton distinguish these concepts, "Your position is something you have decided upon. Your interests are what caused you to so decide" (p. 42). Each side has multiple interests that are easier to reconcile than their fixed positions. Positions represent the answers that participants provide for resolving the issues before them. Interests are the needs, desires, and fears that underlie those positions. Successful negotiators want the parties to focus on the underlying interests in a dispute, because experience shows that interests are more negotiable than positions. For example, in the I–90 dispute, the Mercer Island and Bellevue interests recognized that they could be flexible on their position regarding the ten-lane highway, as long as they protected their interests in increasing the carrying capacity of the highway into Seattle for rush-hour commuters. By conceding their initial position without giving up their underlying interests, they were able to compromise.

Generate a variety of options. A key in negotiating is to search creatively for options that offer mutual gains. Thus it is just as important for managers to broaden the available options as it is to narrow the differences between the parties. Negotiations often fail because the parties rush to a premature judgment on options, search for a single answer rather than creative solutions, and assume that they are allocating a fixed pie (a zero sum) instead of looking for ways to expand the pie (a positive sum). The more the participants in an EDR process can generate options for resolving their differences, the more likely it is that they will succeed.

New options may keep a process moving if they offer the prospect of mutual gain for all the parties. For example, in the regulatory negotiation that developed performance standards for woodstoves, the parties could easily have gotten stuck on the issue of when to phase in the requirements. Manufacturers wanted more time to phase in new products and deal with backlogs in certification by testing labs; the agencies and environmental groups wanted faster implementation. The two-phase implementation schedule and temporary default certification met the industry's concerns and allowed for the standards to take effect within a reasonable period. More generally, mediators often use brainstorming with parties to generate creative new options that lead to consensus. Managers would do well to emulate this strategy.

Insist that the results be based on objective criteria. Often the parties become so wrapped up in their own issues and needs that they lose sight of the merits of different results. No matter how hard they search for win-win options, people "will almost always face the harsh reality of interests that conflict" (Fisher, Ury, and Patton, 1983, p. 84). But in the end, the parties must be able to walk away with a result they can live with and that they are able to sell to their constituencies.

An effective technique that managers can use to keep parties focused on the substantive issues and merits is to agree on criteria for evaluating options. An example is the Storm King and Hudson River controversy that former EPA administrator Russell Train mediated in the late 1970s. The issue was the adverse effects on fish of water that power plants withdrew from the river then discharged after cooling operations. The water was several degrees warmer when it returned to the river and thus harmed the fish. The EPA insisted that the power plants' operators should construct large cooling towers to lower the temperature of the cooling water before it was returned to the river. The operators opposed the towers because of the expense of building and maintaining them. After a long series of negotiations, the EPA finally agreed to consider other options. It did so, however, with one condition attached: these options had to achieve 50 percent of the reduced fish mortality that the cooling towers would have achieved. Although the 50 percent test was not used in the final agreement, it opened the door to another option that became a deal maker: the plants' operators agreed to planned shutdowns during the spawning season, when the fish were most vulnerable (Talbot, 1983, pp. 6–24).

CONCLUSION

In this chapter we have chronicled how growing frustration with conventional dispute resolution processes, especially litigation, has stimulated interest in alternative means for resolving environmental and natural resources disputes. Consequently, techniques and processes developed for resolving many different kinds of societal disputes— collectively referred to as alternative dispute resolution—have been adapted to EDR. As we defined it, EDR is a process that brings representatives of different interests together in the presence of a neutral mediator with the goal of resolving an existing or potential dispute. The parties enter into the process voluntarily and reserve the right to reject the outcome. Anything less is not EDR.

We also argued that managers should understand that EDR processes may be usefully distinguished along two dimensions: the scope of the dispute involved (site-specific or policy-level) and the objective of the process (to make a formal decision or to recommend one to decision makers). Many of the initial applications of EDR (such as those profiled in Talbot, 1983) were to site-specific disputes, usually with a formal decision as the objective. With more experience, however, EDR has increasingly been applied to policy-level disputes, either to agree on a formal decision (such as regulatory negotiation) or to make policy recommendations (such as the Wetlands Forum).

Finally, we contended that EDR is not appropriate for all circumstances, parties, and kinds of disputes. Experience with it suggests that EDR is most likely to work when there are a manageable number of identifiable interests, when there are no major issues of scientific uncertainty, when the core dispute raises no fundamental value or symbolic issues, when the parties are able to achieve a level of trust and shared purpose, and when there is a rough parity in power among the participants. Moreover, experienced mediators have found some strategies and techniques that increase the likelihood of success once EDR is selected as an option. These include separating people from substantive issues, focusing on interests rather than positions, generating new and creative options for reconciling interests, and defining objective criteria for evaluating proposed outcomes.

With this discussion of the logic, strengths and weaknesses, and dos and don'ts of EDR behind us, our discussion of various ways that managers can work with the public is complete for now. Importantly, each of the strategies we have chronicled (working with the media, working with communities, communicating risk, and resolving conflicts) is premised on a two-way iterative flow of communication between agency experts and citizens. In essence our aim in making this case has been to attenuate for managers the downsides of an era of adversarial legalism, a legacy of morality-play-driven priorities, and a labyrinth of balkanized bureaucracies structured more for control than for effectiveness. To this end we have advocated an environmental management approach in which policies and programs are coproduced by "seamless" agencies, key external stakeholders, and increasingly attentive publics.

But whether managers are trying merely to react defensively to regulatory demands for accurate information or to pursue aggressively the coproduction ethic we advocate, the challenge they face is a daunting one. Their organizations must be able to get accurate environmental management information to the right people (such as managers, legislators, regulatory agencies, and citizens), in usable and understandable formats, and in timely ways for policymakers to make decisions. Thus it is to strategic environmental information systems in organizations— their promise, the obstacles that complicate them, and the tactics for building them—that we turn next in Chapter Nine.

PART THREE

DELIVERING
ENVIRONMENTAL VALUES

9

BUILDING STRATEGIC ENVIRONMENTAL INFORMATION SYSTEMS

*King rules or barons rule; We have suffered various oppression,
but mostly we are left to our own devices, and we are content if
we are left alone . . . preferring to pass unobserved.*

—T. S. Eliot[1]

As we have noted throughout this book, the single-medium, single-risk, and single-pollutant regulatory framework used in the United States sorely challenges even the most environmentally committed managers. On the one hand, these statutes inappropriately reinforce tendencies to compartmentalize environmental issues. On the other hand, they reinforce the balkanizing of information within bureaucracies and networks charged with both implementing and complying with them. As such, the dominant predisposition in most conventionally organized organizations is contentment—as T. S. Eliot puts it, being "left alone . . . preferring to pass unobserved."

The rub, of course, is that today's emphasis on multimedia, results-oriented, and risk-prioritized regulation requires free flows of accurate and reliable information about an organization's operations, as well as about those of its partnering network. Regulatory compliance, too,

Note: This chapter was coauthored by Thomas A. Darling.

depends on real-time environmental data. Moreover, these data must flow across media programs, in useful formats, in timely ways, to the right decision makers, and be linked to long-term organizational goals. This means that strategic environmental information systems (SEIS) must be designed. SEIS are strategic information resource management (SIRM) systems that collect and collate data that are useful for attaining an organization's goals and objectives. They are needed in organizations of all sizes and with all levels of complexity, albeit on scales matching each of these organizational characteristics.

In turn, organizations must premise these systems on knowing what managers "need to accomplish, where [they] are now, and where [they] must be at future points in order to meet [organizational] goals" (U.S. General Accounting Office, 1992d, p. 13b). SEIS planning is thus the linchpin of organizational compliance and learning, stakeholder involvement, and public communication and education. It is also a critical tool necessary for improving accountability, in both organizations and their partnering networks.

But multimedia communication is not the only environmental information management problem extant in most organizations. Indeed, even within media programs in regulatory agencies, debilitating data collection gaps, inconsistencies, and measurement decay are common. Then, because these agencies set (or fail to set) the requirements for what kinds of information the regulated community collects or reports, data deficiencies are typically rife in public, nonprofit, and for-profit entities.

In all this, of course, is great irony. As the promise of today's astounding information age technology spirals geometrically, the performance of environmental information resource management (IRM) systems—which merely collect and store data for specific program purposes and are often unrelated to overall organizational goals and priorities—progresses only arithmetically, unevenly, and sometimes not at all. Thus, managers still face considerable human, technological, and financial obstacles to improving their SEIS capabilities. Moreover, they confront these obstacles whether they are hoping to implement environmental laws, cope defensively with them as regulatees, or proactively inculcate a coproduction environmental ethic within their organizations.

Consider, for example, the critical role that strategic information resource management (SIRM) systems must play when managers try to embrace—or encourage others to adopt—the environmental management system (EMS) standards promulgated in the ISO 14000 series (see

Chapter Four). As Table 9.1 summarizes, an effective EMS advances a coproduction environmental ethic in an organization in a variety of ways requiring real-time, accurate, and user-friendly IRM systems. For example, organizations must demonstrate that they have timely, easily accessible, and user-friendly data related to such things as source reduction objectives and targets, monitoring and measurement of results, legal requirements, noncompliance and corrective actions taken, and management reviews of operations. Moreover, and consonant with our focus on creating a coproduction environmental ethic in organizations, managers must be able to use IRM systems to communicate this information swiftly to internal and external organizational stakeholders.

The purpose of this chapter is thus twofold. First, we summarize the kinds and sources of obstacles to organizational learning that managers are likely to encounter in building SEIS. Reviewed in the first half of the chapter are four common bureau pathologies: information deficiencies, power politics, subcultural politics, and the paradoxes of privatizing. Second, we offer a template for those trying to develop SEIS planning in their organizations—one that deals strategically with the realpolitik of each of these four dysfunctions.

Because we have already summarized in Chapter Four the kinds of data that any effective SEIS needs (lagging, leading, outcome, and stakeholder feedback indicators), we will not review them again in this chapter. Neither will we offer advice on hardware or software purchases; these must be tailored to divergent user needs that are too multiple to consider in this book. Finally, lengthy, detailed, and informative accounts of widely accepted approaches to developing information systems (such as rapid prototyping, systems development life cycle, and requirements analysis) can be found in most IRM and decision support system (DSS) textbooks (see, for example, Sauter, 1997). Consequently, we limit our discussion to a brief overview of major considerations for managers in choosing among these approaches, in designing DSSs, and in acquiring SEIS in the face of formidable organizational biases against doing so.

THE SEIS DATA CHALLENGE

At a minimum, four enduring data-related challenges typically plague those bent on enhancing the stature of environmental management in their organizations. First, accurate data—whether related to environmental management outputs or outcomes—are often hard to come by.

Table 9.1. ISO 14000 Environmental Management System Elements.

1	**Environmental Policy**
2	**Planning**
	2.1 Environmental aspects
	2.2 Legal and other requirements
	2.3 Objectives and targets
	2.4 Environmental management programs
3	**Implementation and Operation**
	3.1 Structure and responsibility
	3.2 Training, awareness, and competence
	3.3 Communication
	3.4 Environmental management system documentation
	3.5 Document control
	3.6 Operational control
	3.7 Emergency preparedness and response
4	**Checking and Corrective Action**
	4.1 Monitoring and measurement
	4.2 Nonconformance and corrective and preventive action
	4.3 Records
	4.4 Environmental management system audit
5	**Management Review**

Source: Fredericks and McCallum, 1995.

Second, a maze of information technology (IT) and information systems (IS)—each with its own program requirements and often incompatible software—foils integrated environmental management approaches. Third, mismatches between professed environmental management goals and analytical capabilities are rampant. Finally, capacity problems frequently plague efforts to redress any data problems encountered.

A Lackluster Data Legacy

How bad has the SEIS situation been in most public agencies? As the organization primarily responsible for telling the states and regulated community what data to collect, in what ways, and in what format, the EPA's systems set the tone intergovernmentally. Unfortunately, the EPA has repeatedly joined sister agencies in citing environmental data quality and IRM systems as agencywide weaknesses under the Federal Managers' Financial Integrity Act.

Using terms such as *dysfunctional* and *approaching a crisis level,* the EPA's own Science Advisory Board averred as recently as the early 1990s that the agency's IRM focus had been on "bean-counting administration rather than mission-achieving management." In addition, the EPA's "vertical management tracking of projects and human and financial resources [have made accountability] nearly impossible." Meanwhile, among its media programs, the EPA's data collection mechanisms have been so inconsistent that they "defy rational analysis" ("EPA Science Advisory Board. . .," 1994).

Compromised, as well, because of the self-reporting nature of many media programs are the comprehensiveness and integrity of the data the states collect. Indeed, so suspect were these data in the mid–1990s that National Enforcement and Investigation Center (NEIC) models (such as the Multimedia Priority Ranking of Selected Federal Facilities) provided to EPA regions to help them set enforcement priorities failed to incorporate noncompliance histories at all. Things are getting better now, but Gene Lubienecki of the NEIC lamented at the time, "I don't know who puts the data in the computer or if it is quality controlled. I think you have to be careful on how you use that information. If you take each individual facility and look at it, you may not have an accurate picture" (G. Lubienecki, interview with author, National Enforcement Investigation Center, Denver, Colorado, April 22, 1992). Lubienecki's perceptions are bluntly reinforced by those of Peter Guerrero (U.S. General Accounting Office, 1995, p. 1): "Many of EPA's scientific data sets are either incomplete, obsolete, or missing altogether, a problem that extends across all media areas."

Part of Lubienecki's and Guerrero's dilemma stems as well from the legacy bequeathed to public agencies by the EPA's historical approach to overseeing data collection. For instance, although the EPA monitored the states' efforts to identify CERCLA sites, the agency did little until the Bush Administration to set reporting standards. The states, in turn, adopted their own policies and practices, some of which discouraged full and consistent reporting (U.S. General Accounting Office, 1988a, 1988b, 1995; National Academy of Public Administration, 1995; U.S. General Accounting Office, 1995).

An IRM Morass

Coding problems such as these aside, managers are likely to encounter even more daunting challenges from the existing information technology in many organizations, especially in public agencies. Again, these challenges arise partially—albeit not exclusively—from public and private organizations having to collate information for any of the EPA's major environmental databases. Table 9.2 summarizes some of the primary regulatory databases that managers will encounter when dealing with the EPA during their careers.

What has this reporting interdependency wrought? According to the U.S. General Accounting Office (1991a, 1991b, 1991c, 1992a, 1992b, 1992c, 1992d, 1992e, 1993), a hodgepodge of incompatible IRM computing programs, standards, and systems presently litter our intergovernmental system. Consider the EPA's plight. As late as the mid–1990s, and despite efforts by Administrator Carol Browner to develop a strategic plan for IRM at the agency, the EPA still had more than five hundred separate IT systems. Moreover, as the summary of IRM databases in Table 9.2 illustrates, separate program offices maintained and controlled most of the agency's major environmental IRM systems. Finally, many of these media offices used different definitions and methods for data gathering and processing.

So dire was the state of the EPA's SIRM capacity in the early 1990s that its inspector general wrote, "Despite statutory requirements and repeated criticism from 50 previous reports and testimonies, fragmented management, lack of an integrated long-range planning process and inadequate internal control still keep EPA from developing and operating reliable, cost effective, and secure [SIRM] systems for effective program administration, critical decision making[,] and compliance with federal requirements" (Inspector General, 1992). Similarly, in the mid-1990s, Douglas Brown (1994, p. 139) characterized the EPA's data sets as "overpowered and underinformative."

Managers should also be aware, however, that the Clinton administration has made a concerted effort to redress the IRM obstacles standing in the way of effective, integrated, cross-media environmental management. In particular, Administrator Browner created the Interim Center for Environmental Information and Statistics within the EPA and charged it with ensuring that media-specific databases could also provide integrated cross-media information to decision makers and the public (Center for Environmental Information and Statistics, 1997). Still, these efforts remain at a very nascent stage of development, and to

Table 9.2. Illustrative EPA Program Databases.

Permit Compliance System	Tracks EPA region and state compliance and enforcement data for the National Pollution Discharge Elimination System program under the Clean Water Act.
Comprehensive Environmental Response, Compensation, and Liability Information System (CERCLIS)	Primary Superfund database tracking compliance with CERCLA by individual facilities.
Resource Conservation Recovery Information System	Tracks hazardous waste handlers under RCRA's transportation, storage, and disposal regulations. Replaced the Hazardous Waste Data Management System in FY91.
Hazardous Waste Compliance Docket	Contains a listing of federal facilities affected by hazardous waste legislation.
RCRA Administrative Tracking System	Tracks violations and penalties by enforcement action taken at RCRA facilities.
Aerometric Information Retrieval System (AIRS)	Tracks data on airborne pollution in the United States, including aerometric emissions and compliance data for all point sources monitored by the EPA, the states, and local government agencies.
National Compliance Data Base	Stores data on compliance and enforcement collected by EPA regions and headquarters. Data include those culled under the Federal Insecticide, Fungicide, and Rodenticide Act and the Toxic Substances Control Act Tracking System.
Federal Reporting Data System	Tracks public water supply systems' compliance and enforcement under the Safe Drinking Water Act. Data are collected by EPA regions and the states.
Toxics Release Inventory	Compiles releases of listed chemicals under the Emergency Planning and

Table 9.2. (continued)

	Community Right-to-Know Act (EPCRA). Data is collected according to chemical type, quantity, and nature of release.
Integrated Data for Enforcement Analysis	An EPA initiative to tie together compliance data across programs, including CERCLIS, RCRA, and AIRS.
Facility Index System	Maintains a central inventory of facilities regulated or monitored by different programs within the EPA. Provides a cross-reference ID number for each facility so that performance can be tracked across databases.
Federal Facilities Tracking System	Provides cross-media compliance information on federal facilities. Data are drawn from various program databases (for example, CERCLIS, RCRA, and AIRS).
Federal Facilities Information System	A national database containing budget and project information on all environmental planning activities conducted by federal agencies under Executive Order 12088.

Source: U.S. Environmental Protection Agency, 1994, 1995.

be successful they will require the sustained attention and commitment of agency leaders for many years to come.

Design Disconnects

Even if these data quality problems were nonexistent, proponents of change would still be likely to encounter four basic disconnections between IRM systems and organizational needs. The first disconnection is between individual program needs and the broader SEIS needs of the organization. It stems, quite understandably, from purchasing IRM systems geared entirely toward an organization's or program's core mission, rather than toward environmental management needs more generally.

A second disconnection that managers are likely to find occurs between their organization's IRM procurement priorities and their own programmatic needs. Many organizations put the IT buggy before the management horse. That is, they buy information systems first and analyze their managerial processes later. Consequently, two things happen: "modernizing" becomes little more than making existing processes work faster (U.S. General Accounting Office, 1992e). Organizations thus wind up with systems that "are developed late, fail to work as planned, and cost millions—even hundreds of millions—more than expected" (p. 10).

A third disconnection occurs when organizations design programs and systems that fail to meet managers' needs. For example, they may design systems that collect data that are of marginal use or that are meaningless to managers, or that come too late in the decision-making process to aid managers. Perhaps program offices do not collect certain information because they deem the collection process to be too resource intensive or time-consuming. Alternatively, perhaps they are storing data in timely, useful, and cost-effective ways but they are not sufficiently linking this information to other important managerial systems (such as procurement, accounting, or budget systems).

A final disconnection between data and organization needs might be labeled an "analytical disconnection." For example, as we noted in Chapter Two, a 1987 statistical analysis of the relationship between Hazardous Ranking System scores for Superfund sites and actual risks concluded that they were "poorly correlated" (Doty and Travis, 1990). Seventy percent of all Superfund sites remediated during the 1980s had preremediation risk levels ranging between 10^{-4} and 10^{-7}. Curiously, these were levels that the EPA accepted as satisfactory after remediation took place at less contaminated sites. Moreover, when researchers calculated the relationship between actual cleanup activity and hazardous risk rankings, they again found low correlation coefficients (Doty and Travis, 1990). Similarly, the baseline data necessary for assessing progress in a variety of programs are lacking. For example, conceptual fuzziness and complex and cumbersome reporting requirements rendered many RCRA waste minimization baselines "invalid and unreliable" in the early 1990s (U.S. General Accounting Office, 1992c).

Capacity Problems

As we noted in Chapter Two, the EPA and many state enforcement staffs historically have experienced shortfalls and high rates of turnover among inspectors. These shortfalls compromised—and continue to challenge—effective data collection on the scope, nature, and severity of the pollution problem at many facilities. Average tenures of two years were common as inspectors moved on to higher salaries in the private sector. This in turn required constant hiring and training of recent college graduates as replacements. As well, ever-expanding regulatory universes sorely strained organizational resources. In the process, the quantity and quality of inspection data suffered immeasurably (C. Lundstrom, Department of the Environment, State of New Mexico, interview with author, Albuquerque, Dec. 15, 1992). Relatedly, capacity problems such as these made it nearly impossible to update records appropriately to reflect changes in a regulatory target's compliance. Because inspectors were stretched so thin, reinspections were often long in coming. In the interim, a facility might have come into, or gone out of, compliance. It retained its initial rating, however, for a year or longer until a follow-up visit occurred.

Implications

If managers affected by environmental management regulations conclude that this woeful regulatory data legacy redounds to their benefit, they must think again. To begin with, despite the large problems it inherited, the regulatory community has made significant strides lately in filling these data gaps. The EPA, for example, has developed its Integrated Data for Enforcement Analysis and Facility Index systems. Moreover, as part of its "Reinventing EPA" initiatives, the agency's "Managing for Results" report highlights the EPA's intent to integrate more effectively its planning, budgeting, and accountability management systems in mutually reinforcing ways (Hansen, 1997). Any movement in this direction will certainly advance the EPA's capabilities for dealing with polluters—public, for-profit, or nonprofit.

But even without these efforts, environmental data deficiencies may come back to haunt managers. In the absence of data, risk-averse regulators tend often and more rigidly to go by the book (Bardach and Kagan, 1982). At the same time, if managers lack the data they need to counter the claims of regulators or litigants, they and their organizations suffer appreciably. Finally, as we discussed in Chapters Six and Seven, when citizens do not understand the nature of the risk they confront, when they feel overwhelmed by its mysteries, or when they feel they cannot control a risk, they assume the worst. Accurate data systems can, to an extent, attenuate these perceptions.

For significant SEIS improvements to occur, however, all organizations will have to assess systematically their IT systems architecture on a regular basis. Especially noteworthy in this analysis is information regarding necessary technologies, the location of key functions, and their interfaces. Managers will then have to sell the utility of improving these IT systems to turf-protecting program managers, competing bureaucratic subcultures, and perhaps legislative sovereigns who are wary from IRM fiascoes in the past. Unfortunately, they will usually have to start this campaign from a position of relative weakness within their agencies.

POLITICS, POSITION, AND SIRM

One look at its typical position on most organizational charts tells precisely how much of an afterthought SIRM has been in most public agencies. As students of bureaucracy have long appreciated, an agency's or program's power is directly related to its organizational location. Weakest are those entities whose responsibility is fragmented, who are located deep in the administrative labyrinth of an organization, and who are frequently reorganized. They lack stability, focus, and ready access to the key decision makers who specify their budgets, staffing, and decision rules (Rourke, 1984; Tobin, 1990; Clarke and McCool, 1985). Historically, SIRM functions have not done well on any of these counts at the federal, state, or local levels of government.

Cognizant of this problem, Congress, in the Paperwork Reduction Act, tried to raise the visibility of SIRM within federal organizations and departments. Similar statutes in the states have also interacted with a growing recognition of how important SIRM is to realizing agency missions. Under these laws and initiatives, departments and agencies must designate a senior official for SIRM who reports to the agency or department head.

Still, too often the persons designated are either titular figures with little SIRM experience or with primary program responsibilities lying elsewhere (U.S. General Accounting Office, 1993). In turn, these designees tend to delegate their responsibilities to mid-level SIRM managers, who themselves are bogged down in day-to-day personnel and procurement system operations. Moreover, until recently designees have seldom played major roles in any organization-wide strategic planning that occurs.

Begun as a backroom operation supporting payroll and personnel functions, SIRM has become increasingly more salient to agency heads.

Because of a legacy of neglect in most agencies, however, SIRM functions are still too commonly housed within general offices of administrative services. Thus, most SIRM functionaries must still negotiate their budgets as one function among a variety of functions competing for resources in administrative service offices. In turn, they typically have insufficient resources and staffing to show program offices how information technology can assist them in meeting their needs—environmental or otherwise. Moreover, even if an organization has something called a "strategic technology plan," it often only lists ongoing computer acquisitions divorced from organizational goals.

Nor do mundane project management realities make SEIS planning any easier. For instance, organizations commonly change project managers quite frequently. Consequently, incumbents often defer SIRM problems to their successors or to managers in other programs within the environmental management implementation structure. Consequently, any SIRM projects that do result tend mostly to reflect the parochial interests of individual offices and organizations. This of course does not bode well for environmental management, where the need for interprogram and interorganizational integration is frequently great.

Managers may also find that the quality of SIRM initiatives in their organization suffers from a fundamental tension: quite often inimical are the demands of the acquisition process and those of technology development. The former treasures certainty and eschews risk; the latter is inherently uncertain and fraught with risk. Software development, for example, is inherently unpredictable in terms of advances, costs, development time, and performance. Likewise, large-scale computer systems are extremely complex and time-consuming to design, test, develop, deploy, and learn. Finally, and relatedly, the perverse incentives driving many acquisition management and budgeting processes can compromise quality. Project managers vying with others for scarce resources have an incentive to be overly optimistic when they estimate IT costs, capacity, and delivery schedules.

THE POLITICS OF SUBCULTURES

The clash between management and SIRM system needs is not the only clash that change agents will encounter when trying to develop an effective SEIS. Equally important for improving the chances of developing such a system is understanding how the clash between worldviews of conventional IRM staff and program managers can further complicate SEIS aims. Indeed, these types of subcultural clashes (managerial versus technocratic) have proven fatal in the past.

As we argued in Chapter Four, an aggressive total quality environmental management (TQEM) effort is premised partially on ameliorating these (and other) types of barriers to change. But even if such an effort is successful, cultural changes on this scale take years—some say decades—to take hold. In the interim, they may affect only certain programs or processes within an organization as proponents try to leverage small TQEM successes into larger ones.

Consequently, those who are trying to advance SEIS thinking will have to deal effectively with the well-known and well-founded challenges of meshing competing professional worldviews and marshaling them for common purposes (see, for example, Mosher, 1982; Hodges and Durant, 1989). Fortunately, a rich and varied research tradition exists to guide these efforts. This literature is elaborated and integrated most thoughtfully by Edgar Schein (1992). Schein offers three sets of competing assumptions and perceptions that conventional IRM and managerial cohorts hold about each other. These views relate to how information, people, and work are communicated, learned, and organized best. In Chapter Ten we talk more generally and at greater length about the challenges of managing scientific and technical personnel for effective environmental management. Presently, however, Schein's points are useful to review, because they relate directly to environmentally oriented SEIS initiatives. Indeed, successful SEIS planning may depend on bridging these disparate subcultural assumptions and perceptions.

Information and Communication

Managers tend to look askance at several assumptions that are implicit or explicit in conventional IRM worldviews. For example, they do not necessarily believe that more information is better. Nor do they necessarily see quantitative information as better than qualitative information (Mintzberg, 1996). Many are dubious as well that managerially useful information is compressible into binary computer formats. Finally, many managers know that communicating faster does not necessarily mean communicating better.

Their logic on these matters is straightforward. Managers tend to believe that the binary sharing of information hides meaning that only complex patterns of data sharing can convey. Moreover, they often worry that too much information can create overload. Quality of information, not quantity, is what most frustrates their ability to realize organizational missions. Additionally, they worry that one-point-in-time data collection becomes quickly obsolete. Management situations are too fluid, changeable, and dynamic for databases to remain current— and hence useful to managers. Recall, for example, the data collection problems we chronicled earlier that were rife in compliance reports at polluting facilities.

In addition, mid-level managers are not always sure that their own (and their programs') interests are best served by giving superiors more information. This fear is especially pronounced whenever they think that their superiors will use these bytes of information to construct relative rankings of performance (personnel or programmatic) that lack context. Finally, organizational leaders and managers may not share an IRM staff's verve for speedy information flows. To wit, the costs (both administrative and political) may outweigh the benefits of rapidly transmitting information. As Schein puts it, "who sees what at what time" is a paramount concern of most managers.

How People and Organizations Learn

Strikingly dissimilar as well are the worldviews that managers and SIRM personnel tend to hold about how and what people should learn. Most irritating to SIRM novices are the jargon boundaries and divergent views of human adaptability that are inherent in the two subcultures. Too often SIRM system professionals, as well as organizational purchasing officers, design systems and make purchases as though they believe that "technology leads and people adapt" to it (Schein, 1992, p. 282). Equally frustrating to managers is a perceived SIRM emphasis on data-handling efficiency over other values. Managers, for example, inhabit a world in which they must balance values (such as efficiency, equity, responsiveness, and due process), not persistently maximize one over another (Rosenbloom, 1983). What is more, many managers also resent what they see as an SIRM attitude that technicians know better than managers how to improve organizational operations.

Relatedly, managers often see SIRM professionals as propounding subcultural values that fly in the face of their own "theories-in-practice" (Lynn, 1996). Indeed, many find these assumptions alien, unrealistic, and off-putting in particular circumstances. As Schein (1992, p. 283) summarizes, these assumed values include

- Quests for optimal and final solutions
- Low tolerance for ambiguity
- Small tolerance for negotiated rather than "one best way" decisions
- Predilections for rule and procedural clarity
- Orientations toward clear and quick feedback
- Predispositions for long-range planning in a short-term managerial world
- Quests to reduce human error in data collection and coding
- Interests in hardware and systems rather than in people problems (that is, their goal is to make systems people proof)

To be sure, recent progress in cultivating more user-oriented worldviews among IT professionals is notable. Moreover, private companies that have recently contracted to work with public agencies in IRM system design have formally involved users in the design process (E. J. Seely, Automated Systems Coordinator, Department of Employment, Training and Rehabilitation, interview with author, June 28, 1997). But managers may also find that as users they also share subcultural values that need readjusting if their organization is going to build an effective SEIS.

Sometimes, for example, managers may short-shrift efficiency and economy in favor of responsiveness to constituencies. Sometimes they and their subordinates are technophobes who are unduly anxious about learning new technologies—despite obvious benefits to their organization. And alas, managers may fear that SIRM initiatives will diminish the role their judgment and (most importantly) their discretion play in decision making.

Creating an environmentally responsible SEIS in an organization thus requires considerable legerdemain. Somehow proponents must strike a balance between these two sets of subcultural values and perceptions. Moreover, anyone pursuing an SEIS commitment in a large organization should expect no sudden epiphany on these issues by SIRM staff, program managers, or their staffs and subordinates. Even if individuals want to change, the roots of these subcultural predispositions go beyond personal or professional predilection. They are deeply rooted and routinely reinforced in the perverse incentive structures that conventional bureaucratic structures afford.

Organizing People and Work

SEIS proponents must also be prepared, as with TQEM, to reconcile divergent subcultural values regarding hierarchy, information sharing, and automation. As Schein discusses, two implicit assumptions of conventional IRM subcultures in most organizations are that program goals are better realized through flatter organizations, and that managers value the changes that flattening brings. Yet managers are also well aware that the delayering of hierarchical levels can also be dysfunctional. When spans of control grow too wide, when lines of accountability and authority grow too vague, and when delayering does not involve levels of political appointees as well, the downside repercussions for organizational goals are well-chronicled and wisely avoided (Light, 1995).

Managers often bridle, as well, at the assumption that organizations with open information channels are inherently better than those without them. Indeed, many managers have encountered instances in which free-flowing information *diminishes* their power to influence subordinates, budgets, or policies. More admirably, managers are well acquainted with instances in which hierarchy and bounded rationality are necessary for service delivery to succeed. To be sure, the innovation that can develop when information flows freely in an organization can be precisely what is needed (such as when experimentation with or benchmarking of alternative cleanup technologies is pursued). But this too depends on how executives, senior managers, and political appointees use the information afforded by SIRM system improvements.

Most feared by managers are SIRM improvements that can *centralize* control rather than improve organizational learning (see Prechel, 1994). When this happens, managers and their subordinates are not without their defenses. But these too can undermine organizational goals. For example, subordinates can sabotage data collection or lose a sense of personal responsibility for their actions ("they'll tell me when I'm not performing up to speed"). Goal displacement often accompanies these perceptions as employees "work to the rule" and do no more. Finally, senior organizational leaders may inappropriately divert themselves from strategic thinking by focusing on the minutiae of micromanaging day-to-day operations.

THE PARADOXES OF PRIVATIZING

If these pathologies were peculiar to the public sector, privatizing environmental SIRM functions would soften their edges. They are not. Most of what we have described in this chapter incorporates findings from research on private companies as well. Moreover, even if this were not the case, faulty contract management long ago joined obsolete IRM systems as among the most frequently cited shortcomings of organizations at all levels of government (Kettl, 1993).

Nor can anyone cavalierly discount a major paradox of privatization: while prescribed to reduce the size of government, privatizing creates a need for even better public management as contracts are let out. Yet contract management within the federal government has been among the functions most often downsized in public agencies in recent years (Kettl, 1993; Milward, 1994). Meanwhile, Donald Kettl's (1993) analysis of contracting in states and localities shows similarly alarming trends: capacity shortfalls mean that desperately little systematic follow-up takes place, especially at the local level, on whether contractors perform as they have promised.

Consider the EPA's plight in the early 1990s. As financial support for in-house computer service and contract management dwindled, the agency contracted with Computer Sciences Corporation (CSC) to provide technical and operational computer systems support. By 1992, the EPA inspector general concluded that CSC was "running a large part of EPA's information systems, independent of any federal controls" (Smolonsky, Dickson, and Caplan, 1993, p. 139). Indeed, by the time Congress terminated CSC, the company was, in effect, managing its own contract, assigning work tasks, preparing work statements, and alas, billing the EPA for work it did not perform.

DESIGNING DECISION SYSTEMS

Before turning to how managers can cope with these organizational dynamics when developing SEIS plans for their organizations, it is important to understand some of the more technical choices they face.[2] These choices in turn depend on the purpose or purposes for which the organization's environmental information systems are designed. For simplicity's sake, managers might think of two analytically distinct types of information needs: generating regular reports and supporting decision making.

Routinized Information Needs

In environmental management, standardized reporting situations require a management information system (MIS) that is capable of storing, retrieving, and integrating data. Examples of these situations include marshaling data for periodic reporting on continuous process improvement, ISO 14001 requirements regarding pollution prevention, environmental audits, and Toxics Release Inventory requirements. The downside of these MIS systems is that they are often slow, batch-processing systems. Still, they are fine for meeting routine, structured, and anticipated reporting requirements and decision support needs.

Because of the critical nature of this information, managers need to use system development life cycle (SDLC) analysis and prototyping when designing MIS systems. Otherwise, the likelihood that they will fail increases. As we noted earlier, the most common sources of system failure are inadequate end-user involvement in system design, patchwork fix-ups that perpetuate the use of fundamentally flawed designs that are unstable and user unfriendly, and poor systems integration. To combat these problems, SDLC prompts managers to follow six procedures: analyze current systems, define new system requirements, design and develop new systems, and implement, evaluate, and maintain the new system (Thistle, 1997).

In the upcoming discussion of designing SEIS plans, we illustrate how managers can apply each of these procedures to their organization's and network's benefit. For now it suffices to note how managers can use different techniques during each stage of the process to reduce the likelihood of MIS failure. For example, when analyzing current systems managers would do well to interview and survey users, observe operations, collect document samples, and use data-flow diagrams to map where they should collect information about the system. In turn, when defining new requirements managers should use system flowcharts that map input, storage, and output needs, with an eye toward using this information as a basis for obtaining bids from equipment and software vendors.

Designing and developing new systems requires managers to turn to computer specialists and systems analysts who can take identified needs and match them to existing or new hardware and software system designs. These specialists may use a variety of design tools to guide and document the process and to speed it up by providing graphics tools, prototypes, and programming codes. These tools include hierarchy-input-processing-output tools or computer-aided software engineering packages. Then, before developing the MIS, managers have to decide whether software can be written or purchased, and what types of employee training (by the organization, by vendors, or by both) they will have to provide. They also cannot begin implementing new systems until after months of prototyping have worked out any bugs in the system.

Finally, managers can use four different approaches to implementing new MIS systems. In smaller organizations, or after systems have been thoroughly tested in larger ones, they can make the change all at once. This is called *direct implementation*. In contrast, should they wish to remain cautious in the face of uncertainty, they can keep the old MIS system running even as they introduce the new system. This is called *parallel implementation*. Should they wish to be even more cautious, they can phase in parts of the new system sequentially as each proves satisfactory, an approach known as *phased implementation*. And when an organization has widely dispersed locations or offices, managers can implement the new system one location at a time. This ensures satisfaction before implementing the new MIS system organization-wide, a process called *pilot* or *rolling implementation*.

Decision Support Needs

In contrast, both DSSs and executive information systems (EISs) allow decision makers to retrieve, analyze, and model data that they believe can help them address problems that are poorly structured and underspecified (Sauter, 1997). Given the capabilities of these systems, there are a variety of excellent reasons why managers should consider designing them for their organizations (Sauter, 1997, pp. 19–20):

- To look at more facets of a decision
- To generate better alternatives
- To respond to situations quickly
- To solve complex problems
- To consider more options for solving a problem
- To brainstorm solutions
- To utilize multiple analyses in solving a problem
- To generate new insights into problems and eliminate the tunnel vision associated with premature evaluation of options
- To implement a variety of decision styles and strategies

- To use more appropriate data
- To better utilize models
- To consider what-if analyses

In environmental management, for example, these kinds of systems can use sensitivity analyses to determine the likely impacts on ecosystems of managerial actions if various assumptions are altered. Thus managers can ascertain the impacts on aquatic life of allowing different levels of nonpoint source pollution from municipalities or farms. Moreover, they can assess these impacts either individually or as they combine with other factors (such as acid deposition and nitrogen oxides).

Examples of these types of DSS and EIS technologies abound. The Geographic Environmental Modeling System (GEMS) developed by Carnegie-Mellon University, for instance, models regional air quality. Users can select from various scientific models and different pollution control strategies and compare results to help them choose the best one. Similarly, the EPA's Better Assessment Science Integrating Point and Nonpoint Sources (BASINS) CD-ROM offers watershed models for each of the agency's ten regions.

Not unlike traditional MISs, DSSs and EISs can be developed using SDLC approaches. A second major approach, however, to IRM development—rapid prototyping (RP)—is also used under particular circumstances. Managers would do well to use RP when there are no key components of any DSS or EIS that can inform decision making on environmental matters, and when quick turnaround time is needed to address pressing issues.

These circumstances apply in two situations. When no database management system or user interface exists that would allow users to access data in the format they desire for analysis, RP is appropriate. Likewise, RP is useful when no model-based management system exists to keep track of all the environmental models that could be run for analyses, that could be input into different models, and that could perform sensitivity analyses like the GEMS program does. In turn, the need to start from scratch might arise in three situations: when existing systems fail, when organizations do not have existing platforms on which to build, or when managers are trying to model unique or complex phenomena (such as the effects of a particular toxic pollutant on humans) that preclude building on existing systems.

What is involved in RP? After users express the needs and preferences they have for the DSS or EIS, designers produce prototypes based on those needs and preferences. They later modify them as continuing feedback from users is provided. This iterative cycle continues until the user is satisfied. The advantages for managers relative to the problems we noted earlier are obvious: constant interaction of technicians with users produces rapid turnaround premised on empirical feedback. This substantially reduces the chances of miscommunication among users, managers, and technical personnel holding different perceptions of problems and needs. Moreover, the technical advantages of customizing systems to user needs are profound.

Still, RP is less necessary in designing DSS and EIS operations when systems on which to build already exist or when commercially available tools and technologies are capable of handling the problem. Known as DSS *generators,* these tools and technologies are constructed using two fundamental approaches: the *quick-hit* and *evolutionary* methods. Using the first approach, managers can address narrow (and often one-of-a-kind) problems. They can do so using microcomputers, in systems designed quickly to meet pressing needs with well-understood parameters, and with high payoffs. In contrast, the evolutionary approach assumes that systems will continue to evolve over the years, long after RP ends, as legal requirements, managerial needs, software, and commercially available equipment evolve.

What technological factors must managers consider when using these systems to advance an environmental ethic? In doing requirements analysis, for example, they should consider the following questions:

- What key decisions will decision makers have to make?
- On what information (such as performance analyses and regulatory requirements) will such decisions be based?
- Who will make these decisions and what levels of computer sophistication must they have?
- What existing or commercially available equipment will be used?
- In what ways will the DSS be linked to other management systems (such as personnel and budgeting MIS systems)?

Similarly, when selecting generators managers should consider the following factors:

- How well will the DSS generator connect with existing systems to permit such processes as data sharing, document sharing, Internet use and searching devices, and firewall availability?
- How compatible will the generator be with such things as available equipment, operating systems, and network configurations?
- How costly will it be in terms of initial purchase and licensing, maintenance, conversion, and upgrades?

Finally, in selecting vendors, managers should consider a host of factors, including

- How long has the company been in existence?
- Does it appear financially stable and viable for the long term?
- What are the quality, size, and customer orientation of its technical support staff?
- Does it have an ongoing commitment to the product purchased or the service contracted?
- Is there an organized user group that can be contacted to assess product or service quality?

DEVELOPING AN SEIS PLAN

All of this is not to suggest that cost-effective SEIS in organizations are the product of a series of *ad hoc* decisions by managers. To the contrary, managers hoping to use their SEIS to build a coproduction environmental ethic must deal with system acquisition and development in a comprehensive way. Planning is both critical and a challenge to accomplishing this.

Proponents will thus have to develop SEIS that are premised on the organizational dynamics and design considerations we have identified. Systems must be designed to ensure that organizational heads buy into the final product. Moreover, they must neither take too long to implement nor make excessive demands on program resources. Most successful as well will be SEIS that provide short-term and first-order benefits to other organizational functions, ensure user friendliness, bridge competing subcultural values, break down functional balkanization, and afford adequate stakeholder representation. The SEIS planning process we offer addresses each of these concerns. It is a top-down and, normally, a six-month process offering three primary benefits:

Understanding. Organizations will be able to craft a shared understanding among senior managers of the role of IRM in facilitating environmental management. In the process, employee buy-in to whatever plan emerges will be facilitated.

Reconnaissance. Organizations will be able to recognize existing IRM environmental strengths that they can exploit, to note weaknesses they must address, and to identify where more money and training will reap environmental benefits.

Priority setting. Organizations will be able to develop a list of IT investment priorities premised on environmental goals and maximizing high rates of return on investment.

We believe that, given competing claims on the time and resources that organizations have available for the planning process, a top-down approach to developing the plan is most appropriate. The IT and environmental management directors inevitably serve in the organization as hubs in this exercise; these roles are too important for them to delegate to others. But both directors must also create bottom-up SEIS planning teams that elicit buy-in and active, thoughtful participation in the process. Included on these teams should be the organization's head, critical stakeholders, senior managers, environmental management liaisons and spokespersons (if any), and senior IT and environmental management staff support. Ideally, some cross-fertilizing with stakeholder members of the organization's advisory board also occurs (see Chapter Six).

We are not suggesting that a firm guiding hand from above precludes broad-based participation in SEIS planning. Indeed, three key aspects of the process actually require it:

Reality testing. An accurate assessment of the current SIRM situation requires careful attention to the concerns of a wider set of environmental stakeholders. Alternate methods of eliciting such information are considered later in the chapter and build on approaches we offered in Chapter Six, on working with communities.

Understanding. At some point, including all IT and environmental personnel in SEIS planning becomes unwieldy, too costly, and counterproductive. Nevertheless, nonparticipants must understand not only the activities they will have to perform when the SEIS is implemented, but also the rationale behind those activities. Merely giving those who do not participate in SEIS planning a copy of the completed product will not suffice.

Support. Senior managers from departments directly affected by the SEIS must also be on board. As we noted earlier, their diffidence or outright opposition to SEIS planning can be fatal.

As we have already noted, time is always a formidable constraint in any SIRM exercise. Such an exercise cannot go on forever. Moreover, it must produce timely results that participants and stakeholders can use and value. Finally, busy organizational members and stakeholders must not have to give more time than they feel comfortable giving, considering their other responsibilities.

An organization can complete the SEIS planning process in as few as three months, although six months is the norm. Never, however, should it take more than nine months. Participating on the project team means that an organization's top leadership (elected, appointed, or careerist) must commit to between five and seven days of work. Their time is divided almost equally between team meetings and individual preparation (review of draft materials) for meetings.

SIRM exercises typically use five-year planning horizons. In developing an SEIS plan, however, a variety of nested time horizons is better. When anticipating long-term technology trends, the appropriate horizon is between five and seven years. For example, with movement toward client-server-based systems becoming quite common, organizations must carefully consider a variety of alternatives before upgrading their existing and overburdened mainframe systems. Likewise, when considering major technology and communications infrastructure systems, organizations should try to look ahead five years. This is wise for two reasons: they will have to make large investments in such systems, and they will need time to plan and implement them astutely. In contrast, organizations need not look much beyond three years when purchasing software and smaller technology systems.

Typically, organizations envision three stages in the SEIS planning process: preplanning activities, formal planning, and postplanning activities. The *formal planning* stage involves primarily activities performed by the planning team. As noted earlier, it is critical to minimize the time needed for team members to prepare and meet during this phase. SEIS planning, done correctly, is highly labor intensive.

This is why *preplanning* activities are so important. Although it requires a minimal commitment from team members, the preplanning stage will consume approximately two-thirds of the time and effort expended by the IT and environmental management directors and their staffs. The directors must have high-quality materials available for team members to review well in advance of scheduled meetings. The final product of this stage is a *preliminary technology vision* (PTV) statement drawn up jointly by the IT and environmental management directors and buttressed with supporting documentation. This vision statement provides the broad contours of subsequent deliberations over the terms of the ultimate SEIS plan.

The *postplanning* stage involves producing, implementing, and evaluating the final document. During this phase, organizational leaders explain the tentative SEIS plan to broader segments of stakeholders and constituencies who may not have participated in or been represented on the panel. These key stakeholders then get an additional opportunity to comment formally on the penultimate draft. Team members may or may not choose to alter the plan on the basis of these reactions, but they ought to respond to them before it is implemented and as it is evaluated.

Preplanning Stage Activities

As we have just noted, the end product of the preplanning stage is the PTV statement—the directors' best assessment of how IRM can improve an organization's ability to meet its primary mission or missions. The statement emphasizes how to do this most cost-effectively, in environmentally sensitive and innovative ways, and in full compliance with evolving environmental regulations. IT and environmental management directors face three critical challenges in making the preplanning stage a success.

• *They must keep their minds open.* Above all, the SEIS process should be a learning experience for both IT and environmental management directors, as well as for all involved on the planning team. Thus, both leaders must remain open to information that challenges their impressions and intuitions about daily operations. Moreover, they must assist team members in recognizing emerging environmental management pressures, cutting-edge environmental management innovations, and new or existing IRM capabilities tailored to these innovations.

• *They must manage stakeholder relations.* Beyond the obvious need to manage relationships between the organizational head and the planning team, the IT and environmental management directors should also become conduits for, and consider the opinions of, nonteam members. In particular, they should solicit input from organizational program members and other key stakeholders, often in face-to-face discussions. This involvement serves three purposes: the directors learn firsthand the organization's needs and the challenges that program managers face, stakeholders not formally involved in the process get a sense that they too can influence deliberations, and other team members avoid excessive demands on their time.

- *They must manage the process.* Both the IT and environmental management directors must manage the logistics of the entire SEIS process and keep things moving. An organization's attention span is short. Thus, the quicker the planning process moves forward, the more likely it is that it will succeed. Part and parcel of this management is what analysts call the planning-for-planning process.

Following are the key activities involved in this process.

GAIN TOP-LEVEL COMMITMENT Without question the single most important key to successful SEIS planning is a committed organizational head. The IT and environmental management directors must make every effort to have this person (or her high-level designee) become an active member of the planning team. The head's participation in the process, or lack thereof, symbolically signals to the organization's members how important SEIS planning is to their leader. What is more, research shows that even organizational heads initially committed to SIRM fail to support recommendations when they (or their designees) are not actively involved in developing them.

Sometimes an organizational head (or high-level designate) is unwilling or unable to participate. Should this happen, the top-down, organization-wide approach is best jettisoned in favor of the bottom-up approach suggested in Chapter Four for similarly handicapped TQEM efforts. In the bottom-up approach, smaller-scale (that is, program-specific) efforts are pursued that are most likely to succeed without top-level support (the "pick the lowest hanging fruit first" strategy).

In any event, at their first meeting with the organizational head, the IT and environmental management directors should

- Outline the logic, utility, and advantages of the SEIS process
- Outline the steps in the process and the organizational head's role in them
- Modify the steps on the basis of the organizational head's reactions

- Garner the organizational head's advice about which stakeholders to include on the team and which to informally consult (especially legislators)
- Gain the organizational head's approval to proceed under his or her imprimatur

ASSESS ORGANIZATIONAL MISSION, PRIORITIES, AND ENVIRON-MENTS An organization's existing mission and priorities are typically a good place to begin developing a *technology vision*. If a strategic plan exists, there are at least five reasons not to rely on it alone to identify organizational goals and priorities: it may be outdated; it may serve only public relations purposes; it may reflect only consensus views that avoid rather than confront priority setting; it may leave unstated very critical understandings or hidden agendas; or it may lack input from the IRM and environmental management directors.

To be safe, the directors and their staffs must review any existing plans for accuracy and validity. Their organizational head, legislative overseers, constituency groups, and program managers should be consulted in the process. Also considered should be any other written documents related to the organization's mission (such as enabling statutes, legislative reports, annual reports, and organizational guidance documents).

ASSESS EXISTING SIRM SYSTEMS As we have noted, up-to-date assessments of existing environmental management databases must inform all subsequent stages of SEIS deliberations. The directors must include in these assessments the current condition of organizational databases, information systems, and technology as they relate to environmental management. Moreover, given the problems we outlined in previous chapters regarding balkanized systems, this review has to include SIRM conditions both in and out of the control of the IT and environmental management directors. This is important for three reasons:

> *As reality checks and education for leaders.* For the IT and environmental management directors, knowing the state of environmental IRM systems is critical. Such knowledge is not systematically acquired during normal performance reviews.
>
> *As reality checks and education for team members.* Similarly, other members of the planning team must develop their own holistic impression of the scope and current state of the

organization's environmental IRM capabilities. Otherwise they will be familiar with only those portions of the system they use most.

To marshal evidence. The information garnered is needed to support SEIS initiatives as they compete within the general budgetary process, as the press covers them, and as stakeholders react to them.

Background on the current status of mission-critical environmental management information and technology systems is culled in two phases. During the first phase, IT and environmental management staff identify existing critical systems, inventory their capabilities, and evaluate them relative to environmental management priorities. Noted in this phase are the names and locations of all major end users of environmental management information. In phase two, these listings become the "sampling universe" for a survey of end users regarding the pluses and minuses of existing IRM systems. Respondents are also asked to identify any mission-critical information and technology systems they operate or maintain, and to suggest ways to improve them.

ASSESS TRAINING NEEDS Training is often overlooked in SIRM planning, for both systems professionals and end users. Yet training is critical, especially when managers are attempting to develop an effective SEIS plan in an organization historically disinclined to emphasize environmental management issues. IT, environmental management, and program managers must therefore assess SIRM training needs as a basis for subsequent team-based priority setting.

ASSESS UNFOLDING IRM INITIATIVES The directors and their staffs must also concertedly assess the evolving status of ongoing environmental management-related IRM projects in the organization. Team members should also receive regular updates as new information becomes available. If time, resources, or information gaps preclude extensive data collection in this regard, the IT and environmental management directors should estimate the status of these projects.

ASSESS THE FUTURE STATE OF ENVIRONMENTAL IRM Using the time frames suggested earlier, IT and environmental management directors must work with their senior staff to prepare a summary of long-term trends related to environmental IRM needs. The SEIS team should be thoroughly versed on these trends before they begin setting priorities for SEIS initiatives. What is more, the PTV statement should discuss these trends in depth and relate them explicitly to organizational missions. Future iterations of SEIS planning can revisit these trends for accuracy and correct course appropriately.

IDENTIFY POTENTIAL SEIS INITIATIVES Identifying future IRM initiatives is, of course, the crux of SEIS planning. During the preplanning stage, the directors should work with each program manager, their respective staffs, and environmental media liaisons (if any, as we discussed in Chapter Five) to create a set of initiatives that advance organizational missions. The decision-making heuristic they use in selecting these initiatives will vary, taking into account differences in circumstances and needs.

Fundamentally, however, three principle criteria must drive the selection of projects in order for a coproduction environmental ethic to prevail. SIRM applications must align well with an organization's environmental priorities, as expressed in the PTV statement; they must offer a high environmental return on investment to managers, stakeholders, and regulators; and they must add value to an organization's capacity to ensure environmental learning among its members without compromising its primary mission or missions.

It is also imperative that all program managers understand that the order of most future SEIS initiatives will follow the planning team's final priority rankings. This order creates a strong incentive for them to take the SEIS planning process seriously. To foster this understanding, the directors—with the organizational head's imprimatur—should provide a brief training session for program managers and their staffs. Trainers, as well, should show participants how to develop and justify SEIS initiative lists for their programs.

Individual program managers must then rank their initiatives in terms of overall benefit to their programs (such as more cost-effective compliance with environmental regulations). Also stressed heavily, however, should be how these IRM projects provide organizational leaders with accurate environmental information stored in compatible databases and in understandable formats, when they need it.

To facilitate this effort, the IT and environmental management directors must help translate program needs into SEIS technological capabilities. Without guaranteeing that program managers' preferences will prevail during the planning stage, the directors must show the managers how to make the best possible cases for them. Taking this approach helps to address several of the obstacles to information flow that we identified earlier:

- Program managers can become better informed about IRM technology. Most especially, they can increase their understanding of its capabilities and limits in integrating the organization's primary mission with environmental management sensitivities and requirements.

- IT and environmental management directors can improve their understanding of the daily operational issues that program managers confront. This will in turn improve their ability to identify organization-wide trends, developments, and needs.

- IT and environmental management directors can better respond to questions raised by team members, stakeholders, and the media about any SEIS initiatives pursued. This helps program managers to understand better their users' needs and to sell their initiatives to key stakeholders, legislators, the press, and the public.

- Discrepancies in the way managers try to justify projects can be reduced. This helps to level the playing field and makes systematic project comparisons possible.

- Stakeholders, in turn, are more likely to believe in the fairness of the process. This makes it easier for them to buy into the final SEIS.

Formal Planning Stage Activities

When the background information and proposed SEIS projects from the preplanning stage are ready and incorporated in the PTV statement, the planning team's work begins.

THE ORIENTATION MEETING One major purpose of the first planning session is to develop among SEIS team members an understanding of the PTV statement that the IT and environmental management directors have developed with broad-based input. Critical is an understanding of the substance, logic, and role of that document in establishing the broad parameters of subsequent SEIS planning. In the process, they can discuss amending the vision and do so if needed.

A second purpose is to explain and begin preliminary discussions related to prioritizing the proposed SEIS projects submitted by program managers. In these discussions, team members get a feel for how to proceed in this task as they prepare for the next meeting (the preliminary prioritizing meeting). They learn that their efforts will ultimately produce a prioritized list of SEIS-grounded initiatives across program areas. But to get to that point, members have to identify relatively narrow areas where formal feasibility studies are likely to reveal environmental investment opportunities.

To accomplish this, they identify and access available organizational funding, personnel, and technological expertise. Experience suggests that conducting expensive and labor-intensive feasibility studies on all proposed projects is not cost-effective. Instead, waiting until team members decide which projects merit in-depth study allows the staff to focus their limited resources on initiatives that members feel are best aligned with, and able to add value to, an organization's evolving environmental priorities.

Team members also learn in these discussions that they must individually rate SEIS project proposals before the next meeting and collectively rate them during that meeting. They are to do so according to the three priority-setting criteria listed earlier. At this point, however, they are to prioritize the initiatives only within (not across) various programs or departments. Once these rankings are settled, team members will find it easier to rank priorities across programs and departments. Still, at this point they should also begin looking for possible synergies both within and across programs. Some of these synergies may be new SEIS initiatives that might benefit several offices within programs or across disparate programs. Alternatively, they might piggyback on existing IRM systems.

Finally, team members learn that they must rank SEIS proposals in order of increasing rate of return (using benefit-cost ratios), not by benefit alone. To be sure, a more expensive initiative often provides greater benefits than a less expensive one. But several less expensive initiatives taken together often cost less and add greater environmental benefit. Of course a common dilemma occurs at this point: formal feasibility studies are probably not available to inform preliminary judgments about cost-effectiveness. Moreover, waiting for these results, even for a select set of initiatives, might cause planning to drag on beyond its useful lifetime.

Fortunately, however, research and experience suggest that team members are usually able to make accurate subjective judgments about relative cost-effectiveness among SEIS initiatives. Critical here are the informed judgments that the IT and environmental management directors afford team members from the preplanning stage. Formal feasibility

studies then validate or invalidate these judgments as they become available, and revisions are made accordingly as SEIS planning proceeds. In
the interim, however, team members rank initiatives into broad categories ranging from least to most cost-effective. Noted are any estimates
in which possible costs or benefits have wide margins of error.

THE PRELIMINARY PRIORITIZING MEETING Assuming that tasks were
well understood from the last meeting, the team can hit the ground running in the preliminary prioritizing meeting. Ideally this meeting can end
with team members agreeing on priorities within each program or
department. If not, the process merely carries over to the third (cross-
program priority-setting) meeting.

Research on group dynamics suggests that priority-setting meetings
tend to go through five analytically distinct phases: *forming* (introduc-
tions and identity building), *storming* (conflicts arise and members test
each other's positions, strengths, and weaknesses), *norming* (establishing decision rules and assigning tasks), *conforming* (making choices),
and *parting* (group members disengage from the group and move on to
other tasks).

Research also shows, however, that storming problems can be miti-
gated. First, game theory, according to Robert Stoker (1989), suggests
that "foreshadowing the future" is quite effective. As we noted in our
discussion in Chapter Eight, on dispute resolution, team members
must understand and expect that they will continue to interact as a
team during repeated SEIS exercises in future years. As Stoker notes,
persons so engaged are less likely to be uncooperative, to obstruct, or
to desert deliberations. This is especially true if the stakes of deliberations are high, as they are in the SEIS planning process. Other research
suggests that storming subsides when organizational leaders limit
acceptable alternatives or set inviolable parameters around decision
making. These alternatives and parameters might include values worthy of special protection (such as distributional fairness) or IRM initiatives that are not worth considering (such as off-site waste disposal in
minority neighborhoods).

Finally, the single most critical component of success is ensuring that
members have a basic trust in the process, despite their disagreements.
Consequently, everyone has to have access to the same information.
Moreover, all participants must see "side deals" as impossibilities. If
access is uneven or side deals seem feasible, good-faith participation
and consensus building will die aborning.

THE CROSS-PROGRAM PRIORITY-SETTING MEETING Aside from their limited search for synergistic opportunities, team members have to this point treated each SEIS proposal as an independent entity. But different high-ranking items may address similar environmental management issues that are better approached from a cross-program or cross-media perspective. In these instances, team members can consider piggybacking on existing IRM systems, sharing existing technology, or purchasing new IRM technology with sharing in mind. Synergies thus may make certain initiatives less or more costly than initially expected, as may shifting trends (technological, political, or regulatory). In turn, SEIS proposals may move up or down on the team's list of priorities.

Anticipating these possibilities, the IT and environmental management directors revisit the preliminary list of priorities from the previous meeting. More precisely, they list the synergies and emergent trends they see and present their impressions for other team members to ponder. As part of this presentation, they note any additional SEIS initiatives necessary to realize these synergies or to capitalize on these trends. From all this may or may not come a reordered set of priorities within programs or departments.

Thus informed, the team is now ready to begin prioritizing SEIS projects across programs or departments. As in the preliminary ranking phase, teams can use any of a variety of widely recognized group decision-making techniques to facilitate this process (see, for example, Van Wart, Cayer, and Cook, 1993). A useful decision rule, however, for teams having trouble moving toward consensus on rankings is this: the next initiative that the team adds to the organization-wide priority list must come from the top of one of any of the within-department-rated SEIS projects lists.

THE FINAL PRIORITY-SETTING MEETING Assuming that all has gone well in prior stages of the SEIS planning process, only a small amount of cleanup work will remain for team members in this final meeting. Prior to the meeting, however, the IT and environmental management directors must still complete several important tasks. They must

- Produce the final working version of the SEIS plan
- Meet with IT and environmental management program staffs to review and further elaborate the rationale behind the plan and look for kinks

- Meet with other nonparticipating stakeholders to review and further elaborate the logic, findings, and recommendations of the plan
- Meet with the organizational head for reactions
- Revise (or let stand) the document based on these comments

Once they have incorporated, amended, or rejected entirely these suggestions, the team moves on to the postplanning stage of the SEIS process.

Postplanning-Stage Activities

This stage begins with a general meeting in which the organizational head launches the final SEIS plan. If done well, the final priority list of SEIS initiatives in that document provides a flexible tool to work from as an organization's SIRM resources and responsibilities wax and wane. Implemented in descending order of importance should be those SIRM projects that most cost-effectively allow an organization to meet its primary mission in environmentally sensitive ways.

As time passes, of course, this list will less accurately reflect changing circumstances, strategic plans, environmental requirements and priorities, and currently available technology and software. This might occur within a year, and is almost inevitable after two years. As such, and in order to foreshadow the future, organizations should institutionalize SEIS team meetings at regular intervals. Moreover, well in advance of these meetings the IT and environmental management directors should prepare a *reassessment evaluation*. Premised on a "mixed scanning" model of decision making (Etzioni, 1975), reassessments focus broadly on whether or not a full-scale SEIS planning effort is necessary at this point. More narrowly, they should determine whether an organization needs, either partially or totally, to rerank IRM initiatives. But regardless of the scale of reassessment necessary, the directors must offer team members a clear picture of what has happened (positively or negatively) since they last met.

Informing this reassessment should be both summative and formative evaluations produced jointly by the IT and environmental management directors, their staffs, the organization's environmental spokesperson, and program EMLs. Summative evaluations look at which SEIS initiatives the organization actually undertook, the extent to which they fully implemented them, the value they seem to add to environmental management decision making, any obstacles to success that have arisen, and how the organization might redress these obstacles.

In turn, and informing these questions, a formative evaluation linked to TQEM principles asks the following question: How well have the organization's short-term actions been linked to the long-term goals expressed in its SEIS plan?

When changes occur, and when SEIS projects must recompete for organizational resources, the template we have afforded positions these changes as best as possible for success. This is true for several reasons. First, the SEIS planning process makes every effort to ensure that the organizational head, the stakeholders, and the public buy into projects. Second, it provides clear links between these parties and an organization's mission and goals. Thus, justifying projects becomes infinitely easier. Finally, feasibility studies ensure that organizational leaders originally selected projects that were the most economically, environmentally, and politically defensible.

CONCLUSION

This chapter has drawn the broad contours of an SEIS planning process designed to cope with the formidable and protean obstacles to organizational and network learning typically encountered by actors that carry out environmental management activities. Still, management's success in hard wiring environmental values into any organization's or network's daily operations depends on more than SIRM technology. It also depends on managing people. We therefore turn next to how managers might best approach the management of the technical and scientific personnel on whom their success in delivering environmental values critically depends.

10

MANAGING SCIENTIFIC AND TECHNICAL PERSONNEL

With scientific and technical people your basic commodity is knowledge. That is the capital of your enterprise. If you don't treat them right and they walk—there goes the capital of your enterprise. That argues strongly for a manager paying a lot of attention to the personal relations aspect of dealing with knowledge workers. They can't be replaced easily.

—Former deputy regional administrator, EPA[1]

This chapter addresses a topic that is rarely covered in the management literature but that is of paramount importance for persons having anything to do with environmental management. The question, put most succinctly, is how can managers effectively communicate with, motivate, and coordinate scientific and technical personnel within their organizations? Included among these professionals are engineers, scientists, MIS workers, technical service staff, and research and development personnel. If managers are to have any hope of institutionalizing environmental sensitivities in their organizations, in their interorganizational partnering networks, or in their communities, they must be able to marshal, meld, and reward the services of these important professionals. From these professionals will come critical contributions, some of which we have referred to in prior chapters, including but not limited to data collection and analysis, pollution modeling, information resource management, selection of remedies at RCRA and Superfund sites, and contract and grant monitoring.

In previous chapters we have also chronicled many of the legal, political, organizational, and cultural obstacles that managers face when dealing with these professionals. Diminished in the process are prospects for adding cost-effective environmental value to the goods, services, and opportunities that their organizations provide. What remains, however, is for managers to appreciate the nurturing and interprofessional challenges that also await them whenever they deal with these personnel. Knowing these challenges will give managers only a compass, not a road map, for encouraging the creativity and hard work of these professionals. But even this will put them a step closer to incorporating environmental values in their organizations.

Thus, we begin this chapter by fully explaining the importance to managers of nurturing better work environments and interprofessional relations among scientific and technical personnel. Next we cull from practitioners and the literature general personality traits for scientific and technical staff that will help managers motivate these important personnel. Then we review what various practitioners and research reveal about how scientists say they want to be managed. We supplement this analysis with findings culled from twenty-one in-depth interviews with environmental managers, scientists, and technicians who similarly assess this relationship. The discrepancy between conventional managerial principles and these perceptions is emphasized and its implications are evaluated. Next we review how rivalries among various professions can both advance and retard environmental management—often reinforced by organizational incentive structures. We conclude by summarizing the general lessons learned from our analyses and by providing proactive guidelines for managers.

Before we begin, however, a few caveats are in order. First, the label *scientific and technical personnel* encompasses a broad and varied group of individuals. For example, a computer technician is different from a research chemist. Of necessity, therefore, this chapter is a broad-brush portrayal of how to manage these workers. Scientists and technicians tend to be more alike than different because of their educational and organizational socialization and because of the types of tasks they perform in organizations. At the same time, their personalities may vary widely. Managers are encouraged to look at scientists as individuals, even though the scientists' socialization may account for many similarities among them.

Second, all work environments are different. Managing an engineer at the EPA, for example, will pose different challenges than managing an engineer working for a city or private corporation. The saying that "Working environments matter!" cannot be emphasized enough. Thus, managers should be aware of, and take into consideration, their unique work environments when applying the tactics and strategies we review in this chapter.

Third, the ideas we offer in this chapter tend to be culture bound. When managers are in situations where scientific and technical personnel within their organizations come from different (that is, non-Western) countries, their task becomes even more complicated. They must take time to understand the different cultural backgrounds of these valuable personnel.

Finally, managers in the public realm must keep the realities of government life in mind. Although most of the ideas presented here for managing scientific and technical personnel are laudable, not all are implementable in an era of cutback management. Practitioners are urged to tailor these ideas to their own distinctive situations.

Despite these caveats, managers should understand and avoid stresses and strains in their interactions with technoscientific professionals, because they may dampen the enthusiasm, creativity, and morale of these professionals. Fortunately, managers can take steps to avoid these stresses and strains. Likewise, managers should not be naive about the sources of tension among professionals. They will have to cope with these tensions and use them constructively. Otherwise, these tensions can also be dysfunctional for an organization if left unchecked, unbridled, or unchanneled.

THE IMPORTANCE OF WORK ENVIRONMENTS AND INTERPROFESSIONAL RELATIONS

Although many do not realize it, many of the innovations and scientific discoveries we take for granted today were initially nurtured, cocooned, and developed in public scientific and technical organizations (Waldo, 1988). In many cases, the initially high start-up costs for, or dangers of, these projects meant that only public organizations could subsidize their costs or socialize their risks—at least until they became profitable or their risks became more manageable. Partnering relationships (whether explicit or implicit) thus have a long and storied history in the science and technology community.

Contemporary trends in this partnering relationship, however, are not encouraging. For example, with the increased interest in contracting out and reinventing government, we are seeing an erosion of our scientific and technical staffs in many public organizations (Kettl, 1988; O'Leary, 1993a, 1996). Accordingly, to the extent that high costs or risks militate against the private sector launching scientific or technological initiatives, society has a vested interest in public managers creating attractive work environments for their scientific and technical personnel. These can attenuate, if not prevent, what many now call the brain drain of expertise from public organizations.

Relatedly, of the scientific and technical projects that are still undertaken by government organizations and their contractors, much of what gets done requires new knowledge. To be sure, good data are not available concerning exactly how much "new" science and technology is currently generated by our government organizations, either directly or indirectly. One older research project, however, found that only two-thirds of the scientific and technical knowledge needed to construct a typical weapons system was available at the initiation of the project. In-house expertise had to develop the other one-third of the knowledge during the course of the project (Sherwin, 1972).

No doubt as projects grow more scientifically and technologically sophisticated in the future, this need will become even more acute. Thus public managers will need to join their for-profit and nonprofit partners in nurturing this invaluable pool of talent. All managers will need to maintain and develop ever more user-friendly environments in which technoscientific professionals can flourish as either in-house doers or contractual overseers of such work.

Unfortunately, evidence suggests that some organizations and managers tend to depress rather than enhance scientific and technical creativity when they interact with these types of professionals (O'Leary, 1994a). If interaction between managers and technoscientific personnel were limited, this would not be much of a problem. But scientific creativity is increasingly mediated through interpersonal processes with nonscientific personnel. Moreover, scientists rarely work on their own anymore, without managerial supervision of sorts. Consequently, it is more important than ever for managers to be attuned to the creative needs of scientific and technical personnel. Otherwise, they may stifle the latter's creativity altogether.

Philip Meyers and David Wilemon (1992), for example, argue that high-technology organizations must renew and transform for these professionals what we have highlighted as critical in previous chapters: their commitment to organizational learning geared toward innovation. Likewise, these authors refer to many of the same barriers to organizational and network learning that we have already noted and supplied ways to address (see especially Chapters Four, Six, and Nine): noninnovative organizational cultures; inability to relinquish outmoded systems, structures, strategies, and technologies; bureaucratic rigidity and fragmented departments; lack of integration among functional groups; overcentralized decision making; and parochial views that value only ideas and information generated internally (see also Steele, 1989).

Their work further elaborates and extends earlier research by Jack Gibb (1972) and Jeffrey Liker and William Hancock (1986). Gibb found that four factors tend to depress the creativity of scientists and technical personnel in organizations: latent fear and distrust, restricted flow of communication, attempts to impose motivation, and attempts to control behavior. Similarly, Liker and Hancock reported six organizational barriers that hinder the performance of engineers: inadequate support systems and staff, time pressures arising from extensive engineering changes that require bypassing organizational control systems, lack of information, lack of initial training, lack of continuity in job assignments (career patterns), and a reward system that discourages technical competency while it encourages moves into management.

Managers should be clear, however, that the sources of these problems may lie more with the legal and political contexts within which organizations operate (see, especially, Chapters Three through Six) than with the ham-handedness of their leaders. Indeed, even efforts to reform these pathologies can have perverse effects (Light, 1997). Consider, for example, how the Clinton administration's reinventing-government initiatives have interacted with a Republican Congress's "Contract with America" to demoralize many scientists at the EPA. In a 1996 article in the British journal *Nature,* a top senior EPA researcher alleged that a one-third cut in research staff had combined with a sharp increase in the administrative duties assigned to scientists to jeopardize sound biological research at the agency. Moreover, many disgruntled researchers were either "waiting out their time until retirement or actively looking for new jobs" (Lee, 1996, p. A27).

Further demoralizing was a move during the early 1990s to privatize the EPA's research functions. Between 1992 and 1994, for example, the EPA's Office of Research and Development (ORD) contracted out nearly two hundred research projects laden with short-term funding mechanisms. In a Kafkaesque scenario, the EPA's diminished numbers of in-house scientists had to ensure that these extramural research grantees complied with EPA regulations. In effect, scientists—without experience or predilection to oversee grants—were turned into grant monitors. Moreover, with less time to do their own research and less money to travel to conferences, they had fewer opportunities to inter-act with peers who did not work at the EPA. Finally, to add insult to injury, because they were now policing compliance by external peers with contract regulations, they were forbidden to work with them on funded research. To do so would raise nasty conflict-of-interest issues (see O'Leary, 1993a).

Meanwhile, a move by the Clinton administration to reduce Repub-lican criticisms of the quality of the research that was done under these circumstances brought EPA scientists under further scrutiny. Spe-cifically, the General Accounting Office (1995) found that EPA regions were inconsistently implementing a policy of exposing in-house re-search to external peer review. In addition, the results of the peer review that did take place were often uninspiring. In regions that were accustomed to peer review, the process was proceeding quite well. In those without such a culture, however, inexperience with peer review processes was a problem. Interestingly, however, foiling the process most often were factors less amenable to managers' control—namely, statutory mandates, judicial and budgetary constraints, and a lack of qualified objective reviewers.

There are also normative and practical reasons why managers need to anticipate, know the sources of, and find ways to cope with the be-havioral predispositions of the scientific and technical professionals in their organizations.

Ensuring Accountability

At its best, the presence in public organizations of professionals such as scientists and technical personnel corroborates the early progressive reform era's faith in technocracy as the triumph of competence, politi-cal insularity, and public-interest-oriented expertise in pursuit of soci-etal values. At the same time, however, the paradox of professionalism presciently predicted by early scholars such as Frederick Mosher (1968), York Willbern (1954), and Alvin Gouldner (1957) endures, abounds, and plagues organizational operations. Indeed, when it runs amuck it sullies the memory and belies the optimism of the reformers' vision. Professionalism produces instead "the diminution of public control, the allegiance to professional rather than democratic or organizational norms and values, and the 'tunnel vision' of narrowly trained techno-cratic elites" (Hodges and Durant, 1989, p. 474).

Thus all managers—public as well as those in for-profits and non-profits who act on behalf of government—who deal with environmental issues need to take seriously and counteract with aplomb what Mosher (1968) saw as a major downside of professionals in public organizations: professional experts "can subtly, gradually, but profoundly mov[e] the weight [of political power] toward the partial, the corporate, the professional perspective and away from that of the general interest" (p. 210). What is more, there is evidence that managers can be successful in these efforts (O'Leary, 1994a). Outside the environmental management field, for example, researchers have demonstrated how professional values can serve the public interest when adroitly marshaled by managers (see, for example, Kearney and Sinha, 1988).

Combating Micromanagement

Managers should also understand, however, that the typical way that elected officials tend to combat these tendencies can also raise serious problems for managers. Often, in their oversight of agency operations, elected officials will focus on compliance accountability (that is, issuing mandates that limit discretion). Largely eschewed is oversight stressing performance accountability (that is, outcomes) or capacity accountability (that is, what professionals need to get things done) (Light, 1995). Although understandable, this micromanaging of discretion can sap the energies, creativity, and morale of scientific and technical personnel dealing with environmental issues (Durant, 1995a, 1995b). As we document in this chapter, scientific and technical personnel tend to hold precious the logic of scientific discovery—a process decidedly unamenable to rules, regulations, and standards.

Compliance oversight can also create perverse incentives for scientific and technical personnel that militate against good environmental stewardship. Consider, for example, the plight of professional foresters in the U.S. Forest Service in the late 1980s. Congress specified statutorily that the agency had to allocate monies according to funding formulas that provided a perverse incentive to harvest timber. The more timber harvested, the more money the organization got for wildlife habitat improvement (O'Toole, 1988). Thus, at a minimum managers should persistently be on the lookout for ways in which the management policies they are developing or implementing are consistent with—or at least do not undermine—the environmental management goals they espouse for their organization. They should also be prepared to point out these perverse incentives to elected officials when statutes, appropriation bill riders, legislative vetoes, or executive orders are having the same effect.

Coping with Challenges to Authority

By the same token, managers dealing with scientific and technical professionals must also be aware of and cope with the challenges that the latter's presence can pose to hierarchical authority. Attachments to particular worldviews, routines, and behaviors learned during scientific or technical training can cause these professionals to resent and challenge instructions by managers to do otherwise. Moreover, this tendency can become acutely destructive when managers are nonspecialists in the professional fields involved.

To be sure, challenges of this kind can be beneficial if political appointees or managers issue orders premised on flawed technoscientific principles. But as Alvin Gouldner (1957) so cogently summarizes, managers may face challenges to their authority for decidedly less noble reasons. More precisely, should cosmopolitans (that is, professionals identifying purely with their profession) come to dominate locals (that is, professionals identifying more closely with their organization), the obstinacy of the former can displace appropriate goals, managerial authority, and organizational purpose. As we have noted throughout this book, management relative to environmental issues is about balancing competing values, not about maximizing one or a selected few values touted by specialists. A manager's job is to stay alert to these dynamics and to attenuate them when possible. We say much about how to do this in later sections of this chapter.

Combating Bureaucratic Pluralism

Relatedly, it is important for managers to understand and ameliorate the role that science and technical professionals can play in the time-consuming and deliberation-reducing bureaucratic pluralism we noted in Chapter Five. Recall how bureaucratic pluralism arises when program and technical subunits within an organization pursue their own narrow professional, budgetary, and personnel interests without regard to overall organizational accomplishment (Landy, Roberts, and Thomas, 1994). Unfortunately, these tendencies grow even more acute as budgets contract rather than expand. In essence, a kind of "goal displacement" occurs as differences in professional views of what constitute the primary problems facing one's organization and the best ways for dealing with them get reified in organizational structures. This in turn occurs as particular kinds of scientific and technical professionals are segregated from other professionals in separate units, which then compete with one another in a zero-sum competition for power, resources, and influence in conventional Weberian bureaucracies.

Importantly, the way managers handle bureaucratic pluralism can determine whether tensions among different professionals are creative or dysfunctional. On the dysfunctional side, either stalemate or logrolling can result. Illustrative of these problems was the EPA's enforcement situation during the Reagan years when both stalemate and logrolling took place among the four units that had to work together to bring enforcement actions: the Office of Solid Waste and Emergency Response (OSWER), the Office of Enforcement (OE), the Office of General Council (OGC), and the Office of Planning and Program Evaluation (OPPE). These were staffed respectively by engineers (OSWER), attorneys (OE and OGC), and (for the most part) economists (OPPE) with widely disparate worldviews and enforcement priorities. Engineers, for example, saw solutions in terms of best engineering practices; lawyers saw their role as ensuring that whatever action was taken could pass judicial scrutiny if challenged; and economists saw solutions in terms of the marginal benefits to be derived from each additional dollar spent (Durant, 1993).

Obviously, from an organizational perspective each of these values should be represented in enforcement actions. Indeed, if handled adroitly, the tensions among these worldviews can be quite creative. But again, the perverse incentives created by conventionally organized bureaucracies made creative tension nearly impossible. At times, deadlock ensued when the separate units could not resolve their differences over enforcement priorities, stringency, and tools. At other times, logrolling took place among the units.

For example, the EPA's organizational guidance documents were designed to help the EPA set state enforcement priorities and to permit states to tailor enforcement emphases to their particular circumstances. Quite rationally, OSWER, OE, OGC, and OPPE worried that their own budgets and priorities would suffer if their disparate program priorities were not included in these documents. As a consequence, every program's priorities were included, without setting priorities among them.

Certainly the TQEM principles that we discussed in Chapter Four are tools that managers can use to try to break down bureaucratic pluralism. But short of a full-scale TQEM effort, managers can also try to institutionalize cooperation rather than competition as a guiding principle in their organization. Among various ways to do so is incorporating the requirement of cooperating with other units as part of individual and subunit performance appraisals. Other ways involve repeatedly recognizing in visible ways efforts that break down these barriers, and premising promotions partially on the basis of this behavior. What managers cannot afford to do is ignore the likelihood that bureaucratic pluralism will occur short of these reforms. They will never be able to remove professional and subunit tensions of this kind from their organizations. Yet they must be able to channel them in constructive ways to take advantage of the creativity of their scientific and technical personnel.

Matching Individual Goals with Organizational Needs

Managers are well acquainted with the difficulties of reconciling organizational needs with individual goals. In the environmental policy arena, this issue manifests quite often in regulatory agencies, where scientists who want—and enjoy doing—more basic research watch instead as their budgets shrink and they are asked to spend more of their time doing "regulatory research." Basic research might involve long-term issues such as global warming; regulatory research might deal with short-term organizational needs for accurate information to inform (and defend in court) its regulations and enforcement actions.

As one EPA official put it so well in discussing the perceptual differences on this issue that can arise between managers and scientists, "You don't get too many complaints about inadequacies in the Environmental Mapping and Assessment Program. . ., but we get our pants sued off and our reputations damaged when we write regulations that are not backed up by good science" ("Shrinking Research Budget. . .," 1994, p. 10). Another official added, illustrating the passionate budgetary conflicts that regulatory managers increasingly have to face when trying to increase funding for basic research, that the EPA's ORD "has already skimmed so many resources off the top [that] you can't get much [regulatory science] done in a timely manner" (p. 10). To this change ORD officials responded that funding for basic research has (until recently) fallen steadily in percentage terms.

Regardless of who is correct, the issue of basic versus regulatory science is also typical of the kind of imbroglios that regulatory managers can expect in their organizations when dealing with scientific and technical staff. Most often they will have to come to some understanding that satisfies neither themselves nor their technoscience associates. What is more, budgeting shortfalls for research only increase the stakes involved in fighting these battles. Indeed, one reason that these conflicts have grown so heated at the EPA is that its research budget—excluding funding for construction grants—plummeted from 20 percent to 7 percent of the organization's total budget between 1980 and 1994.

CHARACTERISTICS OF SCIENTIFIC AND TECHNICAL PERSONNEL

Because we have already dealt heavily with strategies for dealing with the negative effects on behavior of conventional bureaucratic structures, the remainder of this chapter deals exclusively with the interpersonal dimensions of managing scientific and technical professionals. The best place to start, we feel, is with the personality traits of technoscientific personnel. In Chapter Nine we began this process by examining how vastly differently computer professionals and managers saw the MIS process. But that was just the tip of the iceberg of the cultural differences that managers can expect when working with scientific and technical professionals.

Managers would do well to understand that these professionals tend to share some characteristics. As IBM founder Thomas Watson once said, scientists and technicians tend to be "wild ducks" (Caudron, 1994, p. 103). Wild ducks are not usually motivated by traditional incentives, including promotion, title, and in some circumstances, pay. They want room to be creative and innovative, and they want recognition for their work. They tend to be more committed to their disciplines than to their organizations. Wild ducks can usually fly to other organizations, yielding brain drain and a loss of institutional memory in the organizations they leave. Wild ducks are often regarded by themselves and their employers as being a group apart and therefore deserving of preferential treatment in terms of their conditions of employment (Jones, 1996).

The psychology and organizational behavior literatures paints a vivid picture of the typical scientist and the typical technical worker. Early on, Anne Roe (1951, 1952, 1953, and 1956)—in a series of classic and often-cited studies—found that scientists tend to be highly independent and self-sufficient, perform well on aptitude and intelligence tests (see also Vernon, 1989, p. 98), and work very hard. More recently, John Koning—a scientist who became a manager—writes that "pregnant egos are greater among scientists than people in many fields" (1988, p. 74). Other researchers have found that scientific and technical workers "expressed the strong belief that they were people who could do what had to be done and would do it right. In almost every way they saw themselves in an elite class, excelling over their peers. . . ." At the same time, they were all concerned with excellence in their own performance, and "felt that their own personal standards transcended the norm" (Maehr and Braskamp, 1986, p. 97).

Similarly, Morris Stein's 1971 study of creative chemists found them to be more autonomous, integrative, and oriented to achievement and acceptance of their own inner impulses than the rest of the population (Prentky, 1989). More generally, Raymond Cattell (1966) concluded that scientists are more skeptical, detached, critical, intellectually adaptable, and self-sufficient than the general population. Meanwhile, Donald MacKinnon (1967) found that creative scientists are introverted, nonconforming, autonomous yet adaptive, striving and assertive, open-minded or flexible in working style, and intuitive.

Robert Greene (1992) says that scientific personnel exhibit the same characteristics we noted earlier about professionals in general. First, through formal education they have developed a large body of knowledge related to their field, but they generally do not have a broad overview of many fields. They are also keenly dedicated to their profession—a dedication that overrides their loyalty to their organization. Third, their work is often interdependent with the other specialists with whom they must work, a sometimes harrowing experience for managers when worldviews among egotists clash. Finally, their work is often out of sync with annual management cycles, a reality that poses challenges at performance appraisal time (Burns, 1975; Bhalla, 1987).

Focusing on engineers, Nancy Gibson and John Whittaker (1996, p. 37) point out that they "have already made a career choice to work in a field in which their success depends on their personal judgment and creativity." Engineers are usually highly motivated. They tend to respond naturally to opportunities to test their own abilities and prove themselves within the work environment. Meanwhile, a study of computer personnel concluded that they too have low social but high growth needs. Low social need means, in part, that these workers want to interact less with their peers and subordinates, and that their communication skills may not be well developed. High growth need means, in part, that these workers have a high need for stimulating and challenging yet manageable work assignments. In addition, they are highly mobile and usually able to find work rather quickly. They therefore tend to be more vocal about their complaints, and they are not very patient about promised changes (Couger and Zawacki, 1980).

Finally, scientific and technical personnel can be unrealistic. "One of the big problems in research, engineering, and software development," commented one manager, "is the fact these employees want to be very professional and create the most perfect product or system technically possible," whether it is politically or budgetarily realistic or not (Caudron, 1994, p. 105; Kearney and Sinha, 1988; Kunda, 1992).

In sum, managers must understand that they are dealing with very bright, self-motivated, and challenge-oriented persons, who seek opportunities to be creative and who pursue perfection in their work. But patience, modesty, and conviviality are not something managers can expect from the typical technoscientist. She is likely to be iconoclastic, guided more by "inner lights" than by organizational mission statements, and narrowly task-oriented.

HOW DO SCIENTISTS WANT TO BE MANAGED?

How do these characteristics translate into how technoscientists wish to be managed? There is an interesting yet limited literature on this topic written by scientists (and by those who have interviewed scientists). An early study by Calvin Taylor (1972) concluded that scientists want their superiors to be their advocate, not judges who only react to proposals. As Taylor puts it, this raises problems: the "role of judge is contrary to what many scientists expect of their supervisor; they feel he [or she] should take the outwardly active, enterprising role of being the scientist's 'agent'" (p. 15). Yet managers ultimately must make these kinds of judgments or be derelict in their duties.

One eminent chief scientist described his ideal creative organization sarcastically in this way: A creative organization is "(1) one where people enjoy what they are doing; (2) one where people are considered often to be working on the wrong thing; (3) one with a poorly defined program; (4) one where the mission is always changing or not clear; and (5) one that is considered to be relatively unresponsive to management" (Taylor, 1972, p. 14). Although this statement obviously was made tongue-in-cheek, it reflects a strong desire for scientific autonomy.

Koning (1988, p. 1) outlines the optimal work environment for scientists. In his view, the scientist

- Is assigned a significant problem that is directly related to a specific organizational goal and allows the scientist to grow in his or her specialty

- Is allowed independence within his or her own specialty area to acquire knowledge to solve the problem
- Is supervised by knowledgeable scientists and administrators who show interest in their subordinates' work, who attempt to fulfill the individual needs of the scientist, and who make a sincere effort to provide all the physical and technical support needed
- Works in completely open communication networks
- Is generously recognized for work well done, while constructively criticized for work not done well

Comparing these criteria to the actual work conditions experienced by EPA scientists described earlier, we can see how a demoralizing gap can develop in public organizations.

Koning goes on to describe the ideal manager of scientific and technical personnel. "Critical" attributes are flexibility, interpersonal skills, communication skills, vision, enthusiasm, and persistence. "Important," as well, are company interests, outside contacts, organization skills, teamwork values, and inside contacts. A "desirable" characteristic is technical expertise. Finally, a "necessary" ability is paperwork skills. It is interesting to note how low on the list technical expertise is. Both Peter Drucker (1974) and Koning (1988) agree that with effort a non-technical manager can learn enough technical aspects of the job to be effective (although not all scientists agree with this view).

Hans Thamhain's (1992) survey of two hundred engineering managers finds that leadership is the most frequently cited skill (98 percent) needed for effective management, followed by technical expertise (90 percent), team-building skills (85 percent), interpersonal skills (83 percent), administrative skills (60 percent), conflict resolution skills (50 percent), and organizational skills (35 percent). Interestingly, the primary source of such expertise among managers of engineers, Thamhain concludes, is on-the-job training.

Andrew Eschenfelder (1968) maintains that the creative culture that scientists and other researchers require should possess the following:

- Well-defined yet dynamic and flexible objectives
- A managerial commitment to both creativity and progress
- Time for dialogue, education, and introspection
- Leaders who recognize and stimulate creativity
- Tolerance for dissent, nonconformity, and mistakes

- Freedom to act and follow through
- Appropriate recognition and reward systems

Finally, Mortimer Feinberg's (1968) suggestions for managing creative scientists still seem relevant: assisting them in feeling secure and confident, letting them set up their own workplace and schedule, encouraging outside activities (such as conferences), encouraging brainstorming and open communication, evaluating creative ideas promptly (as opposed to ignoring them), tolerating dissent and failure, and recognizing and rewarding creativity.

INTERVIEWS WITH MANAGERS, SCIENTISTS, AND TECHNICAL PERSONNEL

To gather current and in-depth information about how to manage scientific and technical personnel, we interviewed eleven managers of such professionals, as well as ten scientific and technical staff who themselves were managed.[2] Each interview concentrated on ways to manage and motivate scientific and technical personnel, including challenges and tips for new managers. Although no interviewee contradicted the literature review just presented, many of their comments do refine and extend several of its points. The highlights of these interviews follow.

On Different Personality Types

One way to determine whether one's managerial style is consonant with the personality needs of scientific and technical personnel is to compare scores from the Meyers-Briggs Type Indicator. On the basis of these scores, two managers—one trained in engineering and business management, the other trained in biology and public administration—reported new understandings about themselves and the ways in which they should manage scientific and technical staff. The manager trained in biology and public administration stated, "My particular personality is fairly assertive and expressive. The majority of the engineers and scientists were less expressive and less assertive. They scored high as analytic decision makers; I scored high as an intuitive decision maker. It is a fundamentally different way of processing information and arriving at decisions, and that was a real revelation to me. Once I started recognizing these differences, managing became easier. I understood when to push [them] and when to back off."

The engineer trained in business management also gained personal insight, but with a different twist. As an engineer, her score was very similar to the scores of most on her staff. It was only when she compared her scores to those of the other managers in the city—for example, the head of personnel—that she realized the city engineering staff was different. She gave an example: "The discussion turned to social affiliation—things like going out to lunch with colleagues. I could not care less if people ask me out to lunch. I would never expect to socialize on the job. I'm there to work—not to socialize." Personnel staff, however, expressed high needs for social affiliation and belongingness on the job. Not surprisingly, the engineer was expressing the usual low need for affiliation associated with the majority of scientific and technical personnel.

One trainer for the EPA commented that approximately 80 percent of the EPA technoscientific staff who have taken the Meyers-Briggs Type Indicator have exhibited the personality type INTJ. According to David Kiersey and Marilyn Bates (1996), INTJs tend to be introverted, to prefer sensation to intuition, to be thinkers, and to prefer closure and the settling of things to more open arrangements. They are the most self-confident of all personality types, having "self-power" awareness. They tend to be introspective, to place great value on empirical logic, and to appreciate theoretical models. However, they quickly discard theories that do not work.

Authority does not impress the typical INTJ: if an idea makes sense, it should be adopted. INTJs are open to new concepts. They are usually good at generalizing, classifying, summarizing, adducing evidence, proving, and demonstrating. INTJs can be single-minded at times, driving themselves and others hard. They usually have a strong need for autonomy and can be indifferent to criticism if they believe they are right.

On Managing in a Political Environment

Interviewees were also quick to note that managers have different perceptions than technoscientific personnel of the role of politics in their work. The latter can accept some compromise, as long as decisions are not premised on "bad," misapplied, or ignored science. The importance of ensuring that these professionals have an opportunity to have their concerns heard was evident in several interviews. "I've seen a number of managers get into trouble by blowing off staff concerns and not being willing to debate the issues with them," said a former EPA deputy regional administrator. His perspective was supported by other EPA interviewees. "If the scientists feel that you are ignoring the science, they will get really upset. Often the really good technical staff feel like the politicians are essentially ignoring the data. Generally, they will accept the reality of making political accommodations on occasion as long as you don't get too cavalier with the facts. The important thing is to be willing to sit down with them and . . . explain your decisions to them."

On Retribution

Interviewees also strongly suggested how foolish it was for managers either to threaten their professionals or underestimate how aggressively and effectively they can undermine decisions. As one interviewee put it, "Any manager who tries to bully scientific and technical personnel is really a fool because they can do it to you in ways that you'll never know. Any technical person can give you less than their best effort and it's hard to tell. Or in the worst case, if they were angry enough, they could set you up. They are very smart people—you don't want to fool them. You need to treat them with respect in a participatory way." Another interviewee opined, "Staff have figured out that if they don't like the decision the manager makes, they can go to the press, or to Congress, or to an environmental interest group. When that happens, you've got a real big problem. If you take the position that you are going to take on an issue that is contrary to staff recommendations, you damn well better go in and explain it with them in depth before you make [that is, announce] the decision. Otherwise you are going to find yourself defending your decision in the press or at a congressional hearing."

On Providing Testimony and Holding Press Conferences

Other interviewees dealt with the question of how much "face time" they should give to technoscientific staff members at hearings or before the press. Illustrative of these comments were these of one manager:

> If the issue is a very technical one, let the staff argue their own case. My attitude is, they are the experts—not me. On the other hand, a lot of managers are uncomfortable with letting the staff speak for themselves. They are worried that [the staff] will say something that is not politically acceptable. And there are circumstances where that

is a legitimate concern. If I have a group of reporters in and we are talking about a technical study, generally I will start off the briefing with an overview statement and then when we start talking about the technical details, I turn it over to the staff. I will then make summarizing comments, consistent with what the staff said. If there are any questions, I will throw them back to the staff and let them answer them.

On Congress, Courts, and Scientists

Another problem that surfaced in these interviews is linked to the adversarial legalism we have discussed in this book. Put most simply, scientists and judges are not always in sync. One former EPA manager gave the example of developing radionuclide regulations. When the Sierra Club sued the EPA for not promulgating these regulations by a statutory deadline, organization experts asked for a nine-year extension. Instead, a federal judge gave the EPA 180 days to promulgate the regulations. Pressured, the organization hastily issued the regulations without letting its Science Advisory Board review them. When the latter finally did, it found them scientifically flawed. The EPA administrator responded by withdrawing the regulations and was held in contempt of court. To purge itself of the contempt-of-court citation, the organization then issued "sham" regulations that conformed with the letter of the court's order but in fact increased the amount of radionuclides that could be emitted into the atmosphere (see O'Leary, 1993a).

Another manager commented that this was fairly typical: "The scientists want more data and the public wants an answer. It's like the push for the Transportation Safety Board to explain the crash of TWA Flight 800. They can't. There is too much uncertainty in the data and it usually takes longer to get to an answer than the nonscientists are comfortable with."

On Tangible Use of Scientific Data

Other interviewees spoke to an issue dear to the hearts of scientific and technical personnel: Is their work being taken seriously and making a difference in the real world? One manager noted, "I saw a real hunger on the part of EPA scientists for some sort of evidence that someone was using the information they were generating. They were doing all this good science, but was anybody really paying attention to the data? They wanted to see some closure. So I think it's incumbent on management to show the staff how it [their information] is being used. They want to be taken seriously."

On Managing High Expectations

Other managers interviewed stressed the ways they try to take advantage of the scientists' high expectations of themselves and of others to improve their own managerial styles. One consistent theme was to give scientific and technical personnel the opportunity to provide feedback to managers. One manager described his experience with this technique: "They would tell me when they thought I was wrong, but I invited that. At least once a year I would offer the staff an opportunity to critique me and my performance and what I was doing. It was to be anonymous, but many times they would want to speak face-to-face."

On Being a Nurturing Manager

Interviewees also suggested a need to think of the relationship between professionals and managers in a quite different way. Using a familial analogy, one manager said

> If one of my staff members ever learned that I said this, they would cringe. But it is true: being a human resource manager is like being the head of a family. Your employees are not children, but closer to teenagers. Scientific and technical personnel will test the limits of authority, wanting to show their independence, and you've got to give it to them if they are going to grow. And just like a teenager, they want to know why they can or cannot do something. You have to let them make mistakes, as long as they are not disastrous, and you have to let them make their own decisions or it will arrest their development.

On Why Scientific and Technical Personnel Deserve a Lot of Attention

Other interviewees—noting how high maintenance scientific and technical staff can be—were quick to explain why managers should not scrimp on the attention they give these professionals. One manager noted

> With scientific-technical people your basic commodity is knowledge. That is the capital of your enterprise. If you don't treat them

right and they walk—there goes the capital of your enterprise. That argues strongly for a manager paying a lot of attention to the personal relations' aspect of dealing with knowledge workers. They can't be replaced easily. These people are the bedrock of your decisions, and they deserve a lot of attention they don't normally get. They often get ignored because they are in the back room, not on the front line, and I think that's a big mistake. They have to have someone in there as their manager who understands all of this and is willing to pay attention to them and take care of their needs.

On Scientists and Technical Persons as Managers

Commonly in organizations, persons with the greatest scientific and technical skills are moved into management positions. Often this is done because the only way to get promoted is to move into management. Yet skill in scientific and technical matters often does not translate into being a skillful manager. This is especially true when one remembers the introverted personality traits, high ego, and impatience of many of these professionals. Specialists do not always become quality managers. One interviewee suggested, "It is a fairly common practice to promote the most technically competent person into a position of supervising the technical people. I personally think that is a mistake. There should be a dual-career track to reward and challenge our best scientists and technical persons without forcing them to become managers." To address this problem, the EPA has used lateral moves to create a two-track system. For example, an exemplary engineer in the water division might move laterally to the air division. This helps create a holistic view of the environment and addresses the balkanizing problem that is endemic to most organizations. One former deputy administrator of the EPA explained, "At first it was really challenging when somebody moved from the toxics area to the air area. All of a sudden they had to learn a whole new set of issues and things. On the other hand, you'd see a new quickness in their step and an enthusiasm about the job they were doing. In the end, the organization and the employee benefited immensely.

Other Management Tips

Finally, one manager expressed a general feeling of our interviewees prosaically:

The greatest management principle in the world: people do what they get rewarded for.

The golden rule: do unto others as you would have them do unto you.

The platinum rule: do unto others as they would like to be done unto.

WHAT NOT TO DO From the literature on managing scientific and technical personnel, as well as from the interviews highlighted here, we have culled fifteen specific rules of thumb concerning how not to manage scientific and technical personnel:

- Do not assume that all people have the same personality traits.
- Do not focus only on salary and fringe benefits, ignoring the job itself. Studies of what creative professionals value conclude that recognition and increased self-esteem are much more highly valued than monetary reward (see, for example, Farid, El-Sharkawy, and Austin, 1993).
- Do not keep the scientific and technical person so busy that he or she cannot think (Taylor, 1972).
- Do not nip all new ideas in the bud. One researcher wrote sarcastically, "If you, as a supervisor, really do want to stop something, be alert, be sensitive to the problem. *Nip it in the bud* because not many people will see you kill it—just the person with the idea and you" (Taylor, 1972, p. 20).
- Do not "assign the scientist a task without any explanation for the assignment, then accept his report on the completed work and tell him you are too busy to discuss it" (Koning, 1988, p. 29). The scientist will take this as "apparent disinterest . . . [as a] discouraging indication that his work is not important[,] and that the supervisor is not concerned about his development" (Koning, 1988, p. 29).
- Do not fail to buy the scientist or the technical worker the equipment that he or she needs to carry out his or her work effectively—at least not without a good explanation of resource constraints.
- Do not evade decision making or let the scientist or technical person drown in a quagmire of bureaucratic rules and regulations.
- Do not duck responsibility or delay action by setting up a multitude of committees to deal with the scientists' or technical workers' concerns.

- Do not inundate the scientist or technical person with meaningless busy work.
- Do not make project goals, scope, resources, and roles of team members as ambiguous as possible (Farid, El-Sharkawy, and Austin, 1993).
- Do not assign tasks arbitrarily without consulting with the scientist or technical person (Farid, El-Sharkawy, and Austin, 1993).
- Do not distribute workload inequitably (Farid, El-Sharkawy, and Austin, 1993).
- Do not fail to give scientists or technical personnel the opportunity to apply their expertise and experience (Farid, El-Sharkawy, and Austin, 1993). As we noted earlier, because of more contracting out EPA scientists are increasingly becoming liaisons with and supervisors of consultants, rather than doing the scientific research themselves (O'Leary, 1993a). Indeed, this problem may be one that for-profit managers will find among their own contractors.
- Do not ignore the data or the science, or make environmental decisions solely on the basis of politics.
- Do not plagiarize the work of your scientific and technical people, or neglect to credit or recognize them for their work.

WHAT TO DO The literature on managing scientific and technical personnel, as well as the interviews highlighted earlier, also suggest several specific guidelines on how best to manage these professionals.

Guideline 1. Establish a work climate that fosters free expression and encourages independent thought (Martin and Shell, 1988).

Guideline 2. Manage ends, but not means (Raelin, 1985).

Guideline 3. Realize that scientific and technical personnel are generally "different." Protect and nurture them as you would any other capital resource in your organization.

Guideline 4. Let scientists and technical workers participate in policy discussions that will affect their work (Raelin, 1985). Explain your decisions to them. To get scientific and technical personnel to work together with management, utilize communication, training, and teamwork. Educate the scientific and technical staff about factors that affect management. Educate management about the challenges of being a scientist or technical worker. Put the diverse groups together in project teams, thus penetrating barriers to integration. (Our tips in Chapters Four, Six, and Nine on building a coproduction environmental ethic in organizations and networks will go a long way toward making sure these things happen.)

Guideline 5. More generally, provide ample avenues for input from scientists and technical personnel. Do not ignore their criticisms or suggestions. Realize that a creative idea can come from any part of the organization, and that unless the right supervisors are selected most ideas will be killed while traveling up the organizational ladder (Kanter, 1983). Also, always keep informal channels of communication open between you and these professionals (Taylor, 1972, p. 12). Finally, always keep Gibb's (1972, p. 28) advice from the early 1970s in mind: "Managers release creativity by trusting, open, allowing, and interdependent [not controlling] actions."

Guideline 6. Take steps to see that the most creative minds do in fact rise to the top of the organization (Taylor, 1972, p. 9).

Guideline 7. Support scientific and technical employees who are action oriented, even if they fail. Especially support proactive behavior (Taylor, 1972, p. 13). One early study showed that, in many instances, organizations were just about to fire their most creative people right before those people produced their most important ideas (Taylor, 1972, p. 8). Similarly, more recent work has noted how important it is not to punish mistakes made once risk taking is encouraged (Hammer, 1996). Also, be sure that you give emotional support to creative persons so they can consistently function at their highest levels of creativity.

Guideline 8. Recognize and give fair credit to scientific and technical personnel when it is due, in ongoing and continuous ways (Caudron, 1994). "Most scientists are driven by their need to discover and then get praise and recognition for those discoveries," said one manager (Caudron, 1994, p. 105). As J. Scott Long and Mary Fox (1995) contend, getting recognized by peers is an important indication of a scientist's contributions to his or her field, and serves both as a reward for past performance and as an inducement for future performance. Koning (1993) agrees, saying that it is the most important component in managing scientists and engineers.

For the reader's convenience, Table 10.1 lists different forms of recognition and rewards adapted from Koning (1988, p. 46). Among the most useful of these forms is setting up roundtables or seminars to give the scientists an opportunity to discuss their research with their peers in open sessions. Another is to give scientists the chance to work together once they demonstrate their ability to conduct research independently. Finally, it is useful to give scientists and technical persons opportunities to author papers and publications, to obtain new equipment, and to gain awards or pats on the back when they do well. Mean-

Table 10.1. Different Forms of Recognition and Rewards for Scientific and Technical Personnel.

Recognition	Rewards
Praise	*Income*
Feedback	Salary increase
Private praise	Equity position
Not taking scientist for granted	Profit sharing
Enthusiasm and support from top management	Promotion
	Pay-for-performance
Appreciation	Bonus
Company praise	Patent royalties
Public praise	Merit salary
More responsibility and authority	Percentage of savings
Freedom to develop solutions to solve problems	Bonus for patents
	Cash awards
Freedom of action	Incentive award
Responsibility	Cost-of-living salary adjustment
Authority to carry out responsibilities	Improved working conditions
Budget control	Satisfying scientists' needs
Expense account	Flexible schedule
New position	Adequate resources to run projects
Professional recognition	Earned time off
Authorship on papers	Professional development
Association awards	Trip to meeting
Fellows program	Membership in professional association
Honors dinner	
Plaque or trophy	Paid education
Title	Benefits
Certificate	Fringe benefits
Work situation	Retirement plan
Meeting personal goals	
Sense of accomplishment	
Challenging research	
Interesting or meaningful research	

Table 10.1. (continued)

Setting joint objectives

Team membership

Dual ladder

Personal interaction with upper
management

Special parking

Source: Adapted from Koning, 1993. Used with permission of the publisher.

while, a simple showing of confidence in their judgment and giving credit where credit is due can go a long way.

Guideline 9. Realize that the scientific process is often at tension with the political process, as well as with the realities of running large bureaucracies. This is especially true in regulatory agencies, where a constant tension exists between scientists wanting to do basic research but finding their time and resources skewed toward regulatory science. Be sensitive to these concerns, and try to foster as much of the former as is possible under these constraints. At a minimum, understand the frustrations of these professionals in this regard.

Guideline 10. Give scientific and technical personnel the opportunity to provide feedback to managers.

Guideline 11. Strive to provide innovative dual-career ladders so that scientists and technical personnel may continue to do their creative work (Raelin, 1985; Greene, 1992). Another way to allow employees to advance while they remain in a technical role is to reward them consistently with status, salary, and incentives that are equivalent to those enjoyed by managers. Finally, at all times allow employees to explore and assess their interests and strengths so they can make informed career choices (Caudron, 1994, p. 106).

Guideline 12. Use regulatory compensation to recruit and retain scientific and technical staff. In 1986, the Federal Technology Transfer Act mandated that employee-inventors working in federally funded research laboratories should be granted a royalty of at least 15 percent of any licensing income the laboratory receives. One study estimated that one-sixth of all scientists and engineers in the United States, or about 100,000 workers, might be eligible for such rewards (Caudron, 1994, p. 104). One of the advantages of such an approach is that it allows managers to use markets rather than organizational budgets as reward mechanisms.

Guideline 13. Provide formal training in people skills (especially communication skills) whenever you promote technoscience professionals to management positions.

Guideline 14. Instill pride by promoting the strengths of the organization and the contributions of professionals to those strengths (Rastogi, 1995; Gibson and Whittaker, 1996).

Guideline 15. Give scientific and technical people tools and resources that allow their skills and work to shine. Especially valued are the technology and resources needed to work on cutting-edge projects. Legend has it that Chuck Yeager stayed in the Air Force because he loved to fly experimental new aircraft that he could not afford to buy himself (Caudron, 1994, p. 106). Many scientific and technical staff feel this way about their high-tech equipment. Tied in with this, managers can attract and keep scientific and technical personnel by promising to fund "one of their pet projects. . . . Give them the toys they need to continue the projects they're interested in," suggests one manager (Caudron, 1994, p. 106). In this regard, some organizations use "innovation banks" to fund special projects that normally might not be funded (Caudron, 1994, p. 106).

Guideline 16. Practice task assignment through "managed volunteerism." Here the goal is to foster a personal commitment among professionals to do the job correctly and well (Gibson and Whittaker, 1996). Thomas McFarland (1994) maintains that the most important factor in managing engineers is matching individual abilities and motivations with the development and goals of the organization. This can often be accomplished through managed volunteerism.

Guideline 17. Allow flexibility within whatever structures (administrative, responsibility, and accounting) must exist (see Chapter Four). This can allow an atmosphere of creativity to flourish (Sankar, 1991).

Guideline 18. Make sure that supervisors of scientific and technical staff understand the basic science and technical issues that are the subject of their workers' projects.

Guideline 19. Invest in job enrichment and job enlargement. High salary and fringe benefits are not the only solutions to keeping scientific and technical personnel. Rather, the job itself is the major motivator. Job enrichment refers to a "planned change of job content to provide the worker with a greater variety of work that requires a higher level of knowledge or skill, generally providing an opportunity for personal growth and development" (Couger and Zawacki, 1980, p. 46). In a job enrichment program, the worker is brought into the planning, organizing, and controlling aspects of the job, as opposed to just doing the work he or she is told to do. Job enlargement refers to a situation in which the worker is given "a greater variety of work (such as job rotation) without increasing the need for a higher level of knowledge and skills" (Couger and Zawacki, 1980, p. 46). The focus here is not on autonomy; rather, it is on horizontal movement from job to job.

CONCLUSION

Although there are no administrative quick fixes or magic recipes for successfully managing scientific and technical personnel, this chapter has offered suggestions that managers have found useful. We first provided a general personality portrait of these professionals. They tend to be highly analytical "wild ducks" who oftentimes are not motivated by traditional incentives. They have strong commitments to their disciplines, which can clash with organizational and political norms and demands. Wild ducks usually can fly to other organizations, yielding brain drain and loss of institutional memory. They are often regarded by themselves and their employees as being a group apart and therefore deserving preferential treatment in terms of their conditions of employment. We then highlighted what scientific and technical workers say they want in terms of a creative environment and competent managers. From this review, we culled lessons about what—and what not—to do.

Clearly, managing scientific and technical personnel will continue to provide immense challenges to managers as they try to deal effectively, prudently, and responsively with today's and tomorrow's environmental management issues. Moreover, this will be true whether they are environmental specialists or nonspecialists, regulators or regulatees, government contractors or contract managers. But as daunting as this challenge to institutionalizing a commitment to environmental values can be within organizations, it pales in comparison to the challenges that public managers face when trying to institutionalize this ethic among their partnering networks of for-profit and nonprofit contractors and grantees. Moreover, an even more fundamental threshold question must be answered by those who are thinking about employing contractors, subcontractors, and grantees to do the public's business for them: Under what conditions is it prudent to use contracts, subcontracts, and grants in this fashion? It is to these issues that we turn next in Chapter Eleven.

11

MANAGING CONTRACTS
AND GRANTS

What I do not see I do not know.

—Hildegard von Bingen[1]

In the early 1990s there were approximately 160,000 people working for the U.S. Department of Energy (DOE). Only about 19,000 civil servants, however, were on the DOE payroll at that time. The difference in numbers is attributed to the contracting out of important DOE work, including the cleanup of hazardous and toxic wastes at plants that at one time produced nuclear weapons. In 1992 there were more than fifty such contracts that cost taxpayers an estimated $14 billion (Hickox, 1992; Goldstein, 1992). In 1996, the DOE awarded another $19.5 billion to private contractors for the cleanup of hazardous and toxic wastes (Rubin and Wright, 1996). These primary contractors in turn subcontracted some of their work to other firms.

The case of DOE nuclear waste cleanup is only one of thousands of examples of the use of contracts or grants (also known as *outsourcing*)— or more consonant with our theme, partnering—to get the business of government done. This chapter addresses the issues of awarding and managing those contracts, subcontracts, and grants effectively. It thus speaks foremost to government policymakers and managers. But for-profit and nonprofit organizations also must consider the promise and pitfalls of subcontracting out parts of the awards they receive from government, as well as the wisdom of other partnering arrangements they might be contemplating. Moreover, when acting as agents on behalf of government, managers from each of these sectors will be held accountable for the full range of values that citizens expect in a democracy.

We begin the chapter by examining the pros and cons of utilizing contracts and grants to provide government goods and services. We then review recent U.S. Supreme Court cases concerning the rights of independent contractors. Next we distill lessons learned from both practitioners and prior research about managing contracts and grants. Finally we provide a list of questions that the thoughtful policymaker and manager should ask when deciding whether and how to utilize contracts or grants.

PROXIES, PROGRAMS, AND THE PUBLIC INTEREST

As noted, it is not just the DOE that utilizes contracts and grants. The EPA's Superfund program to clean up hazardous waste sites has contracted out more than $10 billion in business to private firms (U.S. General Accounting Office, 1991b). The Department of Interior's Bureau of Reclamation has distributed $75 million in grants for projects to reduce the salinity of the Colorado River (Rosenbaum, 1996). Water treatment programs contracted out in Indianapolis both improved service and saved money (Goldsmith, 1997). Many nonprofit charities derive a large portion of their income from government grants and contracts, amounting to an estimated 40 percent of all charitable spending (Spencer, 1995).

Contracts and grants are a form of what Donald Kettl (1988) calls "government by proxy." These proxy partnerships include private and nonprofit contractors and subcontractors who do work previously done by government agencies; state, county, and local government agencies that receive grants to provide goods and services previously afforded by higher levels of government; and individuals who receive grants and contracts to carry out research, develop new products, and provide services. Sometimes proxy government is genuinely seen as a more efficient, effective, and equitable way to do the public's business (DeHoog, 1984; Donahue, 1989; Kelman, 1990). At other times, it is merely an attempt to satisfy critics of government who demand a pound of flesh in exchange for letting an agency survive. At still other times, it is an attempt by governments to "load shed" (that is, to shift responsibilities to others) in order to reduce budget expenditures. But whatever the reason in specific cases, managers who think that proxy government is a passing fad are making a serious mistake (O'Leary, 1996).

It is important to distinguish between contracts and grants. Kettl (1988) points out that contracts are negotiated documents. The contractor provides an agreed-upon service or product for an agreed-upon price. Contracts typically are competitive. If one agent fails to deliver, at least in theory it is possible to turn to another agent. In contrast, grants to states or localities are set up differently. The federal government often agrees to grant money to state or local governments if they will conduct certain programs. If the governments do not pursue the programs or if they perform poorly, it is usually difficult for federal administrators to turn to another grantee to get the job done. A similar conundrum confronts state governments that issue grants to their localities. Hence grants generally imply less of a master-servant relationship than contracts do (O'Leary, 1996).

THE PROS AND CONS OF UTILIZING CONTRACTS AND GRANTS

Why do policymakers, elected officials, and managers pursue contract and grant partnership arrangements with providers outside of government? Primarily they do so with four expectations: to save money, to promote flexibility, to further social objectives, and to garner political support. At the same time, several potential disadvantages to utilizing contracts and grants must be kept in mind. Thus, weighing the pros and cons of such arrangements is important.

Potential Advantages

Contracting can be a powerful environmental management tool with the following strengths.

SAVES MONEY Policymakers often find that contracts and grants are a less expensive way to deliver goods and services than providing them through government agencies (Seidenstat, 1996; Johnston, 1996). Public choice scholars argue that competition in the marketplace produces goods and services efficiently, whereas monopolies such as government bureaucracies tend to be both inefficient and unresponsive. Purchaser power and cost savings may increase when there is competition for a service. Labor may be less expensive because private firms do not have to follow civil service requirements. Layers of public laws, red tape, and bureaucracy also may not encumber them.

But one need not be an ideologue to see the advantages of market-based alternatives to service delivery. As Indianapolis Mayor Stephen Goldsmith (1997) argues, often what public agencies see as expenses, businesspersons see as cash cows. In these instances, both sides win. Outsourcing or partnering means that agencies (and ultimately, perhaps, taxpayers) pay less for products and services while businesses use economies of scale to expand their markets and improve profit margins.

Goldsmith's observations are borne out in many empirical studies across all levels of government and a full range of products and services, including savings on in-house administrative costs, sanitation services, solid waste treatment plants, prisons, bus systems, airports, and port authorities (Savas, 1987, 1995; Goodman, 1990; Hakim, Seidenstat, and Bowman, 1996; Hatry, Brounstein, and Levinson, 1993). Indeed, there is also evidence that under certain circumstances outsourcing modestly increases quality as well, as long as proper accountability measures are maintained (see, for example, Hatry, Brounstein, and Levinson, 1993; Durant, Legge, and Moussios, 1998).

How widespread are Goldsmith's sentiments? A 1987 survey by the International City/County Management Association (ICMA) found general support by local government officials for contracting of some services. Seventy-four percent of the 1,086 cities and counties that responded to the survey indicated that cost saving was a major reason to contract out services (International City/County Management Association, 1989). Another study concluded that nearly 80 percent of all cities and counties in the United States contract out some services in order to save money (David, 1988). Since then, surveys of states, counties, and cities have shown that officials have persistently and increasingly opted for outsourcing across the nation (Seidenstat, 1996).

ENHANCES FLEXIBILITY Policymakers may also find that contracts and grants yield greater flexibility. In some circumstances, starting up new programs is easier for a contractor or grantee than for a government bureaucracy encumbered by mandated standard operating procedures, demanding interest groups, and bureaucratic red tape. Contractors and grantees may also be better able to tailor a program to a given community. Steven Smith and Michael Lipsky (1993, p. 192) give the example of job counseling for Spanish-speaking teenagers and point out that it may be easier for government to hire a private Hispanic firm to provide the needed services than to have a government agency retool or hire new staff.

PROMOTES GOOD POLITICS Under certain circumstances, contracting and grantmaking can also be good politics for policymakers. Critics among conservative politicians tend to support these measures, in part as a way to curb permanent big government. The size of government bureaucracy is kept in check, theoretically (Harney, 1992). This approach can thus be a profitable way for policymakers to sell the delivery of environmental goals, services, and opportunities to conservative politicians, who might not otherwise support them. In turn, "new Democrats" may sign on to reap cost-effective environmental management, as long as the concerns of public employee unions and environmental justice activists are met.

PROMOTES SOCIAL OBJECTIVES Policymakers can also use contracting and grantmaking to promote social and economic objectives while pursuing environmental benefits (MacManus, 1992). Examples include nurturing small businesses, the use of minority businesses, the use of recycled materials, and the employment of physically challenged citizens. In some areas, contracting and grantmaking have even bolstered Buy American campaigns.

MAINTAINS OR IMPROVES QUALITY There are numerous examples of programs that have improved through contract and grant arrangements while saving money. The Department of Defense has successfully hired private contractors to handle sanitation services (B. G. Peters, 1996). Similarly, a series of grants from the EPA to fifteen cities is credited with improving their Brownfields programs (see Chapter Six). Laredo, Texas, for example, developed a Brownfields inventory and cleanup plan, while Louisville, Kentucky, used a geographical information system to locate development areas ("Brownfields Grants," 1995). Hundreds of cities have upgraded their wastewater treatment plants using federal and state grants (as well as state revolving fund loan programs). More broadly, one 1984 study of twenty cities in California found that for seven services—street cleaning, janitorial services, signal maintenance, street paving, refuse collection, tree maintenance, and grounds maintenance—contracting saved money while maintaining a reasonable level of service. In only one circumstance—preparing payrolls—were no savings achieved by contracting out (Stevens, 1984).

Most interesting in the environmental management arena are two cases: Indianapolis's experience in contracting out operating expenses for its already advanced wastewater treatment plants, and Mt. Vernon, Illinois's experience in franchising construction and operation of an expanded wastewater facility. In the former case, Indianapolis realized reduced operating costs of 44 percent, totaling $65 million, over the five-year life of the contract (Goldsmith, 1997). In the Mt. Vernon case, the city saved $3 million when the contractor completed the project far ahead of schedule (Seidenstat, 1996).

Why did better environmental management emerge in these cases at seriously less cost? To an extent, public choice theorists are correct: even otherwise well-managed agencies are still buffered from market competition, as well as from the consequences of their actions. But agencies are not always monopoly providers of services. Moreover, benchmarking, the use of revolving funds, and intra-agency service comparisons are ways to gain quasi-market competition without contracting out.

Far more significant in these cases, we argue, are two commodities that public agencies are finding it difficult to maintain during downsizing and attrition: institutional memory and highly skilled personnel. In the Indianapolis case, for example, the contractor—White River Environmental Partnership—had years of experience treating wastewater in Europe (where contracting out these services is routine). At the same time, it had more civil engineers with Ph.D. degrees than Indianapolis had employees. As the city's director of public works put it, this firm had "resources our guys in city government only dream of" (Goldsmith, 1997, p. 116).

Potential Disadvantages

Despite these many advantages, contracting is not always a wise environmental management choice. It may have the following drawbacks for policymakers and their agencies.

DOES NOT ALWAYS SAVE MONEY Contracting and grantmaking can expose a government to excessive costs and give contractors little incentive to control expenditures if adequate safeguards are not imposed (U.S. General Accounting Office, 1991c). The profit motive of the private sector "should not automatically be correlated with efficiency in the private sector" (Prager, 1994). In some cases, such as the procurement of large weapons systems, there simply is no preexisting market for the goods the government wishes to purchase. In the absence of a market to determine the appropriate value for such a good, the burden falls on government to make such a determination. It is not at all clear that government is able to do this effectively (Kettl, 1993). Using contracts and grants may also increase litigation costs. Charles Wise (1990) points out that if there are severe differences in contractor performance and government expectations, the contract dispute is likely to reach the courts.

MAY INCREASE SIZE OF GOVERNMENT Policymakers should also understand that in some circumstances contracting and grant letting have expanded government programs. This occurs because they are "unconstrained by the difficulties public agencies [ordinarily] would experience in hiring a huge number of new workers for new tasks" (Smith and Lipsky, 1993, p. 204). Without popular opposition, investigations by the press, and legislator scrutiny, it is easier for government programs to thrive. In this sense, government has not really become smaller, only different. Moreover, the "pinstripe patronage" it occasions among contractors creates a ready and powerful constituency to expand government services.

REQUIRES MONITORING Policymakers should also expect accountability problems. A general consensus exists that for the most part contractors and grantees have not been adequately monitored. The U.S. General Accounting Office (GAO) (1991b, 1991c), for example, has concluded that oversight of contracts and grants at the federal level has generally been inadequate because of limits on staffing and resources. Kettl (1993) points out that sometimes the information needed to monitor contractors thoroughly is difficult to obtain—a situation that is even more outlandish at the state and local levels.

The reasons for this situation are multiple. The oversight of contracts and grants, for both financial and technical compliance, is time-consuming and resource intensive. This in turn often reduces the resources available for uses deemed more productive by managers in the organization (Milward, 1994). In addition, new regulations often must be promulgated to regulate the contracting processes. Moreover, staff must often be allocated—and sometimes reallocated from unrelated tasks—to oversee contracts (recall the experience of EPA scientists). And much too often those transferred have no experience in monitoring contracts.

Work of uneven or poor quality subsequently results. If contracts are broken or grant guidelines are not followed, contractors, subcontractors, and grantees must be penalized in some fashion. If they are not, the potential for mischief spirals apace.

PERMITS COLLUSION AND ABUSE Collusion among bidders for contracts is another serious danger that policymakers should anticipate. Competition should not be assumed (Prager, 1994), because in some areas there is no competition (Kettl, 1993). Contracts and grants can also be abused after they are awarded. One inspector general, for example, found that some contractors for the EPA were receiving compensation for work outside the scope of their contract or agreement. Other contractors had become such good friends with EPA employees that they had insider status and were treated preferentially in the contracting process. Finally, other contractors subdivided contracts in order to take advantage of noncompetitive small-business bidding rules (U.S. House of Representatives, Committee on Government Operations, 1993).

There has been significant documentation of abuse in contractor-grantee spending. One company that contracted with the EPA to clean up Superfund hazardous waste sites spent taxpayer money on baseball tickets, Disneyland tickets, flowers, and lavish Christmas parties. The company defended its actions by maintaining that they were needed to maintain positive employee morale (U.S. House of Representatives, Committee on Government Operations, 1992, p. 54). This loss of control over how taxpayer funds are spent should be a major worry for managers awarding or overseeing contracts, subcontracts, and grants. Other problems they should worry about include conflicts of interest, problems with accountability of contractors and grantees, reduced quality of services or products, private consultants making public policy decisions, and reduced citizen participation (Goldstein, 1992; MacManus, 1992).

MAY BE RESISTED BY LABOR UNIONS Policymakers should expect that one of the major sources of resistance to the utilization of contracts and grants will be public labor unions. Many union members fear the loss of jobs if excessive contracting and grantmaking are used (Chandler and Feuille, 1994). Indeed, nearly one-half (47 percent) of respondents to a 1987 ICMA survey cited such union opposition as a reason not to use contracts and grants (International City/County Management Association, 1989). Since then, however, the use of contracting has spiraled, with at least grudging union support once members' concerns are taken into account. For example, sizable contracting efforts in Phoenix, Arizona, and in Massachusetts and New York proceeded once unions were afforded "safety nets" for their members. Contracts, for instance, had to stipulate that displaced workers would be given priority in hiring by contractors. Guarantees that those displaced would get other jobs somewhere else in government have also eased union opposition and lessened employee anxiety.

REQUIRES KNOWLEDGE OF THE ORGANIZATION Contractors, their subcontractors, and grantees often know more about a task than those who are awarding contracts and grants. This information asymmetry can cause implementation problems that policymakers cannot always adequately address either by carefully selecting contractors and grantees or by monitoring them (Prager, 1994). The flip side to this phenomenon is that contracting and grantmaking can yield a brain drain from certain types of public agencies (a phenomenon we noted in Chapter Ten). Managers at the EPA, for example, report a hiring preference for individuals with abilities to oversee contractors, rather than individuals with scientific and technical expertise (U.S. House of Representatives, Committee on Post Office and Civil Service, 1989; O'Leary, 1993a). In turn, and as we have noted, EPA employees with scientific and technical expertise are frustrated by their extensive oversight responsibilities (Lee, 1996; see also Goldstein, 1992; Kettl, 1993; O'Leary, 1993a).

MAY CAUSE EXTERNALITIES Externalities can occur when contracting (Kettl, 1993). A negative externality is an unintended and undesirable social effect of production or consumption. For example, as we noted earlier and in Chapter Three, environmental contamination occurred when federal agencies contracted out the production of nuclear weapons. In these instances, and because of the erosion of the "contractor defense" in lawsuits (whereby contractors were assumed to share sovereign immunity when acting on behalf of government agencies), contracts yielded greater problems for government. They can now be responsible for fines levied against contractors for violating environmental laws. Because it cannot be proven, however, that contamination would not have occurred if production had remained in-house, these kinds of externalities may not be unique to contracting. Still, all managers need to be vigilant about the environmental sensitivity of their contractors, subcontractors, and grantees when making awards.

MAY DISRUPT SERVICES AND LACK CLEAR DEFINITION OF NEEDS
Policymakers should also expect that continuity of services can be a
problem when utilizing contracts and grants. Services may be inter-
rupted, for example, because of financial problems or because of strikes
by consulting firm employees (see later discussion for ways to protect
against this). Moreover, switching from one contractor to another may
yield service gaps, which in turn may affect the health or safety of government clients (Allen and others, 1989).

**MAY INCREASE GOVERNMENT INTERVENTION IN PRIVATE ORGANI-
ZATIONS** Policymakers should also understand that contracting and
grant letting have yielded unprecedented government involvement in the
affairs of private organizations. "Instead of shrinking the role of government and making the provision of public services subject to market
discipline, contracting has actually diminished and constrained" certain
organizations that contract with government agencies (Smith and Lipsky,
1993, p. 204). Likewise, many in the nonprofit community worry that
their increasing dependence on government grants may distort their priorities or divert them from their original missions (Herzlinger, 1994). In
both cases, this has in some circumstances lessened innovation and fur-
thered the gulf between the provider and the recipient of services.

MAY BE GIVEN LOW JOB STATUS Although contract and grant management are increasing in importance in private firms and local, state,
and federal government agencies, they are usually not regarded as high-
status jobs (Milward, 1994). Indeed, the prestige associated with overseeing contracts and grants has remained static despite their increased
use. Simply put, there are few rewards for quality contract and grant
managers. One GAO report, for example, cited a lack of high-level attention in the federal government to contract management. Agency leaders often delegate contract management to U.S. government regional
offices that lack sufficient oversight and accountability measures (U.S.
General Accounting Office, October 1991c). Consequently, policymakers must anticipate difficulty in getting workers who are enthusiastic
about monitoring contracts, who will stay with the job for a long time,
and who will take the job seriously. This will be true at least until they
raise the salience of contracting and reward it accordingly.

GOVERNMENT MAY BE BEST Some goods and services are best provided by government (O'Leary, 1996; Donahue, 1989; Savas, 1987).

Smith and Lipsky (1993), for example, maintain that solid waste disposal may sensibly be provided by contractors or grantees only under certain circumstances (discussed shortly). Access to environmental services for the disadvantaged may also be reduced as contractors avoid clients for whom services are likely to be difficult or expensive (Allen and others, 1989). Policymakers should be wary of contracting under these circumstances.

In addition, government may provide services of greater quality or quantity than the private sector. For example, a private contractor providing solid waste collection and disposal services may pick up bags weekly in a residential area. In contrast, a government entity may provide the same service twice a week and provide additional valued services, including bulk waste collection and disposal, composting, household hazardous waste disposal, and recycling.

One city public works director interviewed explained that privatizing solid waste services in his city produced marginal financial benefits. Moreover, bulk waste collection and disposal, as well as street sweeping, were no longer offered after privatization. Contracting in such circumstances may be politically popular for policymakers in the short term, but it may have indirect and unforeseen costs that outweigh benefits in the long run. One such cost might be the kinds of environmental lawsuits we noted in Chapters Two, Three, and Six. It is therefore of paramount importance to stipulate in any contract that all services will be provided in an environmentally sensitive fashion. Otherwise, taxpayers may have to incur costs for fines, penalties, and remedial actions assessed against their contractors.

MAY PRODUCE HOLLOW GOVERNMENT There has been little research about the impact of contracting and grant letting on an organization's overall functions, as well as its impact on the legitimacy of government organizations (Milward, 1994). Serious questions remain. What do contracting and grant letting mean for the future of government agencies? How will public programs be held accountable for the results that contracting or grantmaking produce (Milward, 1994; Durant, 1998a)? Will the result be "hollow government, where public organizations are separated from their output" (Milward, Provan, and Else, 1993)? Clearly the pros and cons of the use of contracts and grants pose formidable but as yet largely uninvestigated challenges for environmental policymakers concerned about the larger implications of these actions for democratic values.

RECENT COURT DECISIONS

By the same token, the courts have addressed issues involved in contracting that can affect democratic values and taxpayers' wallets. Managers can ill afford to remain ignorant of the lessons these issues afford. How far, for example, can a contractor go in criticizing policymakers before they can fire him? During its 1995–96 term the Supreme Court decided two cases concerning the First Amendment rights of independent contractors. Both cases strengthened the rights of private contractors.

In *Board of County Commissioners* v. *Umbehr* (1996), Umbehr was a contractor hauling trash for the county. He was also an outspoken critic of the board of county commissioners. The commissioners voted to terminate or prevent the automatic renewal of the contract. Umbehr brought suit, alleging that he was terminated because of his criticism and that the commissioners had thus violated his First Amendment free speech rights. The district court granted summary judgment in favor of the commissioners, but the Tenth Circuit reversed and remanded the decision. The Supreme Court affirmed the appeals court.

The Court said that the First Amendment protects independent contractors from termination or prevention of automatic renewal of at-will government contracts whenever governments are retaliating against an exercise of free speech. It justified its decision by citing the balancing test previously applied to government employees in *Pickering* v. *Board of Education* (1968). This test requires governments to weigh their interests as contracting party against the free speech interests of their employees. In Umbehr's case, the commissioners had tried to differentiate between independent contractors and public employees, but the Court rejected the distinction.

The majority also set guidelines for lower courts to use when applying the *Pickering* test. For contractors to prevail, they must show initially that termination of the contract was motivated by what they said on a matter of public concern. They must also prove more than that they criticized officials before they were terminated. In contrast, local government officials will have a valid defense if they can show by a preponderance of evidence that they would have terminated the contract regardless of what was said. Importantly, this proof rests on the officials' knowledge, perceptions, and policies at the time they terminated the contractor. They will also prevail if they can demonstrate that their legitimate interests as contracting party, deferentially viewed, outweigh any free speech interests at stake. At the same time, however, they cannot argue that they would have fired the contractor anyway based on information obtained after the firing. They also cannot depend on other or new contracts they grant to the contractor to offset their financial obligations to the contractor if they lose the case.

The issue in the second First Amendment case was contract termination predicated on campaign support for policymakers. In *O'Hare Truck Service* v. *City of Northlake* (1996), the contractor operated a towing service and his business was on a rotation list maintained by the city to perform towing services upon request. The contractor refused to contribute to the mayor's reelection campaign and instead supported his opponent. Subsequently, the city removed the contractor's business from the rotation list. The contractor filed suit, alleging that the removal was in retaliation for his campaign stance and as such it violated his First Amendment rights.

The district and appeals courts found in favor of the city. Citing previous case law, these courts held that the general notion that government officials may not discharge public employees for refusing to give them political support does not extend to independent contractors. On appeal, the Supreme Court reversed the lower courts' ruling, stating that public employee precedents now apply to contractors as well. The Court stressed that the question to be answered is whether the hiring authority can demonstrate that party affiliation is an appropriate requirement for the effective performance of the service involved. The Court stated that if the government terminates its affiliation with a service provider for reasons unrelated to political association, there is no First Amendment violation.

LESSONS LEARNED

Managers can glean a variety of lessons from our review of the literature on contracting and grantmaking. These lessons are presented here as *macro* (big picture) and *micro* (contract specific) guidelines. The review of these lessons is followed by a checklist of questions for policymakers to ask when considering the use of contracts and grants.

Macro Lessons

1. *Critically examine the circumstances under which outsourcing is proposed* (O'Leary, 1996; Donahue, 1989; Savas, 1987, 1995). For example, contracts, subcontracts, or grants may be most appropriate when a program or service is either too small or too large to take

advantage of economies of scale or scope. Criteria favoring the use of contracts or grants rather than direct service provision by public agencies include the following:

- Money will be saved.
- Service will be enhanced.
- The environment will be protected.
- Other programs will not be negatively affected.
- Citizens' needs will be met.
- Increased flexibility will result.
- Objectives can be measured and tasks can be monitored.
- Political support is high.
- Competition is present and is likely to remain so.
- Continuity of services will not be disrupted.
- Legal impediments will be minor.

Do not hesitate to argue against the use of contracts or grants if they do not make sense on these terms.

2. *Be aware of the politics of your specific situation* (O'Leary, 1996; Donahue, 1989; Seidenstat, 1996; Osborne and Plastrik, 1997). On the one hand, make sure that political support exists for using contracts and grants. Remember that contractors, subcontractors, and grantees often have political clout with legislators, which can be both positive and negative. Still, outsourcing can be contentious, given the stakes for those who benefit from the status quo. Managers can therefore anticipate that they will likely have to privatize functions in an "ad hoc, piecemeal, opportunistic fashion" (Windsor, 1995). As Paul Seidenstat (1996, p. 471) notes, elected officials and citizens are not likely to embrace "rapid, comprehensive, wholesale efforts" to outsource.

If privatization is successful, however, understand that the pinstripe patronage that outsourcing and partnering create can be either a help or a hindrance later. For example, switching contractors or grantees can be difficult, thus reducing your flexibility in the long run. However, if political support for valuable programs is an aim, contracting and grantmaking may help.

Finally, in the environmental arena, it is critical that managers develop contingency plans when contracting out infrastructure responsibilities. Practically and politically, poor performance or breakdowns in essential services (such as water and wastewater treatment) can be devastating. Contracting agencies must be prepared to take over these functions again if problems such as strikes, other work stoppages, bankruptcies, or business terminations arise.

3. *Make sure that there is competition for contracts, and do not be afraid to consider other government agencies as contractors, if appropriate* (O'Leary, 1996; Donahue, 1989; Prager, 1994). Another option is to pit existing government providers against private bidders. "There is little if any advantage to be gained from turning over a public service to a private monopolist" (Prager, 1994). Relatedly, be sure to advertise widely in order to promote competition. Finally, even if competition exists, contract specificity and monitoring are critical, as is allowing contractors a reasonable time to show results before the contract is rebid.

4. *Create a learning situation for rebidding* (Donahue, 1989; Osborne and Plastrik, 1997). Even when competition is not present initially, there are ways to create quasi-competition that can help inform future rebidding or requests for proposals (RFPs). For example, in contracting out services, see if there are opportunities to divide the community into different districts and award multiple contracts for later comparisons. Alternatively, reserve a district in the community for a government agency provider, and then let the agency bid for the other districts when rebidding begins. Each of these alternatives can afford unit costing or activity-based cost accounting, information that most agree is critical to advancing environmental values in the most cost-effective ways possible.

5. *When screening contractors, subcontractors, and grant seekers, utilize findings by other programs or organizations (such as inspectors general, comptrollers, and even the contractors' or grantees' own internal audit departments) to gain insight into their performance history* (O'Leary, 1996). Check out their reputation as well. For example, have they adequately implemented contracts or grants in the past? Have they been environmentally responsible? Do they informally follow, or are they formally certified as complying with, ISO 14000 standards? Do they follow due process procedures when dealing with clients? Do they strive for excellence and product quality? Has their performance reflected positively or negatively on the reputation of government in the past? Have they upheld all requirements for seeking a diverse workforce in terms of such goals as gender equity—especially as environmental justice issues come to the forefront?

6. *In certain circumstances, it may make more sense to move incrementally in the hiring of contractors and grantees* (O'Leary, 1996). The

EPA's Superfund program, for example, has been criticized by the GAO for hiring too many contractors at once and thus yielding confusion and excessive program management costs (U.S. General Accounting Office, 1991c).

7. *Be sure to target opportunities for outsourcing and partnering.* As Seidenstat (1996) summarizes, experiences across the nation suggest that outsourcing will be successful if the number of public employees affected is relatively small, if the service is specialized, if the outputs and outcomes are easily defined and measured, if the entry of other bidders is relatively easy, and if there are more rather than fewer beneficiaries. Also, be aware of a fundamental tension. The market must be large and broad enough to ensure that multiple bids will occur; but the market should not be so large that coalitions of interests can defeat the proposal to outsource. This can be a difficult balancing act (Johnston, 1996).

8. *Ensure that, when feasible, contractors and grantees obtain private insurance to protect the government from possible lawsuits* (O'Leary, 1996). Not only should managers monitor contractors to be sure that their insurance does not lapse, but they should also set limits on indemnification.

9. *Make contractors and grantees the first line of defense in detecting and preventing waste, mismanagement, and environmental mischief* (O'Leary, 1996; Donahue, 1989; Osborne and Plastrik, 1997). Require them to oversee management and financial systems and to document compliance with governmental regulations—environmental and otherwise. It is important but hardly sufficient that contractors and grantees oversee themselves, to prevent wrongdoing. Outside, periodic, and meaningful monitoring of these systems and processes is also necessary. Managers should understand that "efficient monitoring, though costly, pays for itself by preventing overcharges and poor quality performance in the first place, by recouping inappropriate outlays, and by disallowing payment for inadequate performance" (Prager, 1994, p. 176). Thus, astute policymakers will resist pressures to outsource unless it is clear that adequate resources are available to monitor and manage contracts and grants. Otherwise, policymakers may avoid waste and mismanagement better by sticking with only the "continuous process improvement" tools associated with Total Quality Environmental Management that we discussed in Chapter Four, and with the quasi-market options outlined earlier in this chapter.

10. *Always try to buy outputs and outcomes, rather than inputs* (Donahue, 1989; Goldsmith, 1997). Put differently, if you focus on outsourcing only the individual services needed to produce a given

outcome, you will leave in place all of the cross-functional problems with which you started. Indeed, you may even make the situation worse (Goldsmith, 1997). As B. Guy Peters (1996) points out, a fundamental irony of contracting out is that a balkanizing of project parts replaces the balkanization of bureaucracy that reformers are bent on correcting.

11. *Move quickly when waste, fraud, and abuse are suspected, but within the boundaries of due process* (O'Leary, 1996). One study concluded that by waiting up to five years to address grant problems, the Long Island Railroad more than doubled its estimated project costs (U.S. General Accounting Office, 1992a). Likewise, when these problems are found, managers must act aggressively to compel grantees and contractors to correct noncompliance and pay back misspent funds. In the interim, they should withhold funds where appropriate and within the law. A clear message has to be sent that meeting government standards is important, and that not doing so will have immediate negative consequences for those involved.

12. *Periodically review overhead costs (including contract design, letting, and monitoring costs), audit costs, contractor costs, and grant costs* (Goldsmith, 1997). Use benchmarking with best-in-class providers (but see micro-lesson six for a caveat). Another option is to compare actual costs continually with projected program expenses if the service or product is provided in-house. As Jonas Prager (1994) notes, "Contracting out is inappropriate when the combined contract price and the cost of contract management exceed the cost of in-house production." Policymakers should also not shy away from paring down or ending the services provided by the contractor or grantee if savings or environmental performance are lackluster. Finally, never hesitate to use other noneconomic points of comparison, such as the manageability of alternative arrangements and whether they better serve the public interest (Wise, 1990).

13. *Be certain to investigate all laws involved.* In addition to meeting diversity requirements in hiring and contracting, managers also face a host of specific environmental laws and executive orders. For example, must paper goods be provided on recycled paper? Have all mandated processes been followed? Also, managers should be certain to think through possible legal challenges, which might include contractor liability for injury incurred on the job, financial problems of contractors or subcontractors that may make them unable to perform, termination for breach of contract (Sweeney, 1996), fraud (Morenberg, 1995), and the First Amendment rights of contractors.

14. *Be sure that your efforts to use outsourcing do not make the services for which you contract responsive to customers but not to citizens* (Osborne and Plastrik, 1997). As Ronald Moe (1994) worries, in customer-based, market-oriented reforms it is easy for customer satisfaction and economic values to drive out political and legally based values. Charles Goodsell (1993) is even more blunt: as customers become more valued, the concerns of the larger citizenry can become severely disadvantaged.

15. *Be alert that contractors and beneficiaries do not subtly—and not so subtly—begin defining what environmental management becomes* (DeHoog, 1984; Donahue, 1989). This has happened occasionally when governments have outsourced aspects of social service programs. Ruth DeHoog (1984) reports that in Michigan, for example, contractors and beneficiaries began defining clients' needs and determining how to evaluate programs to meet those needs. Much the same can happen in environmental management.

Micro Lessons

1. *The type of contract used should be appropriate for the type of service sought* (O'Leary, 1996; Donahue, 1989). For example, many firm-fixed-price contracts would be inappropriate for the design and testing of first-of-a-kind services because of the inherent uncertainty of these activities.

2. *Whenever possible, make contract and grant terms clear and unambiguous* (O'Leary, 1996). For example, if government contracts (or government contractors subcontract) for the design and manufacture of an item, the ownership of patent rights to that item should be clearly articulated. Of course, this desired clarity might not always be possible, such as in the development of unproven environmental technologies or in grants to medical investigators. Nevertheless, precision should always remain a primary aim.

3. *Think through the sequence of desired activities and enunciate them clearly in contracts* (O'Leary, 1996). For example, if regulatory approval is needed for an item, do not allow final manufacturing of that item until approval is granted. Biotechnological applications, among others, may also be relevant here.

4. *Set specific target dates for accomplishing all contract or grant activities, including dates for audits* (O'Leary, 1996; Donahue, 1989). Likewise, establish enforceable milestones for closing out inactive and

completed grants and contracts. Managers should be sure that they have a tracking process in place to ensure that these deadlines are met.

5. *Whenever possible, be sure to include performance assessment measures in contracts and grants* (O'Leary, 1996; Donahue, 1989; Osborne and Plastrik, 1997). But also be sure to avoid process measuring or "bean counting" of inputs (such as numbers of inspections completed) or outputs (such as notices of violation issued) unless there are paramount reasons to do so. Such reasons might include the need to link inputs and outputs to measures of outcomes (such as tons of waste eliminated).

6. *Avoid benchmarking solely against government service providers when private businesses produce the same service* (Goldsmith, 1997). Such benchmarking could cause managers to miss tremendous opportunities for cost savings. For example, before Indianapolis outsourced its wastewater treatment plants, the city-county council asked a Big Six accounting firm to assess the government's performance against government-operated plants across the country. The firm found that they compared very well and could shave off only an additional 5 percent in operating costs by altering operations. As noted earlier, however, when Mayor Goldsmith then insisted that they benchmark their plants against European private operators, what the city learned wrought savings of 44 percent.

7. *Relatedly, when issuing RFPs, specify outcomes desired rather than systems to implement* (Goldsmith, 1997). If policymakers do otherwise, they may only be outsourcing a bad system. What they should want the private sector to produce are improved ideas, approaches, and management systems. Again, Indianapolis's experience is instructional. The review work for issuing drainage permits was the slowest part of the process for the city's planning office. The city therefore tried outsourcing the review process to an engineering firm. The results were uninspiring: turnaround time improved marginally while costs increased dramatically. When confronted by these results, the firm said that the contract had only allowed its employees to run the existing system, not create a better one. Subsequently, the planning department rewrote the RFP, this time asking the same company to redesign the entire permitting system. The results were substantial: turnaround time dropped from 4 weeks to 4.3 days, while costs plummeted 40 percent.

8. *Insist that contractors and grantees use professional and orderly processes.* Contracts should stipulate that recipients promptly answer phone calls from either government officials or clients. As part of this

professionalism, be sure that contractors and grantees provide status updates on these and other agreed-upon performance measures in a timely fashion.

QUESTIONS TO ASK WHEN CONSIDERING UTILIZING CONTRACTS OR GRANTS

To summarize, participants in and research on contract and grant management suggest that thoughtful policymakers will want to get affirmative answers to a number of questions before proceeding to make decisions about contracts and grants:

- Will the government clearly save money by using contracts or grants?
- Will the service received be of high quality?
- Will the program be more effective than it would be if administered in-house?
- Will contractors or grantees implement programs in an environmentally safe fashion? Do the chosen contractors have a positive record in this regard?
- What will be the impact of the contract or grant on the government's other programs, services, products, organizational subunits, or organizations?
- Will responsiveness to citizens' concerns or needs (not just those of the customers served) be enhanced by outsourcing?
- Will the government gain greater flexibility by using contracts or grants?
- Are the government's objectives narrow enough to be easily defined and measured? Can it articulate with specificity what its communities need and want from potential contractors, subcontractors, and grantees?
- Are there specifiable tasks with identifiable milestones that can be monitored at a reasonable price?
- Is there political support for outsourcing?
- Are there enough providers to ensure competition? If not, can forms of quasi-market competition be created that can enhance the government's learning when rebidding contracts or grants?

Can the same be said for nonprofits and for-profits when they subcontract for services or products?

- Are reimbursable costs robust enough to ensure that many potential suppliers are likely to bid? A general rule (with some exceptions) is that the larger the potential government contract or grant is, the greater will be the number of firms or individuals that are likely to bid (Smith and Lipsky, 1993).

- If the government needs to ensure continuity of services or the provision of goods, will its contractors, their subcontractors, and grantees be around to provide those goods or services? If not, will a change in contractor or grantee not substantially diminish the effectiveness of the program? If it will, are there contingency plans for reassuming service provision?

- Is there an arms-length relationship between the government and the contractors or grantees? If the parties to a contract, subcontract, or grant become too involved in each other's affairs, the potential for corruption spirals. What is more, the government may become the de facto provider of the goods or services while paying the outside entity. Also, contractors or grantees may become too involved in structuring market demand, thereby diminishing competition (Smith and Lipsky, 1993). This is likely to happen where there are long-term relationships between government organizations and contractors or grantees (Milward, Provan, and Else, 1993). Be wary of these situations.

- Will the government be able to keep sufficient control of the service (Morgan and Hirlinger, 1991)?

- Is the public, for-profit, or nonprofit organization capable of enforcing fair rules—substantively, procedurally, and distributionally?

- Will it encounter legal impediments to using contracts and grants?

- Will racial, gender, and other diversity goals be advanced or protected?

CONCLUSION

Clearly, grant and contract management will continue to be an important aspect of environmental management in the years to come. The hollowing of the administrative state is likely to continue apace. Some proponents will seek to do so for ideological reasons, primarily to shrink the proportion of the gross domestic product spent by government relative to the private sector. In reality, however, they may only be changing the nature of the administrative state, creating powerful pressures to embrace additional public expenditures, and diminishing accountability for what is spent by not ensuring strong contract management. Other proponents, however, will be seeking to learn how—and under what conditions—society can best harness the dynamism of markets with the public service ethic of civil servants to improve environmental quality and life opportunities for all citizens. Our goal in this chapter has been to help inform the judgments of this latter group.

The motives of proponents aside, however, the momentum behind privatization and partnering means that it is imperative for public, for-profit, and nonprofit managers and elected officials to update the quality of these processes continually. This is true whether they seek merely to avoid future liabilities or to institutionalize a commitment to a coproduction environmental ethic in their organizations. At a minimum, they must become smarter buyers, award contracts and grants premised more centrally on environmental management and performance, and oversee this largesse more assiduously in terms of these values.

But contracts and grants are not the only new policy tools or instruments that challenge managers today and to which they must further adapt in the future. Indeed, a variety of emerging approaches to environmental management are already offering managers challenges, choices, and opportunities. We turn next, in Chapter Twelve, to several of the more intriguing tools that will continue to vie for attention in the twenty-first century.

12

ADAPTING TO ENVIRONMENTAL CHALLENGES

A Policymaker's Tool Kit

Give us the tools, and we will finish the job.

—Winston Churchill[1]

Workers in nuclear power plants are screened daily as they leave their jobs for signs of unusual exposure to radiation. In 1984, when Stanley Watras left his job each day at a nuclear plant in eastern Pennsylvania, he activated the alarm on the plant's radiation monitors. Unsure about why he was triggering the alarm, Watras decided one day to test the source of the problem by turning around and passing through the monitor *before* entering the plant. The alarm went off, suggesting that the cause of his exposure lay somewhere outside the plant rather than inside. To track down the source of the problem, officials tested the air inside Watras's home, where they discovered the highest level of radioactivity found in any home in the world—with health effects equal to smoking 135 packs of cigarettes a day.

The cause of the high radioactivity was radon seeping into the house from underground. Radon is an odorless, invisible, naturally occurring gas that is associated with some geological formations more than with others. The most common source of indoor radon is uranium in the rock or soil on which homes are built. As uranium naturally breaks down it releases radon, which is a colorless, odorless, reactive gas. Radon travels freely and moves easily through small spaces.

Although researchers had for years known the potential risks of exposure to high levels of radon, these risks were associated primarily with certain occupations, such as uranium mining. To be sure, scientists were also well aware that radon occurs naturally under homes, builds up when soil conditions are right, and poses danger when ventilation in the house is inadequate. Exposure to naturally occurring radon in homes, however, was not seen as a major public health threat until the Watras incident and other events in the mid-1980s. In particular, and as we noted in Chapter Seven, the danger was realized when EPA risk assessments suggested that residential radon caused an estimated seven thousand to thirty thousand deaths from lung cancer annually (U.S. Environmental Protection Agency, 1992; Cole, 1993).

Once radon emerged on the policy agenda, the issue for policymakers was what to do about it. In the past they had responded to most such problems by setting a regulatory standard and requiring sources either to meet it or incur government sanctions. This strategy of direct regulation may have been an appropriate response to problems such as industrial sources of air pollution, which are large, visible, and relatively limited in number. To apply a direct regulatory strategy to a problem like residential radon, however, would have been disastrous. The EPA would have had to issue a national rule requiring homeowners to test radon levels in their homes. Those with dwellings exceeding acceptable levels would have had to make the necessary corrections (such as sealing cracks in the foundation and improving ventilation), retest their homes, and certify to regulatory authorities that they had reduced radon to acceptable levels. The expense, intrusiveness, and complexity of such a plan would have been a nightmare. Thus, as we discuss in greater detail later in this chapter, Congress and the EPA used a different approach to deal with the radon problem: providing information and assistance to homeowners.

Radon, of course, is only one of many newly salient environmental problems for which traditional approaches seem anemic. For example, to address one of the newest and potentially biggest environmental problems of all time—global warming—policymakers are considering new and innovative solutions. What is more, even with older problems, such as industrial sources of air and water pollution, policymakers are today improvising new methods that draw on principles of market economics.

It is to these newer options in policymakers' tool kits that we now turn. Understanding the logic, promise, and performance of these initiatives is critical to public, nonprofit, and for-profit managers alike—whether they are regulators or regulatees searching for more cost-effective, responsive, and equitable solutions to today's dynamic environmental challenges.

In this chapter we refer to tools or approaches for responding to environmental problems as *policy instruments*. This term draws on Richard Elmore's (1987) distinction between two levels of policy response. On one level are strategies, which are "planful, calculated behavior in concert with others whose interests differ" (p. 180). At another level, these more or less well-defined strategies are composed of policy instruments—"an authoritative choice of means to accomplish a purpose" (p. 175). Put most simply, a strategy is a plan for attacking a problem, and a policy instrument—an emissions limit, tax, or warning label, for example—is a means for carrying out that attack (Fiorino, 1995). Thus, in this chapter we focus initially on instruments and turn later to how policymakers can combine these to form strategies. We conclude by discussing instruments that should be most useful to managers in the future—instruments that stress flexibility, performance, participation, and trade-offs by affected parties. These are issues and trends that we noted in Part One as central to the future of environmental management.

AN INVENTORY OF POLICY INSTRUMENTS

Many treatments of policy instruments have tried to distinguish regulatory approaches to solving environmental problems from nonregulatory approaches, or traditional from nontraditional approaches. In contrast, a 1995 Office of Technology Assessment (OTA) report does not attempt such tricky distinctions. It therefore allows us to present more cogently the range of policy instruments available to policymakers, and the strengths and weaknesses of each instrument.

As Table 12.1 illustrates, OTA's framework lists twelve classes of policy instruments. Seven of these classes prescribe particular pollution reduction goals, which makes them more certain, predictable, and likely to enjoy political and public support. At the same time, however, these policy instruments have been less flexible and adaptable than many people have wished them to be. In contrast, the remaining five

Table 12.1. Brief Definitions of Environmental Policy Tools.

Tools That Directly Limit Pollution

Single-Source Tools

Harm-Based Standards	Describe required end results, leaving regulated entities free to choose compliance methods.
Design Standards	Describe required emissions limits based on what a model technology might achieve; sources use the model technology or demonstrate that another approach achieves equivalent results.
Technology Specifications	Specify the technology or technique a source must use to control its pollution.
Product Bans and Limitations	Ban or restrict manufacture, use, or disposal of products that present unreasonable risks.

Multisource Tools

Integrated Permitting	Incorporates multiple requirements into a single permit rather than having a permit for each individual emissions source at a facility.
Tradeable Emissions	Allow regulated entities to trade emission control responsibilities among themselves, provided that the aggregate regulatory cap on emissions is met.
Challenge Regulations	Give target group of sources responsibility for designing and implementing a program to achieve a target goal, with a government-imposed program or sanction if goal is unmet by the deadline.

Tools That Do Not Directly Limit Pollution

Pollution Fees	Require regulated entity to pay fixed dollar amount for each unit of pollution emitted or disposed of, no ceiling on emissions.
Liability	Requires entities causing pollution that adversely affects others to compensate those harmed to the extent of the damage.
Information Reporting	Requires entities to report emissions or product information publicly.
Subsidies	Provide financial assistance to entities, either from government or private organizations.
Technical Assistance	Provides additional knowledge to entities regarding consequences of their actions, and what techniques or tools reduce those consequences.

Source: U.S. Congress, Office of Technology Assessment, 1995.

types of instruments do not set fixed pollution reduction goals. Consequently they are less certain about what they will accomplish. Thus the trade-off between certainty and flexibility is one of the central choices that policymakers face when deciding how to respond to environmental problems.

These instruments can be further subdivided into three major categories: those that set fixed pollution-reduction targets and apply to single sources, those that set fixed targets but apply to multiple sources, and those that do not set fixed pollution targets. The more conventional instruments fall into the first category, while several of the newer and more innovative ones fall into the second and third categories.

Instruments with Fixed Targets That Apply to Single Sources

Not surprisingly, simplicity is often seen as a virtue in devising solutions to policy problems. When people become aware of an environmental problem that requires government intervention, they want assurance that authorities understand the causes of the problem, that they will hold the people causing the problem responsible, that they will reduce the effects of the problem to acceptable levels, and that they will punish any failure by the people responsible to redress the situation. This first group of policy instruments—which we have referred to as *command-and-control regulation*—have been popular precisely because they meet these needs. They provide some assurance that government will hold pollution sources accountable and make them change their behavior (Mitnick, 1980; Bardach and Kagan, 1982).

HARM-BASED STANDARDS The first class of instruments in this category is *harm-based* standards. They specify a result that pollution sources must achieve and are usually the basis for design or technology standards (which we refer to together as *technology instruments*). The best examples of harm-based standards are the National Ambient Air Quality Standards (NAAQS). As noted in Chapter Two, these standards define maximum levels of several common pollutants allowable in the ambient (surrounding) air. NAAQS are currently set for sulfur oxides, particulates, ozone, lead, carbon monoxide, and nitrogen oxide. These are all common pollutants that are found to some degree in most parts of the world, especially in urban areas. As we also noted, the Clean Air Act of 1970 directed the EPA to set the NAAQS for each pollutant at a level sufficient to protect the most sensitive parts of the population, such as asthmatics, infants, and the elderly. In setting the NAAQS, the EPA relies extensively on available studies of the health effects of a pollutant at different levels of exposure. By law, NAAQS are based entirely on health effects; the economics of achieving the standards cannot be considered (Portney, 1990).

The NAAQS do not on their own make people do anything. They are goals, but they have the weight of the law behind them. The federal government sets the NAAQS, then assigns responsibility to the states for achieving them. If parts of a state exceed the NAAQS, state regulators must impose control measures in order to meet the standards. In doing this, states may of course draw on other policy instruments.

The NAAQS illustrate a harm-based standard that applies to all of the legally covered polluting sources in a given area—be they public, nonprofit, or for-profit. At times policymakers have applied harm-based standards to individual sources, based on a judgment of the risk that will be caused by the release of pollutants by those sources. In implementing this kind of harm-based standard, regulatory authorities specify an acceptable level of risk for exposure to a given pollutant (for example, no more than one excess statistical case of cancer annually per million people exposed). They then require sources to take whatever steps are necessary to keep their emissions below that risk level. As we noted in Chapters Two and Seven, such risk-based standards have been notoriously hard to develop and implement, as shown by the EPA's experience with hazardous air pollutants in the 1980s. The tasks of deciding what is "acceptable" risk, determining what that means in emissions for each source, and verifying that each source has achieved the needed level of emission reduction impose huge burdens on both the regulatory and regulated communities.

DESIGN AND TECHNOLOGY STANDARDS The workhorses of U.S. policy in this category have been *design and technology instruments*. Recall from Chapter Two how these instruments are expressed in a legion of terms that define the legal criteria applied to sources, such as best available control technology, lowest achievable emission rate, maximum available control technology, best demonstrated available technology, and many others. Among all of the available environmental policy instruments, these offer the most direct and verifiable assurance that sources are changing their behavior to protect the environment. Technology instruments can also, however, place enormous discretionary burdens on regulators and significant costs on regulatees, as we discuss shortly.

By the same token, however, technology instruments do provide some certainty that a problem will be addressed; they define enforceable obligations for regulated entities; and they apply the same or similar standards to similar sets of economic activities. They also allow regulators to take advantage of a division of labor that permits them to focus expertise on air, water, and waste issues. Many regulators, however, also criticize technology instruments for their deficiencies, especially now that the first generation of major industrial sources have come under regulatory control. Indeed, nearly every advisory panel that has evaluated environmental policy in recent years has stressed the need to improve on the nation's conventional, single-source, technology focus (see, for example, National Academy of Public Administration, 1995; President's Council on Sustainable Development, 1996; Environmental Law Institute, 1998). Their criticisms fall into four areas: cross-media transfers, overcontrol and undercontrol, the emphasis on controlling rather than preventing pollution, and the problem of "regulatory lag."

- *Cross-media transfers.* As we noted in Chapter Four, in practice a single-source focus means that the big picture is lost (Haigh and Irwin, 1990). All too often, pollution problems are solved in one medium by moving them to another. For example, the standard method for removing sulfur oxides from industrial processes that burn fossil fuels creates sludge that must be disposed of as solid waste. A single-source focus also means that pollution controls often are more expensive than they need to be. The cost per unit of controlling emissions of a chemical released into the air may be several times higher than the cost per unit of controlling discharges of the same chemical into water. Rather than specifying a performance result and allowing the source to come up with the best overall mix of controls, the technology approach requires specific technologies to control particular releases. Policymakers may solve an air pollution problem only to find that they have created a waste or water pollution problem instead.
- *Overcontrol and undercontrol.* Because conventional single-source instruments require regulators to specify exactly where and in what form pollution will be controlled, such instruments may lead to the use of stringent technologies in one area while opportunities for reducing emissions in another are neglected. An important consideration here is the law of increasing marginal costs: as the allowable emissions approach zero, the costs per unit of pollution control increase, often dramatically. For example, consider the lessons learned from a project

that the EPA and the Amoco Corporation conducted at a petroleum refinery in Yorktown, Virginia, in the early 1990s (National Academy of Public Administration, 1995).

Participants in the project identified all the sources of environmental releases from the refinery, determined what the best outcome (in economic and environmental terms) would be for reducing those releases, then compared the outcome to what was required under existing rules. They found that under the existing clean air regulations Amoco had reduced airborne hydrocarbon emissions by about 7,300 tons per year at a cost of $2,400 per ton. If, however, Amoco could have greater flexibility than the rules allowed, it could reduce its hydrocarbon emissions by about the same amount at a cost of only $500 per ton. Nevertheless, citing specific provisions in the Clean Air Act, the EPA decided that it could not authorize Amoco to implement the less expensive approach.

• *Controlling rather than preventing pollution.* As we have noted, the basic appeal of technology instruments is this: they allow regulators to identify pollution sources and force action to control them on the basis of judgments about best available technologies. Whatever the merits of this approach in the 1970s, policymakers began to realize by the early 1980s that something was fundamentally amiss. Regulations were applied only when pollution was released into the environment. Practices and decisions leading to those releases—the choice of raw materials, the recycling of materials for reuse—were taken as givens. Yet according to experiences documented throughout the 1980s, choices made upstream in production processes are important in reducing what comes out at the end. As we noted in Chapter Four, this recognition was the midwife for the pollution prevention movement. Still, the statutory emphasis on technology controls continues to impede pollution prevention.

• *Regulatory lag.* Technology instruments are labor- and information-intensive for regulators. They require knowledge of the operational processes of polluters, of widely used (as well as state-of-the-art) technologies for controlling pollution, and of the costs and feasibility of installing and maintaining these technologies across a wide range of facilities. Additionally, the administrative process for developing and issuing technology standards is long, cumbersome, and difficult. Finally, even if regulators have the necessary information to issue a state-of-the-art standard at some point, that standard may be badly out of date by the time it is implemented.

The consequence of all this is a problem known as *regulatory lag*. For products and processes that change little over time, this lag may be manageable. But for dynamic industries, the lag can be serious. In the electronics sector, for example, one expert remarked to one of the authors that by the time the EPA issues an environmental standard affecting the industry, it is already eight years out of date.

Instruments with Fixed Targets That Apply to Multiple Sources

After nearly three decades of national regulatory programs, it is clear that harm-based and technology-based command-and-control instruments have forced significant and positive changes in polluters' behavior. The limitations of these instruments, however, have stimulated interest in complementary and alternative approaches. Another set of instruments—those that specify fixed pollution reduction targets but apply to multiple rather than single sources—offer ways to improve on conventional regulatory approaches. Managers in both the regulatory and regulated communities must understand the promise and the performance of these instruments.

As noted in Table 12.1, this category includes three instruments designed to overcome weaknesses associated with a single-source approach. The first instrument, *emissions trading,* has been implemented to a large degree, especially in the clean air program. The two other instruments—*integrated permitting* and *challenge regulation*—are more nascent in origin. All three promise to be important in future environmental management.

EMISSIONS TRADING From the early days of the national regulatory programs in the 1970s, people have been interested in a class of policy instruments that apply market incentives to environmental protection. Long a favorite of academic economists, market instruments now command attention from a wider audience, including legislators and regulatory agency officials. The case for market incentives comes from environmental economics. Regulation arises in response to failures in private markets when participants treat air, water, land, and other common property resources as free goods. The result is an imbalance between the prices of goods and services sold in markets and the true costs to society of producing and consuming them. Because uses of common property resources do not carry a price, private markets encourage their overuse, and "the price system conveys the false message that society places no value on clean air and water" (Kneese and Schultze, 1975, p. 6). Thus market instruments are designed to make pollution sources internalize the costs of the damages they impose on society.

Several instruments qualify as market incentives. Some attach a fee directly to the behavior in question—such as releasing tons of air pollution or disposing of pounds of waste. Other instruments, such as emissions trading, create artificial markets by giving sources incentives to reduce pollution, earn emission credits, and buy and sell them (Carlin, 1992; U.S. Environmental Protection Agency, 1991). We consider emissions trading to be an instrument with fixed reduction goals. Pollution fees, discussed later in the chapter, are considered instruments without fixed reduction goals.

Emissions trading has been the most successful application of market incentives to environmental protection in the United States (Ackerman and Stewart, 1988; Stewart, 1988). It is a policy innovation that was born of political necessity in the 1970s, a product of restrictions that the Clean Air Act imposed on nonattainment areas (that is, those that have failed to meet National Ambient Air Quality Standards). As we discussed in Chapter Two, the EPA and state officials could not grant permits for new or expanded facilities as long as an area was in nonattainment status. In areas such as Southern California, this restriction in effect prohibited economic growth.

To ensure progress toward cleaner air and to allow for carefully managed growth, the EPA developed a policy that would let companies build new or expanded facilities, but under two conditions. The first condition was discussed previously in Chapter Two—that companies had to install technology that would produce the lowest achievable emission rate. The second condition (and the origin of emissions trading) was that companies had to demonstrate that existing sources in the area would reduce their emissions by more than enough to offset the new source's emissions. Typically, the new source would pay existing sources to install required technology or take other measures to reduce its emissions by the required amount. Initially called the *offset policy*, it became known as emissions trading as the EPA expanded its use and as markets emerged across the country. Congress in turn codified the policy in the 1977 Clean Air Act Amendments (Cook, 1988; Meidinger, 1989).

Today, air emissions trading consists of four programs: bubbles, offsets, banking, and netting. *Bubbles* allow trading across different points of release of the same pollutant, as long as they are in the same "facility," as defined under the law. *Offsets* allow firms in nonattainment areas to build new facilities if they obtain emission reduction credits from other sources that more than offset their own emissions. *Banking* allows firms to save or bank emission credits for later use or sale. *Netting* enables sources to modify their facilities, in some cases without going through the full new-source review process that applies to new facilities. Each of these programs is designed to give firms an incentive to find cost-effective ways to reduce emissions. Because most trading programs require that a percentage of emissions be retired each time a trade is made, they also lead to less overall pollution than technology instruments can produce on their own.

Recall as well that trading was implemented even further in the acid rain provisions of the 1990 Clean Air Act Amendments. In that act, Congress directed the EPA to create a market for sulfur dioxide emissions. In this case, the problem was not localized air pollution. Rather, it was the long-range transport of sulfur dioxide releases, mostly from utilities in the Midwest, to the Northeast and Canada, where the sulfur dioxide returned to the ground as acid rain. Congress could have relied entirely on a standard technology solution, directing the EPA to issue standards that required each utility to install state-of-the-art controls. Instead, it created an acid rain allowance trading program that combined technology and trading instruments.

The law set an initial national cap of about ten million tons annually for sulfur dioxide emissions, a cap that would decline to less than nine million tons by the year 2000. It assigned emission allowances to utilities on the basis of their historic emission levels, emission rates, fuels used, and other factors. Sources can overcomply by installing technology, switching to cleaner fuels, or reducing production at older, dirtier plants and increasing it at newer, cleaner ones. They may sell their unused allowances to other utilities (those with higher control costs) that undercomply. The result should be progress toward better environmental quality at less overall cost to society. The EPA originally estimated that acid rain allowance trading would save $0.7 to $1.0 billion annually. After about five years, the cost savings of the trading program compared to those from conventional regulation have been estimated at one billion dollars annually (Hockenstein, Stavins, and Whitehead, 1997).

In recent years policymakers have extended trading to water pollution as well. In May 1996, the EPA issued the *Draft Framework for Watershed-Based Trading*. It had issued guidance on implementing a national policy earlier that year. The framework outlines five different types of trades and provides case studies that illustrate how they may occur. One of the first trades under this program took place as part of an EPA pilot project in New Jersey in 1997. Two chemical processors agreed on a transaction in which one sold to the other its permitting authority to emit copper into the local sewage treatment system. As a condition of the trade, the buyer's permit retired 20 percent of the allowable copper discharge. The expectation was that over time such trades would allow these and other processors to operate more efficiently and still reduce the amounts of copper and other metals that enter the sewage system.

Despite its efficiency value, however, trading has been criticized on ethical grounds. First, many critics view trading as simply a license to pollute. Why, they ask, should sources be allowed to benefit by selling the right to pollute to others? One answer, of course, is that any environmental permit is a license to pollute, almost by definition. Trading programs are no different from traditional permitting, except that they allow additional flexibility and incentive for firms to achieve the expected level of pollution reductions less expensively. Unless one takes the view that any level of pollution is morally unacceptable and should be prohibited—a view that is not widely shared in our society—trading programs should be no more ethically objectionable than technology-based permitting. What is more, trading allows for better results and gives sources slightly more discretion.

A second criticism has more merit. Trading of emission credits among sources often has the effect of geographically redistributing pollution and its risks. To be sure, overall emissions may decrease as a trading program is implemented. Yet the risks to certain populations within the geographical area in which trading is allowed may increase over what they would be under conventional, technology-based regulation. For example, we know that ambient air pollution levels within an area vary widely, depending on such factors as the number of sources, the weather, and the topography. With technology instruments, in contrast, there is the assurance that sources are doing the most that is technically feasible to control their emissions.

At the same time, if the sources buying the credits are concentrated in the same neighborhoods, the result may be higher emissions in some areas than in others. As a result, trading can easily and appropriately become fodder for challenges by environmental justice groups. In southern California, for example, there are already complaints that air trading is leading to higher pollution around older sources that had bought credits from newer ones, and that more of these sources are located in minority communities. For this reason, national or global problems such as acid rain and global climate change may be better candidates for trading instruments, possibilities that we consider later in this chapter.

INTEGRATED PERMITTING Another innovative instrument is integrated permitting. Trading is designed to address one weakness of technology instruments—their inflexibility. Yet trading has always been applied on a single-source and single-contaminant basis. For example, volatile organic compounds (VOCs) are traded only with other VOCs, while sulfur dioxide allowances are bought and sold only for sulfur dioxide emissions. Policymakers have not implemented trading either across environmental media or among pollutants emitted in the same medium. The results are often onerous for larger and smaller polluters alike. For example, Schering, a large pharmaceutical company in New Jersey, operated under some six hundred separate environmental permits prior to 1991.

But even small firms, such as chemical processors with fewer than forty employees, often have to obtain, comply with, and renew forty to fifty permits across different media and sources. Hence the purpose of an integrated permit is to deal with fragmentation on the ground, within a facility, where critical environmental choices are made. It is different from other efforts to streamline (by simplifying the process) or consolidate permitting (by packaging forms and processes but maintaining multiple permits). In integrated permitting, air, water, and land releases are combined into a single permit at a facility.

In pursuing this strategy, states such as New Jersey and Massachusetts have experimented with innovative permitting processes that set overall emission and discharge limits for an entire facility rather than for each point of release within that facility (New Jersey Department of Environmental Protection, 1995; Rabe, 1991). For instance, New Jersey authorized facilitywide permitting pilots in its Pollution Prevention Act of 1991. To implement the pilot program, the state's Department of Environmental Protection (DEP) had to replace existing permits at ten to fifteen facilities with a facilitywide permit that combined air, water, hazardous waste, and pollution prevention planning requirements. The goals were to maximize opportunities for pollution prevention, to give additional flexibility to find cost-effective solutions, to streamline permitting and compliance, and to improve overall environmental results by allowing facilities to manage across rather than within media (New Jersey Department of Environmental Protection,

1995, 1996). Accordingly, regulators gave facilities flexibility to make operational changes without prior regulatory approval, as long as they met three conditions: their emissions were within an assigned cap, they developed a pollution prevention plan, and they used materials accounting analysis to account for what materials entered and left the facility for each of their production processes.

New Jersey's program is still relatively new, but the DEP's preliminary assessment is that integrated permitting offers several important benefits that managers need to know about, including the following:

- Improved identification of previously unregulated emissions and multimedia transfers
- Increased understanding of whole-facility risks
- Development of better relationships between facilities and regulators
- Increased pollution prevention
- Increased accountability resulting from consolidated reporting
- Improved integration of environmental management into long-range planning

Conversely, the time and expense of facilitywide permitting seems to increase significantly. After all, developing the permit requires a complete environmental evaluation of the facility. Moreover, the process of accounting for materials, relating these data to permits and compliance, and projecting production and pollution prevention trends involves substantial work for facilities (New Jersey Department of Environmental Protection, 1996).

On balance, however, integration seems to reduce administrative costs and complexity for both regulators and regulatees. Although Schering's facilitywide permit cost it about $1 million and required a special team from the New Jersey DEP to develop it, further progress up the learning curve may reduce these costs substantially. Second, polluters with the incentive and flexibility to seek pollution reductions find that rather than just comply with single-medium technology requirements, they can achieve better performance at less cost. An evaluation of the pollution planning process in New Jersey, which includes elements of integrated permitting, concluded that many firms saved (in reduced materials use and compliance costs) several times what they had invested (New Jersey Department of Environmental Protection, 1996). Third, integration may provide more capacity for continued improvement. If performance across all media is the test of compliance, there should be better environmental outcomes in the long run.

CHALLENGE REGULATION Another policy instrument builds on emissions trading and integrated permitting. The 1995 OTA report describes it as *challenge regulation* because "government *challenges* a group of sources to take the lead in designing and implementing a program for meeting environmental goals" (p. 113). The distinctive characteristics of this approach are that it establishes clear, measurable targets and timetables for performance; it sets targets for multiple facilities (usually by industry sector or geographical area) rather than just for individual facilities; it assigns collective responsibility to sources for designing and implementing a program to meet performance targets; and it prescribes alternative programs or sanctions for use if progress toward achieving the targets is unsatisfactory.

As with the existing command-and-control regulatory regime, government still sets standards with fixed goals that sources must meet or else face sanctions. Challenge regulation differs, however, in two important ways. First, it prescribes what sources must do rather than how they must do it. Second, it assigns collective responsibility to groups of firms that must cooperate to achieve a result. The role of government is to set measurable performance targets, devise methods for tracking progress toward the targets, verify that the targets are achieved, and impose sanctions if the targets are not met.

Challenge regulation is designed to overcome some of the core weaknesses of conventional, single-source instruments. By setting performance goals but not telling sources specifically how to achieve them, it grants flexibility for polluters to determine collectively the best way to control the environmental effects of their activities. They can decide whether or not they prefer, for example, to develop and install new technologies, use different raw materials, recycle existing materials, or discontinue old or introduce new products. With additional flexibility, and with the certainty that comes from knowing what their obligations are over given periods, polluters have an incentive to think and manage innovatively. Government regulators are in a different position as well. Instead of guessing what the achievable or best available technology standard should be three or four years down the road, they focus on results and on whether or not companies are achieving them.

Another innovative aspect of challenge regulation is that it imposes collective obligations on regulated entities. U.S. environmental regulation has always been a two-party relationship. Each polluter is legally bound to meet requirements to the satisfaction of the regulator or else face sanctions (see Bardach and Kagan, 1982). What a polluter's peers achieve or fail to achieve is irrelevant, except that failures by out-of-compliance firms can create pressure for more stringent controls on firms that are complying. Relatedly, companies are also reluctant to share information with peers because they fear losing confidentiality and proprietary rights. In contrast, challenge regulation affords incentives for similarly situated polluters to move toward collective responsibility for environmental results. In fact, sharing information on technologies and best practices now makes eminently more sense. Large firms with greater resources can serve as mentors for smaller firms. Trading and other programs that lead to greater overall efficiency and better performance become more attractive. It is even possible that the adversary nature of industry-government relations can be reduced. Following are some examples of challenge regulation.

The 33/50 program

To date, the closest that U.S. policymakers have come to implementing challenge regulation is the 33/50 program. Created in the early 1990s, this program built on the information provided by the Toxics Release Inventory (TRI). The EPA selected seventeen high-priority chemicals from the TRI. Using 1988 emissions as a baseline, the agency then challenged industry to voluntarily reduce these emissions by 33 percent by 1992, and by 50 percent by 1995. Polluters were encouraged to join the program by making a public commitment to the 33 percent and 50 percent targets and to self-certify that they had achieved the reductions. In developing the program, however, the EPA also used a formidable threat from its traditional tool kit. More precisely, it warned industry that a failure to achieve these voluntary goals could lead the agency to impose mandatory emission reductions through technology regulation.

Was the 33/50 program an incremental step toward a system of challenge regulation? Probably not, for several reasons. The most obvious is that 33/50 was voluntary. Polluters were not obligated to participate. Moreover, most of those that did participate were large companies with the resources to invest in the program, the confidence to commit publicly to the targets, and a desire to reap the public relations benefits of participation. An unwillingness to participate or a failure to achieve the targets brought no government sanctions other than a general threat to possibly issue regulations.

The 33/50 program also differed from challenge regulation in setting performance targets for individual companies rather than for groups of polluters. Although it may have spurred companies to take measures they otherwise would not have taken, it did not promote cooperation among firms by creating a collective responsibility for better performance. Lost were the potential benefits of companies working together to achieve sectorwide or regional performance goals.

Nevertheless, the apparent success of the 33/50 program triggered many sequels. The ClimateWise program, for example, encourages polluters to commit publicly to achieving reductions in releases of carbon dioxide that contribute to global warming. The Green Lights program asks them to commit to replacing their existing lights with more energy-efficient alternatives. WasteWise encourages specific targets to cut back on the generation of solid wastes. Although the form of the commitment and the obligations on polluters vary, each of these (and several other) voluntary programs builds on 33/50. All encourage firms to achieve a level of environmental performance beyond their legal obligations. The principal reward for companies is public recognition. The major problem with all of these voluntary programs is that none of them offers the kind of regulatory relief (such as less oversight or increased flexibility) that might enhance their corporate profits (or their agency's budget). Yet many in industry and government view incentives like these as necessary for future programs to work (Davies and Mazurek, 1996).

The Dutch sector approach

For managers to appreciate fully how far 33/50 and similar programs fall short of challenge regulation in critical respects, they need only to examine the efforts of the Netherlands in this regard (Fiorino, 1996). Among industrialized nations, the Netherlands faces especially difficult challenges. It is one of the most densely populated countries in the world and is highly industrialized. Moreover, because much of the country is below sea level, the Dutch have a long tradition of state involvement and public-private cooperation in resource planning and management. Understandably, global warming and the associated prospect of rises in sea level are a special worry. Thus, when the Dutch recognized in the 1980s that conventional regulation would not, in the long run, yield needed levels of environmental protection, they implemented the National Environmental Policy Plan (NEPP). The NEPP set national environmental goals and created an innovative, industry-sector approach for achieving them.

The Dutch initially targeted twelve industry sectors. For each sector (primary metals, printing, and chemicals were the first three), the government and the trade associations representing industry negotiated sector goals. For example, in the chemical sector, the goals for the year 2010 are to reduce 1985 levels of air emissions of benzene, ethylene, and toluene by 97.5 percent, 97 percent, and 90 percent, respectively. Within a sector, each company negotiates an agreement, or covenant, with the government for achieving the company's share of pollution reduction. The covenant defines a comprehensive plan for managing the company's environmental performance. Once the industry and the government have both signed the covenant, it is legally enforceable. Together, the covenants define a framework within which local licensing agencies can then grant permits (Layman, 1994; Von Zijst, 1993; Hersch, 1996; Hajer, 1995).

The sector and company goals challenge industry to achieve ambitious levels of environmental performance. They extend until the year 2010 to allow industries to take a long-term perspective in their planning. In exchange, the government "has pledged to not unilaterally change its standards or requirements during this time" (Layman, 1994, p. 11). Companies are collectively responsible to some degree for meeting their sector's performance targets. Moreover, failure to achieve those targets as a sector translates into more stringent requirements for individual firms. In essence, the Dutch approach stresses performance— meeting the national, sector, and company goals—and it challenges companies to achieve the goals collectively during a set period and in the most efficient ways they can.

Instruments Without Fixed Pollution Reduction Targets

For reasons that we have already discussed, the United States has historically been wary of policy instruments that do not prescribe fixed targets. Moreover, when such instruments are used, they are typically combined with instruments that do set fixed targets. The OTA report lists five instruments in this category: pollution fees, statutory liability, information reporting, subsidies, and technical assistance. Of these five, we focus on the first and the third, with most of our attention going to information reporting. We do so because, arguably, these two instruments promise to provide a foundation for a new generation of environmental policy instruments. Consequently, public, nonprofit, and for-profit managers should understand their promises and pitfalls.

POLLUTION FEES Like emissions trading, *pollution fees* apply the principles of market economics. They force sources to internalize the costs of the damages they impose on society by making them pay for each unit of pollution they generate (Opschoor and Vos, 1989). As we have noted, technology instruments make polluters in similar categories control to the same level of stringency, whatever the costs. Pollution fees, in contrast, recognize that some polluters can control emissions at lower costs than others can. The goal of such fees is to allocate control costs efficiently across sources. A well-designed pollution fee induces sources to control emissions or use raw materials in such a way that the marginal cost of control equals the amount of the fee. Sources with low costs typically stay within the emission limits and pay less in fees. Firms with high control costs typically fall short of the standards but pay higher fees. The result should be the same or less pollution, but at less total cost to society.

There is an obvious theoretical appeal to fees—the more you pollute, the more you pay. But they have not been used widely, in part because it is so difficult to set fees at levels that ensure a certain level of pollution reduction. If policymakers do not accurately predict behavioral responses to the fees, they may find lots of sources paying fees on pollution levels that are unacceptably high. Another problem with fees is the need they generate for accurate, continuous monitoring of emissions. This kind of information is expensive, yet it is essential to know how much pollution a source is generating.

Two kinds of pollution fees, however, illustrate applications that are more feasible administratively. One type is a raw materials fee exacted on inputs into production processes, such as a tax on the carbon content of fossil fuels. The amount of carbon in fuels determines how much carbon dioxide is emitted from a combustion process. The more carbon dioxide that is emitted, the greater are the effects on global warming. Hence any fee should increase with the fuel's carbon content and provide an incentive for sources to reduce their fuel use or shift to fuels with lower carbon content. Moreover, the effects on emissions could be large. The EPA estimated in 1990 that a $25 fee per ton of carbon would reduce emissions by 8 to 17 percent and raise $38 to $50 billion in revenue annually by the year 2000 (U.S. Environmental Protection Agency, 1991). As President Clinton learned to his dismay in 1993, such a fee faces formidable political obstacles in the U.S. Congress.

Also more effective are fees applied to municipal waste disposal. These typically are packaged as volume-based pricing initiatives. In most areas, trash services are covered through general tax revenues or a flat fee. Each household pays the same fee, whatever the amount and kind of waste it generates. Volume-based pricing, in contrast, links service rates to the amount of waste generated; households pay for the direct costs of disposal and (in theory) for the social costs of the environmental damage that results from the disposal of the waste they produce.

Consider, for example, Seattle's approach to municipal waste disposal. Households pay according to the number and size of trash cans they use each week. In 1990, for example, people paid nearly $11 to use a nineteen-gallon can and $14 for a thirty-two-gallon can. They then had to buy stickers to cover waste in excess of their standard level of service. Recyclables were separated and collected free of charge. Seattle initially based its rates on the direct costs of collection and disposal, including tipping fees paid at landfills. Later, however, it increased these fees above the costs of direct service to give households more incentive to recycle and reduce the volume of wastes they generate. But pollution fees are by no means applicable only to municipal waste disposal. Other governments have used them to discourage fuel use (such as a gas tax), congestion (variable tolls assessed on drivers using congested roads), and toxic pesticide applications (Repetto, Dower, Jenkins, and Geoghegan, 1992).

INFORMATION REPORTING A second old yet potentially most innovative policy instrument eschewing specific reduction targets is *information reporting*. It is old in that governments have been providing warnings about environmental hazards for many years, in such forms as product labels and public information campaigns. This instrument is also novel, however, in that recent requirements for public accountability, such as the federal TRI and state community right-to-know laws, are transforming environmental policy in many ways. Indeed, policymakers are looking at information-based instruments more systematically than they have ever done in the past.

As Susan Hadden documents in *Read the Label* (1986), product warnings have long been a staple of government efforts to protect public health and safety. Federal requirements for warning labels on cigarette packages were a central issue in the struggle over smoking policy. Indeed, long before policymakers began restricting smoking in public areas, they used an information approach to influence public behavior, with great success. Product warnings have been central to environmental policy as well. As we noted in Chapter Two, when the EPA registers a pesticide for use, it also prescribes the conditions under which citizens may use it, including whether or not special training and certification are required. Likewise, the Toxic Substances Control Act authorizes the EPA to require, among other measures, that manufacturers include information in their packaging about the risks and appropriate uses of a chemical. Finally, a cursory look at common household cleaners, solvents, and coatings shows how extensive information reporting has become in our lives.

The most systematic use of information in responding to an emerging problem was federal policy for radon in the 1980s. As we discussed at length in Chapter Seven, it was then that the field of risk communication came into being, with radon as a principal application. As our look at Stanley Watras's predicament in 1984 suggested, environmental problems and solutions sometimes come from almost nowhere to emerge suddenly on the policy agenda. In the case of radon, policymakers wisely recognized that a standard technology-based regulatory instrument was inappropriate. Instead, the core of the strategy for responding to the radon problem is based on information and technical assistance. Government provides homeowners with user-friendly sources of information. It then encourages them to take action when radon levels exceed a recommended "action level" (four picocuries per liter). Finally, it recommends reliable test kits for measuring radon and certifies contractors for making structural and ventilation fixes that reduce its levels.

The radon case exemplifies one application of information as a policy instrument: using it to influence directly the behavior of people at risk. Government provides information and advice, but leaves it up to citizens to act on that information and advice. Another way to use information, however, is to require its disclosure in order to force accountability from pollution sources. Community right-to-know laws, including Title III of the Superfund Amendment and Reauthorization Act (EPCRA) of 1986, exemplify this new use of information (Hadden, 1989b; Baram, Dillon, and Ruffle, 1990).

To understand the origins of the community right-to-know laws that we discussed in Chapters Two, Three, Six, and Seven, we need to go back to an explosion at a Union Carbide chemical plant in Bhopal, India. This 1984 event was one of the most significant in contemporary environmental policy. The rapid release of a highly toxic chemical in the early morning hours killed three thousand people instantly and caused thousands of others injury in the poor settlements around the plant (Shrivastava, 1992). If Bhopal was a tragedy for the local residents, it was what John Kingdon (1995) calls a *focusing event* for the rest of the world. It forced the industrial nations to confront the hazards posed by large manufacturing facilities, many of which were located in highly populated areas. Indeed, just as Three-Mile Island provoked public concern about nuclear power in the late 1970s, so Bhopal crystallized public fear about the petrochemical and other industries in the 1980s.

The lesson that policymakers drew from Bhopal was this: residents of communities near manufacturing facilities that may pose hazards have a right to know what toxic materials are being used and released into the environment, in what amounts, and (to some degree) with what possible consequences. Until the passage of community right-to-know laws, there was no public accounting of chemicals discharged into air, water, and land. Not surprisingly, given the concentration of these plants within its borders, New Jersey was the first state to pass a right-to-know law (in 1984), and it served as a model for EPCRA. Other states soon followed.

As noted, the centerpiece of EPCRA is the TRI. It requires manufacturing facilities listed under standard industrial codes (SIC) to track and report annually on their use, storage, and release of some three hundred potentially hazardous substances into the air, water, land, and underground injection wells. They must also report any quantities transferred off-site. The EPA compiles the information and publishes a summary in an annual report, which the media has extensively covered from the beginning. Moreover, the information is gradually becoming accessible to residents and community groups in electronic form. Importantly, the TRI does not require firms to install technology or change their production processes; it is purely an information requirement. It can result, however, in changes in production processes if the data are unflattering (Hadden, 1989a).

This reporting is costly. The EPA estimates that U.S. businesses spend approximately eighty million hours annually to comply; this translates into $3.2 billion in compliance costs. Nevertheless, in 1996 the EPA expanded the TRI's coverage by adding chemicals to the list; then, in 1997 it proposed to increase the categories of firms covered. In addition, although the TRI has been heralded as a victory for the public, it still has significant limitations. First, it covers only a subset of U.S. polluters. Iron and steel plants, chemical processors, and metal fabricating plants must report; yet polluters in other SIC categories do not have to report. This gives a biased view of releases. Second, TRI accounts for a small proportion of releases of many pollutants. VOCs—common air pollutants—are an example. Most come from motor vehicles (not included in the TRI), so only 2 percent of VOCs released are covered. Third, the TRI reports only on volumes of substances released, not on their toxicity. Early on, sulfuric acid releases dominated the reporting in terms of volumes of releases from many facilities. Yet sulfuric acid is much less harmful than many other substances released in much smaller amounts. Thus, TRI numbers distort the actual health and environmental impacts of the different substances (sulfuric acid was later dropped from the TRI). Finally, the reliability of TRI reports is questionable. They rely on a system of self-reporting by facilities, with limited verification of accuracy. An EPA analysis revealed that a large proportion of TRI reports from facilities might be inaccurate by a factor of two or more times the numbers reported—either over or under the reported amount.

Despite these limitations, many commentators credit the TRI for promoting environmental management and improving community relations. At a minimum, most observers initially viewed EPCRA as an expression of the principle of the public's right-to-know. But what the public would do with this information and what its effects would be on companies were uncertain. Experience with the TRI has confirmed the old adage that information is power. The disclosure of information on chemicals and releases has indeed created a measure of accountability. Assessments of the TRI and similar programs suggest that when many firms are forced to inform the public about the effects of their activities, they try harder to minimize those effects and to respond to public concern about them (see, for example, Baram and Dillon, 1993; Durant, Legge, and Moussios, 1998).

Whatever the promise of disclosure instruments, however, managers should keep two issues in mind. First, disclosure works best within a framework of performance requirements, implemented with technology or other instruments. Some polluters will not respond to public disclosure on their own. Moreover, even otherwise-responsible entities need to know that competitors will not derive an economic advantage from poor environmental performance. Second, performance targets are necessary to assure the public that desired levels of environmental protection will be achieved. Information instruments do not ensure particular levels of pollution reduction. Consequently, for information instruments to be legitimate and successful, policymakers need to combine their information tools with other instruments.

EVALUATING POLICY INSTRUMENTS

Before we consider how to determine the best fit between instruments and problems and the use of instruments in combination, here are some general observations for managers about the use of policy instruments and strategies.

Design and technology standards, combined with harm-based standards, have dominated U.S. policy. They remain the policy instruments of choice. Their virtues are that they clearly assign responsibilities to sources, they reflect knowledge of the best technological solutions, and they give some assurance that a pollution reduction target will or may be achieved. At the same time, three decades of experience with these command-and-control instruments revealed weaknesses: a single-source focus, lack of flexibility, high cost, and a tendency to stifle innovation. These weaknesses stimulated a search for alternatives.

The use of market instruments to complement conventional instruments has grown incrementally. Beginning with offsets in the 1970s and continuing with acid rain allowance trading, volume-based pricing for solid waste, and trading options for reducing greenhouse gas emissions, market instruments have become a valuable adjunct to conventional regulation. Moreover, with the advent today of water pollution trading, their continuing and expanding salience to policymakers seems ensured.

Information instruments that use disclosure to create accountability are transforming environmental management in the United States and Europe. Changes in environmental management set off by the Bhopal tragedy affected government and industry in different but related ways. Government saw mandatory information disclosure as a major new mechanism for increasing public awareness and corporate accountability. Importantly, it was also a way to do so without having to issue detailed design or technology standards. For its part, industry grew convinced that maintaining public confidence and trust was essential for doing business. Firms convinced of this need aggressively developed environmental management systems, integrated environmental issues into operations and planning, and improved public reporting, often well beyond existing legal requirements. Finally, many turned for guidance in doing these things to Europe, where policy strategies such as the Eco-Management and Audit Scheme (EMAS) flourish (Orts, 1995; Irwin, 1997). EMAS sees quality environmental performance as a function of public reporting, third-party auditing, and internally coherent strategic environmental information systems and management systems—much like what we describe.

The concept of challenge regulation offers a foundation for a new generation of instruments and strategies. The OTA concept of challenge regulation provides a framework for integrating several trends. It allows policymakers to overcome weaknesses in conventional regulation. Moreover, it capitalizes on the movement toward integrated environmental management, information disclosure that creates accountability, and flexibility within and across facilities. The Dutch version of challenge regulation is appealing because it retains the assurances of technology instruments but allows for greater flexibility and creativity among sources as they work cooperatively toward achieving performance targets.

MAKING THE SOLUTION FIT THE PROBLEM

This chapter opened with the radon example because it illustrates an important principle: different kinds of environmental problems need to be addressed by different policy instruments. Consider the following scenarios. Had any policymaker seriously tried to implement a strategy based on technology instruments, using government inspection and testing to address the radon problem, he would have been run out of office. Conversely, anyone proposing in 1970 that voluntary commitments from industry, along the lines of the 33/50 program, were the key to reducing industrial pollution would have been pilloried for naivete. Similarly, no one would seriously think that what works in preserving wetlands would necessarily work in reducing hydrocarbon emissions at a paint factory, or that the strategies that worked in 1975 would be as efficient or as effective today. Finally, no one would seriously argue that what is effective for large firms with sophisticated management and technological capabilities is appropriate for small firms with limited resources. What follows, then, are four rules of thumb that managers should find useful when trying to match instruments to problems.

The more dispersed the sources of a problem are, the less likely it is that design and technology instruments will succeed. The extensive use of design and technology instruments reflects in part the kinds of problems that environmental policymakers initially had to solve. In the 1960s and 1970s, as we have noted, the leading concerns were air and water pollution from large industrial sources—power plants, steel mills, petrochemical facilities, smelters, and so on. Policymakers had to deal with a limited number of sources, whose compliance, for the most part, they could monitor and against whom they could take corrective action. As policymakers had to respond to more diffuse and dispersed sources of problems, however, they recognized the limits of a conventional technology approach. Water pollution today, as we have noted, is more the result of agricultural runoff or stormwater drainage than of large industrial polluters. For these problems, specifying technologies, issuing detailed permits, and exercising close regulatory oversight is infeasible. Market, information, subsidy, and technical assistance instruments are more likely to achieve the desired results.

The more dynamic a sector is, the greater is the need for flexibility and innovation. Most regulated industries today are more dynamic and complex than they were thirty years ago. Electronics is an example. Rapid changes in products, technologies, and applications mean that most technology or design standards formulated today will quickly be outdated. Even more dysfunctional is the likelihood that by the time a regulatory agency formally issues technology standards, those standards will be several years out of date. For these sectors, alternatives to technology instruments are a must. Among the options are fees applied to substances for which uses and disposal are concerns. Equally plausible are labels on electronic products (like nutrition labels on food) that describe the environmental effects of the manufacture and use of these products. Finally, product stewardship requirements, such as those noted in Chapter Four regarding ISO 14000 standards, can make manufacturers accountable for a product throughout its life cycle.

Problems that are local or regional in scope require local or regional responses. A general trend in U.S. environmental policy over the last thirty years has been the shift of responsibility and authority from the state and local levels to the national level. For some problems, such as global warming or regional air and water pollution, a national, even global approach to selecting and applying policy instruments is appropriate. For many other problems, however, there has been too much emphasis on national uniformity and too little regard for local variations in conditions, capabilities, and preferences. As we have noted in previous chapters, the EPA and state environmental agencies have recognized this problem by placing growing emphasis on place-based policies that rely more on bottom-up than on top-down strategies. This emphasis enables local policymakers and communities to draw more creatively on a range of policy instruments (U.S. Environmental Protection Agency, 1997).

Policymakers may combine various policy instruments to fashion effective strategies for responding to environmental problems. The trend over the last thirty years has been unmistakable: policymakers are combining different kinds of instruments to create more effective and less expensive strategies for environmental protection. Managers must understand that only rarely should one instrument be used on its own to deal with a given problem. Information disclosure through the TRI, for instance, was effective only against a backdrop of technology standards. Likewise, emissions trading can help make technology instruments more cost-effective and flexible, while technical assistance may complement any other strategy. The latter is particularly useful when regulated entities include a large number of small polluters. Finally, harm-based standards help define a goal and framework for using other policy instruments. Thus, more and more the key to successful environmental management lies in skillfully combining different policy instruments.

Consider a brief example of how policymakers may combine instruments to respond to a complex problem. Although the rate, magnitude, and consequences of change are unclear, most scientists agree that higher concentrations of many substances in the atmosphere are causing the gradual increases in global temperatures that we noted in the Introduction. What is more, nearly all products of modern industrial society are contributing to this phenomenon. More than half of the increase is attributable to carbon dioxide emissions from combustion of fossil fuels. Thus, scientists say that a key to reducing the rate of warming is to lower these emissions.

Among the options that policymakers have to address this problem are

- Across-the-board technology requirements that would apply to different categories of sources emitting carbon dioxide (fixed target, single source)

- An input fee on carbon content for use of fuels, to encourage industries to switch to natural gas and other fuels with lower carbon content (no fixed target)

- An output fee applied to carbon dioxide emissions, with the amount of the fee increasing per unit of emissions (no fixed target)

- A system of trading in greenhouse gas emissions that sets a ceiling for each country and allows trading among them in order to achieve a more efficient result (fixed target, multiple sources)

A program for slowing the rate of global warming by reducing carbon dioxide emissions could be built by combining at least some of these instruments. Technology requirements could define a baseline that facilities would have to meet or else face sanctions. An input fee based on the carbon content of fuels could encourage sources to find alternatives that would allow them to perform even better than the technology standards require (as long as they could deviate from those standards if they achieve a better result). An output fee could be combined with technology standards to reward sources that find ways to perform even better than the standards require. A trading system could accommodate variations in national policies that encourage creative solutions within the context of clear performance targets. Within nations, trading among sources could help achieve more efficient results, as acid rain allowance trading has done under the 1990 Clean Air Act Amendments.

But combining policy instruments to achieve better results is presently more art than science. Some principles that could be followed include

- Technology standards (if they are defined in terms of results rather than specific technologies) could be used with emissions trading to achieve desired levels of performance more flexibly and efficiently.
- Information instruments could be combined effectively with a variety of other instruments as a way to achieve greater accountability and encourage more responsible performance.
- A strategy based on challenge regulation (along the lines of the Dutch model) could be applied on a sectoral or regional basis and used jointly with baseline technology requirements and information instruments.
- Integrated permitting could offer a means of achieving better environmental results on a facility basis.
- Harm-based standards could be combined with several other instruments as a way of defining targets and determining what levels of source performance are really necessary.

CONCLUSION

The instruments discussed in this chapter make up a formidable tool box for responding to environmental problems. All public, nonprofit, and for-profit managers—whether regulators or regulatees—would do well to understand the following advantages and disadvantages of these instruments:

- *Technology instruments* offer a degree of certainty, an assurance that some action will be taken, and definable standards for determining whether or not sources are in compliance. At the same time and on their own, they may be costly and inflexible and discourage innovation.
- *Emissions trading* is quite effective within a framework of technology instruments, and it is typically more flexible and cost-efficient than technology standards that are applied uniformly.
- In spite of the many implementation issues it has to overcome, *integrated permitting* can lead to more cost-effective strategies for managing and preventing pollution.
- *Challenge regulation* maintains high standards of performance but gives sources flexibility in determining how to achieve them. It provides an overall approach and a way to use other instruments—such as trading, fees, and information—to achieve better overall results.
- *Pollution fees* harness market incentives to change behavior in environmentally beneficial ways. Although technical issues have limited the use of fees to controlling such problems as industrial air pollution, fees are more feasible when applied to inputs to production or to wastes that are easily measured, such as municipal waste.
- *Information instruments* are especially promising options for the future. Policies for residential radon illustrate one use of information— as a way to influence directly the behavior of people at risk. A recent trend has been to require disclosure of information to force accountability, as exemplified in community right-to-know laws. Information disclosure in combination with other instruments may prove very effective. But reporting costs can be substantial.

If managers are to respond to environmental problems more effectively, fairly, and efficiently, they must understand the effects of these different tools under different circumstances and both alone and in combination with other instruments. Before this can happen, however, there must be much more systematic evaluation of these dynamics. Moreover, as we have chronicled in previous chapters, a whole host of political, legal, organizational, psychological, and communication barriers must be overcome as well. Nonetheless, we do know a great deal today about effectively managing public, nonprofit, and for-profit organizations in environmentally prudent ways. It is to a summary of these broad principles, practices, and priorities—as well as to the perplexing trends that complicate managers' jobs in realizing them—that we turn next in Chapter Thirteen.

PART FOUR

LESSONS

13

PRINCIPLES, PRACTICES, AND PRIORITIES FOR A NEW CENTURY

The first rule of intelligent tinkering is to save all the pieces.

—Aldo Leopold[1]

Writing in 1947, John Gaus cogently chronicled how fundamental and momentous social, economic, technological, and environmental discontinuities and challenges had historically led citizens in the United States to turn toward the federal government for sustenance, succor, and redress. Intrinsic to these developments was the ascendancy of the positive state philosophy and the institutionalization of the administrative state[2] in Washington, D.C. (Waldo, 1948). Only the latter was viewed as being capable of marshaling the will, wherewithal, and countervailing power necessary to protect and promote the interests of otherwise marginalized citizens in the face of forces beyond their power to influence, let alone control.

Over the past two decades the United States has experienced wrenching transformations akin to those that Gaus maintained had led to the rise of the administrative state. To use Alvin Toffler's (1980) terms, "third-wave" transformations (such as global capitalism, the information revolution, and global warming) have shaken social, economic, and political systems in ways comparable to when the U.S. shifted from an agricultural (the first wave) to an industrial (the second wave) society. Yet dominant today is a downsizing, defunding, and devolution

(D³) agenda decidedly at odds with the agenda that originally propelled the rise of the administrative state. Indeed, much of this book has chronicled precisely how these trends have affected environmental management in the United States.

The consequences of this larger agenda are growing clearer every day: intentions aside, politicians in the United States are not so much dismantling the administrative state as they are changing its metes, bounds, and complexity. Indeed, efforts to shrink the administrative state have produced fewer federal bureaucrats, but not fewer bureaucracies involved in the networks of public, for-profit, and nonprofit organizations now charged with either delivering some services, regulating other actors, or voluntarily complying with the law.

In this final chapter we address the implications of this trend for environmental management in the twenty-first century. We begin by thinking globally. We note the uncertainties presented and the controversies ignited for managers worldwide by third-wave transformations in the environmental policy arena. Next we narrow our focus to examine the political economy driving the D³ agenda in the United States in the wake of these challenges. We analyze the ways in which the agenda is already affecting environmental management, and what its prospects are for continuing in the future. We then examine the problems and prospects posed by the D³ agenda for managers bent on developing what we have argued is essential for their organizations: a coproduction environmental ethic. These uncertainties notwithstanding, we conclude by reviewing what we do know about what managers will have to do in the twenty-first century to deal effectively with environmental issues—whether the D³ agenda prevails or not.

THINKING GLOBALLY

If Steven Jay Gould (1983) is correct, paleontologists and managers dealing with environmental issues have much in common. Paleontologists, he notes, have to make inferences from databases that are disastrously incomplete and biased. Fossil records sometimes have gaps of centuries, and certain fossils have a better chance than others of surviving or being discovered. Thus, paleontology is like trying to understand a book when you can read only every tenth page and can recognize only vowels. Certainly managers trying to deal with the issues, trends, and trade-offs in environmental management that we have chronicled know this feeling well. In fact, they may even envy paleontologists, for they at least can turn the pages by themselves, at their own pace, and without lawyers or micromanaging legislators looking over their shoulders.

Nor is their task likely to grow any easier as the D³ agenda interacts with third-wave transformations in the twenty-first century. Consider, for example, the globalization of world markets and disputes over its impact on environmental quality—locally, regionally, and globally. Some worry that environmental concerns have played and will continue to play second fiddle to opening world markets (see, for example, Rich, 1994; Korten, 1996; Karliner, 1997; Piven and Cloward, 1997). These authors say that the International Monetary Fund (IMF) and the World Bank force cash-strapped and export-crop-dependent developing nations into environmentally destructive activities.

Relatedly, other authors argue that governance effectively shifts under globalization to regulatory regimes (to regions, states, and special districts domestically, or to the IMF, the ISO, and the World Bank internationally) in which corporations have the advantage over downsized, defunded, and devolved national and subnational governments. The leaders of these governments know that these corporations are unencumbered by loyalties to localities or local employees in a global economy in which capital is mobile. Consequently, governments have to design their tax policies and environmental regulations as though corporations will relocate, shift production, or assign profits to jurisdictions that impose the fewest costs on them.

Equally straightforward, however, is the argument marshaled by critics of this perspective. They say that the economic growth that globalization of world markets inspires in these nations is a prerequisite to environmental protection efforts. They point as well to loans that the IMF and World Bank make to poor and developing countries for sustainable development efforts. Similarly, they tout the contributions that the ISO 14000 standards will make to enhancing free trade. Critics of globalization in turn reply that the process of "greening" attitudes is hardly automatic, that it requires political mobilization on a large scale, and that it demands an end to the fast-tracking of global economic agreements negotiated with insufficient environmental input (such as the North American Free Trade Agreement).

Concomitantly, as our understanding of ecological interdependencies continues to grow and spread in the third wave's dynamic information age, uncertainty and contentiousness often spiral rather than dissipate. Consider, for example, how this occurs worldwide to challenge three critical dimensions of environmental management: institutional boundaries, time horizons, and policy implementation (Wells, 1996). Recognizing through computer modeling, satellite imagery, and scientific advances that ecosystem connections exist has not made it any easier for policymakers and managers to identify precisely the boundaries of a given ecosystem (Chase, 1995). Relatedly, this recognition has not advanced their understanding of the best kinds of institutional arrangements for meeting these challenges, and it offers little advice for deciding how best to overcome political resistance to institutional change. Likewise, realizing the intergenerational consequences of decisions has not made settling arguments over proper discount rates more facile or less conflict-ridden. And the recognition that nonpoint source pollution from farms into waterways is a major obstacle to future progress has not reduced as yet the technical, political, and legal challenges managers face in altering behavior.

We do not mean to suggest that no progress has been made in coping with these complexities, uncertainties, and challenges. For example, worldwide recognition of global environmental problems has wrought international agreements nurtured by, among other institutions, the United Nations Environmental Programme. Similarly, at the regional level the European Community has profoundly affected and strengthened the environmental policies of its members. Meanwhile, in the United States many states have put significant amounts of money into programs designed to induce farmers to cut back on fertilizer use voluntarily (Warrick and Goodman, 1998). Still, these efforts are notable for the absence of progress they highlight in other areas of the world. They are also notable for the obstacles they have all had to overcome, and for the substantial hurdles that lie ahead for them in the new millennium.

Likewise, while international consensus existed among nations at the 1997 Kyoto Global Climate Conference that something has to be done about global warming, disparate national interests made solutions problematic. More precisely, developed and developing nations disagreed over who should bear what proportion of the burdens and benefits of attenuating the problem. In the end, each nation was given an individual target for attaining a worldwide greenhouse-gas reduction of 5.2 percent below 1990 levels. But only thirty-eight developed countries had to reduce these emissions, and developing nations had only to set voluntary limits. Jeopardized in the process is ratification of the treaty by the U.S. Senate; ninety-five members voted in 1997 to require developing nations to participate.

THINKING POLITICALLY

What is not in question or conflict presently, however, is the depth and breadth of the political commitment in the United States today to the D^3 agenda. Consider, for example, the recommendations of an important 1995 study of environmental regulation by the National Academy of Public Administration (NAPA). In this congressionally commissioned report, NAPA avers that regulatory power, authority, and discretion must be redirected out of Washington, D.C., and into states, local communities, and markets. NAPA urges that in turn Congress must reprioritize environmental concerns, goals, and resource allocations to reflect the most serious risks as well as the individuals and communities who are most seriously at risk. Urged as well is the evaluation of programs in terms of the environmental outcomes they produce, and especially in terms of the risks they reduce. Finally, NAPA says that bureaucracies at all levels of government must strive to empower affected stakeholders and in the future will have to rely on alternative regulatory tools (such as voluntary compliance, tax incentives, and ADR) to a greater degree.

As previous chapters have illustrated, a host of very good reasons exists for moving in this direction. Among these reasons are the inadequacies of command-and-control regulation in meeting third-generation environmental problems, the fiscal realities of tight operating budgets, the costs of adversarial legalism, the inefficiencies of bureaucratic pluralism, and the inherent worth of developing civic capital. But managers wishing to understand present trends and to anticipate the future must also place these reasons within the larger context of the D^3 agenda and its ultimate fate. At a certain level, both the D^3 agenda and managers' environmental management fate are interconnected politically.

To date, two very distinctive philosophical camps have supported the D^3 agenda, each for very different reasons. For simplicity, and ignoring the nuances within each camp, we refer to these groups as minimalists and positivists.[3] Philosophically, *minimalists* are devotees of limited government who see the D^3 agenda as a vehicle for realizing their goals by limiting the resources on which agencies can draw, by shifting decisions to political arenas that are less prone to government expansion, and by forcing a dialogue over what governments should and should not do. In contrast, *positivists* see the D^3 agenda as a vehicle partially for mending bureaucratic pathologies and partially for preserving activist government in the face of the minimalist assault. In terms of the latter, they see the D^3 agenda as refocusing the debate away from what government should do and toward running better whatever government does exist at whatever level. For environmental managers, this debate often gets framed in terms of the extent to which the so-called precautionary principle (that government should take action now before dire consequences result) should prevail in given situations. It also indirectly informs conflicts over the amount of resources to allocate to basic, as opposed to regulatory, science in agencies.

Descriptively, both groups point to government failures. What is more, each wishes to see agencies evaluated more on the extent to which they think long-term rather than short-term, and to focus on results rather than on program inputs and outputs. For minimalists pushing the D^3 agenda, however, government failures are the norm rather than the exception (Niskanen, 1971). Indeed, they view nonmarket (that is, government) rather than market failures as the primary source of contemporary public problems (Wolf, 1979). Thus, rather than government being the solution to market failures, as positivists since the Progressive Reform era have seen it, minimalists see markets and market competition as the solutions to government failures. Moreover, they herald efficiency as the principle criteria for evaluating performance. In environmental management, this perspective informs the property rights (or "wise-use") movement that we discussed in Chapters Five and Six.

In contrast, positivists tout the advantages of an approach to structuring agencies (for example, enterprise funding as a defunding alternative to the "general fund mentality") and delivering services that is more market-oriented than bent on ending them altogether (see Barzelay, 1992).[4] What is more, they see government's bottom line as value maximization, with efficiency balanced—if not trumped—by responsiveness, equity, and other values (see Denhardt, 1993, for an elaboration of this argument). In environmental management, these assumptions find their way into such disparate and often conflictual emphases as the environmental indicators, environmental justice, and market-based pollution control initiatives that we discussed in Chapters Two, Three, Six, and Twelve.

Both minimalists (philosophically) and positivists (by either conviction or political expediency) aver that government must do more with less. Where they differ, however, is over the extent and the focus of retrenchment. Minimalists insist that bureaucrats implementing the largely administrative and monitoring responsibilities that do remain at the federal level must be forced to tether their appetites drastically. So too must those engaged in service delivery within state and local agencies. Managers must therefore respond to unrelenting demands for relief or succor from everyday and third-wave externalities with Spartan virtuosity—that is, with scaled-back administrative overhead, smaller staffs, reduced layers of management between political appointees and line workers, additional analytical and reporting requirements, and proposals for privatizing services. Most recently, this philosophy emerged in failed environmental legislation mandating full-scale cost-benefit and risk analyses for all proposed regulations, with de novo review of each regulation by federal judges.

For positivists, third-wave technological developments—in particular, the information revolution—make the D^3 agenda feasible, but on nowhere near the scale that minimalists envision. What is more, in the expenditure of whatever funds are available, their focus is less on compliance accountability (Was the money spent as prescribed?) than on capacity (Are sufficient resources available?) and performance accountability (What did funding accomplish?) (Light, 1995). In environmental management, this predisposition has most recently arisen in EPA proposals to strengthen the agency's internal analytical capabilities, to make better use of external panels of scientists, to improve the agency's peer review process, and to create a new environmental statistics center (Johnson, 1998). Similar proposals, however, have run into minimalist roadblocks and gone down to defeat.

THINKING AHEAD

How enduring will this coalition and its D^3 agenda be in the future? There are at least two scenarios for managers to contemplate. The first, based on recent political and economic events, is that in sight is an end to the more draconian minimalist inclinations of the D^3 agenda (Dionne, 1996). Stalled Republican attempts to eviscerate federal programs coupled with budget surpluses may allow for new agency initiatives. Among these would be windfalls for environmental causes.

The second scenario is much more pessimistic. Pay-as-you-go budgeting decision rules in Washington could continue to force trade-offs among agency budgets and competing programs. Meanwhile, the looming demographic time bomb regarding entitlement programs for the baby-boom generation, $14 trillion in unfunded retirement and health care benefits still outstanding for that generation (Broder, 1998), and the interest on a $5.5 trillion national debt all portend less money for agency operating budgets—regardless of which party dominates.

But is not a third scenario possible, one in which devolution has a positive influence on environmental management? After all, most states today are reporting budgetary surpluses, some particularly large (Texas, for example, reported a projected surplus of more than one billion dollars in 1998). Obviously, if the economy continues to grow at its present pace, a necessary but still insufficient condition for growth in environmental budgets is satisfied. But if a downturn in the national economy occurs, problems could still lie ahead. Moreover, even if prosperity continues, it is not entirely clear what states will do with their surpluses. Some may react as Maryland has by putting some additional resources into environmental programs. Others, however, talk of tax cuts or (Texas, for example) of returning the surpluses to taxpayers. Still others (such as Michigan and Wisconsin) talk of putting major shares of their money into welfare programs, given the continuing focus they intend to give to this highly salient policy area. Thus, as has typically been the case, the fate of environmental funding and programs will vary across the states.

Managers would thus do well to expect that certain factors will drive the aggressiveness of state efforts. These factors include the severity of pollution that exists in a state, the relative strength of environmental and industry groups within its borders, the state's historical commitment to environmental protection, the size of its population, the aggressiveness of the EPA region within which it is located, and the degree of organizational integration of environmental programs in the state's government (see, for example, Bacot and Dawes, 1997; O'Toole and others, 1997; Bowman and Kearney, 1986; Davis and Feiock, 1992; Davis and Lester, 1987; Lester, Franke, Bowman, and Kramer, 1983; Lowry, 1992; Ingram and Mann, 1989; Hedge and Scicchitano, 1992).

Regardless of which scenario prevails, managers should understand that reforming environmental management is no longer a choice. The only question remaining is what the nature of those reforms will ultimately be. As we have stressed, widespread consensus exists among both regulators and regulatees that environmental problems do not respect single-medium regulatory regimes; that addressing problems one risk, one pollutant, and one medium at a time is inefficient, ineffective, and (often) inequitable; and that resource constraints and third-generation problems require market and partnering approaches, with scientifically and community-informed trade-offs made among competing risks.

THINKING STRATEGICALLY

Most reform proposals thus call on managers to *reconnect* with citizens, to *reconceptualize* priorities and agency operations, and to *reengage* environmental resources and responsibilities accordingly (the R³ agenda). Indeed, these are critical dimensions of what, we have argued, encapsulates the primary principles, practices, and priorities that managers must pursue to be successful in the twenty-first century—a coproduction environmental ethic. Does the D³ agenda help or hinder the goals of this R³ agenda?

As you may recall, a coproduction environmental ethic imbues an organization's members with an abiding awareness of the five cutting-edge issues introduced in Chapter One. Employees are cognizant of how their activities and operations affect present and future generations in the communities they serve. In addition, they are sensitive to the impact that the benefits and burdens produced by those activities have historically had on disadvantaged members of these communities. At the same time, employees have a sense of the efficiency and effectiveness gains that are possible in an era of unfunded mandates by focusing on pollution reduction and prevention, on ecosystems, and on prioritized risks. Finally, they understand that meeting each of these objectives starts with, and ultimately depends for success on, mutually defining with their communities a sense of the environmental issues, trends, and trade-offs they confront.

Reconnecting with Citizens

Minimalists touting the D³ agenda often talk about the advantages for accountability that stem from government closest to the people. Yet they simultaneously try to disempower citizens by reducing reporting requirements, delimiting their access to technical advice, and reducing the capacities of counterbureaucracies (such as the General Accounting Office, the Congressional Research Service, and the now dismantled Advisory Commission on Intergovernmental Relations) to evaluate their operations. Meanwhile, positivists focused on customers say little about how policy-challenged citizens can make these important decisions in informed ways in the absence of complete information, meaningful competition, and prices that reflect the true social and environmental costs of production.

If the perestroika in citizen-agency relationships that we envision for effective environmental management is to occur, these attitudes must change. Merely shifting responsibilities closer to the people (as the minimalists would have it) or being responsive to the unfiltered wishes of one's customers (as the positivists would like to see) are Lilliputian in proportion to the task at hand. As the literature amply documents, government that is closer to the people is not necessarily as populist in effect or accountable under all circumstances as minimalists suggest it will be (Golembiewski, 1977). Nor are people merely customers (Osborne and Plastrik, 1997) or owners (Frederickson, 1997) of government.

As Michael Hammer (1996) notes, even private firms do not rush to meet consumer demands that threaten other values (such as stock dividends, share prices, market shares, or opening up new market niches). Alternatively, for public agencies customers are also individuals with rights to be protected, clients with needs for professional experts to address, and citizens with responsibilities to carry out. What is more, an agency's primary customers may not be the clients with whom it has direct contact but rather the larger citizenry it serves as trustee.

Becoming policy entrepreneurs is also not sufficient for managers who are trying to reconnect citizens with their agencies to improve accountability. As Marc Landy (1995) suggests, entrepreneurialism involves selling one's policies, programs, and predilections. This in turn means selectively marshaling evidence to support and advance existing or new policies, programs, claims, and interests. Managers must begin tutoring citizens in the complexity of the issues their agencies face; in the intricacies of the agency decision-making processes that managers must traverse; and in the very real legal, ethical, and financial constraints that managers must factor into their decisions. In essence, managers must come to realize that demystifying technocratic complexities for citizens is in their own, and in society's, best interest. This may yet happen, but proponents of the D³ agenda offer little to advance the cause, despite mounting evidence that citizen aptitudes and attitudes are influenced by information provided to them (Yankelovich, 1991).

Reconceptualizing Priorities and Operations

As we have stressed repeatedly, single-medium regulatory regimes are the most important obstacles to managers' moving toward environmental risk-based priority setting, ecosystem management, and sustainable development. To date, however, principled disagreement has reigned over the wisdom of developing an integrated, or organic, environmental statute to overcome this dilemma. To some, to do so would open the possibility for too much mischief on the part of implementers with questionable environmental values. To others, there is enough discretion in existing statutes to allow for trade-offs, if implementers will only exercise the will to do so. Moreover, doing nothing avoids opening each existing statute to amendment by friends or foes of vigorous environmental regulation. Thus, with few exceptions at the state level (such as in California), the one pollutant, one medium, and one risk regulatory regime prevails and is likely to do so for the foreseeable future.

But might not managers expect that the complexity and exorbitant compliance costs of the present system will push polluters toward source reduction and pollution prevention? Certainly the cost savings we have cited for private companies and the pilot projects associated with the EPA's Project XL (see Chapter Four) or with New Jersey's and Massachusetts's integrated permitting systems (see Chapter Twelve) have demonstrated how attractive these strategies can be. All of these programs show how more flexibility in setting compliance priorities can combine with source reduction and pollution prevention initiatives to bring about significantly more cost-effective environmental quality. Moreover, as we have noted in Chapter Two, one of the only explicitly multimedia statutes presently in existence—the Pollution Prevention Act of 1990—affords a mandate and vehicle for pursuing these ends. Meanwhile, the Toxics Release Inventory adds additional pressures on some managers to reduce pollution from their operations, as do stringent toxic release standards and pollution prevention efforts in the states (Folz, 1991; John, 1994; O'Toole and others, 1997; Bacot and Dawes, 1997).

In the future, success in environmental management will also depend on how well managers apply what we already know from the first rounds of reinvention and reengineering in the public and private sectors (Radin, 1995). First, what matters in reinvention efforts is the consolidation of programs rather than departments and agencies (Kettl and DiIullio, 1995; Thompson, 1993; Osborne and Plastrik, 1997). Second, a focus on flow-of-work processes rather than on discrete functions is most advantageous (Golembiewski, 1987; Rainey, 1990; Hammer and Champy, 1993; Hammer and Stanton, 1995). Third, a focus on implementation structures rather than on single departments, agencies, or functions is often necessary for change to occur in an era of proxy or hollow government (Hjern and Porter, 1981; Stoker, 1989; Kettl, 1993; Milward and Provan, 1993; O'Toole, 1997). Fourth, finding ways to measure and attribute responsibility for results in often opaque interorganizational networks is of critical importance (O'Toole, 1997; Milward and Provan, 1993; Stoker, 1989; Kettl, 1997; Durant, 1998a). Finally, the amount of "delayering" (of political appointees and careerists) that takes place in bureaucracies is more critical for reinventing them than are the number of employees cut, agencies restructured, or functions devolved (Light, 1995; Thompson, 1993; Kettl and DiIullio, 1995).

Astute environmental management in the twenty-first century will also depend on whether or not managers make the same mistakes that private corporations did early on and later had to correct. In many corporations, research and development cutbacks eventually jeopardized future competitiveness in world markets to the point where organizations were becoming anorexic or bulimic (Davenport, 1995). Later these capacities had to be rebuilt. At the same time, many companies cut highly paid mid-level managers, only to replace them with significantly less experienced and lower-salaried employees. In the process, institutional memory was lost and took time to rebuild. Presently, however, we cannot say whether these lessons—or the others noted earlier—will inform efforts to reconceptualize environmental management in the future.

Reengaging Resources

To date, both minimalist and positivist proponents of the D³ agenda have talked a great deal about shifting resources to high-priority items. Minimalists, for example, talk passionately about deciding what government should and should not do. As we have noted, however, sorting these things out in the environmental policy arena requires significant investment in such things as "good science," strategic environmental information systems that incorporate or use ISO 14000 standards as guidelines, and monitoring data. These are all items, however, that are low on any minimalist's wish list of expenditures. Meanwhile, positivists talk (albeit less) about shifting responsibilities to other levels of government and sectors of the economy (for-profits and nonprofits), about setting priorities, and about measuring results. Yet their implicit assumption is that results-oriented environmental management alone will bring about needed changes in structures, expenditures, and priorities—a precarious assumption in our Madisonian system of checks and balances.

Consider, for example, the early political dynamics surrounding the EPA's Environmental Performance Agreement (EnPA) initiative, the environmental indicators movement. As we noted in Chapter One, in return for negotiating outcome measures with the EPA, states participating in EnPA were to receive reduced reporting requirements. Relatedly, the agency's Performance Partnership Grant (PPG) program allowed states to shift money among media-specific federal grants to address local priorities. But to succeed, both EnPA and PPG had to overcome the single-medium statutory approach taken by Congress in regard to both regulation and intergovernmental grants. Yet these grants worked in direct opposition to both programs.

Similarly, even though many managers have embraced the environmental indicators movement as a means for becoming more outcomes based, only a handful of states have the rudiments of a system that can be used in multimedia environmental management (Bernard, 1996). Meanwhile, obstacles to reengaging resources come from regulatory targets as well as from agencies and legislatures. All of these groups are sometimes reluctant to give up familiar regulatory procedures (such as permitting) for promising but unfamiliar ones.

Finally, the EPA's Common Sense Initiative (CSI) to make environmental decision making produce cleaner, cheaper, and smarter regulations is illustrative of the trust problems among stakeholders that have to be overcome ("Michigan Abandons. . . ," 1996). A recent study by the U.S. General Accounting Office (1997) of fifteen of the EPA's forty CSI projects emphasizes the substantial time needed to collect and analyze data requested by stakeholders. It also chronicles how difficult it has been to gain consensus on complex policy issues (as opposed to more successful efforts on more specific projects such as redesigning the emergency response planning process).

As these vignettes indicate, successful environmental management in the twenty-first century will also require managers to be skilled in connecting to, communicating with, and coordinating a sense of purpose and trust among a wide variety of actors. Moreover, they will have to do so within nonhierarchical networks composed of disparate public, for-profit, and nonprofit actors. And alas, this will be true whether the D^3 agenda prevails or not.

Research on networks in general indicates that managers will be better able to foster cooperation and trust among network actors under four conditions: when programmatic rewards are linked explicitly to cooperative behavior, when linkages are made to other issues dear to implementers' hearts, when large program goals and programs are broken down into smaller parts to reduce the gains realizable from defection or exploitation, and when implementation processes are "transparent" (that is, when they formally provide for information

sharing and routine external evaluations of cooperation among participants). Still uncertain, however, is whether there will be enough sufficiently talented managers of goodwill and good faith to work these
complex seams of government effectively.

MANAGING FOR THE ENVIRONMENT IN THE TWENTY-FIRST CENTURY

With all this uncertainty, what can we say with confidence about how
effective managers will deal with environmental management issues in
the years and decades to come? Most important, we know that there is
not a stereotypical environmental manager. Many public, for-profit,
and nonprofit managers who are not trained professionals in this field
deal with the important challenges addressed in this book. Effective
environmental management is a challenge facing all of us.

Effective managers will prudently carry out two broad and important tasks when dealing with environmental issues. First, they will take
vague, ambiguous, or even conflicting laws, translate them into programs, and take steps to implement them within an environment of
adversarial legalism. Second, they will serve as intermediaries among
scientists, technical personnel, politicians, contractors, stakeholders,
and the general public. In turn, the most effective among them will
focus on results, not on program inputs or outputs. Importantly, they
will go beyond merely "counting things." They will focus instead on
what is measured, on how it is measured, and on whether these measures really tell them what they need to know in order to manage
effectively.

The environmental results that effective managers will want to see
must not merely involve improvements in individual programs or on
behalf of generations or classes of people. Effective managers will think
holistically, intergenerationally, and distributionally. Thus they will
manage ecosystems, not programs. They will manage for future generations, not merely for their own. And they will manage in the interests of
all races, genders, and income levels. All this of course requires them to
involve diverse groups in the environmental decisions they contemplate,
make, and implement.

Intelligent managers will be concerned about equitable and sustainable development. *Sustainable development* means meeting the needs of
the present without compromising the ability of future generations to
meet their own needs. This in part means behaving as a steward of our
natural resources and seeing that accurate measurements of the bene-

fits, costs, and differential impacts of our policy decisions are determined, analyzed, and utilized in decision-making processes.

The effective manager will be aware that environmental laws and recent developments in case law have prompted nothing less than a fundamental change in public, for-profit, and nonprofit management practices. Thus, savvy managers will

- Educate themselves and their staffs about their legal responsibilities and potential liabilities

- Carry out environmental assessments of their organizations that examine and pinpoint areas in need of environmental strengthening

- Follow through by seeing that the needed changes are made

- Monitor compliance with environmental laws and integrate environmental policies into their daily work environment

- Seek out the assistance of federal, state, and local regulatory agencies and work in tandem with them to address environmental problems

Effective managers will implement total quality environmental management (TQEM) but will be more or less successful to the extent to which they apply its principles realistically and strategically. TQEM values cost-effective environmental management initiatives that are multimedia focused, that emphasize source reduction and pollution prevention, and that depend on continuous environmental quality improvements that managers incorporate into their operations. An effective manager will encourage her organization to become a learning organization in order both to incorporate TQEM changes and to improve on such innovations continuously.

An effective manager will also work proactively and strategically with the media on environmental issues. This means anticipating reporters' needs, holding press conferences, providing outlines of key points, and promptly answering inquiries. This also means using the media as a management tool to improve public understanding of environmental issues, and to get out to citizens the positive news of innovations, changes, and opportunities. Thus, the savvy manager will know the news media in general, and the characteristics and needs of the local media in particular. Specifically, he will be willing to understand the journalist's point of view and will build credibility through honesty, consistency, and availability; he will respect the agenda of the media, even though it may be at variance with that of the manager's particular public, for-profit, or nonprofit organization; and he will dedicate sufficient staff time to planning and implementing environmental information campaigns, to developing and distributing information, and to making media contacts.

Relatedly, managers dealing successfully with environmental management issues will work proactively with communities. Managers do not and should not work in a vacuum. Rather, they have a both noble and self-interested obligation to build environmental decisions with the public, not for the public. This translates into tutoring the public if needed; listening to key stakeholders; building a coproduction environmental ethic that is translated into internal decision-making processes; fostering two-way communication (a process that encompasses problem identification, eliciting values, validating values, generating options, and developing discrete criteria for evaluating these options and final choices); and avoiding closed-door meetings whenever possible.

Success in working with communities on environmental issues will depend on able risk communication. An effective manager will realize that risk means different things to different people, and that most individuals tend to ignore or discount discrete, familiar, voluntary, and low-probability risks. He will realize that feelings of control and opportunities for participation influence evaluations of the acceptability of risk. He will understand that risks are not perceived and evaluated in a vacuum; rather, people evaluate risks as members of a community. He will know that trust is important for influencing risk perceptions.

Consequently, the savvy manager will try to communicate clearly about environmental risks by

- Using simple nontechnical language
- Using vivid, concrete, and easily understood images
- Using examples and anecdotes that make technical data come alive
- Avoiding distant or abstract language
- Acknowledging fears and anxieties
- Using comparisons in order to put risks in perspective
- Being open about discussing actions under consideration
- Being honest about what she can and cannot do

The effective manager will utilize a host of environmental dispute resolution (EDR) techniques. EDR incorporates a variety of approaches that allow parties to meet face to face to reach a mutually acceptable resolution of the issues in a dispute or potentially controversial situation. It is often viewed as intervention between conflicting parties or viewpoints to promote reconciliation, settlement, compromise, or understanding in the environmental arena. Such interventions include mere assistance from a neutral third party to the negotiation process. Assistance can be directed toward settling disputes arising out of past events, or it can be directed toward establishing rules to govern future conduct, such as in the case of regulatory negotiation.

A savvy manager will know that EDR will most likely work when certain conditions are met, including when

- There are a manageable number of identifiable interests
- There are no major issues that involve scientific uncertainty or controversy
- The core dispute raises no fundamental value or symbolic issues
- The parties are able to achieve a level of trust and a sense of shared purpose
- There exists a rough parity of power among the participants

Such a manager will know that there are four principles for successful negotiation: separate the people from the problem; focus on interests, not on positions; generate a wide variety of options for reconciling interests; and insist that the result be based on objective criteria.

The effective manager will also build strategic environmental information systems. Moreover, the most astute among them will do so while keeping an eye on ISO 14000 standards as guidelines. This means seeking out accurate data, matching environmental management goals and analytic capabilities, streamlining information technology, and maintaining information technology capacity. A savvy manager will also be aware of the different professional worlds of her computer and noncomputer staffs, and will seek to bridge those worlds. Toward these ends, an effective manager will

- Develop a strategic environmental information plan that is user friendly
- Break down functional balkanization

- Afford adequate stakeholder representation
- Gain support from agency heads
- Continually assess and address information technology training needs
- Ensure that the evolving information system is modified, if necessary, to meet the organization's needs
- Ensure that the information technology system offers a high return on the investment of managers, stakeholders, and regulators

The effective manager will pay attention to the issue of managing scientific and technical personnel for environmental ends. This means establishing a work climate that fosters free expression and encourages independent thought; managing ends, not means; protecting scientific and technical personnel as a major capital resource of the organization; letting scientists and technical workers participate in policy discussions that concern their work; explaining decisions to them; emphasizing communication, training, and teamwork; providing ample avenues in the organization for input from scientists and the technical staff; supporting proactive behavior; and giving ample credit and recognition to staff when it is due.

Relatedly, a successful manager will also realize that the scientific process is often in tension with the political process, as well as with the realities of running large bureaucracies. Thus, whenever possible she will give scientific and technical people the tools and resources that will allow their skills and work to shine; she will practice task assignment through managed volunteerism that includes allowing employees to volunteer for assignments; she will foster a personal commitment among the workers to do the job right and well; and she will invest in job enrichment and job enlargement.

The effective manager will also pay close attention to the issue of managing environmental contracts, grants, and partnerships. He will critically examine the criteria for determining whether outsourcing or partnering may be appropriate, including

- Will money be saved?
- Will service be enhanced?
- Will other programs be negatively affected?
- Will citizens' needs be better met?
- Will more flexibility be yielded?

- Designing, building, and maintaining strong internal program, organizational, and information systems

- Managing scientific, technical, and other personnel in pursuit of environmental ends

- Managing environmental contracts and grants rigorously

- Working proactively with communities and the media to define environmental issues, understand alternative solutions, and measure progress on agreed-upon choices in light of existing constraints

- Honing finely tuned alternative dispute resolution skills and applying them to environmental situations when appropriate

- Knowing how to use available environmental policy instruments productively

Thus we end this book where we began, with the centrality of dynism, communication, and adaptation as enduring themes of envimental management. Attaining the literacies we have suggested is rmously challenging for all managers as they try to adapt to the ironmental dynamism they confront. Yet armed with the principles, ctices, and priorities we have summarized, they will be better able to derstand, coproduce, and deliver the kinds of added environmental ue that a sustainable economic future requires. Put differently, they be better able to demonstrate and communicate to others how so- institutions can best reconcile humankind's needs and aspirations h the limits that the natural world places on them. And that, it is e to say, will be no modest accomplishment.

- Can objectives be measured and tasks monitore
- Is political support high?
- Is there competition?
- Will continuity of services be preserved?
- Will legal impediments be minor?

Relatedly, the most astute among these managers
of the politics of each situation. Moreover, when s
tors, grant seekers, and potential partners, he will
other programs or organizations that provide insig
history of the organizations that are seeking gove
partnerships.

The savvy manager will also make contractors and
line of defense in detecting and preventing waste and
She will do this by requiring them to provide oversight
and financial systems, and to document compliance
ment's environmental regulations. She will move quicl
fraud, and abuse are suspected, albeit always within th
due process. She will periodically review overhead co
contractor costs, and grant costs.

Finally, the effective manager will utilize a broad ar
mental policy instruments, including technology instrum
trading, integrated permitting, challenge regulation, pol
information instruments. She will know that instrumen
bined in various ways to form effective environmental
will strive to match policy instruments to problems; she
that the more dispersed the sources of a problem are, the
that technology and design instruments will succeed; she
that the more dynamic a sector is, the greater will be the
bility and innovation; she will be aware that problems th
regional in scope require local and regional responses;
stantly evaluate and improve on the use of such policy
realizing that different instruments will yield different ou
different circumstances.

In sum, what makes an effective manager—whethe
for-profit, or nonprofit organization—can be boiled d
key literacies:

- Knowing today's environmental challenges, including
  laws, and regulations

NOTES

INTRODUCTION

1. By *transboundary* we mean that environmental problems cross political boundaries, thus requiring institutional coordination. By *multimedia* we mean that environmental problems that begin in one medium often shift to another medium, necessitating a holistic approach to environmental management.

CHAPTER ONE

1. U.S. Senate Environment and Public Works Committee. Confirmation Hearing on Lee Thomas, Feb. 13, 1985.
2. Dwivedi (1988, p. 8) makes this point when stating that "man is viewed by disciplinary ecologists as being 'outside nature.'"
3. It seems that environmentalists and policymakers were also not concerned about the efficiency of responses to environmental and public health risks demanding the minimization (and in some cases elimination) of pollution regardless of the costs of the law. See, for example, the Clean Air Act Amendments of 1970 and the Federal Water Pollution Control Act Amendments of 1972.
4. On the concept of social capital, see Putnam, 1995a and 1995b; and Edwards and Foley, 1997.
5. See Fromm, 1992; Allenby and Fullerton, 1991/1992, 2(1), 51–61. See generally *Pollution Prevention Review*.

CHAPTER THREE

1. DiNunzio, M. R. (ed.). *Theodore Roosevelt: An American Mind.* New York: Penguin Books, 1994, p. 145.
2. An exception was included for mixed hazardous and radioactive wastes generated and stored at DOE nuclear facilities. The DOE has three years to comply with RCRA regulations pertaining to these wastes before enforcement actions can be taken against it.
3. See *United States* v. *Conservation Chemical Co.*, 1985; *United States* v. *Ottati & Goss*, 1985; *United States* v. *Reilly Tar*, 1982; *United States* v. *NEPACCO*, 1984; *United States* v. *Waste Ind.*, 1984; *United States* v.

Seymour Recycling Corp., 1984; *United States* v. *Vertack Chemical Corp.*, 1980; *United States* v. *Hardage*, 1982. But see also *Outboard Marine Corp.* v. *Thomas*, 1985.

4. 42 U.S.C. 9601; *United States* v. *M/V Big Sam*, 1982; *United States* v. *Lebeouf Bros. Towing Co.*, 1980, cert. denied, 1981; *Steuart Transportation Co.* v. *Allied Towing Corp.*, 1979; *Burgess* v. *M/V. Tamano*, 1977, cert. denied 1978; *United States* v. *Bear Marine Services*, 1980, reversed on other grounds, 1983; *United States* v. *Tex Tow*, 1978; *United States* v. *Ward*, 1985; *United States* v. *Mirabile*, 1985; *United States* v. *Conservation Chemical Co.*, 1985; *United States* v. *South Carolina Recycling and Disposal, Inc.*, 1984; *United States* v. *Price*, 1983; *United States* v. *NEPACCO*, 1984; *United States* v. *Chem-Dyne Corp.*, 1983; *City of Philadelphia* v. *Stephan Chemical Co.*, 1982; *United States* v. *Argent Corp.*, 1984; *United States* v. *Cauffman*, 1984; *United States* v. *Dickerson et al.*, 1986; *In Re T.P. Long Chemical, Inc.*, 1985; *United States* v. *Ottati & Goss*, 1985; *United States* v. *Miami Drum Services, Inc.*, 1986; *Violet* v. *Picillo*, 1986; *United States* v. *Tyson*, 1986.

5. For case law defining *indivisible*, see *United States* v. *South Carolina Recycling and Disposal, Inc.*, 1984; *United States* v. *Ottati & Goss*, 1985; *United States* v. *A & F Materials, Inc.*, 1984; *United States* v. *NEPACCO*, 1984; *United States* v. *Dickerson et al.*, 1986; *United States* v. *Northernaire Plating Co.*, 1989. For case law concerning joint and several liability, see *United States* v. *Mirabile*, 1985; *United States* v. *South Carolina Recycling and Disposal, Inc.*, 1984; *United States* v. *Chem-Dyne*, 1983; *United States* v. *Conservation Chemical Co.*, 1985; *New York* v. *Shore Realty*, 1985; *United States* v. *Ward*, 1985; *United States* v. *Shell Oil Company*, 1985; *United States* v. *Miami Drum Services, Inc.*, 1986.

6. Exceptions to this rule include the "innocent landowner" defense and the EPA's de minimis policy.

7. For representative cases concerning municipal landfills, see *South Macomb Disposal Authority* v. *United States Environmental Protection Agency*, 1988; *New Castle County* v. *Hartford Accident and Indemnity Company*, 1988; *The City of New York* v. *Exxon Corporation*, 1988; *City of Stoughton, Wisconsin* v. *U.S. Environmental Protection Agency*, 1988; and *Robert Ayers et al.* v. *Township of Jackson*, 1987.

8. CAA, CERCLA, CWA, FIFRA, RCRA, SDWA, and TSCA are examples of major environmental statutes that contain felony sanctions.

CHAPTER FOUR

1. Hayward, S. F. *Churchill on Leadership: Executive Success in the Face of Adversity.* Rocklin, Calif.: Forum/Prima, 1997.

CHAPTER FIVE

1. Aurelius, M. *Meditations* (M. Staniforth, trans.). New York: Penguin Books, 1964, p. 104.

CHAPTER SIX

1. Paraphrased in Norris, K. *The Cloister Walk*. New York: Riverhead Books, 1996, p. 165.

CHAPTER EIGHT

1. U.S. Senate Confirmation Hearings of Manuel Lujan and William K. Reilly. Washington, D.C., Feb. 13, 1989.

CHAPTER NINE

1. Eliot, T. S. *Murder in the Cathedral*. Orlando: Harcourt Brace, 1935, p. 12.
2. This section relies heavily on Sauter, 1997, and Thistle, 1997.

CHAPTER TEN

1. Interview with author, 1998.
2. The persons interviewed include the following: a former deputy administrator, chief of staff, and general counsel of the EPA; a former deputy regional administrator of the EPA; a former biologist for the Bureau of Reclamation in the U.S. Department of the Interior; a vice president of a national wildlife preservation organization; two former commissioners of a state environmental organization; a former director of policy and planning for a state environmental organization; a city engineer; a city manager; a director of public works for a city; a supervisor of a laboratory; two engineers; two environmental scientists; two information systems workers; a manager of a regional air pollution control organization; and three managers in environmental consulting firms. Each interview lasted from one-half hour to two hours.

CHAPTER ELEVEN

1. Quoted in Norris, K. *The Cloister Walk*. New York: Riverhead Books, 1996, p. 9.

CHAPTER TWELVE

1. Hayward, S. F. *Churchill on Leadership: Executive Success in the Face of Adversity.* Rocklin, Calif.: Forum/Prima, 1997.

CHAPTER THIRTEEN

1. Leopold, A. *Sand County Almanac.* New York: Oxford University Press, 1949.
2. The *positive state* philosophy purports that government is and should be the ultimate provider, promoter, and guarantor of goods, services, and opportunities to its citizenry. The term *administrative state* refers to the idea that large-scale government bureaucracies, staffed by nonelected public managers, wield discretionary power on behalf of society in ways that challenge democratic accountability.
3. Contemporary political proponents of the minimalist philosophy include, but are not limited to, House Republicans and conservative Democrats backing the principles enunciated in the 1992 Republican Contract With America. Contemporary political proponents of the positivist philosophy (such as Vice President Gore) see activist but reinvented government as playing an important role in society.
4. Enterprise funding consists of administrative support units (such as printing offices, motor pools, and personnel offices) selling their services to departmental "customers." This system replaces traditional reliance on appropriations from legislatures.

REFERENCES

PUBLICATIONS CITED

Ackerman, B. A., and Stewart, R. B. "Reforming Environmental Law: The Democratic Case for Market Incentives." *Columbia Journal of Environmental Law,* 1988, *13,* 171–199.

Administrative Conference of the United States. *Sourcebook: Federal Agency Use of Alternative Means of Dispute Settlement.* Washington, D.C.: Office of the Chairman, Administrative Conference of the United States, 1987.

Administrative Conference of the United States. *Negotiated Rulemaking Sourcebook.* Washington, D.C.: Office of the Chairman, Administrative Conference of the United States, 1995.

Advisory Commission on Intergovernmental Relations. *Protecting the Environment: Politics, Pollution and Federal Policy.* Washington, D.C.: Advisory Commission on Intergovernmental Relations, 1981.

Allen, J. W., and others. *The Private Sector in State Service Delivery: Examples of Innovative Practices.* Washington, D.C.: Urban Institute Press, 1989.

Allenby, B. R., and Fullerton, A. "Design for the Environment: A New Strategy for Environmental Management." *Pollution Prevention Review,* 1991/1992, *2*(1), 51–61.

Almond, G. A., and Verba, S. *The Civic Culture: Political Attitudes and Democracy in Five Nations.* Princeton: Princeton University Press, 1963.

Amy, D. *The Politics of Environmental Mediation.* New York: Columbia University Press, 1987.

Anderton, D., Anderson, A., Oakes, J., and Fraser, M. "Environmental Equity: The Demographics of Dumping." *Demography,* 1994, *31,* 229.

Andrews, R. "Hazardous Waste Facility Siting: State Approaches." In C. Davis and J. Lester (eds.), *Dimensions of Hazardous Waste Politics and Policy.* New York: Greenwood Press, 1988.

Bacot, A. H., and Dawes, R. A. "State Expenditures and Policy Outcomes in Environmental Program Management." *Policy Studies Journal,* 1997, *25*(3), 355–370.

Bacow, L., and Wheeler, M. *Environmental Dispute Resolution.* New York: Plenum Press, 1984.

Balaton Group. "Indicators and Information Systems for Sustainable Development." Unpublished manuscript, 1996.

Ball, H. *Justice Downwind: America's Atomic Testing Program in the 1950's.* New York: Oxford University Press, 1986.

Baram, M. S., and Dillon, P. S. "Corporate Management of Chemical Accident Risks." In K. Fischer and J. Schot (eds.), *Environmental Strategies for Industry: International Perspectives on Research Needs and Policy Implications.* Washington, D.C.: Island Press, 1993.

Baram, M. S., Dillon, P. S., and Ruffle, B. *Managing Chemical Risks: Corporate Response to SARA Title III.* Boston: Tufts University Center for Environmental Management, 1990.

Bardach, E. *The Implementation Game: What Happens After a Bill Becomes a Law.* Cambridge, Mass.: MIT Press, 1977.

Bardach, E., and Kagan, R. A. *Going by the Book: The Problem of Regulatory Unreasonableness.* Philadelphia: Temple University Press, 1982.

Barzelay, M. *Breaking Through the Bureaucracy: A New Vision for Managing in Government.* Berkeley: University of California Press, 1992.

"Beauty for America." Proceedings of White House Conference on Natural Beauty, Washington, D.C., May 24–25, 1965.

Been, V. "Locally Undesirable Land Uses in Minority Neighborhoods: Disproportionate Siting or Market Dynamics?" *Yale Law Journal,* 1994, *103*(6), 1383–1407.

Been, V. "Analyzing Evidence of Environmental Justice." *Journal of Land Use and Environmental Law,* 1995, *11*(1), 1–36.

Bemelmans-Videc, M., Rist, R. C., and Vedung, E. (eds.). *Carrots, Sticks, and Sermons: Policy Instruments and Their Evaluation.* New Brunswick, N.J.: Transaction Books, 1998.

Berman, E. M. "The Challenge of Total Quality Management." In C. Ban and N. Riccucci (eds.), *Public Personnel Management: Current Concerns, Future Challenges.* (2nd ed.) White Plains, N.Y.: Longman, 1997.

Berman, E. M., and West, J. P. "Municipal Commitment to Total Quality Management: A Survey of Recent Progress." *Public Administration Review,* 1995, *55*(1), 57–66.

Bernard, J. R. "Environmental Indicators: An Integral Tool for the Future of Environmental Management." *State Environmental Monitor,* 1996, *1*(4), 26–28.

Berry, J. M., Portney, K. E., and Thomson, K. *The Rebirth of Urban Democracy.* Washington, D.C.: Brookings Institution, 1993.

Bhalla, S. K. *The Effective Management of Technology: A Challenge for Corporations.* Reading, Mass.: Addison-Wesley, 1987.

Bingham, G. *Resolving Environmental Disputes: A Decade of Experience.* Washington, D.C.: Conservation Foundation, 1986.

Bingham, G., and Mealey, T. "Overview: Negotiating Hazardous Waste Facility Siting and Permitting Agreements." In G. Bingham and T. Mealey (eds.), *Negotiating Hazardous Waste Facility Siting and Permitting Agreements.* Washington, D.C.: Conservation Foundation, 1988.

Bingenheimer, K. "Jury Rules California Liable for Cleanup." *Waste Tech News,* 1989, p. 1.

Blackburn, J. W. "Environmental Mediation as an Alternative to Litigation: The Emerging Practice and Limitations." In M. K. Mills (ed.), *Alternative Dispute Resolution in the Public Sector.* Chicago: Nelson-Hall, 1991.

Boerner, C., and Lambert, T. "Environmental Injustice." *The Public Interest,* 1995, *118,* 61–82.

Bosso, C. *Pesticides and Politics: The Lifecycle of a Public Issue.* Pittsburgh: University of Pittsburgh Press, 1987.

Bowen, E. "The Pressman-Wildavsky Paradox." *Journal of Public Policy,* 1982, *2,* 1–22.

Bowman, A. O'M., and Kearney, R. C. *The Resurgence of the States.* Englewood Cliffs, N.J.: Prentice-Hall, 1986.

Bowman, J. S. "At Last, an Alternative to Performance Appraisal." *Public Administration Review,* 1994, *54*(2), 129–136.

Boynton, S. P. "A Dozen Tips for Working with the Media." *PM,* Mar. 1989, 27–28.

Broder, D. S. "The Good, the Bad and the Budget." *Washington Post,* Feb. 8, 1998, p. C7.

Brown, D. A. "Thinking Globally and Acting Locally: The Emergence of Global Environmental Problems and the Critical Need to Develop Sustainable Development Programs at the State and Local Levels in the United States." *Dickinson Journal of Environmental Law and Policy,* 1996, *5,* 175–214.

Brown, D. M. "Results First: An Integrated Approach to Environmental Policy." In J. Greenberg and W. Kistler (eds.), *Buying America Back.* Tulsa, Okla.: Council Oak Books, 1992.

Brown, D. M. "Environmental Regulatory Enforcement: Are Public and Private Facilities Treated Differently?" Unpublished doctoral dissertation, Department of Political Science, American University, 1994.

Brown, P. "When the Public Knows Better: Popular Epidemiology Challenges the System." *Environment,* 1993, *35,* 16–20, 32–41.

"Brownfields Grants," *ENR,* 1995, *235*(8), 65.

Bullard, R. D. "Solid Waste Sites and the Black Houston Community." *Sociological Inquiry,* 1983, *53,* 273–288.

Bullard, R. D. *Dumping in Dixie: Race, Class, and Environmental Quality.* (2nd ed.) Boulder, Colo.: Westview Press, 1994.

Bullard, R. D. "Environmental Justice: It's More Than Waste Facility Siting." *Social Science Quarterly,* 1996, *77*(3), 493–499.

Burnett, M. L. "The Pollution Prevention Act of 1990: A Policy Whose Time Has Come, or Symbolic Legislation?" Paper presented at the Annual Meeting of the Western Social Science Association, Reno, Nevada, Apr. 17–20, 1996.

Burnham, J. "Of Science and Superstition: The Media and Biopolitics." In

C. L. LaMay and E. E. Dennis (eds.), *Media and the Environment.* Washington, D.C.: Island Press, 1991.

Burns, R.O. *Innovation: The Management Connection.* San Francisco: New Lexington Press, 1975.

Cairncross, F. *Costing the Earth: The Challenge for Governments, the Opportunities for Business.* Cambridge, Mass.: Harvard Business School Press, 1992.

Caldwell, L. K. "An Ecosystems Approach to Public Land Policy." In P. O. Foss (ed.), *Public Land Policy: Proceedings of the Western Resources Conference.* Boulder, Colo.: Colorado Associated University Press, 1970.

Carlin, A. *The United States Experience with Economic Incentives to Control Environmental Pollution.* Washington, D.C.: U.S. Environmental Protection Agency, 1992.

Carnevale, D. G. *Trustworthy Government: Leadership and Management Strategies for Building Trust and High Performance.* San Francisco: Jossey-Bass, 1995.

Carr, D., and Littman, I. *Excellence in Government: Total Quality Management in the 1990s.* New York: Coopers and Lybrand, 1990.

Carson, R. *Silent Spring.* New York: Fawcett, 1962.

Cattell, R. B. *The Scientific Analysis of Personality.* Hawthorne, N.Y.: Aldine, 1966.

Caudron, S. "Motivating Creative Employees Calls for New Strategies." *Personnel Journal,* 1994, 73(5), 103–106.

Cawley, R. M. "Collaborative Stewardship and the Bureau of Land Management." Paper presented at the Annual Meeting of the American Society for Public Administration, Seattle, Washington, May 9–13, 1998.

CEEM, Inc. "FAQS About ISO 14000." [http://www.ceem.com/faq.htm]. Mar. 13, 1998.

Center for Environmental Information and Statistics, [http://www.epa.gov/reinvent/notebook/ceis.htm]. Sept. 13, 1997.

Chandler, T. D., and Feuille, P. "Cities, Unions, and the Privatization of Sanitation Services." *Journal of Labor Research,* 1994, 15(1), 53–71.

Chase, A. *In a Dark Wood: The Fight over Forests and the Rising Tyranny of Ecology.* Boston: Houghton Mifflin, 1995.

Chase, G., and Reveal, E. C. *How to Manage in the Public Sector.* Reading, Mass.: Addison-Wesley, 1983.

Chess, C., Salomone, K. L., and Hance, B. J. "Improving Risk Communication in Government: Research Priorities." *Risk Analysis,* 1995, 15, 127–135.

Chess, C., Salomone, K. L., Hance, B. J., and Saville, A. "Results of a National Symposium on Risk Communication: Next Steps for Government Agencies." *Risk Analysis,* 1995, 15, 115–125.

City of Corvallis, Oregon. "The City: Special Report—United Chrome." *Federal Register,* 1988, 53, 28.

Clark, R. "E.P.A. Presses Sweeping Plan to Detail Factory Pollution." *New York Times,* Aug. 12, 1997, pp. A1, C20.

Clarke, J. N., and McCool, D. *Staking Out the Terrain: Power Differentials Among Natural Resource Management Agencies.* Albany: State University of New York Press, 1985.

Cohen, S., and Brand, R. "Total Quality Management in the U.S. Environmental Protection Agency." *Public Productivity and Management Review,* 1990, *14,* 99–133.

Cohen, S., and Brand, R. *Total Quality Management in Government: A Practical Guide for the Real World.* San Francisco: Jossey-Bass, 1993.

Cohen, S., and Eimicke, W. "Project-Focused Total Quality Management in the New York City Department of Parks and Recreation." *Public Administration Review,* 1994, *54*(5), 450–456.

Cohen, S., and Eimicke, W. *The New Effective Public Manager: Achieving Success in a Changing Government.* San Francisco: Jossey-Bass, 1995.

Cohen, S., and Eimicke, W. "Roundtable on TQM." National Conference of the American Society for Public Administration, Atlanta, Georgia, June 29–July 3, 1996.

Cohrssen, J. J., and Covello, V. T. *Risk Analysis: A Guide to Principles and Methods for Analyzing Health and Environmental Risks.* Washington, D.C.: Executive Office of the President, 1989.

Cole, L. A. *Element of Risk: The Politics of Radon.* Oxford University Press, 1994.

"Colorado, Utah Opt for Consolidated Environmental Grants." *State Environmental Monitor,* June 3, 1996, *1*(4), 12–13.

Commoner, B. "Pollution Prevention: Putting Comparative Risk Assessment in Its Place." In A. M. Finkel and D. Golding (eds.), *Worst Things First? The Debate over Risk-Based National Environmental Priorities.* Washington, D.C.: Resources for the Future, 1994.

Conlan, T. J. "And the Beat Goes On: Intergovernmental Mandates and Preemption in an Era of Deregulation." *Publius: The Journal of Federalism,* 1991, *21*(3), 43–57.

Conlan, T. J., Riggle, J. D., and Schwartz, D. E. "Deregulating Federalism? The Politics of Mandate Reform in the 104th Congress." *Publius: The Journal of Federalism,* 1995, *25*(3), 23–39.

Congressional Budget Office. *Federal Liabilities Under Hazardous Waste Laws.* Washington D.C.: Congressional Budget Office, 1990.

Conservation Foundation. *Protecting America's Wetlands: An Action Agenda (The Final Report of the National Wetlands Policy Forum).* Washington, D.C.: Conservation Foundation, 1988.

"Consolidated Environmental Data Reporting Would Reduce Burden for Industry, EPA Says." *BNA Environment Reporter,* 1995, *25,* 1998.

Cook, B. J. *Bureaucratic Politics and Regulatory Reform: The EPA and Emissions Trading.* Westport, Conn.: Greenwood Press, 1988.

Cook, D. S. "An Education in Managing Change Includes Analysis and Creativity." *Warfield's,* Aug. 5, 1996, p. 15.

Cormick, G. W., and Patton, L. K. "Environmental Mediation: Defining the Process Through Experience." In L. Lake (ed.), *Environmental Mediation: The Search for Consensus.* Boulder, Colo.: Westview Press, 1980.

Couger, J. D., and R. A. Zawacki. *Motivating and Managing Computer Personnel.* New York: Wiley, 1980.

Covello, V. T., McMallum, D. B., and Pavlova, M. *Effective Risk Communication: The Role and Responsibility of Government and Nongovernmental Organizations.* New York: Plenum Press, 1989.

Covello, V. T., Sandman, P. M., and Slovic, P. *Risk Communication, Risk Statistics, and Risk Comparisons: A Manual for Plant Managers.* Washington, D.C.: Chemical Manufacturers Association, 1988.

Covello, V. T., von Winterfeldt, D., and Slovic, P. "Communicating Scientific Information About Health and Environmental Risks: Problems and Opportunities from a Social and Behavioral Perspective." In J. C. Davies, V. T. Covello, and F. W. Allen (eds.), *Risk Communication.* Washington, D.C.: Conservation Foundation, 1987.

Crowfoot, J. E., and Wondolleck, J. M. *Environmental Disputes: Community Involvement in Conflict Resolution.* Washington, D.C.: Island Press, 1990.

Crozier, M., Huntington, S. P., and Watanuki, J. *The Crisis of Democracy: Report on the Governability of Democracies to the Trilateral Commission.* New York: New York University Press, 1975.

"Current Developments: GAF, New York County Agree to Site Cleanup." *BNA Environment Reporter,* 1987, *18,* 15.

D'Antonio, M. *Atomic Harvest: Hanford and the Lethal Toll of America's Nuclear Arsenal.* New York: Crown, 1993.

Davenport, T. H. "Why Reengineering Failed—and What Comes Next?" *Fast Company,* Premiere Issue, 1995, pp. 69–74.

David, I. T. "Privatization in America." In International City/County Management Association, *The Municipal Year Book, 1988.* Washington D.C.: International City/County Management Association, 1988.

Davies, T., and Mazurek, J. *Industry Incentives for Environmental Improvement: Evaluation of Federal Initiatives.* Washington, D.C.: Resources for the Future, 1996.

Davis, C. "Implementing the Resource Conservation and Recovery Act of 1976: Problems and Prospects." *Public Administration Quarterly,* 1985, 218–236.

Davis, C., and Feiock, R. "Testing Theories of State Hazardous Waste Regulation." *American Politics Quarterly,* 1992, *20,* 501–511.

Davis, C. E., and Lester, J. P. "Decentralizing Federal Environmental Policy." *Western Political Quarterly,* 1987, *40,* 555–565.

"Defense Attorney Warns Transport Group of Environmental Noncompliance Consequences." *BNA Environment Reporter,* 1994, *18,* 157.

DeHoog, R. H. *Contracting Out for Human Services: Economic, Political, and Organizational Perspectives.* Albany: State University of New York Press, 1984.

Deming, W. E. *Out of the Crisis.* MIT Center for Advanced Engineering Study. Cambridge, Mass.: MIT Press, 1986.

Denhardt, R. B. *The Pursuit of Significance: Strategies for Managerial Success in Public Organizations.* Belmont, Calif.: Wadsworth, 1993.

Dennis, E. E. "In Context: Environmentalism in the System of News." In C. L. LaMay and E. E. Dennis (eds.), *Media and the Environment.* Washington, D.C.: Island Press, 1991.

Dickens, C. *Bleak House.* London: Penguin, 1996. (Originally published 1853)

Dionne, E. J. Jr. *They Only Look Dead: Why Progressives Will Dominate the Next Political Era.* New York: Simon & Schuster, 1996.

DiNunzio, M. R. (ed.). *Theodore Roosevelt: An American Mind: A Selection of His Writings.* New York: St. Martin's Press, 1994.

Donahue, J. D. *The Privatization Decision: Public Ends, Private Means.* New York: Basic Books, 1989.

Doniger, D., and National Clean Air Coalition. "Clean Air Act Amendments of 1989." *Hearings Before the Senate Committee on Environment and Public Works,* 101st Cong., 1st sess., Sept. 21, 1989, pp. 28–30.

Doty, C. B., and Travis, C. C. "Is EPA's National Priorities List Correct?" *Environmental Science and Technology,* 1990, 24(12), 1778–1780.

Douglas, M. *Risk Acceptability According to the Social Sciences.* New York: Russell Sage Foundation, 1985.

Douglas, M., and Wildavsky, A. *Risk and Culture: An Essay on the Selection of Technological and Environmental Dangers.* Berkeley: University of California Press, 1982.

Downs, A. "Up and Down with Ecology: The 'Issue-Attention Cycle.'" *Public Interest,* 1972, *28,* 38–50.

Drucker, P. F. *Management: Tasks, Responsibilities, Practices.* New York: HarperCollins, 1974.

Dunlap, R. E. "Public Opinion and Environmental Policy." In J. P. Lester (ed.), *Environmental Politics and Policy: Theory and Evidence.* Durham, N.C.: Duke University Press, 1989.

Dunlap, R. E., and Van Liere, K. D. "The 'New Environmental Paradigm': A Proposed Measuring Instrument and Preliminary Results." *Journal of Environmental Education,* 1978, *9,* 10–19.

Durant, R. F. *When Government Regulates Itself: EPA, TVA, and Pollution Control in the 1970s.* Knoxville: University of Tennessee Press, 1985.

Durant, R. F. "Fire Alarms, Garbage Cans, and the Administrative Presidency." *Administration & Society,* 1991, *23,* 94–122.

Durant, R. F. "Beyond Markets, Hierarchies, or Clans: Lessons from Natural Resource Management in the Reagan Era." *Administration & Society,* 1992a, *24*(3), 346–374.

Durant, R. F. *The Administrative Presidency Revisited: Public Lands, the BLM, and the Reagan Revolution.* Albany: State University of New York Press, 1992b.

Durant, R. F. "Hazardous Waste, Regulatory Reform, and the Reagan Revolution: The Ironies of an Activist Approach to Deactivating Bureaucracy." *Public Administration Review,* 1993, *53,* 550–560.

Durant, R. F. "Public Policy, Overhead Democracy, and the Professional State Revisited." *Administration & Society,* 1995a, 27(2), 165–202.

Durant, R. F. "The Democratic Deficit in America." *Political Science Quarterly,* 1995b, *110*(1), 25–47.

Durant, R. F. "Agenda Setting, The 'Third Wave,' and the Administrative State.: *Administration & Society,* 1998a, 30(3), 211–247.

Durant, R. F. "Total Quality Management." In S. Condrey (ed.), *Handbook of Human Resource Management.* San Francisco: Jossey-Bass, 1998b.

Durant, R. F., Legge, J. S. Jr., and Moussios, A. "People, Profits, and Service Delivery: Lessons from the Privatization of British Telecom." *American Journal of Political Science,* 1998, 42(1), 117–140.

Durant, R. F., Thomas, L. W., Brown, R. G., and McClellen, E. F. "From Complacence to Compliance: Toward a Theory of Intragovernmental Regulation." *Administration & Society,* 1986, *17,* 433–459.

Durant, R. F., and Wilson-Gentry, L. "Public Management, TQM, and Quality Improvement: Toward a Contingency Strategy." *American Review of Public Administration,* 1993, 23(3), 215–245.

Dwivedi, O. P. "Man and Nature: An Holistic Approach to a Theory of Ecology." *The Environmental Professional,* 1988, *10,* 8–15.

Edwards, B., and Foley, M. W. (eds.). "Social Capital, Civil Society, and Contemporary Democracy." *American Behavioral Scientist,* 1997, 40(5).

Elmore, R. F. "Instruments and Strategy in Public Policy." *Policy Studies Review,* 1987, *7,* 174–186.

Environmental Law Institute. *Barriers to Environmental Technology Innovation and Use.* Washington, D.C.: Environmental Law Institute, Jan. 1998.

"EPA Cumulative Risk Guide Inaugurates More Holistic Assessments." *Risk Policy Report,* 1997, 4(8), 3–5.

"EPA Science Advisory Board Says Agency Science Effort Near 'Crisis.'" *Inside EPA Weekly Report,* 1994, *15*(24), 1, 13–14.

Eschenfelder, A. H. "Creating an Environment for Creativity." *Research Management,* 1968, *XI*(4), 231–241.

Etzioni, A. *A Comparative Analysis of Complex Organizations.* New York: Free Press, 1975.

Fallows, J. *Breaking the News: How the Media Undermine American Democracy.* New York: Pantheon Books, 1996.

Farid, F., El-Sharkawy, A. R., and Austin, L. K. "Managing for Creativity and Innovation in A/E/C Organizations." *Journal of Management in Engineering,* 1993, *9*(4), 399–409.

Feinberg, M. R. "Fourteen Suggestions for Managing Scientific Creativity." *Research Management,* 1968, *11*(2) 83–93.

Findley, R. E., and Farber, D. A. *Environmental Law in a Nutshell.* (4th ed.) St. Paul, Minn.: West, 1996.

Fiorino, D. J. "Regulatory Negotiation as a Policy Process." *Public Administration Review,* 1988, *48,* 764–772.

Fiorino, D. J. "Environmental Risk and Democratic Process: A Critical Review." *Columbia Journal of Environmental Law,* 1989, *14,* 501–547.

Fiorino, D. J. "Can Problems Shape Priorities? The Case of Risk-based Environmental Planning." *Public Administration Review,* 1990a, *50,* 82–90.

Fiorino, D. J. "Dimensions of Negotiated Rulemaking: Practical Constraints and Theoretical Limitations." In M. K. Mills (ed.), *Conflict Resolution and Public Policy.* Westport, Conn.: Greenwood Press, 1990b.

Fiorino, D. J. "Technical and Democratic Values in Risk Analysis." *Risk Analysis,* 1990c, *9,* 293–299.

Fiorino, D. J. *Making Environmental Policy.* Berkeley: University of California Press, 1995.

Fiorino, D. J. "Toward a New System of Environmental Regulation: The Case for an Industry Sector Approach." *Environmental Law,* 1996, *26,* 101–132.

Fischer, K., and Schot, J. *Environmental Strategies for Industry: International Perspectives on Research Needs and Policy Implications.* Washington, D.C.: Island Press, 1993.

Fischoff, B. "Risk: A Guide to Controversy." In National Academy of Sciences, *Improving Risk Communication.* Washington, D.C.: National Academy Press, 1989.

Fischhoff, B. "Risk Perception and Risk Communication Unplugged: Twenty Years of Process." *Risk Analysis,* 1995, *15,* 137–145.

Fischhoff, B., Slovic, P., and Lichtenstein, S. "Lay Fables and Expert Foibles in Judgments About Risk." *American Statistician,* 1982, *3B,* 240–255.

Fisher, R., Ury, W., and Patton, B. *Getting to Yes: Negotiating Agreement Without Giving In.* (2nd ed.) New York: Penguin, 1991.

Fitch, L. "Increasing the Role of the Private Sector in Providing Public Services." In W. D. Hawley and D. Rogers (eds.), *Improving the Quality of Urban Management.* Thousand Oaks, Calif.: Sage, 1974.

Fitzwater, M. *Call the Briefing! Reagan and Bush, Sam and Helen: A Decade with Presidents and the Press.* New York: Times Books, 1995.

"Five States Map the Road to 'Performance Partnerships.'" *State Environmental Monitor,* 1996, *1*(1), 19–21.

Flener, M. "Legal Considerations in Privatization and the Role of Legal

Counsel." In L. Finley (ed.), *Public Sector Privatization: Alternative Approaches to Service Delivery.* New York: Quorum Books, 1989.

Florini, K. L. "Issues of Federalism in Hazardous Waste Control: Cooperation or Confusion." *Harvard Environmental Law Review,* 1982, *6,* 306–337.

Folberg, J., and Taylor, A. *Mediation: A Comprehensive Guide to Resolving Conflicts Without Litigation.* San Francisco: Jossey-Bass, 1984.

Folz, D. H. "Recycling Program Design, Management, and Participation: A National Survey of Municipal Experience." *Public Administration Review,* 1991, *51*(3), 222–231.

Foster, D. "Fuzzy Fungus Out on Forest Survival Limb with Spotted Owl." *Los Angeles Times,* July 31, 1994, p. B3.

Fredericks, I., and McCallum, D. "International Standards for Environmental Management Systems: ISO 14000." [http://www.mgmt14k.com/ems.htm]. Aug. 1995.

Frederickson, H. G. *The Spirit of Public Administration.* San Francisco: Jossey-Bass, 1997.

Freemuth, J. "The Legitimacy Crisis in Federal Land." Paper presented at the Annual Meeting of the American Society for Public Administration, Seattle, Washington, May 9–13, 1998.

Friedman, S. M. "Two Decades of the Environmental Beat." In C. L. LaMay and E. E. Dennis (eds.), *Media and the Environment.* Washington, D.C.: Island Press, 1991.

Fromm, C. H. "Pollution Prevention in Process Design." *Pollution Prevention Review,* 1992, *2*(4), 389–401.

Funk, W. "When Smoke Gets in Your Eyes: Regulatory Negotiation and the Public Interest—EPA's Woodstove Standards." *Environmental Law,* 1987, *18,* 55–98.

Gabel, M. *Interests and Integration: Market Liberalization, Public Opinion, and European Union.* Ann Arbor: University of Michigan Press, 1998

Garnett, J. L. *Communicating for Results in Government: A Strategic Approach for Public Managers.* San Francisco: Jossey-Bass, 1992.

Gaus, J. *Reflections on Public Administration.* Birmingham: University of Alabama Press, 1947.

Gawthrop, L. C. "Civis, Civitas, and Civilitas: A New Focus." *Public Administration Review,* 1984, *44,* 101–107.

Gerbner, G., Gross, L., Morgan, M., and Signorelli, N. "Television's Contribution to Public Understanding of Science: A Plot Study." Philadelphia: Annenberg School of Communications, 1980.

Gibb, J. R. "Managing for Creativity in the Organization." In C. W. Taylor (ed.), *Climate for Creativity.* New York: Pergamon Press, 1972.

Gibson, N., and Whittaker, J. "Rules of Thumb." *Journal of Management in Engineering,* Nov./Dec. 1996, pp. 34–39.

Glasbergen, P. "Learning to Manage the Environment." In W. M. Lafferty and

J. Meadowcroft (eds.), *Democracy and the Environment: Problems and Prospects*. Cheltenham, U.K.: Edward Elgar, 1996.

Glickman, T. S., and Gough, M. (eds.). *Readings in Risk*. Washington, D.C.: Resources for the Future, 1990.

Goldman, B. A., and Fitton, L. *Toxic Wastes and Race Revisited: An Update of the 1987 Report on the Racial and Socioeconomic Characteristics of Communities with Hazardous Waste Sites*. Washington, D.C.: National Association for the Advancement of Colored People, 1994.

Goldsmith, S. "Can Business Really Do Business with Government?" *Harvard Business Review,* 1997, *75*(3), 110–121.

Goldstein, M. *America's Hollow Government: How Washington Has Failed the People*. Burr Ridge, Ill.: Irwin, 1992.

Golembiewski, R. T. "A Critique of 'Democratic Administration' and Its Supporting Ideation." *American Political Science Review,* 1977, *71*(4), 1488–1507.

Golembiewski, R. T. "Public Sector Organization: Why Theory and Practice Should Emphasize Purpose, and How to Do So?" In R. C. Chandler (ed.), *A Centennial History of the American Administrative State*. New York: Free Press, 1987.

Good, D., Kissel, J., Mullins, D., and O'Leary, R. "The Solid Waste Crisis." Washington, D.C.: International City/County Management Association, 1991.

Goodman, J. C. Address to the Third National Conference, Privatization Council, Washington, D.C., June 11, 1990.

Goodsell, C. T. "Reinvent Government or Rediscover It?" *Public Administration Review,* 1993, *53*(1), 85–87.

Goodwin, C. "Reassessing the Local Television News: The Role of Journalists." Paper presented at the Midwest Political Science Association, Chicago, Apr. 1997.

Gordon, G. "The Identification and Use of Creative Abilities in Scientific Organizations." In C. W. Taylor (ed.), *Climate for Creativity*. New York: Pergamon Press, 1972.

Gore, A. *Earth in the Balance: Ecology and the Human Spirit*. New York: Penguin, 1993.

Goss, T., Pascale, R., and Athos, A. "The Reinvention Roller Coaster: Risking the Present for a Powerful Future." *Harvard Business Review,* 1993, *71*(6), 97–108.

Gottlieb, R. *Forcing the Spring: The Transformation of the American Environmental Movement*. Washington, D.C.: Island Press, 1993.

Gould, S. J. *Hen's Teeth and Horse's Toes*. New York: Norton, 1983.

Gouldner, A. W. "Cosmopolitans and Locals: Toward an Analysis of Latent Social Roles." *Administrative Science Quarterly,* 1957, *2,* 281–306.

Government Institutes. *Environmental Law Handbook*. (14th ed.) Rockville, Md.: Government Institutes, 1997.

Graham, J. D., and Hartwell, J. K. *The Greening of Industry: A Risk Management Approach.* Cambridge, Mass.: Harvard University Press, 1997.

Greene, R. J. "Effective Compensation Strategies for Professional and Scientific Personnel." *Compensation and Benefits Management,* 1992, 8(4), 57–65.

Grogan, P. L. "Legislative Evaluations." In H. F. Lund (ed.), *The McGraw-Hill Recycling Handbook.* New York: McGraw-Hill, 1993.

Hadden, S. G. *Read the Label: Reducing Risk by Providing Information.* Boulder, Colo.: Westview Press, 1986.

Hadden, S. G. *A Citizen's Right to Know: Risk Communication and Public Policy.* Boulder, Colo.: Westview Press, 1989a.

Hadden, S. G. "Institutional Barriers to Risk Communication." *Risk Analysis,* 1989b, 9, 301–308.

Haigh, N., and Irwin, F. (eds.). *Integrated Pollution Control in Europe and North America.* Washington, D.C.: Conservation Foundation, 1990.

Hajer, M. A. *The Politics of Environmental Discourse.* Oxford: Clarendon Press, 1995.

Hakim, S., Seidenstat, P., and Bowman. G. W. (eds.). *Privatizing Transportation Systems.* Westport, Conn.: Praeger, 1996.

Hall, G., Rosenthal, J., and Wade, J. "How to Make Reengineering Really Work." *Harvard Business Review,* 1993, 71(6), 119–131.

Hamilton, M. S. "Regulatory Federalism: A Useful Concept for Natural Resources and Environmental Management?" In M. S. Hamilton (ed.), *Regulatory Federalism, Natural Resources, and Environmental Management.* Washington, D.C.: American Society for Public Administration, 1990.

Hamilton, M. S. "Environmental Mediation: Requirements for Successful Institutionalization." In M. K. Mills (ed.), *Alternative Dispute Resolution in the Public Sector.* Chicago: Nelson-Hall, 1991.

Hammer, M. *Beyond Reengineering: How the Process-Centered Organization Is Changing Our Work and Our Lives.* New York: HarperCollins, 1996.

Hammer, M., and Champy, J. *Reengineering the Corporation: A Manifesto for Business Revolution.* New York: HarperCollins, 1993.

Hammer, M., and Stanton, S. A. *The Reengineering Revolution: A Handbook.* New York: HarperCollins, 1995.

Hance, B. J., Chess, C., and Sandman, P. M. *Improving Dialogue with Communities: A Risk Communication Manual for Government.* Trenton, N.J.: Department of Environmental Protection, 1988.

Hanford, P., and Sokolow, A. "Mandates as Both Hardship and Benefit: The Clean Water Program in Small Communities." *Publius: The Journal of Federalism,* 1987, 17(4), 131–146.

Hansen, A. "The Media and the Social Construction of the Environment." *Media, Culture and Society,* 1991, 13, 443–458.

Hansen, F. "Redesigning EPA's Management and Accountability System." [http://www.epa.gov/reinvent/notebook/hansen.htm]. Jan. 29, 1997.

Harney, D. F. Service Contracting: A Local Government Guide. Washington, D.C.: International City/County Management Association, 1992.

Harr, J. A Civil Action. New York: Vintage Books, 1996.

Harter, P. J. "Negotiating Regulations: A Cure for the Malaise?" Georgetown Law Review, 1982, 71, 1–118.

Hartig, J. H., and Hartig, P. D. "Remedial Action Plans: An Opportunity to Implement Sustainable Development at the Grassroots Level in the Great Lakes Basin." Alternatives, 1992, 17(3), 26–31.

Harwood, P., and Williams, D. "Collaborative Planning in BLM: A Different View of Communities and the BLM." Natural Resources & Environmental Administration, 1998, 19(2), 5–7.

Harwood, R. "The Growing Irrelevance of Journalists." Washington Post, Oct. 23, 1992, p. 21.

Hatry, H. P., Brounstein, P. J., and Levinson, R. B. "Comparisons of Privately and Publicly Operated Corrections Facilities in Kentucky and Massachusetts." In G. W. Bowman, S. Hakim, and P. Seidenstat (eds.), Privatizing Correctional Institutions. New Brunswick, N.J.: Transaction, 1993.

Hays, S. P. (in collaboration with B. D. Hays). Beauty, Health, and Permanence: Environmental Politics in the United States, 1955–1985. New York: Cambridge University Press, 1987.

Hays, S. P. "Environmental Political Culture and Environmental Political Development: An Analysis of Legislative Voting, 1971–1989." Environmental History Review, 1992, 16(2), 1–22.

Hayward, S. F. Churchill on Leadership: Executive Success in the Face of Adversity. Rocklin, Calif.: Forum/Prima, 1997.

Hedge, D. M., and Scicchitano, M. J. "Devolving Regulatory Authority: The Federal and State Response." Policy Studies Review, 1992, 11, 81–90.

Henry, J. G., and Heinke, G. W. Environmental Science and Engineering. (2nd ed.) Englewood Cliffs, N.J.: Prentice Hall, 1996.

Hersch, R. A Review of Integrated Pollution Control Efforts in Selected Countries. Washington, D.C.: Resources for the Future, 1996.

Herzlinger, R. E. "Effective Oversight: A Guide for Nonprofit Directors." Harvard Business Review, 1994, 72(4), 52–60.

Hess, S. "The Decline and Fall of Congressional News." In T. E. Mann and N. J. Ornstein (eds.), Congress, the Press, and the Public. Washington, D.C.: American Enterprise Institute and Brookings Institution, 1994.

Hickox, K. "Swords into Bankshares: How the Defense Industry Cleans Up on the Nuclear Build-Down." Washington Monthly, Mar. 1992, pp. 31–34.

Higgins, R. R. "Race and Environmental Equity: An Overview of the Environmental Justice Issue in the Policy Process." Polity, 1993, 26(2), 281–300.

Hird, J. A. *Superfund: The Political Economy of Environmental Risk.*
Baltimore: Johns Hopkins University Press, 1994.

Hjern, B., and Porter, D. O. "Implementation Structures: A New Unit of
Administrative Analysis." *Organization Studies,* 1981, 2(3), 211–227.

Hockenstein, J. B., Stavins, R. N., and Whitehead, B. W., "Crafting the Next
Generation of Market-Based Environmental Tools." *Environment,* 1997,
39, 12–20; 30–33.

Hodges, D., and Durant, R. F. "The Professional State Revisited: Twixt Scylla
and Charybdis?" *Public Administration Review,* 1989, 49, 474–485.

Inglehart, R. *The Silent Revolution: Changing Values and Political Styles
Among Western Publics.* Princeton, N.J.: Princeton University Press,
1977.

Ingram, H. M., and Mann, D. E. "Interest Groups and Environmental Policy."
In J. P. Lester (ed.), *Environmental Politics and Policy.* Durham, N.C.:
Duke University Press, 1989.

Inspector General. "After Twelve Years, EPA's Information Resources
Management Problems Continue." Washington, D.C.: Office of the
Inspector General, U.S. Environmental Protection Agency, Sept. 28,
1992.

Interagency Ecosystem Management Task Force. *The Ecosystem Approach:
Healthy Ecosystems and Sustainable Economies. Volume I: Overview.*
[Location:] Interagency Ecosystem Management Task Force, 1995.

International City/County Management Association. *Trends and Issues in the
Use of Intergovernmental Agreements and Privatization in Local
Government: Baseline Data Report 21.* Washington, D.C.: International
City/County Management Association, 1989.

International City/County Management Association. *Municipal Yearbook.*
Washington, D.C.: International City/County Management Association,
1993.

International Institute for Sustainable Development. "Measurements and
Indicators for Sustainable Development."
[iisd1.iisd.ca/measure/default.htm]. 1997.

International Joint Commission Great Lakes Water Quality Board. *Report on
Great Lakes Water Quality.* Windsor, Ontario: International Joint
Commission Great Lakes Water Quality Board, 1985.

International Standardization Organization. "Advisory Group Recommends
Actions for Greater Compatibility, but No Merging of ISO 9000 and
ISO 14000." [http://www.iso.ch/presse/presse19.htm]. Mar. 13, 1998.

International Symposium on Man's Role in Changing the Face of the Earth.
Man's Role in Changing the Face of the Earth. Chicago: University of
Chicago Press, 1956.

Irwin, F. W. *Charting a Sustainable Course for the Industrial Sector:
Initiatives in the European Union.* Washington, D.C.: World Wildlife
Fund, 1997.

Jackson, D. "Who Speaks for the Land?" In C. L. LaMay and E. E. Dennis (eds.), *Media and the Environment*. Washington, D.C.: Island Press, 1991.

Jamieson, K. H. *Dirty Politics: Deception, Distraction, and Democracy.* New York: Oxford University Press, 1992.

John, D. *Civic Environmentalism: Alternatives to Regulation in States and Communities.* Washington, D.C.: Congressional Quarterly Press, 1994.

Johnson, A. "Working with the Media: A Reporter's View." *PM,* May 1987, 29–30.

Johnson, B. B., and Covello, V. T. (eds.). *The Social and Cultural Construction of Risk: Essays of Risk Selection and Perception.* Dordrecht, Holland: D. Reidel, 1987.

Johnson, M. E. "The EPA in Transition: Reform and Reinvention at the Environmental Protection Agency." *Natural Resources & Environmental Administration,* 1998, *19*(2), 8–9, 12.

Johnston, V. R. "Optimizing Productivity Through Privatization and Entrepreneurial Management." *Policy Studies Journal,* 1996, *24*(3), 444–463.

Jones, O. "Human Resources, Scientists, and Internal Reputation: The Role of Climate and Job Satisfaction." *Human Relations,* 1996, *49*(3), 269.

Juanillo, N. K., and Scherer, C. W. "Attaining a State of Informed Judgments: Toward a Dialectical Discourse on Risk." In B. Burleson (ed.), *Communication Yearbook,* no 18. Thousand Oaks, Calif.: Sage, 1995.

Juran, J. *Juran on Planning for Quality.* New York: Free Press, 1988.

Kagan, R. A. "Adversarial Legalism and American Government." In M. K. Landy and M. A. Levin (eds.), *The New Politics of Public Policy.* Baltimore: Johns Hopkins University Press, 1995.

Kanter, R. M. *The Change Masters: Innovation and Entrepreneurship in the American Corporation.* New York: Simon & Schuster, 1983.

Kanter, R. M. *Rosabeth Moss Kanter on the Frontiers of Management.* Boston: Harvard Business School Press, 1997.

Kaplan, R. S., and Norton, D. P. "Using the Balanced Scorecard as a Strategic Management System." *Harvard Business Review,* 1996, *74*(1), 75–85.

Karliner, J. *The Corporate Planet: Ecology and Politics in the Age of Globalization.* San Francisco: Sierra Club Books, 1997.

Kasperson, R. E. "Six Propositions on Public Participation and Their Relevance for Risk Communication." *Risk Analysis,* 1986, *6,* 275–281.

Kearney, R. C., and Sinha, C. "Professionalism and Bureaucratic Responsiveness: Conflict or Compatibility?" *Public Administration Review,* 1988, *48*(1), 571–579.

Keiter, R., and Boyce, M. (eds.). *The Greater Yellowstone Ecosystem: Redefining America's Wilderness Heritage.* New Haven, Conn.: Yale University Press, 1991.

Kelman, S. *Procurement and Public Management: The Fear of Discretion and the Quality of Government Performance.* Washington, D.C.: American Enterprise Institute Press, 1990.

Kempton, W., Boster, J. S., and Hartley, J. A. *Environmental Values in American Culture.* Cambridge, Mass.: MIT Press, 1995.

Kenworthy, T. "Conservationists Challenge Ranchers' Hold on State Lands." [http://www.washingtonpost.com/wp-srv/WPlate/1997–09/09/1181–090997–idx.html]. Sept. 9, 1997.

Kerwin, C. M. *Rulemaking: How Government Agencies Write Law and Make Policy.* Washington, D.C.: Congressional Quarterly Press, 1994.

Kettl, D. F. *Government by Proxy: (Mis?)Managing Federal Programs.* Washington, D.C.: Congressional Quarterly Press, 1988.

Kettl, D. F. *Sharing Power: Public Governance and Private Markets.* Washington, D.C.: Brookings Institution, 1993.

Kettl, D. F. "Reinventing Government: Past, Present, But Is There a Future." Lecture and Discussion, University of Baltimore, May 5, 1997.

Kettl, D. F., and DiIulio, J. J. (eds.). *Cutting Government: A Report of the Brookings Institution's Center for Public Management.* Washington, D.C.: Brookings Institution, 1995.

Kiersey, D., and Bates, M. Personality Indicator Web Page. [http://keirsey.com/personality/ntij.html]. Del Mar, Calif.: Prometheus, 1996.

Kingdon, J. W. *Agendas, Alternatives, and Public Policies.* (2nd ed.) New York: HarperCollins, 1995.

Kneese, A. V., and Schultze, C. L. *Pollution, Prices, and Public Policy.* A study sponsored jointly by Resources for the Future and the Brookings Institution. Washington, D.C.: Brookings Institution, 1975.

Knott, J. H., and Miller, G. J. *Reforming Bureaucracy: The Politics of Institutional Choice.* Englewood Cliffs, N.J.: Prentice Hall, 1987.

Koehler, J. W., and Pankowski, J. M. *Quality Government: Designing, Developing, and Implementing TQM.* Delray Beach, Fla.: St. Lucie Press, 1996.

Koning, J. W. *The Manager Looks at Research Scientists.* Madison, Wis.: Science Tech, 1988.

Koning, J. W. "Three Other R's: Recognition, Reward, and Resentment." *Research Technology Management,* 1993, 36(4), 19–29.

Korten, D. C. *When Corporations Rule the World.* West Hartford, Conn., and San Francisco: Kumarian Press and Berrett-Koehler, 1996.

Kraft, M., and Clary, B. "Citizen Participation and the NIMBY Syndrome: Public Response to Radioactive Waste Disposal." *Western Political Science Quarterly,* 1991, 44, 299–328.

Krimsky, S., and Plough, A. *Environmental Hazards: Communicating Risks as a Social Process.* Dover, Mass.: Auburn House, 1988.

Kriz, M. "A New Ball Game?" *National Journal,* Jan. 2, 1993, p. 391.

Kunda, G. *Engineering Culture: Control and Commitment in a High-Tech Corporation.* Philadelphia: Temple University Press, 1992.

Kupchella, C. E., and Hyland, M. C. *Environmental Science: Living within the System of Nature.* (3rd ed.) Englewood Cliffs, N.J.: Prentice Hall, 1993.

Kurtz, H. *Media Circus: The Trouble with America's Newspapers.* New York: Times Books, 1994.

Kurtz, H. *Spin Cycle: Inside the Clinton Propaganda Machine.* New York: Free Press, 1998.

LaMay, C. L., and Dennis, E. E. (eds.). *Media and the Environment.* Washington, D.C.: Island Press, 1991.

Landy, M. K. "The New Politics of Environmental Policy." In M. K. Landy and M. A. Levin, (eds.), *The New Politics of Public Policy.* Baltimore: Johns Hopkins University Press, 1995.

Landy, M. K., Roberts, M. J., and Thomas, S. R. *The Environmental Protection Agency: Asking the Wrong Questions: From Nixon to Clinton.* (Expanded ed.) New York: Oxford University Press, 1994..

Larkin, J. "Spreading the Word: Improving Government/Media Relations Means a Better Image for Public Service." *Public Administration Times,* 1992, *15,* 3.

Lasswell, H. D. *Politics: Who Gets What, When, How.* New York: Meridian Books, 1958.

Lave, L. B. (ed.). *Quantitative Risk Assessment in Regulation.* Washington, D.C.: Brookings Institution, 1982.

Lawler, E. E. III, Mohrman, S. A., and Ledford, G. E. *Employee Involvement and Total Quality Management: Practices and Results in Fortune 1000 Companies.* San Francisco: Jossey-Bass, 1992.

Layman, P. "Dutch Plan Sets Environmental Targets for Chemical Industry." *Chemical and Engineering News,* Nov. 1, 1994, pp. 11–13.

Lazarus, R. "The Meaning and Promotion of Environmental Justice." *Maryland Journal of Contemporary Legal Issues,* 1993/1994, *5*(1), 1–12.

Lazarus, R. "Understanding and Pursuing Environmental Justice." ALI-ABA Course of Study, Feb. 15, 1995, pp. 531–557.

Lee, G. "Agency Takes a Hit from One of Its Own." *Washington Post,* June 27, 1996, p. A27.

Lee, K. N. *Compass and Gyroscope: Integrating Science and Politics for the Environment.* Washington, D.C.: Island Press, 1993.

Lee, K. N., and others. "Little Bumps and Guard Rails: Searching for Indicators of Sustainability." Unpublished manuscript, 1996.

Lester, J. P., Franke, J. L., Bowman, A. O'M., and Kramer, K. W. "A Comparative Perspective on State Hazardous Waste Regulation." In J. P. Lester and A. O'M. Bowman (eds.), *The Politics of Hazardous Waste Management.* Durham, N.C.: Duke University Press, 1983.

Levin, M. A., and Ferman, B. *The Political Hand: Policy Implementation and Youth Employment Programs.* New York: Pergamon Press, 1985.

Lichter, S. R., Lichter, L. S., and Rothman, S. *Prime Time: How TV Portrays American Culture.* Washington, D.C.: Regnery, 1994.

Light, P. C. *Thickening Government: Federal Hierarchy and the Diffusion of Accountability.* Washington, D.C.: Brookings Institution, 1995.

Light, P. C. *Tides of Reform: Making Government Work, 1945–1995.* New Haven: Yale University Press, 1997.

Liker, J. K., and Hancock, W. M. "Organizational Systems Barriers to Engineering Effectiveness." *Institute of Electrical and Electronics Engineers Transactions on Engineering Management,* 1986, *33*(2), 82–91.

Linsky, M. *Impact: How the Press Affects Federal Policymaking.* New York: Norton, 1986.

Lipset, S., and Schneider, W. *The Confidence Gap: Business, Labor, and Government in the Public Mind.* New York: Free Press, 1983.

Lipset, S., and Schneider, W. "The Confidence Gap During the Reagan Years, 1981–1987." *Political Science Quarterly,* 1987, *102,* 1–X.

Long, J. S., and Fox, M. F. "Scientific Careers: Universalism and Particularism." *Annual Review of Sociology,* 1995, *21,* 45–72.

Loveless, S., and Bozeman, B. "Innovation and the Public Manager." In W. B. Eddy (ed.), *Handbook of Organization Management.* New York: Dekker, 1983.

Lowry, W. R. *The Dimensions of Federalism: State Governments and Pollution Control Policies.* Durham, N.C.: Duke University Press, 1992.

Luke, J. S. *Catalytic Leadership: Strategies for an Interconnected World.* San Francisco: Jossey-Bass, 1998.

Luton, L. S. *The Politics of Garbage: A Community Perspective on Solid Waste Policy Making.* Pittsburgh: University of Pittsburgh Press, 1997.

Lynn, L. E. Jr. *Public Management as Art, Science, and Profession.* Chatham, N.J.: Chatham House, 1996.

Maas, J. "Region 9 Brownfields Partnership Action Agenda." [http://www.epa.gov/region09/waste/brown/brown.html#national]. July 1997.

MacKenzie, S. H. *Integrated Resource Planning and Management: The Ecosystem Approach in the Great Lakes Basin.* Washington, D.C.: Island Press, 1996.

MacKinnon, D. W. "The Study of Creative Persons." In J. Kagan (ed.), *Creativity and Learning.* Boston: Houghton Mifflin, 1967.

MacManus, S. A. *Doing Business with Government.* New York: Paragon House, 1992.

Maehr, M. L., and Braskamp, L. A. *The Motivation Factor: A Theory of Personal Investment.* San Francisco: New Lexington Press, 1986.

Manchester, L. "Alternative Service Delivery Approaches and City Service Planning." In L. K. Finley (ed.), *Public Sector Privatization: Alternative Approaches to Service Delivery.* New York: Quorum Books, 1989.

Maney, A. L., and Hadwiger, D. F. "Taking 'Cides: The Controversy Over Agricultural Chemicals." In T. H. Peterson (ed.), *Farmers, Bureaucrats, and Middlemen.* Washington, D.C.: Howard University Press, 1980.

Mani, B. G. "Old Wine in New Bottles Tastes Better: A Case Study of TQM Implementation in the IRS." *Public Administration Review,* 1995, *55*(2), 147–158.

Mansbridge, J. M. "Politics as Persuasion." In L. C. Dodd and C. Jillson (eds.), *The Dynamics of American Politics: Approaches and Interpretations.* Boulder, Colo.: Westview Press, 1994.

Marsh, G. P. *Man and Nature.* Cambridge, Mass.: Harvard University Press, 1965. (Originally published 1865.)

Martin, D. D., and Shell, R. L. *Management of Professionals: Insights for Maximizing Cooperation.* New York: Dekker, 1988.

Maser, C. *Resolving Environmental Conflict: Towards Sustainable Community Development.* Delray Beach, Fla.: St. Lucie Press, 1996.

Mazmanian, D., and Morell, D. *Beyond Superfailure: America's Toxics Policy for the 1990s.* Boulder, Colo.: Westview Press, 1992.

McCabe, A. S., and Fitzgerald, M. R. "Media Images of Environmental Biotechnology: What Does the Public See?" In G. S. Sayler, R. Fox, and J. W. Blackburn (eds.), *Environmental Biotechnology for Waste Treatment.* New York: Plenum Press, 1991.

McFarland, T. D. "Managing Performance of Engineers." *Journal of Management in Engineering,* 1994, *10*(5), 28–33.

McLuhan, M. *The Medium Is the Message.* New York: Bantam, 1970.

Meidinger, E. "The Development of Emissions Trading in U.S. Air Pollution Regulation." In K. Hawkins and J. M. Thomas (eds.), *Making Regulatory Policy.* Pittsburgh: University of Pittsburgh Press, 1989.

Melnick, R. S. *Regulation and the Courts: The Case of the Clean Air Act.* Washington, D.C.: Brookings Institution, 1983.

Melnick, R. S. "The Courts, Congress, and Programmatic Rights." In R. Harris and S. Milkis (eds.), Remaking American Politics. Boulder, Colo.: Westview Press, 1989.

Melnick, R. S. "Administrative Law and Bureaucratic Reality." *Administrative Law Review,* 1992, 44(2), 245–259.

Melnick, R. S. "Separation of Powers and the Strategy of Rights: The Expansion of Special Education." In M. K. Landy and M. A. Levin (eds.), *The New Politics of Public Policy.* Baltimore: Johns Hopkins University Press, 1995.

Meyers, P. A., and Wilemon, D. "Learning in Dominant Technological Firms."

In D. F. Kocaoglu (ed.), *Management of R&D and Engineering.* Amsterdam: North-Holland, 1992.

"Michigan Abandons High-Priority EPA Regulatory Reinvention Project." *Inside EPA Weekly Report,* 1996, *16*(26), 1, 11.

Milakovich, M. E. *Improving Service Quality.* Delray Beach, Fla.: St. Lucie Press, 1995.

Milbrath, L. W. *Environmentalists: Vanguard for a New Society.* Albany: State University of New York Press, 1984.

Mills, M. K. *Alternative Dispute Resolution in the Public Sector.* Chicago: Nelson-Hall, 1991.

Milward, H. B. "Implications of Contracting Out: New Roles for the Hollow State." In P. W. Ingraham, B. S. Romsek, and Associates, *New Paradigms for Government: Issues for the Changing Public Service.* San Francisco: Jossey-Bass, 1994.

Milward, H. B., and Provan, K. G. "The Hollow State: Private Provision of Public Services." In H. M. Ingram and S. R. Smith (eds.), *Public Policy for Democracy.* Washington, D.C.: Brookings Institution, 1993.

Milward, H. B., Provan, K. G., and Else, B. A. "What Does the 'Hollow State' Look Like?" In Barry Bozeman (ed.), *Public Management: The State of the Art.* San Francisco: Jossey-Bass, 1993.

Mintz, J. "Scandal Management of Campaign Finance Investigations." *Washington Post,* July 2, 1997, p. A4.

Mintzberg, H. "Managing Government, Governing Management." *Harvard Business Review,* 1996, *74*(3), 75–83.

Mitnick, B. M. *The Political Economy of Regulation: Creating, Designing, and Removing Regulatory Forms.* New York: Columbia University Press, 1980.

Moe, R. C. "The Reinventing Government Exercise: Misinterpreting the Problem, Misjudging the Consequences." *Public Administration Review,* 1994, *54*(2), 111–122.

Moe, T. M. "The Politics of Bureaucratic Structure." In J. E. Chubb and P. E. Peterson (eds.), *Can the Government Govern?* Washington, D.C.: Brookings Institution, 1989.

Mohai, P. "The Demographics of Dumping Revisited: Examining the Impact of Alternate Methodologies in Environmental Justice Research." *Virginia Environmental Law Journal,* 1995, *14*(4), 615–653.

Mohai, P. "Environmental Justice or Analytic Justice? Reexamining Historical Hazardous Waste Landfill Siting Patterns in Metropolitan Texas." *Social Science Quarterly,* 1996, *77*(3), 500–507.

Mohai, P., and Twight, B. W. "Age and Environmentalism: An Elaboration of the Buttel Model Using National Survey Evidence." *Social Science Quarterly,* 1987, *68*(4), 798–815.

Moore, M. H. *Creating Public Value: Strategic Management in Government.* Cambridge, Mass.: Harvard University Press, 1995.

Morell, D., and Magorian, C. *Siting Hazardous Waste Facilities: Local Opposition and the Myth of Preemption.* Cambridge, Mass.: Ballinger, 1982.

Morenberg, P. W. "Environmental Fraud by Government Contractors: A New Application of the False Claims Act." *Boston College Environmental Affairs Law Review,* 1995, 22(3), 623–669.

Morgan, D. R., and Hirlinger, M. W. "Intergovernmental Service Contracts." *Urban Affairs Quarterly,* 1991, 26(2), 128–144.

Mosher, F. E. *Democracy and the Public Service.* New York: Oxford University Press, 1968.

Mosher, F. E. *Democracy and the Public Service.* (2nd ed.) New York: Oxford University Press, 1982.

Motavalli, J. "The Virtual Environment." *E: The Environmental Magazine,* 1996, 7(3), 34–35.

Moyers, B. *A World of Ideas II: Public Opinions from Private Citizens.* New York: Doubleday, 1990.

Nash, R. F. *The Rights of Nature: A History of Environmental Ethics.* Madison: University of Wisconsin Press, 1989.

National Academy of Public Administration. *Setting Priorities, Getting Results: A New Direction for the Environmental Protection Agency.* Washington, D.C.: National Academy of Public Administration, 1995.

National Academy of Sciences. *Improving Risk Communication.* Washington, D.C.: National Academy Press, 1989.

National Research Council. *Risk Assessment in the Federal Government: Managing the Process.* Washington, D.C.: National Academy Press, 1983.

"Navy Air Station Hit with Fine Under New Federal Law Provisions." *BNA Environment Reporter,* 1993, 24, 190.

Nelkin, D. *Technological Decisions and Democracy: European Experiments in Public Participation.* Thousand Oaks, Calif.: Sage, 1977.

New Jersey Department of Environmental Protection. *Industrial Pollution Prevention Planning: Meeting Requirements Under the New Jersey Pollution Prevention Planning.* Trenton: Office of Pollution Prevention, August 1995.

New Jersey Department of Environmental Protection. *New Jersey Department of Environmental Protection Report to the Legislature: Overview of the Impact of the 1991 Pollution Prevention Act* (draft). Trenton: Office of Pollution Prevention, June 1996.

Niskanen, W. A. Jr. *Bureaucracy and Representative Government.* Chicago: Aldine-Atherton, 1971.

Novick, S. M. "The Twenty-Year Evolution of Pollution Law: A Look Back." *The Environmental Forum,* Jan. 1986, pp. 12–18.

Odum, E. *Fundamentals of Ecology.* (3rd ed.) Philadelphia: Saunders, 1971.

O'Leary, R. "The Impact of Federal Court Decisions on the Policies and

Administration of the U.S Environmental Protection Agency." *Administrative Law Review,* 1989, *41*(4), 549–574.

O'Leary, R. "The Courts and the EPA: The Amazing Flannery Decision." *Natural Resources and Environment,* 1990a, *5*(1), 18–22, 54–55.

O'Leary, R. "Will Hazardous Waste Cleanup Costs Cripple Our State and Local Governments?" *State and Local Government Review,* 1990b, *22,* 84–89.

O'Leary, R. *Environmental Change: Federal Courts and the EPA.* Philadelphia: Temple University Press, 1993a.

O'Leary, R. "Five Trends in Government Liability Under Environmental Laws: Implications for Public Administration." *Public Administration Review,* 1993b, *53*(6), 542–554.

O'Leary, R. "The Progressive Ratcheting of Environmental Laws: Impact on Public Management." *Policy Studies Review,* 1993c, *12*(3/4), 118–136.

O'Leary, R. "The Bureaucratic Politics Paradox: The Case of Wetlands Legislation in Nevada." *Journal of Public Administration Research and Theory,* 1994a, *4*(4), 443–467.

O'Leary, R. "What Every Administrator Should Know About Environmental Law." In D. Rosenbloom and R. Schwartz (eds.), *Handbook of Administrative Law and Regulation.* New York: Dekker, 1994b.

O'Leary, R. "Environmental Mediation: What Do We Know and How Do We Know It?" In J. W. Blackburn and W. M. Bruce (eds.), *Mediating Environmental Conflicts—Theory and Practice.* New York: Quorum Books, 1995.

O'Leary, R. "Managing Contracts and Grants." In J. Perry (ed.), *Handbook of Public Administration.* San Francisco: Jossey-Bass, 1996.

Olsen, M. E., Lodwick, D. G., and Dunlap, R. E. *Viewing the World Ecologically.* Boulder, Colo.: Westview Press, 1992.

Opschoor, J. B., and Vos, H. P. *Economic Instruments for Environmental Protection.* Paris: Organization for Economic Co-operation and Development, 1989.

Osborne, D., and Plastrik, P. *Banishing Bureaucracy: The Five Strategies for Reinventing Government.* Reading, Mass.: Addison-Wesley, 1997.

Orts, E. W. "Reflexive Environmental Law." *Northwestern University Law Review,* 1995, *89,* 1227–1240.

O'Toole, L. J. Jr. "Implementing Public Innovations in Network Settings." *Administration & Society,* 1997, *29,* 115–138.

O'Toole, L. J., and others. "Reducing Toxic Chemical Releases and Transfers: Explaining Outcomes for a Voluntary Program." *Policy Studies Journal,* 1997, *25*(1), 11–26.

O'Toole, R. *Reforming the Forest Service.* Washington, D.C.: Island Press, 1988.

Otway, H. "Experts, Risk Communication, and Democracy." *Risk Analysis,* 1987, *7,* 125–129.

Ozawa, C. P. *Recasting Science: Consensual Procedures in Public Policymaking.* Boulder, Colo.: Westview Press, 1991.

Paehlke, R. "Government Regulating Itself: A Canadian-American Comparison." *Administration & Society,* 1991, 22(4), 424–450.

Page, B. I. *Who Deliberates? Mass Media in Modern Democracy.* Chicago: University of Chicago Press, 1996.

Patterson, T. E. *Out of Order.* New York: Knopf, 1994.

Pearce, D. D. *Wary Partners: Diplomats and the Media.* Washington, D.C.: Congressional Quarterly, 1995.

Perritt, H. H. Jr. "Negotiated Rulemaking in Practice." *Journal of Policy Analysis and Management,* 1986, 5, 482–495.

Peters, B. G. *The Future of Governing: Four Emerging Models.* Lawrence: University of Kansas Press, 1996.

Peters, K. M. "Civilians at War." *Government Executive,* 1996, 28(7), 23–27.

Pettingell, K. "If I'm so Good at My Job, Why Do I Hate It?" *Journal of Systems Management,* 1995, 46(1) 16–21.

Piven, F. F., and Cloward, R. A. *The Breaking of the American Social Compact.* New York: New Press, 1997.

Plough, A., and Krimsky, S. "The Emergence of Risk Communication Studies: Social and Political Context." In T. S. Glickman and M. Gough (eds.), *Readings in Risk.* Washington, D.C.: Resources for the Future, 1990.

Poister, T. H., and Harris, R. H. "The Impact of TQM on Highway Maintenance: Benefit/Cost Implications." *Public Administration Review,* 1997, 57(4), 294–302.

Porter, M. E., and van der Linde, C. "Green *and* Competitive: Ending the Stalemate." *Harvard Business Review,* 1995, 73(5), 120–134.

Portney, P. R. *Public Policies for Environmental Protection.* Washington, D.C.: Resources for the Future, 1990.

Posner, P. "The Politics of Federal Mandates: Congress on the Frontiers of Federalism." Unpublished doctoral dissertation, Columbia University, 1996.

Postman, N., and Powers, S. *How to Watch TV News.* New York: Penguin Books, 1992.

Prager, J. "Contracting Out Government Services: Lessons from the Private Sector." *Public Administration Review,* 1994, 54(2), 176–184.

Prechel, H. "Economic Crisis and the Centralization of Control Over the Managerial Process: Corporate Restructuring and Neo-Fordist Decision-Making." *American Sociological Review,* 1994, 59, 723–745.

Prendergrass, J., Locke, P., and McElfish, J. "The Environment and the Contract." *Environmental Law Review,* 1995, 25, 10350–10366.

Prentky, R. "Creativity and Psychopathology." In J. A. Glover, R. R. Ronning, and C. R. Reynolds (eds.), *Handbook of Creativity.* New York: Plenum Press, 1989.

President's Council on Sustainable Development. *Sustainable America: A New*

Consensus for Prosperity, Opportunity, and a Healthy Environment for the Future. Washington, D.C.: Government Printing Office, 1996.

Price Waterhouse. *The Burden of Unfunded Mandates: A Survey of the Impact of Unfunded Mandates on America's Counties.* New York: Price Waterhouse, Oct. 26, 1993a.

Price Waterhouse. *Impact of Unfunded Federal Mandates on U.S. Cities: A 314–City Survey.* New York: Price Waterhouse, Oct. 26, 1993b.

Putnam, R. "Bowling Alone: America's Declining Social Capital." *Journal of Democracy,* 1995a, *6*(1), 65–78.

Putnam, R. "Tuning In, Tuning Out: The Strange Disappearance of Social Capital in America." *PS: Political Science and Politics,* 1995b, *28*(4), 664–683.

Rabe, B. G. "Environmental Regulation in New Jersey: Innovations and Limitations." *Publius: The Journal of Federalism,* 1991, *21,* 83–103.

Rabin, R. "Federal Regulation in Historical Perspective." *Stanford Law Review,* 1986, *38*(5), 1189–1326.

Rabkin, J. *Judicial Compulsions: How Public Law Distorts Public Policy.* New York: Basic Books, 1989.

Radin, B. A. "Varieties of Reinvention: Six NPR 'Success Stories.'" In D. F. Kettl and J. DiIullio Jr. (eds.), *Inside the Reinvention Machine: Appraising Governmental Reform.* Washington, D.C.: Brookings Institution, 1995.

Raelin, J. A. *The Clash of Cultures.* Boston: Harvard Business School Press, 1985.

Rago, W. V. "Struggles in Transformation: A Study in TQM, Leadership and Organizational Culture in a Government Agency." *Public Administration Review,* 1996, *56*(3), 227–234.

Rainey, G. W. "Implementation and Managerial Creativity." In D. J. Palumbo and D. Calista (eds.), *Implementation and the Policy Process: Opening Up the Black Box.* Westport, Conn.: Greenwood Press, 1990.

Rastogi, P. N. *Management of Technology and Innovation: Competing Through Technological Excellence.* Thousand Oaks, Calif.: Sage, 1995.

Rayner, S., and Cantor, R. "How Fair Is Safe Enough? The Cultural Approach to Social Technology Choice." *Risk Analysis,* 1987, *7,* 3–9.

Reich, R. B. "Public Administration and Public Deliberation: An Interpretative Essay." *Yale Law Journal,* 1985, *94,* 1617–1641.

Reilly, W. K. "New Directions in Environmental Policy." *Risk Policy Report,* 1994, *1*(1), 19–20.

Repetto, R., Dower, R. C., Jenkins, R., and Geoghegan, J. *Green Fees: How a Tax Shift Can Work for the Environment and the Economy.* Washington, D.C.: World Resources Institute, 1992.

Resolve. *Risk Assessment Under FIFRA: Report of the Aquatic Effects Dialogue Group.* Washington, D.C.: World Wildlife Fund, 1992.

Rich, B. *Mortgaging the Earth: The World Bank, Environmental*

Impoverishment, and the Crisis of Development. Boston: Beacon Press, 1994.

Rieser, A. "Ecological Preservation as a Public Property Right: An Emerging Doctrine in Search of a Theory." *Harvard Environmental Law Review,* 1991, *15*(2), 393–433.

Ringquist, E. J. *Environmental Protection at the State Level: Politics and Progress in Controlling Pollution.* Armonk, N.Y.: Sharpe, 1993.

Ringquist, E. J. "Environmental Protection Regulation." In K. J. Meier and E. T. Garman, *Regulation and Consumer Protection.* (2nd ed.) Houston, Tex.: DAME Publications, 1995.

"Risk Commission Stresses Need for 'Integrated' Risk Management." *Risk Policy Report,* 1997, *3*(1), 3–5.

Rodgers, W. H. *Environmental Law.* (2nd ed.) St. Paul, Minn.: West, 1994.

Roe, A. "A Psychological Study of Physical Scientists." *Genetic Psychology Monographs,* 1951, *43,* 121–235.

Roe, A. "A Psychologist Examines Sixty-Four Eminent Scientists." *Scientific American,* 1952, *187*(5), 21–25.

Roe, A. *The Making of a Scientist.* New York: Dodd-Mead, 1953.

Roe, A. *The Psychology of Occupations.* New York: Wiley, 1956.

Rosenbaum, D. B. "Eliminating the Salt and the Pork." *ENR,* 1996, *236*(13), 28–29.

Rosenbaum, W. A. "The Clenched Fist and the Open Hand: Into the 1990s at EPA." In N. Vig and M. Kraft (eds.), *Environmental Policy in the 1990s: Toward a New Agenda.* (2nd ed.) Washington, D.C.: Congressional Quarterly Press, 1994.

Rosenbaum, W. A. *Environmental Politics and Policy.* (3rd ed.) Washington, D.C.: Congressional Quarterly Press, 1995.

Rosenbloom, D. H. "Public Administrative Theory and the Separation of Powers." *Public Administration Review,* 1983, *43*(3), 219–227.

Rosenbloom, D. H., and O'Leary, R. *Public Administration and Law.* (2nd ed.) New York: Dekker, 1997.

Rourke, F. E. *Bureaucracy, Politics, and Public Policy.* (3rd ed.) New York: Little, Brown, 1984.

Rubin, D. K., and Wright, A. G. "DOE Drops $19.5 Billion Bombshell." *ENR,* 1996, *237*(7), 10–11.

Ruckelshaus, W. D. "Risk, Science, and Democracy." *Issues in Science and Technology,* 1985, *1,* 19–38.

Ruckelshaus, W. D. *Inside EPA Weekly Report,* 1993, 14(45), 10.

"Running Cities: Goldsmith's Glitter." *The Economist,* 1966, *340*(7981), 26–27.

Sabatier, P. A., and Jenkins-Smith, H. *Policy Change and Learning: An Advocacy Coalition Approach.* Boulder, Colo.: Westview Press, 1993.

Sandel, M. J. *Democracy's Discontent: America in Search of a Public Philosophy.* Cambridge, Mass.: Belknap Press, 1996.

Sandman, P. M., Sachsman, D. B., Greenberg, M. R., and Gochfeld, M. *Environmental Risk and the Press: An Exploratory Assessment.* New Brunswick, N.J.: Transaction Books, 1987.

Sankar, Y. *Management of Technological Change.* New York: Wiley, 1991.

Sarianni, C., and Friedland, L. "Civic Environmentalism." [http://www.cpn.org/sections/ topics/environment/index.html]. 1995.

Sauter, V. L. *Decision Support Systems: An Applied Managerial Approach.* New York: Wiley, 1997.

Savas, E. S. *Privatization: The Key to Better Government.* Chatham, N.J.: Chatham House, 1987.

Savas, E. S. "Privatization in State and Local Government." Unpublished manuscript, 1995.

Schein, E. H. *Organizational Culture and Leadership.* San Francisco: Jossey-Bass, 1992.

Schmidheiny, S. *Changing Course: A Global Business Perspective on Development and the Environment.* Cambridge, Mass.: MIT Press, 1992.

Schnapf, D. "State Hazardous Waste Programs Under the Federal Resource Conservation and Recovery Act." *Environmental Law,* 1982, *12,* 678–743.

Schoenbrod, D. "Goals Statutes or Rules Statutes: The Case of the Clean Air Act." *UCLA Law Review,* 1983, *30,* 740–828.

Schuck, P. "The Politics of Rapid Legal Change." In M. K. Landy and M. A. Levin (eds.), *The New Politics of Public Policy.* Baltimore: Johns Hopkins University Press, 1995.

Seidenstat, P. "Privatization: Trends, Interplay of Forces, and Lessons Learned." *Policy Studies Journal,* 1996, *24*(3), 464–477.

Shapiro, M. *Who Guards the Guardians? Judicial Control of Administration.* Athens, Ga.: University of Georgia Press, 1988.

Sherwin, C. "Major Weapon System Advances Through Multiple Innovations." In C. W. Taylor (ed.), *Climate for Creativity.* New York: Pergamon Press, 1972.

"Shrinking Research Budget for Rule Support Irks EPA Program Staff." *Inside EPA Weekly Report,* 1994, *15*(6), 10–11.

Shrivastava, P. *Bhopal: Anatomy of a Crisis.* (2nd ed.) New York: Paul Chapman, 1992.

Silbergeld, E. K. "Risk Assessment: The Perspective and Experience of U.S. Environmentalists." *Environmental Health Perspectives,* 1993, *101,* 100–104.

Slocombe, D. S. "Implementing Ecosystem-Based Management." *BioScience,* 1993, *43*(9), 612–622.

Slovic, P. "Informing and Educating the Public About Risk." *Risk Analysis,* 1986, *6,* 403–415.

Slovic, P. "Perception of Risk." *Science,* 1987, *236,* 280–285.

Slovic, P. "Perceived Trust, Risk, and Democracy." *Risk Analysis,* 1993, *13,* 675–682.

Smith, S. R., and Lipsky, M. *Nonprofits for Hire: The Welfare State in the Age of Contracting.* Cambridge, Mass.: Harvard University Press, 1993.

Smolonsky, M., Dickson, D., and Caplan, E. *Annual Review of the U.S. Environmental Protection Agency.* Washington, D.C.: Environmental Working Group, 1993.

Spencer, P. L. "Government Charities?" *Consumers' Research Magazine,* 1995, *78*(3), 1–2.

"States Rebuff USEPA Effort to Craft New Partnership Guidance." *State Environmental Monitor,* 1996, *(1)*3, 5–6.

Steele, L. W. *Managing Technology: The Strategic View.* New York: McGraw-Hill, 1989.

Stevens, B. J. "Comparing Public and Private Sector Productive Efficiency: Analysis of Eight Activities." *National Productivity Review,* 1984, *3,* 395–406.

Stewart, R. B. "Controlling Environmental Risks Through Economic Incentives." *Columbia Journal of Environmental Law,* 1988, *13,* 153–169.

Stoker, R. P. "A Regime Framework for Implementation Analysis: Cooperation and Reconciliation of Federalist Imperatives." *Policy Studies Review,* 1989, *9*(1), 29–49.

Susskind, L., and McMahon, G. "The Theory and Practice of Negotiated Rulemaking." *Yale Journal on Regulation,* 1985, *3,* 133–165.

Susskind, L., and Weinstein, J. "Towards a Theory of Environmental Dispute Resolution." *Boston College Environmental Affairs Law Review,* 1980–81, *9,* 311–357.

Sustainable Seattle. *Indicators of Sustainable Community.* Seattle, Wash.: Sustainable Seattle, 1995.

Swartz, T., and Peck, J. (eds.). *The Changing Face of Fiscal Federalism.* Armonk, N.Y.: Sharpe, 1990.

Sweeney, N. J. "Thinking the Unthinkable: Contemplating Termination for Default in Construction Contracts." *Water Environment and Technology,* 1996, *8,* 62–66.

Talbot, A. R. *Settling Things: Six Case Studies in Environmental Mediation.* Washington, D.C.: Conservation Foundation, 1983.

Taylor, C. W. "Can Organizations Be Creative, Too?" In C. W. Taylor (ed.), *Climate for Creativity.* New York: Pergamon Press, 1972.

Telego, D. J. "Conference Overview and Objectives." Paper presented at the Conference on RCRA Reform: Pollution Prevention and Enforcement—New Policies and Procedures for 1993, sponsored by Inside EPA and Risk Management Technologies, Washington, D.C., Apr. 20, 1993.

Thamhain, H. J. "Developing Engineering/Program Management Skills." In D. F. Kocaogly (ed.), *Management of R&D and Engineering.* Amsterdam: North-Holland, 1992.

Thistle, D. A. "Systems Development Life Cycle—SDLC." [http://cs104.cs.uwindsor.ca/develop.htm]. June 24, 1997.

Thomas, J. C. *Public Participation in Public Decisions: New Skills and Strategies for Public Managers.* San Francisco: Jossey-Bass, 1995.

Thompson, F. J. (ed.). *Revitalizing State and Local Public Service: Strengthening Performance, Accountability, and Citizen Confidence.* San Francisco: Jossey-Bass, 1993.

Thompson, J. D. *Organizations in Action: Social Science Bases of Administrative Theory.* New York: McGraw-Hill, 1967.

Tietenberg, T. H. *Environmental and Natural Resource Economics.* (4th ed.) New York: HarperCollins, 1996.

Tobin, R. *The Expendable Future: U.S. Politics and the Protection of Biological Diversity.* Durham, N.C.: Duke University Press, 1990.

Toffler, A. *The Third Wave.* New York: Bantam Books, 1980.

Tucker, W. *Progress and Privilege: America in the Age of Environmentalism.* New York: Doubleday, 1982.

Tullock, G. *The Politics of Bureaucracy.* Washington, D.C.: Public Affairs Press, 1965.

Udall, S. *Quiet Crisis.* Austin, Tex.: Holt, Rinehart and Winston, 1963.

Underwood, D. *When MBAs Rule the Newsroom: How the Marketers and Managers Are Reshaping Today's Media.* New York: Columbia University Press, 1995.

United Church of Christ Commission on Racial Justice. *Toxic Wastes and Race in the United States: A National Report on the Racial and Socioeconomic Characteristics of Communities with Hazardous Waste Sites.* New York: United Church of Christ Commission on Racial Justice, 1987.

United Nations Conference on Environment and Development. *Agenda 21 and the UNCED Proceedings.* New York: Oceana, 1992.

U.S. Conference of Mayors. *National Survey on Unfunded Federal Mandates.* In U.S. House of Representatives Subcommittee on Investigation and Oversight of the Committee on Science, Space and Technology, *Unfunded Federal Mandates: Who Should Pick Up the Tab?* 103rd Congress, 2d sess., March 22, 1994.

U.S. Congress. *The Safe Drinking Water Act: A Case Study of an Unfunded Federal Mandate.* Congressional Budget Office, 1995.

U.S. Congress, Office of Technology Assessment. *Environmental Policy Tools: A User's Guide.* Washington, D.C.: Office of Technology Assessment, 1995.

U.S. Environmental Protection Agency. *Seven Cardinal Rules of Risk Communication.* Washington, D.C.: U.S. Environmental Protection Agency. 1988.

U.S. Environmental Protection Agency. *The Nation's Hazardous Waste*

Management Program at a Crossroads: The RCRA Implementation Study. Washington, D.C.: EPA Office of Solid Waste and Emergency Response, 1990.

U.S. Environmental Protection Agency. *Economic Incentives: Options for Environmental Protection.* Washington, D.C.: Office of Policy, Planning, and Evaluation, 1991.

U.S. Environmental Protection Agency. *Strategy for Reducing Lead Exposures.* Washington, D.C.: U.S. Environmental Protection Agency. Feb. 21, 1991.

U.S. Environmental Protection Agency. *Citizen's Guide to Radon.* (2nd ed.) Washington, D.C.: U.S. Environmental Protection Agency. 1992.

U.S. Environmental Protection Agency. *The State of Federal Facilities: A Comprehensive Overview of the Environmental Compliance Status of Federal Facilities Through the End of FY 1992.* Washington, D.C.: U.S. Environmental Protection Agency, Feb. 1994.

U.S. Environmental Protection Agency. *The State of Federal Facilities: An Overview of Environmental Compliance at Federal Facilities, FY 1993–94.* Washington, D.C.: U.S. Environmental Protection Agency, Dec. 1995.

U.S. Environmental Protection Agency. *Draft Framework for Watershed-Based Trading.* Washington, D.C.: U.S. Environmental Protection Agency, Office of Water, May 1996.

U.S. Environmental Protection Agency. *Community-Based Environmental Protection: A Resource Book for Protecting Ecosystems and Communities.* Washington, D.C.: Office of Policy, Planning, and Evaluation, September, 1997.

U.S. General Accounting Office. *Siting of Hazardous Waste Landfills and Their Correlation with Racial and Economic Status of Surrounding Communities.* Washington, D.C.: U.S. General Accounting Office, 1983.

U.S. General Accounting Office. *EPA Management Review.* Washington, D.C.: U.S. General Accounting Office, Dec. 1988a. (GAO/RCED–88–101)

U.S. General Accounting Office. *Water Pollution: Stronger Enforcement Needed to Improve Compliance at Federal Facilities.* Washington, D.C.: Government Printing Office, 1988b.

U.S. General Accounting Office. *Geographic Information Systems: Information on Federal Use and Coordination.* Washington, D.C.: U.S. General Accounting Office, Sept. 1991a. (GAO/IMTEC–91–72FS)

U.S. General Accounting Office. *Energy Management: Contract Audit Problems Create the Potential for Fraud, Waste and Abuse.* Washington D.C.: U.S. General Accounting Office, Oct. 1991b.

U.S. General Accounting Office. *Superfund: EPA Has Not Corrected Long-Standing Contract Management Problems.* Washington D.C.: U.S. General Accounting Office, Oct. 1991c.

U.S. General Accounting Office. *Mass Transit Grants: Noncompliance and Misspent Funds by Two Grantees in UMTA's New York Region.* Washington, D.C.: U.S. General Accounting Office, Jan. 1992a.

U.S. General Accounting Office. *Nuclear Waste: Weak DOE Contract Management Invited TRUPACT-II Setbacks.* Washington, D.C.: U.S. General Accounting Office, Jan. 1992b.

U.S. General Accounting Office. *Waste Minimization: Major Problems of Data Reliability and Validity Identified.* Washington, D.C.: U.S. General Accounting Office, Mar. 1992c. (GAO/PEMD–92–16)

U.S. General Accounting Office. *Environmental Enforcement: EPA Needs a Better Strategy to Manage Its Cross-Media Information.* Washington, D.C.: U.S. General Accounting Office, Apr. 1992d. (GAO/IMTEC–92–14)

U.S. General Accounting Office. *Information Management and Technology Issues.* Washington, D.C.: U.S. General Accounting Office, Dec. 1992e. (GAO/OCG–93–5TR)

U.S. General Accounting Office. *Environmental Enforcement: EPA Cannot Ensure the Accuracy of Self-Reported Compliance Monitoring Data.* Washington, D.C.: U.S. General Accounting Office, Mar. 1993. (GAO/RCED–93–21)

U.S. General Accounting Office. *Environmental Protection: EPA's Problems with Collection and Management of Scientific Data and Its Efforts to Address Them.* Washington, D.C.: U.S. General Accounting Office, May 1995. (GAO/T-RCED–95–174)

U.S. General Accounting Office. *The Government Performance and Results Act: 1997 Governmentwide Implementation Will Be Uneven.* Washington, D.C.: Government Printing Office, 1997. (GAO/GGD–97–109)

U.S. House of Representatives, Committee on Government Operations. *The Environmental Protection Agency's Superfund ARCS Contracting Process and Contractor Performance.* Washington, D.C.: Government Printing Office, Apr. 9, 1992.

U.S. House of Representatives, Committee on Government Operations. *Management Problems and Contracting Activities at EPA Laboratories.* Washington, D.C.: Government Printing Office, June 25, 1993.

U.S. House of Representatives, Committee on Post Office and Civil Service. *Contracting at Environmental Protection Agency and Its Effect on Federal Employees.* Washington, D.C.: Government Printing Office, Feb. 23, 1989.

U.S. Senate Committee on Environment and Public Works. *Staff Report: Analysis of the Unfunded Mandates Surveys Conducted by the U.S. Conference of Mayors and the National Association of Counties.* Washington, D.C.: U.S. Government Printing Office, June 14, 1994.

U.S. Senate Environment and Public Works Committee. *Confirmation Hearings of Lee Thomas,* Washington, D.C., Feb. 13, 1985.

U.S. Senate Environment and Public Works Committee. Confirmation
Hearings of Manuel Lujan and William J. Riley, Washington, D.C., Feb.
13, 1989.

Van Dieren, W. (ed.). *Taking Nature into Account: A Report to the Club of
Rome: Toward a Sustainable National Income.* New York: Copernicus,
1995.

Van Wart, M., Cayer, N. J., and Cook, S. *Handbook of Training and
Development for the Public Sector: A Comprehensive Resource.* San
Francisco: Jossey-Bass, 1993.

Vaughan, D. *The Challenger Launch Decision: Risky Technology, Culture,
and Deviance at NASA.* Chicago: University of Chicago, 1996.

Vaughan, E. "The Significance of Socioeconomic and Ethnic Diversity for the
Risk Communication Process." *Risk Analysis,* 1995, *13,* 169–180.

Vernon, P. E. "The Nature-Nurture Problem in Creativity." In J. A. Glover,
R. R. Ronning, and C. R. Reynolds (eds.), *Handbook of Creativity.* New
York: Plenum, 1989.

Vig, N. J., and Kraft, M. E. (eds.). *Environmental Policy in the 1990s.* (2nd
ed.) Washington, D.C.: Congressional Quarterly Press, 1994.

Vig, N. J., and Kraft, M. E. (eds.). *Environmental Policy in the 1990s.* (3rd
ed.) Washington, D.C.: Congressional Quarterly Press, 1997.

Von Zijst, H. "A Change in the Culture." *Environmental Forum,* May-June
1993, pp. 12–17.

Waldo, D. *The Administrative State: A Study of the Political Theory of
American Public Administration.* Somerset, N.J.: Ronald Press, 1948.

Waldo, D. *The Enterprise of Public Administration: A Summary View.*
Novato, Calif.: Chandler & Sharp, 1988.

Warrick, J. "Checkup Time for the Environment: Conference Aims to
Transform '92 Rio Accord 'From Words to Deeds.'" *Washington Post,*
June 22, 1997, p. A06.

Warrick, J., and Goodman, P. S. "EPA Plans to Regulate Livestock Waste:
Clean Water Act Would Be Applied." *Washington Post,* Mar. 5, 1998,
p. A01.

"Washington Fines DOE, Westinghouse Under New Federal Compliance
Statute." *BNA Environment Reporter,* 1993, *23,* 3019.

Weaver, P. H. *News and the Culture of Lying: How Journalism Really Works.*
New York: Free Press, 1994.

Weiland, P. "The Impact of Intergovernmental Environmental Law and Policy
on Local Government." Unpublished doctoral dissertation, Indiana
University, Bloomington, 1996.

Wells, D. T. *Environmental Policy: A Global Perspective for the Twenty-First
Century.* Englewood Cliffs, N.J.: Prentice-Hall, 1996.

Wenner, L. *The Environmental Decade in Court.* Bloomington, Ind.: Indiana
University Press, 1982.

Wenner, L. "Environmental Policy in the Courts." In N. J. Vig and M. E. Kraft (eds.), *Environmental Policy in the 1990s: Toward a New Agenda.* (2nd ed.) Washington, D.C.: Congressional Quarterly Press, 1994.

West, J. P, Berman, E. M., and Milakovich, M. E. "HRM, TQM, and Organizational Policies: The Need for Alignment." In *Proceedings of the Academy of Business Administration: Public Sector Studies.* London: Academy of Business Administration, 1994.

West, W. *Administrative Rulemaking: Politics and Processes.* Westport, Conn.: Greenwood Press, 1985.

Wever, G. H. *Strategic Environmental Management: Using TQEM and ISO 14000 for Competitive Advantage.* New York: Wiley, 1996.

Whittemore, A. "Facts and Values in Risk Analysis for Environmental Toxicants." *Risk Analysis,* 1983, *1,* 23–33.

Willbern, Y. "Professionalization in the Public Service: Too Little or Too Much?" *Public Administration Review,* 1954, *14,* 13–21.

Windsor, D. *Piecemeal Privatization: The United States Domestic Transportation Example.* Paper presented at the meeting of the Western Regional Science Association, San Diego, California, Feb. 23, 1995.

Wilson, J. Q. *Bureaucracy: What Government Agencies Do and Why They Do It.* New York: Basic Books, 1989.

Wilson, J. Q., and Rachal, P. "Can Government Regulate Itself?" *The Public Interest,* 1977, *46,* 3–14.

Wilson-Gentry, L., and Durant, R. F. "Evaluating TQM: The Case for a Theory-Driven Approach." *Public Administration Review,* 1994, *54*(2), 137–146.

Wise, C. "Public Service Configurations and Public Organizations: Public Organization Design in the Post-Privatization Era." *Public Administration Review,* 1990, *50*(2), 141–155.

Wise, C., and Emerson, K. "Regulatory Takings: The Emerging Doctrine and Its Implications for Public Administration." *Administration & Society,* 1994, *26,* 305–336.

Wise, C., and O'Leary, R. "Intergovernmental Relations in Environmental Management and Policy: The Role of the Courts." *Public Administration Review,* 1997, *57*(2), 150–159.

Wolf, C. Jr. "A Theory of Non-Market Failures." *The Public Interest,* Spring 1979, pp. 114–133.

Woodrow, K. D. "The Proposed Federal Environmental Sentencing Guidelines: A Model for Corporate Environmental Compliance Programs." *BNA Environment Reporter,* 1994, *25,* 325.

World Commission on Environment and Development. *Our Common Future.* New York: Oxford University Press, 1987.

Yandle, T., and Burton, D. "Reexamining Environmental Justice: A Statistical Analysis of Historical Hazardous Waste Landfill Siting Patterns in Metropolitan Texas." *Social Science Quarterly,* 1996, *77*(3), 477–492.

Yankelovich, D. *Coming to Public Judgment: Making Democracy Work in a Complex World.* Syracuse, N.Y.: Syracuse University Press, 1991.

Zimmerman, R. "A Process Framework for Risk Communication." *Science, Technology, and Human Values,* 1987, *12,* 131–137.

LEGAL CASES CITED

Babbitt v. *Sweet Home,* 515 U.S. 687 (1995).

Board of County Commissioners v. *Umbehr,* 518 U.S. 668 (1996).

Burgess v. *M/V. Tamano,* 564 F.2d 964 (1st Cir. 1977) (1977) (1978).

C & A Carbone, Inc. et al. v. *Clarkstown, New York,* 511 U.S. 383 (1994).

City of Chicago v. *Environmental Defense Fund,* 511 U.S. 328 (1994).

City of New York v. *Exxon Corporation,* 697 F. Supp. 677 (S.D.N.Y. 1988).

City of Philadelphia v. *Stephan Chemical Co.,* 544 F. Supp. 1135 (E.D. Pa. 1982).

City of Stoughton, Wisconsin v. *U.S. Environmental Protection Agency,* 858 F.2d 747 (D.C. Cir. 1988).

Colorado v. *Idarado Mining Co.,* 735 F. Supp. 368 (D. Colo. 1990).

Colorado v. *United States Department of the Army,* 707 F. Supp. 1562 (D. Colo. 1989).

Dolan v. *Tigard,* 512 U.S. 374 (1994).

Ex Parte Young, 209 U.S. 123 (1908).

First English Evangelical Lutheran Church of Glendale v. *County of Los Angeles,* 478 U.S. 1003 (1986).

Fitzpatrick v. *Bitzer,* 427 U.S. 445 (1976).

Florida Rock Industries, Inc. v. *United States,* 21 Cl. Ct. 161 (1990).

FMC Corporation v. *U.S. Commerce Department,* 29 F.3d 833 (3d Cir. 1994).

In Re T.P. Long Chemical, Inc., 45 B. R. 278 (1985).

Kleeman v. *McDonnell Douglas Corp.,* 890 F.2d 698 (4th Cir. 1989).

Loveladies Harbor, Inc. v. *United States,* 21 Cl. Ct. 153 (1990).

Lucas v. *South Carolina Coastal Council,* 505 U.S. 1003 (1992).

New Castle County v. *Hartford Accident and Indemnity Company,* 685 F. Supp. 1321 (D. Del. 1988).

New York v. *Shore Realty,* 759 F.2d 1032 (2d Cir. 1985).

Nollan v. *California Coastal Commission,* 483 U.S. 825 (1987).

O'Hare Truck Service v. *City of Northlake,* 518 U.S. 712 (1996).

Outboard Marine Corp. v. *Thomas,* 773 F.2d 883 (7th Cir. 1985).

Pennsylvania v. *Frey,* No. 904C1989 (1989).

Pennsylvania v. *Union Gas,* 491 U.S. 1 (1989).

Pennsylvania Coal Co. v. *Mahon,* 260 U.S. 393 (1922).

Pennsylvania DER v. *U.S. Postal Service,* 13 F.3d 62 (3d Cir. 1993).

Robert Ayers et al. v. *Township of Jackson,* 525 A.2d 287 (N.J. 1987).

Pickering v. *Board of Education,* 391 U.S. 563 (1968).

Seminole Tribe of Florida v. *Florida,* 517 U.S. 44 (1996).

South Macomb Disposal Authority v. *United States Environmental Protection Agency*, 681 F. Supp. 1244 (S.D. Mich. 1988).

State of Colorado v. *United States Department of the Army*, 707 F. Supp. 1562 (D. Colo. 1989).

Steuart Transportation Co. v. *Allied Towing Corp.*, 596 F.2d 609 (4th Cir. 1979).

Thomas v. *FAG Bearings Corporation*, 846 F. Supp. 1400 (W.D. Mo. 1994).

Trevino v. *General Dynamics Corp.*, 865 F.2d 1474 (5th Cir. 1989).

United States v. *A & F* Materials Company Inc., 578 F. Supp. 1249 (S.D. Ill. 1984).

United States v. *Argent Corp.*, 21 Env't Rep. Cas. 1354 (D. N.M. 1984).

United States v. *Bear Marine Services*, 509 F. Supp. 710 (E.D. La. 1980).

United States v. *Bogas*, 731 F. Supp. 242 (N.D. Ohio 1990).

United States v. *Brittain*, No. 89–283–P (1990).

United States v. *Carr*, 880 F.2d 1550 (2d. Cir. 1989).

United States v. *Cauffman*, 21 Env't Rep. Cas. 2167 (C.D. Cal. 1984).

United States v. *Chem-Dyne Corp.*, 572 F. Supp. 802 (S.D. Ohio 1983).

United States v. *Colorado*, 990 F.2d 1565 (10th Cir. 1993).

United States v. *Conservation Chemical Co.*, 619 F. Supp. 162 (W.D. Mo. 1985).

United States v. *Curtis*, 988 F.2d 946 (9th Cir. 1993).

United States v. *Dee*, 912 F.2d 741 (4th Cir. 1990).

United States v. *Dickerson et al.*, 640 F. Supp. 448 (D.Md. 1986).

United States v. *Hardage*, 18 Env't Rep. Cas. 1685 (W.D. Okla. 1982).

United States v. *Hoflin*, 880 F.2d 1033 (9th Cir. 1989).

United States v. *Lebeouf Bros. Towing Co.*, 621 F.2d 787 (5th Cir. 1980).

United States v. *Miami Drum Services, Inc.*, 25 Env't Rep. Cas. 1469 (S.D. Fla. 1986).

United States v. *Mirabile*, 15 Env't Law Rep. 20992 (E.D. Pa. 1985).

United States v. *M/V Big Sam*, 681 F.2d 432 (5th Cir. 1982).

United States v. *NEPACCO*, 579 F. Supp. 823 (W.D. Mo. 1984).

United States v. *New Mexico*, 32 F.3d 494 (10th Cir. 1994).

United States v. *Northernaire Plating Co.*, 20 Env't Law Rep. 20200 (W.D. Mich. 1989).

United States v. *Ottati & Goss*, 23 Env't. Rep. Cas. 1705 (D. N.H. 1985).

United States v. *Price*, 577 F. Supp. 1103 (D.N.J. 1983).

United States v. *Reilly Tar*, 546 F. Supp. 1100 (D.Minn. 1982).

United States v. *Seymour Recycling Corp.*, 618 F. Supp. 1 (S.D. Ind. 1984).

United States v. *Shell Oil Company*, 605 F. Supp. 1064 (D. Colo. 1985).

United States v. *South Carolina Recycling and Disposal, Inc.*, 20 Env't Rep. Cas. 1753 (D. S.C. 1984).

United States v. *South Carolina Recycling and Disposal, Inc.*, 21 Env't. Rep. Cas. 1577 (D. S.C. 1984).

United States v. *Stringfellow*, No. 83–2501 JMI (1989).

United States v. *Tex Tow,* 589 F.2d 1310 (7th Cir. 1978).

United States v. *Tyson,* 25 Env't Rep. Cas. 1897 (E.D. Pa. 1986).

United States v. *Union Gas,* 832 F.2d. 1343 (3d Cir. 1987).

United States v. *Vertac Chemical Corp.,* 489 F. Supp. 870 (E.D. Ark. 1980).

United States v. *Wade,* 546 F. Supp. 785 (E.D. Pa. 1983).

United States v. *Ward,* 618 F. Supp. 884 (E.D. N.C. 1985).

United States v. *Waste Ind.,* 734 F.2d 159 (4th Cir. 1984).

United States v. *Windham,* Cr. 1–89–00001 (1989).

United States Department of Energy v. *Ohio,* 503 U.S. 607 (1992).

Violet v. *Picillo,* 648 F.Supp. 1283 (D.R.I. 1986).

Whitney Benefits v. *United States,* 926 F.2d 1169 (Fed. Cir. 1991).

NAME INDEX

A

Ackerman, B. A., 316
Allen, J. W., 294, 295
Almond, G. A., 181, 189
Amy, D., 196, 212
Anderson, A., 12
Anderton, D., 12
Athos, A., 94
Austin, L. K., 278, 279

B

Babbitt, B., 8
Bacow, L., 193
Baker, J., 126
Ball, H., 47
Baram, M. S., 327, 329
Bardach, E., 157, 188, 232, 311, 322
Barzelay, M., 344
Bates, M., 273
Been, V., 11, 12, 13
Bemelmans-Videc, M., 188
Berman, E. M., 88, 93, 100, 138
Bernard, J. R., 7, 351
Berry, J. M., 142
Bhalla, S. K., 269
Bingenheimer, K., 52
Bingham, G., 194, 200, 201, 203, 209, 212
Blackburn, J. W., 213
Boerner, C., 13, 14
Bosso, C., 40
Boster, J. S., 104, 105
Bowen, E., 216
Bowman, J. S., 89, 100
Boyce, M., 8
Bozeman, B., 100
Brand, R., 88, 93, 94

Braskamp, L. A., 269
Broder, D. S., 345
Brown, D. A., 16, 228
Brown, D. M., 37
Brown, P., 147
Browner, C., 155, 228
Bullard, R. D., 11–12, 13, 149
Burnett, M. L., 42
Burnham, J., 109
Burns, R. O., 269
Burton, D., 13–14
Bush, G., 50

C

Caplan, E., 239
Carlin, A., 316
Carson, R., *xxiii*
Cattell, R. B., 269
Caudron, S., 268, 280, 282, 283
Cayer, N. J., 255
Chandler, T. D., 292
Chase, A., 342
Chess, C., 169, 180, 184, 189
Churchill, W., 77, 307
Clark, R., 150
Clinton, B., 150
Cohen, S., 88, 89, 93, 94
Cole, L. A., 171, 178, 184
Commoner, B., 144
Conlan, T. J., 20, 21
Cook, D. S., 94
Cook, S., 255
Cormick, G. W., 194, 200, 202, 207–208
Couger, J. D., 269, 284
Covello, V. T., 170, 174, 176, 183–184
Crowfoot, J. E., 194, 196

SUBJECT INDEX

Note: Literature citations for law cases are included in the References section.

A

Accidents, toxic, 111, 327–328, 330

Accountability in environmental management, 4–7, 320; and contracting and grant letting, 291–292, 293, 295; and measurement challenges, 5–6, 95–96; results-based, 6–7, 324, 345, 352; and right-to-know laws, 39, 84, 189, 322, 327–329, 335; and technoscientific professionalism, 263–264, 266, 345; and TRI, 329; on water quality, 5. *See also* Informational approach to regulation

Accounting, environmental: data-informed, 95–96; and economic growth, 16; and incremental costs of mandates, 20; life-cycle costing, 86; and SEIS project proposals, 253, 255, 256; total cost assessment, 86; and TQEM costing methods, 86; unit or activity-based, 299. *See also* Cost savings; Costs

Acid rain control, 29, 317, 334

Active waste sites. *See* Hazardous and solid wastes regulation

Acts, environmental. *See* Laws, environmental protection

Administrative state, 339–340, 362*n*.2

ADR alternative dispute resolution, 193, 199, 202

Adversarial legalism, 134–136; and indemnification, 300; management implications of, 136–137; positive aspects of, 138–139; problems of, 198–199, 275. *See also* Case law; Lawsuits

Advertising, deceptive, 107

Advisory boards, 155, 227, 275

Advisory Commission on Intergovernmental Relations, 24, 347

Advocacy groups. *See* Groups, environmentalist

AEDG Aquatic Effects Dialogue Group, 205–206

Aerometric Information Retrieval System (AIRS), 229

Agency-forcing provisions of environmental protection laws: on air quality, 30; effects of, 43–44, 98, 135, 264, 275; on pesticides registration, 40–41; on point-source pollution, 42; on prospective waste control, 33–34, 35–36. *See also* Laws, environmental protection

Agenda 21, UN Conference on Environmental and Development, 15

Agreements, international, 15, 342

Agriculture, 41, 342

Air Force Logistics Command, 88

Air quality environmental laws: critique of recent, 30; evolution of, 25–30; the logic of reform in, 27–29; water act differences from, 31. *See also* NAAQS

Air quality modeling, regional, 242

Air toxics. *See* HAPs hazardous air pollutants

Allowance trading. *See* Trading systems

Ambient standards: air quality (NAAQS), 25, 27, 31, 214, 311–312; water, 31

Z